The Moral Economies of American Authorship

OXFORD STUDIES IN AMERICAN LITERARY HISTORY

Gordon Hutner, Series Editor

Family Money
Jeffory A. Clymer

America's England
Christopher Hanlon

Writing the Rebellion
Philip Gould

Antipodean America
Paul Giles

Living Oil
Stephanie LeMenager

Making Noise, Making News
Mary Chapman

Territories of Empire
Andy Doolen

Propaganda 1776
Russ Castronovo

Playing in the White
Stephanie Li

Literature in the Making
Nancy Glazener

Surveyors of Customs
Joel Pfister

The Moral Economies of American Authorship
Susan M. Ryan

After Critique
Mitchum Huehls

The Moral Economies of American Authorship

REPUTATION, SCANDAL, AND THE NINETEENTH-CENTURY LITERARY MARKETPLACE

Susan M. Ryan

Oxford University Press is a department of the University of Oxford. It furthers
the University's objective of excellence in research, scholarship, and education
by publishing worldwide. Oxford is a registered trade mark of Oxford University
Press in the UK and certain other countries.

Published in the United States of America by Oxford University Press
198 Madison Avenue, New York, NY 10016, United States of America.

© Oxford University Press 2016

First issued as an Oxford University Press paperback, 2019

All rights reserved. No part of this publication may be reproduced, stored in
a retrieval system, or transmitted, in any form or by any means, without the
prior permission in writing of Oxford University Press, or as expressly permitted
by law, by license, or under terms agreed with the appropriate reproduction
rights organization. Inquiries concerning reproduction outside the scope of the
above should be sent to the Rights Department, Oxford University Press, at the
address above.

You must not circulate this work in any other form
and you must impose this same condition on any acquirer.

Library of Congress Cataloging-in-Publication Data
Ryan, Susan M., Ph.D.
The moral economies of American authorship : reputation, scandal, and the nineteenth-century
literary marketplace / Susan M. Ryan.
pages cm.—(Oxford studies in American literary history ; 11)
Includes bibliographical references and index.
ISBN 978-0-19-027402-3 (hardback); 978-0-19-006784-7 (paperback)
1. American literature—19th century—History and criticism.   2. Literature—Philosophy.
3. Literature and morals—History—19th century.   4. American literature—Authorship.   I. Title.
PS217.P45R93   2015
810.9'384—dc23   2015020484

Typeset in Minion Pro Regular

For Eden

{ CONTENTS }

Acknowledgments	ix
Introduction: Moral Markets	1
1. Fenimore Cooper, Property, and the Trials of National Authorship	25
2. Paratexts and the Making of Moral Authority	55
3. Frederick Douglass's Marketing of Moral Repair	85
4. The Currency of Reputation	109
5. Stowe, Byron, and the Art of Scandal	137
Epilogue: Reputation Redux	163
Notes	169
Index	213

{ ACKNOWLEDGMENTS }

I almost wish that my authorship of this book included some scandalous backstory, such that I could use this as an opportunity to justify myself and scold my detractors. Alas—I'll have to restrict myself to the usual expressions of thanks, though their conventionality makes them no less heartfelt or deserved.

As is the case with any long project, my debts, both intellectual and personal, have accumulated. For their insightful and challenging comments on segments of the manuscript, not to mention their warm friendship, I'm grateful to Teresa Goddu, Susan Griffin, and Aaron Jaffe. My colleagues Karen Chandler, Ben Hufbauer, and Carol Mattingly were part of a writing group that provided much-appreciated encouragement and critique in the early stages. Bob Levine suggested, also early on, that I look into Fenimore Cooper's land dispute and libel suits, with which I subsequently became obsessed; I thank him for that keen advice and for his encouragement more generally. Philip Gura's generous mentorship continues to shape my work. Meredith McGill deftly led a seminar on copyright at the 2013 C19 conference that helped me to think through the connections between moral and legal properties. A number of anonymous readers—for Oxford University Press and for the venues in which I prepublished portions of the manuscript—provided invaluable and careful feedback. Not least, I wish to thank Gordon Hutner and Brendan O'Neill at Oxford, who have done so much to bring this book to press.

For material support I thank the National Endowment for the Humanities, whose summer stipend program funded a portion of my research. I also received funding from the University of Louisville's Office of the Vice President for Research and Department of English, which allowed me to hire several graduate research assistants over a span of time. Maria Accardi, DaRelle Rollins, Leslie French Harper, and Amy Lueck were unfailingly helpful, even when the work I asked of them verged into tedium. Librarians and other staff members at the University of Louisville and the Library of Congress provided crucial assistance.

Friends and family, in Louisville and elsewhere, have not only given support and advice that helped me to finish this project, but they've enriched my life in countless ways. My daughter's remarkable ability to befriend kids with fantastic parents (Jenny and John Napier, Nisha Gupta and Rich VerWiebe, Bernadette and Bill Johnston, and Sally and Tom McMahon) has given me not just a lovely and unanticipated social circle, but also the peace of mind that comes with knowing she is safe and happy in their homes. Gabriela Alcalde,

Tatjana Soldat-Jaffe, Beth Willey, and Leigh Viner are among the smartest and strongest women I've ever known. I'm more grateful for their friendship than I can express. Family members—my siblings, Marty and Angela Ryan, and my parents, Bill and Mary Ryan—deserve more effusive thanks than this genre comfortably allows. I will simply say that I treasure their seemingly boundless love and support. And while it seems silly to thank one's dog in print, my greyhound mix Libby has been a consistent morale booster and writing companion, though her proofreading skills, I have found, need work.

Finally, I wish to thank Brian Gallup for his patience with this project and for the daily gift of his presence in my life. Eden Gallup, to whom this book is dedicated, is a revelation to me, the joy of which I am slowly learning not to question.

An earlier version of chapter 5 and segments of the epilogue were first published as "Stowe, Byron, and the Art of Scandal," *American Literature* 83.1 (2011): pp. 59–91. Republished by permission of Duke University Press (www.dukeupress.edu). Portions of the introduction and chapter 3 originally appeared as "Douglass, Melville, and the Moral Economies of American Authorship," in *Frederick Douglass and Herman Melville: Essays in Relation*, ed. Robert S. Levine and Samuel Otter (Chapel Hill: University of North Carolina Press, 2012). UNC Press has granted permission to republish. Passages that appear in the introduction and chapter 4 were first included in "Moral Authority As Literary Property in Mid-Nineteenth-Century Print Culture," in *The Cambridge History of American Women's Literature*, ed. Dale Bauer (Cambridge: Cambridge University Press, 2012), pp. 165–84. My thanks to the editors for giving me the opportunity to publish this work and to the presses for their permission to reproduce it here.

The Moral Economies of American Authorship

Introduction

MORAL MARKETS

In the fall of 1853, a white widow named Margaret Douglass was prosecuted in Norfolk, Virginia, for the crime of teaching free African American children to read. Her trial, which resulted in a nominal fine of one dollar and a monthlong jail sentence, was widely noticed in the US abolitionist press, long critical of the South's embrace of antiliteracy laws. A headline that ran in the *National Era*, for example, called Douglass "heroic," while a piece in *Frederick Douglass' Paper* insisted that her conviction would prove more momentous than such landmark events as the Boston Tea Party or the conversion of Martin Luther: "None of these...promised in their introduction to do as much as the imprisonment of Mrs. Douglass now promises."[1] For antislavery activists, Douglass's ordeal evidenced the absurdity and moral bankruptcy of Virginia's (and, by extension, the South's) laws, even as it offered a kind of hope: in a southern white woman's defiance of an unfair statute lay a version of the nation that was not so far gone after all—that was not immune to the promise of righteousness, of a transformative benevolence that belied the more palpable threats of racial animosity and political disintegration.

The Boston-based publisher John P. Jewett soon brought out Douglass's account of her experiences in a slim volume titled *Educational Laws of Virginia* (1854). Still flush with the success of *Uncle Tom's Cabin*, released just two years earlier, Jewett sought to capitalize on the outrage that Douglass's case had elicited by advertising her narrative, modestly priced at twenty cents a copy, in at least three abolitionist venues: *Frederick Douglass' Paper*, the *National Era*, and the *Liberator*. Promising "ASTOUNDING DISCLOSURES!" and highlighting Douglass's imprisonment, the advertisement averred that the work would "astonish the civilized world" (see Figure 1). This mixture of sensationalism and novelty sought to establish the narrative's author as an upstanding—if abused—citizen whose good works landed her in "the common jail." One version of the advertisement further emphasized Douglass's antislavery bona fides by

the employment and enjoyment of his loving and advanced spirit through an immortal existence.

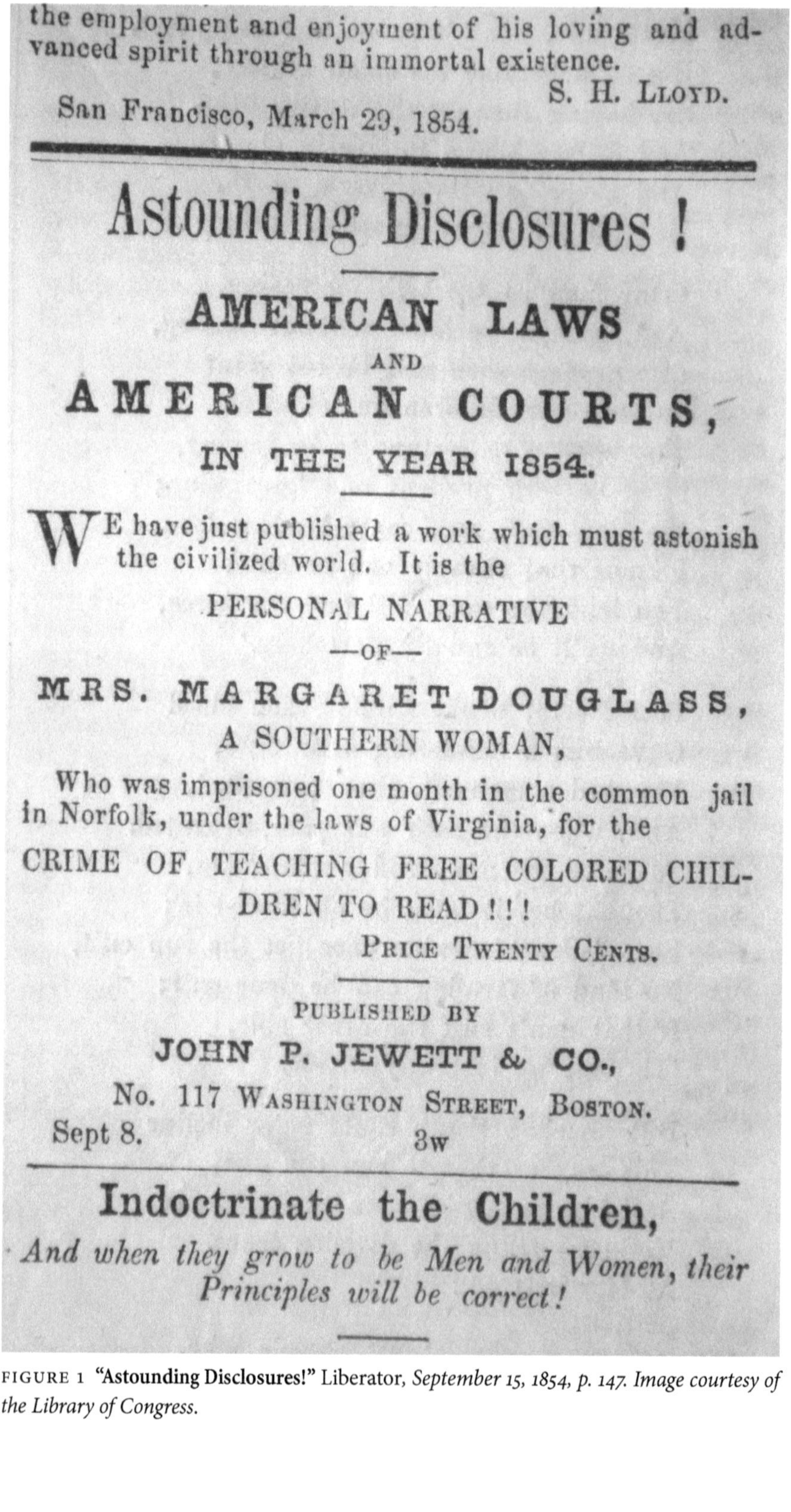

S. H. LLOYD.

San Francisco, March 29, 1854.

Astounding Disclosures!

AMERICAN LAWS

AND

AMERICAN COURTS,

IN THE YEAR 1854.

WE have just published a work which must astonish the civilized world. It is the

PERSONAL NARRATIVE

—OF—

MRS. MARGARET DOUGLASS,

A SOUTHERN WOMAN,

Who was imprisoned one month in the common jail in Norfolk, under the laws of Virginia, for the

CRIME OF TEACHING FREE COLORED CHILDREN TO READ!!!

PRICE TWENTY CENTS.

PUBLISHED BY

JOHN P. JEWETT & CO.,

No. 117 WASHINGTON STREET, BOSTON.

Sept 8.   3w

Indoctrinate the Children,

And when they grow to be Men and Women, their Principles will be correct!

FIGURE 1 *"Astounding Disclosures!"* Liberator, *September 15, 1854, p. 147. Image courtesy of the Library of Congress.*

grouping her book with such titles as *Pictures and Stories from Uncle Tom's Cabin* and *Anthony Burns's Farewell to Boston, June 2, 1854. A Poem Set to Music by J. W.* Meanwhile, the September 15, 1854, issue of the *Liberator*—one of at least five in which Jewett advertised *Educational Laws*—included an excerpt from the presiding judge's odious pronouncements in its "Refuge of Oppression" column, which ran down the left side of the paper's front page, next to a selection from Douglass's own "spirited comments," to quote the editor's headnote, in which she insisted that Judge Baker had "insulted the good sense and generous nature of the community in which he lived, by so cowardly and unmanly a decision."[2] Completing this admirable sandwich-in-print, the right side of the page featured a speech by Senator Charles Sumner titled "Duties of Massachusetts," replete with references to the "Slave Power" that "must be overthrown" by forthright northern voters and legislators.[3]

William Lloyd Garrison's editorial framing of Margaret Douglass as a martyr to conscience in an abolitionist mold accords with the way her story was referenced and repeated in antislavery discourse more broadly.[4] In 1857, the *National Anti-Slavery Standard* went so far as to refashion the southern-born Douglass as a "Yankee bluestocking" in its headnote to a parodic version of her trial transcript.[5] William Craft, who incorporated that parody into the text of *Running a Thousand Miles for Freedom* (1860), framed it as a straight-up account of her persecution and noted that her ordeal would "serve to show how persons are treated in the most enlightened slaveholding community."[6] Indeed, a truncated version of Douglass's history was still being recounted a decade after her trial in a volume titled *The Anti-Slavery Cause in America and Its Martyrs* (1863), where she joined such abolitionist saints as Garrison himself, the much-harassed schoolmistress Prudence Crandall, and the murdered newspaper editor Elijah Lovejoy.[7]

Within her narrative, however, Douglass established a markedly different kind of moral authority. Granted, she discussed at length the injustice of the law she was convicted of violating and emphasized the industriousness and gratitude of her pupils and their families, as antislavery readers would expect. But much of the volume spoke instead to an audience of proslavery southerners, for whom Douglass positioned herself as a loyal coresident.[8] Wishing "to do away with any impression that I was or am an Abolitionist," she insisted that she "was not contending against any of the Southern institutions, but only against a particular law of the State of Virginia." Indeed, she described herself as a former slave owner who "would be again, if [she] felt so disposed." For Douglass white superiority was so fundamental, timeless, and secure that black literacy could not possibly threaten it: "Our slaves and servants," she insisted, "whether bond or free, ... can be nothing else in our community."[9] Why not, then, teach them to read? Turning her attention from free African Americans, the specific "objects" of her instruction, to the enslaved population that formed the controversy's subtext, Douglass then asserted that slave literacy would alter southern society in just one crucial respect: it would undermine the practice of "amalgamation." Antiliteracy laws, she claimed, were specifically designed to ensure white men's sexual access to enslaved women. Slaves "must not read the Bible because that teaches them the sin of their masters.... They must not learn to read and write, for every mental and moral improvement only tends to...improve those feelings...that already repel this gross system of sensuality and licentiousness."[10] Black literacy, in Douglass's rendering, would promote sexual and racial purity, but would perpetuate nothing so shocking as emancipation or social mobility for nonwhites.

This anecdote suggests just how canny antebellum publishers could be in their manipulation of the book market. Jewett played to the expectations and desires of his audience—including the editors whom he paid to run advertisements—and built on the brief, outraged hagiographies that had already appeared in print, marketing "Mrs. Douglass" as an abolitionist true believer and her book as a paean to the transformative potential of literacy, not unlike the cultural work undertaken by a better-known Douglass's narrative, published nine years earlier. Nevertheless, the question of whether Jewett and various abolitionist newspaper editors were deceptive or simply misinformed in their construction of the myth of Margaret Douglass matters less than what her case tells us about the intersection of moral authority and print culture at midcentury. In this era an author's moral reputation emerged as a crucial element in the presentation and marketing of printed material, but in ways that were incomplete, unstable, and above all contingent—contingent on such immediate elements as genre, venue, placement on the page, excerpting practices, paratextual framing, and sponsorship or imprimatur, but also on more amorphous features: the ideological and sectional divisions, not to mention the racial and gendered expectations, that shaped a text's reception.

Margaret Douglass's case also highlights the entanglement of claims to moral authority with the threat, or the fact, of scandal: Jewett promoted Douglass as the victim of a scandalously unjust southern judiciary, even as her text had the potential to reveal the scandal of his misleading marketing campaign. One wonders why she was not broadly criticized as a faux-abolitionist and, more immediately, how an editor as relentless as Garrison in the exposure of hypocrisy could have facilitated her passing.[11] But the more pressing matter, in terms of the era's cultures of print, is how we might understand a set of emerging markets in which investment in authorial character was so intense—and readership so segmented—that it made sense to represent a proslavery author as an abolitionist in the first place.

While few examples are so stark in their contradictions, mid-nineteenth-century authorship entailed complex interrelations between moral authority on the one hand, and various aspects of self-presentation, marketing, and reception on the other.[12] Harriet Beecher Stowe, for example, emerged as an antislavery icon for vast numbers of English and American readers in the 1850s;

in praise of *Uncle Tom's Cabin*, the African American author Frances E. Watkins (later Harper) addressed her reverently in a poem published in *Frederick Douglass' Paper*: "The halo that surrounds thy name/ Hath reached from shore to shore."[13] Whether "shore to shore" was meant to register as transcontinental or transatlantic, Stowe here approached a freakishly expansive saintliness. Meanwhile, proslavery reviewers maligned her character in an attempt to quash the popularity and thus the impact of her work; a piece in the *Southern Quarterly Review* went so far as to replace her halo with a satanic hoof.[14] Frederick Douglass, another polarizing figure in the slavery debates, included an appendix to his 1845 *Narrative* that clarified his views on religion, lest readers take his blistering critique of religious slaveholders to be a wholesale rejection of Christianity, something few would have countenanced. Self-justifying gestures emerged in the era's less overtly political writing as well. Nathaniel Hawthorne devoted *The Blithedale Romance*'s preface to the project of forestalling the book's categorization as a roman à clef, a "reviled and disruptive" literary form, in Sean Latham's words, that is inextricable from scandal: "These characters," Hawthorne insisted, "are entirely fictitious. It would, indeed, (considering how few amiable qualities he distributes among his imaginary progeny,) be a most grievous wrong to his former excellent associates, were the Author to allow it to be supposed that he has been sketching any of their likenesses."[15] While attempting to avoid any insult to Transcendentalism's insiders as well as the suggestion that he was a gossip or a backstabber, Hawthorne nevertheless sparked a cottage industry in correspondences that continues to the present day. Even Thoreau, as impervious to public opinion as he often seemed, used the opening paragraphs of *Walden* to justify what readers might interpret as an unforgivable arrogance in his recurring "I." Working toward some version of moral authority (or working to prevent its disintegration) approached, for midcentury authors, the status of an imperative.

Accordingly, this book advances three linked propositions. The first is that moral authority circulated as a kind of literary property within the mid-nineteenth century's rapidly expanding print markets. By moral authority, I mean the ways in which an author's (perceived) good character came to comprise such elements as credibility, admirableness, and influence—qualities that mattered a great deal in a culture that expected its literary texts to teach moral lessons.[16] *Character* was one of nineteenth-century Americans' keywords: though the term sometimes referred to a sort of moral essence—an individual's unchanging interior worth—more often character was conceived as something to be achieved and maintained through the energetic cultivation of good habits and the relentless rooting out of bad ones. Just as crucially, character had to be communicated to the world beyond the individual self. Thomas Augst addresses this dual obligation when he writes that "'character' provided both a method for development of the self and a standard for social presentation."[17] It is via this presentational mode that character begins to morph into reputation, which we might define as character rendered public, where it not only comes within the purview of others' perceptions but also accrues various forms of value.

If nineteenth-century Americans saw character not just as a means of acquiring capital but as itself a form of capital (a phenomenon that Augst, Judy Hilkey, and others have explored), then it comes as no surprise that strategies for discerning and evaluating character garnered attention well beyond the literary field.[18] As Karen Halttunen claimed in *Confidence Men and Painted Women*, middle-class Americans invested in a range of social rituals and performances that advanced gentility and respectability as proxies for good character. Further, the era's elaborate letters of introduction, whether social or professional, purported to vouch for the bearer's character and thus to preview and promise his or her good comportment. Indeed, as Scott Sandage has noted, in early America such a letter was itself called "a character," a term that collapses the document into that which it purports to guarantee.[19] Moreover, by the middle of the nineteenth century American business practices began explicitly to commodify the matter of character. Sandage's extended case study of the Mercantile Agency, a precursor to our era's ubiquitous credit rating and reporting agencies, reveals the minuteness with which character and by extension worth were measured, as agents solicited "local informants" whose reports would illuminate, with regard to individual merchants and would-be men of business, "a matrix of past achievement, present assets, and future promise," all of which was recorded in the firm's carefully guarded ledgers—the "big red book of third-rate men," in Sandage's sardonic rendering.[20] My interest in authorial character as a kind of currency, then, addresses a specific version of a larger—and, as Sandage asserts, often quite ruthless—national phenomenon.

In referring to these as "moral economies," I invoke the work of the historian E. P. Thompson, whose well-known essay "The Moral Economy of the English Crowd in the Eighteenth Century" argued that so-called food riots were not unselfconscious collective spasms but rather operated within "a popular consensus as to what were legitimate and what were illegitimate practices," beliefs that were "grounded upon a consistent traditional view of social norms and obligations, of the proper economic functions of several parties within the community, which, taken together, can be said to constitute the moral economy of the poor."[21] I share with Thompson the presumption that economic actions, even those that appear to be merely reactive, are grounded in deeply held—if not always explicitly examined—beliefs about social and ethical obligations and risks. That said, the sites I analyze in this book evidence far less consistency and consensus than Thompson attributes to England's hungry masses; further, the transactions that interest me range well beyond traditionally economic matters (e.g., buying, selling, hoarding, or stealing). Within the nineteenth-century literary field, that is, an author's perceived character and the moral authority with which it was endowed took a number of forms, some literally remunerative and others commercial in a more abstract, even metaphorical, sense.²² As the following chapters will demonstrate, moral standing was perceived to be a crucial factor in the numbers of books or magazine pieces an author might sell (though a reputational crash could, paradoxically, yield a *succès de scandale*); by extension, such authority was thought to inform the ease or difficulty with which an author found a publisher or a receptive magazine editor for whom a contributor's moral capital was a means of increasing circulation; and it shaped how less tangible forms of value (e.g., critical esteem, national representativeness or belovedness, positioning within early canonization initiatives like literary anthologies or encyclopedias) were assigned as well. I use "economies" in the plural, then, as a way of marking these overlapping forms of exchange and disparate levels of abstraction. And, in keeping with my emphasis on commerce, I often refer in the following pages to the *moral freighting* of authorship, a term that suggests how burdensome these expectations surely seemed at times, but that also connotes movement, circulation, and distribution, elements of the literary field that were dramatically expanding at midcentury.

While I have been talking about these formations in social and economic rather than explicitly religious terms, by no means were they secular in the current vernacular sense of existing apart from or in opposition to regimes of faith.²³ Nineteenth-century Americans' religious beliefs—and the texts, sermons, and other pedagogical forms that shaped and sustained them—fundamentally influenced their conceptions of moral worth. Indeed, most would have found absurd the notion that morality might exist without religion. That said, this book does not attend to the very specific notions of morality that developed within particular sects, not because Americans—or even American Protestants—enjoyed some sort of theological consensus in those years but rather because notions of personal and public morality, though rooted in divergent faith traditions, were routinely rendered amenable to a realm of commercial exchange that depended upon a flattening or blurring of sectarian distinctions. This phenomenon accords with what historian John Higham has called "pan-Protestant ideology," a set of beliefs that "suffused" nineteenth-century American culture, managing to be sufficiently vague that they were widely embraced and yet sufficiently energizing that they offered distinct Protestant sects a "unifying purpose."²⁴ A similar homogenization emerges in many nineteenth-century conduct and success manuals, which recur to and rely upon the presumption of broadly shared notions of what constitutes a moral self. That "pan-Protestantism" or, in Catherine Albanese's term, "public Protestantism," was always a construct—one that worked to paper over some of the era's most pressing fault lines—does not mean that it lacked social, economic, and political power.

In keeping with these insights, the discourse that this book reconstructs—though uneven, multivalent, even contradictory—involved a subordination of religious differences to the market's many exigencies, among them the need to communicate (and to sell books, magazines, and newspapers) across sectarian lines.[25] While authors, editors, reviewers, and publishers no doubt drew on their specific beliefs, they also transcended them as they went about the business of selling, evaluating, and circulating printed material and, by extension, authors' reputations. It isn't that writers and speakers within this broader community reached anything like agreement with regard to who possessed an enduring moral authority or even what such a thing might look like—my book's case studies and the broader culture's notable fractiousness belie that notion. But their disagreements took place within a "moral background," to borrow sociologist Gabriel Abend's term, which includes a culture's shared notions of "what can and cannot be evaluated from a moral point of view" and its "repertoire of concepts" with which moral judgments might be made. Nineteenth-century Americans, in other words, argued bitterly over the moral tendency of particular authors or books, but they overwhelmingly agreed that such were appropriate objects of moral judgment. An author might be deemed moral or immoral, but it was atypical to say the least for such a figure to be declared "non-moral" (another of Abend's terms)—that is, incomprehensible within or irrelevant to moral registers.[26]

This book's temporal boundaries require clarification as well. My focus on the middle decades of the nineteenth century should not be taken to suggest that Americans cared little about authorial character prior to, say, 1830: Benjamin Franklin's *Autobiography*, to cite an obvious example, is profoundly, if facetiously, concerned with shoring up its author's moral authority even as it makes a case for virtue's broader courtship of capital. Olaudah Equiano's *Interesting Narrative*, too, premises its moral force—not to mention the economic successes it details—on its author's personal character, forged via his experience of the middle passage, the literal truth of which Vincent Carretta's scholarship has intriguingly called into question.[27] And early novelists like Susanna Rowson used their prefaces and narrative intrusions to justify their having written within a morally suspect genre. The antebellum period rewards focused attention not because it originated this nexus of concerns but because its increasingly capacious print marketplace, and especially its periodical culture, accelerated and elaborated the circulation of reputational property through book advertising, reviewing, and other printed forms of literary commentary. Further, these venues paid overt attention to publishing as an interlocking series of markets, remarking explicitly on the material, commercial consequences of waxing or waning reputations. While a precise opening date for this intensification would be impossible to assign, I begin my inquiry in the late 1820s and 1830s, when domestic publication and distribution of books, magazines, and newspapers saw significant expansion, and end it around 1870, when Stowe's scandalous writings on Lord and Lady Byron sparked a transatlantic frenzy of recrimination. That final set piece allows us to examine the (supposed) reputational self-immolation of a key antebellum author—one whose moral authority had long been embattled—even as it offers a glimpse of a later period's anxious disarticulation of the author from the text. Eighteen-seventy, that is, emerges as a moment in which the US literary field was beginning to look more contemporary, at least in terms of its conception of the relationship between authorial reputation and literary value.

Crucial to my investigation is an emphasis on authorial character as it played out in publicly available, printed venues—not because these are the only forms of communication that matter, but because I wish to tell a story *about print* at a historical moment in which reputation and scandal were working to reshape its circulation and value. These public claims to moral authority both align with and depart from the more private, though still economically embedded, forms of moral self-cultivation that Thomas Augst and others have explored. Augst's young urban men, for example, used diary keeping and other informal literary practices as a way of acquiring "the moral identity of manhood... within the marketplace, rather than apart from it in ascetic denial or aristocratic ease."[28] Writing was for them a private regime of moral formation that then went public, insofar as the writer performed and promoted his improved self in the workplace as well as in literary and other social organizations. The figures I emphasize, by contrast—mostly self-styled men and women of letters, but also those, like Margaret Douglass, whose more incidental authorship attracted notice—collapsed that process, constructing and disseminating moral identity as an already-public phenomenon, a kind of coin or commodity that helped to constitute the print markets in which they participated. And, while I take Augst's point that writing was imbricated with white masculinity in myriad and fascinating ways in this period, I wish to explore the extent to which men and women—within and beyond the Anglo-American mainstream—used the language of moral authority to frame and promote their texts and their public personas. Identity categories—not just race and gender but also political and religious orientations, regional origins, and other factors—shaped, but did not in any straightforward way determine, the moral freighting of authorship. All published authors, that is, operated to some extent within the burdens and affordances of the era's moral economies. And, while this notion of reputation as literary property necessarily trains our attention on the figure of the individual author, on his or her personhood, that focus proves illusory insofar as reputation cannot ultimately be located there. It emerges, instead, through networks of dissemination and reception that the author cannot reliably control.

The slipperiness of moral authority yields a second proposition: that this paradigm is most intriguing when it is somehow undermined or exploded, hence this book's attention to scandal. In a general sense, scandal renders visible the boundaries around propriety by transgressing them. Author scandals in particular clarify, within a given cultural moment, what readers and commentators want their admired authors to do, or say, or purport to be. The limits of admiration, in other words, both test and illuminate its core. Nineteenth-century authors' transgressions took any number of forms: the violation of sexual norms, whether literal or rhetorical, of course figured prominently, but so did the misuse (typically through publication) of secrets or confidences; the flouting of gender expectations; and various breaches of social decorum (e.g., writing about politically incendiary topics, maligning the dead, or failing to show deference where it was thought due). More specifically writerly forms of bad behavior entered the conversation as well—Melville and Cooper, for example, were each accused of writing at least one scandalously bad book and charges of plagiarism were leveled against authors as prominent as Longfellow or as now-obscure as Fitz-James O'Brien.[29] Crucially, these transgressions and accusations reverberated within a rapidly expanding print culture. Michael Millner has argued that by the early 1830s, scandal was primarily mediated through print: no longer "a local, face-to-face" phenomenon, he writes, it came to be "understood as an event that the public sphere play[ed] a role in creating" and that individual observers encountered largely through reading.[30] I would revise Millner's claim to say that print did not supersede the local, oral, epistolary, gestural, and observational elements of scandal so much as it extended their reach.[31] That is, these more ephemeral modes of registering disapproval in many cases yielded printed versions or interventions, which were then disseminated—and commented on—well beyond the social arena in which offense was initially taken. Further, many of the authorial transgressions I examine were themselves print phenomena—a poorly gauged publication or printed remark that elicited criticism—such that a recursion ensued, with print sparking anger, disdain, and sometimes amusement, sentiments that then found their way into subsequent printed responses. Author scandals, because their principle figures were already immersed in and beholden to print economies, only intensified the resulting synergy between text and outrage. And because authors at midcentury were widely expected to deliver moral truths to their readers—or at the very least to refrain from causing harm—they experienced a high degree of what media scholars James Lull and Stephen Hinerman call *scandal susceptibility* relative to those whose activities were perceived to be less influential or less morally significant.[32]

My attention to scandal should not, however, be taken as evidence of a fundamentally cynical critical lens. Despite the deceptions animating this introduction's opening vignette, I do not see the assertion of moral authority as inevitably a disingenuous performance, the falseness of which simply awaits discovery. Rather, scandal provides a way of interrogating authorship's moral economies when they are most under pressure. Those moments of recalibration or disintegration matter insofar as readerly expectations, once disappointed, are more starkly legible than when, because satisfied, they remain implicit. The scandals I explore are relatively minor affairs in the annals of human transgression—no axe murders or cannibalism here—but their very mildness suggests how invested readers were in the project of admiring the nation's authors and how readily such investment gave way to a range of affects: disappointment, to be sure, but also schadenfreude, as when a once-lionized figure revealed his or her fallibility; or vindication, as when an author long reviled by some managed to alienate erstwhile supporters. Author scandals on the whole trafficked in subtly corrosive emotions (e.g., resentment, disillusion) rather than in the more bracing realms of shock or horror.

These inquiries into the cultural resonances of reputational collapse ultimately reveal the malleable and recuperable qualities of moral authority in the middle decades of the nineteenth century. Contra the stereotype of the rigid, unforgiving Victorian audience, I have found that readers, commentators, and publishers enabled authors to rebound rather quickly following their scandalous missteps. The "non-compliant" were not so much "branded and expelled," to revise Laura Kipnis's formulation, as they were chastised and reincorporated.[33] In advancing this claim I am working against the grain of much Americanist scholarship, in which assertions of reputational ruin are so widespread that the era's political and moral inflexibility has become an article of faith. James Fenimore Cooper's reputation, for example, is said to have never recovered from the vitriolic attacks of various Whig editors; Lydia Maria Child's promising career, we are told, was irreparably harmed by the publication of her antislavery polemic (*An Appeal in Favor of That Class of Americans Called Africans*) in 1833; and Stowe ruined her popularity when she published "The True Story of Lady Byron's Life" in 1869. The severity and longevity of such crashes have been much exaggerated. After their immediate public relations debacles had passed, these authors and others similarly disgraced continued to publish books with well-regarded, mainstream houses and they subsequently garnered positive reviews, at least in some venues and of some titles. And all enjoyed marks of high status within the literary field: publishers' advertisements listed their names and book titles alongside those of unequivocally esteemed authors; magazines named them as important, audience-attracting contributors; and early chroniclers of US literature identified them as key figures in the formation of the nation's corpus.[34]

Lydia Maria Child is an apt example. She was indeed shunned by much of the literary establishment after the publication of her *Appeal*, but as I have argued in detail elsewhere, her exile was short-lived: not only were reviews of that specific text mixed rather than entirely negative, but mainstream firms in Boston, New York, and London continued to publish her (nonabolitionist) work, belying scholars' claims that she had become toxic or unmarketable.[35] Within just three years, her novel *Philothea* (1836) was warmly received in a range of venues. Even the *Southern Literary Messenger*, though it had deplored Child's abolitionist writings, reviewed the work favorably, referring to her, neutrally, as the author of *Hobomok*, *The American Frugal Housewife*, and *The Mother's Book*, with no mention of her recent controversial status.[36] To judge by her steady pace of publication and republication across the next several decades, Child continued to matter within the US literary field as a children's author, a domestic advisor, an essayist, and a novelist.

Child's case reinforces my sense that the martyrdom paradigm, whereby a principled author sacrifices his or her career to prove a moral point, is largely mythical. Why, then, do these misconceptions persist? For one thing, self-sacrifice—especially in the service of a cause we now admire—makes for a better story than a career that recovers adequately but fails to win riches or overwhelming praise. More to the point, these narratives of decline tend to rely on entrenched, if overly optimistic, counterhistories. That is, we imagine that Lydia Maria Child would have been a fully self-supporting author if she had not published the *Appeal*, despite the fact that few of her contemporaries, abolitionist or otherwise, achieved financial security solely through their writing. Similarly, we suppose that Stowe's immense 1850s popularity would have lasted until and perhaps beyond her death if not for the Byron scandal, even though, as Joan Hedrick has noted, postbellum literary tastes were shifting in ways that disadvantaged all authors who worked in a sentimental mode—not just those who published poorly received essays referencing incest.[37] And scholars have tended to overextrapolate from limited evidence, such as negative reviews or commentary in a few prominent venues or by a handful of influential individuals. Looking at a broader range of sources across a longer time frame—and at underexamined genres within the literary field (e.g., advertisements)—yields a more nuanced picture.

Further, I submit that scholars have overestimated the degree to which the political and ideological issues that we still care about shaped the nineteenth-century literary field. In particular, Americanists retrospectively assign to the slavery debates a controlling influence that the era's primary documents do not fully support. Controversies over slavery absolutely informed authors' careers, but they were not central to every critical judgment, editorial decision, or marketing gambit. Indeed, there seems to have been a tendency to forget or at least bracket an author's position vis-à-vis slavery when he or she chose to write in other modes. Like Lydia Maria Child, Richard Hildreth was well known for his antislavery writings, which included the oft-reprinted narrative *The Slave, or, Memoirs of Archy Moore* (1836) and the polemic *Despotism in America* (1840). That reputation, however, did not stop Harper and Brothers, a firm generally hostile to abolitionist politics, from publishing and energetically promoting Hildreth's multivolume *History of the United States of America* (1849–1852).[38] Antislavery figures and institutions evinced a similar amnesia: John P. Jewett, known for his abolitionist sympathies, published Caroline Hentz's *Ernest Linwood* in 1856, despite the fact that just two years earlier she had released a widely noticed proslavery novel (*The Planter's Northern Bride* [1854], first published by Abraham Hart of Philadelphia). Perhaps more surprisingly, the *Liberator* ran advertisements for the 1856 work, even though Garrison had printed disparaging remarks about *Northern Bride*, including references to its inept caricature of an abolitionist supposedly based on the editor himself.[39] Indeed, antislavery venues were less single-minded overall than one might expect; in addition to its political and social-justice-oriented content, *Frederick Douglass' Paper* routinely incorporated literary reviews and other material without obvious abolitionist import, including a serialization of Charles Dickens's *Bleak House*.[40]

What I have characterized as an imposition of present values and concerns onto these nineteenth-century objects of inquiry might be better understood as an interpenetration of past and present with respect to authorship's moral economies. Antebellum readers' investments in authorial character should not, in other words, compel us to distance ourselves, as twenty-first-century academics, from their habits of mind and modes of reception—to tell ourselves how quaint and unsophisticated they were to have cared about such things. Instead, this book's third organizing claim is that the nineteenth century's moral economies continue to inform and trouble the field of literary studies in ways that invite sustained critical attention. This assertion may seem counterintuitive, given that the disavowal of authorial character as a meaningful evaluative criterion has figured prominently in literary studies since at least the early twentieth century, from modernism's impatience with Victorian pieties, to the New Criticism's dismissal of considerations beyond the text, to less temporally bound eruptions of academic antiearnestness. Scholars often advance the notion that contemporary readers are—or ought to be—too sophisticated to care whether, say, Frederick Douglass was an unfaithful husband or Ralph Waldo Emerson was an elitist. Nevertheless, a preoccupation with authorship's moral economies recurs and, indeed, structures many of the field's scholarly and pedagogical inquiries. Consider the reams of scholarship devoted to examining authors' racial politics and representations (Stowe is an obvious figure here for those working in the antebellum period, though there are many others), or the intensity of their reformist commitments (e.g., Emerson), or the credibility of their claims to empathy (e.g., Whitman). Authors' personal lives enter the conversation, too, though less voluminously—one need look no further for evidence than the controversy that ensued when Elizabeth Renker suggested, in a 1994 article and subsequent book chapter, that Herman Melville had likely beaten his wife.[41] Moral litmus tests, demonstrating varying degrees of nuance and historical grounding, influence matters of canonicity and literary value at the level of the individual author, even as they shape how the field comprehends, assesses, and teaches broader modes and genres (e.g., sentimentalism, the domestic novel, the political essay, nature writing).

Though authors of other eras are not exempt from characterological considerations, these burdens continue to fall especially heavily on mid-nineteenth-century figures, largely because the issues they engaged—slavery; racial hierarchy; woman's rights; national belonging, expansion, and disunion—still resonate with academics, students, and general readers. A contemporary version of literary nationalism undergirds these conversations: however much the nation has been called into question as literature's central organizing category—most recently via transatlantic, transnational, and hemispheric literary and cultural studies—there remains a powerful residue of national orientation, and, indeed, an underacknowledged nationalism, in the field's critical, pedagogical, and curricular practices. This echo is especially obvious in scholarship that focuses on (relatively) admirable authors from the antebellum period, those who embody a version of the national past that is at least remotely encouraging, insofar as they contested the prejudices and injustices rampant in their own historical moment. Further, the aspects of their careers that seem most coherent with a national imaginary tend to garner disproportionate attention: scholars have emphasized Frederick Douglass's combative patriotism, for example, but have largely ignored his engagement with the prospect of Haitian emigration, as Robert S. Levine has shown.[42] This emplotment of admirable figures within a national outline is only part of the story; the scholarly ritual of excoriating canonized authors for their ideological failings contributes as well. The national project, rather than being jettisoned, is recuperated through these recurring attempts at dissecting how it went so far wrong. On some level we want our representative authors, however the field argues over that designation, to be good people, people whose politics—racial, cultural, and otherwise—do not embarrass us. If they fail to live up to those standards, the apparent alternatives are to expose and analyze those failings or to exile the offending parties. Consider the example of Sarah Josepha Hale. Though a pioneering editor and prolific author, she appears less frequently on university syllabi or in the pages of scholarly journals than do such contemporaries as Child, Stowe, or even Catharine Maria Sedgwick, perhaps because, as Nina Baym has pointed out, Hale was on the "wrong" side of nearly every nineteenth-century controversy that readers still consider important.[43] And when she has entered the scholarly conversation as a novelist, it has largely been as an apologist for white supremacy or for domesticity's alignment with imperialism.[44] Similarly, the relative marginalization of a figure like William Gilmore Simms has less to do with his aesthetic shortcomings or with some transhistorical bias against southern authors than with his proslavery politics. It is difficult enough to navigate the troubling racial representations in texts like *Uncle Tom's Cabin* or Melville's *Benito Cereno* or William Wells Brown's *Clotel*; what are we to do with *The Sword and the Distaff*? And yet, a serious attempt at understanding the nineteenth century's literary-cultural matrix can ill afford to exclude every author who elicits ideological discomfort in twenty-first-century readers. Who would remain for us to talk about?

I am hardly the first to identify this conceptual trap. Indeed, a number of critical interventions over the last twenty years have urged scholars to move beyond it, as when June Howard asserted in her 1999 essay "What Is Sentimentality?" that the question of whether sentimentalism should be conceived as progressive or retrograde, compassionate or appropriative, had grown so consuming as to disable productive analysis.⁴⁵ Others have specifically positioned their work as abandoning the binaries of hagiography and condemnation, acquittal and conviction, as when Meredith McGill proposes an alternative to the scholarly reflex of figuring Edgar Allan Poe either as entirely resistant to or entirely complicit with the literary cliques of his day.⁴⁶ While the "getting past it" model that these interventions endorse has informed some excellent scholarship, *Moral Economies* argues instead for delving in—that is, for recovering and interrogating the genealogy of these investments rather than isolating them as habits of mind that astute readers ought to avoid. As long as we believe that literature has the potential to do cultural and political work—or, at the very least, as long as we study a period in which that belief was active—we will be obliged to contend with authorship's moral economies.

If the contemporary academy's linkage of authorial character and literary nationalism is largely implicit, in the middle decades of the nineteenth century the connection was openly acknowledged. The *American Quarterly Review* may have referred to literary renown as "the most enduring of a nation's ornaments," but authors could not afford to be merely attractive. They were expected to render their good character legible in print and were especially well regarded if they did so while demonstrating a distinctive Americanness through their treatment of native themes, settings, and characters (e.g., Sedgwick's New England settlers, Cooper's peripatetic woodsman).⁴⁷ In myriad ways, an author's claims to moral authority figured into and aligned with the larger project of becoming nationally representative, even as the collapse of such claims fueled insecurity over the viability of a vibrant US national literature. Authorship's moral compacts, I argue, bridge a crucial historiographical gap in the mid-nineteenth century between an often expressed, if amorphous and inconsistent, desire for a national literature—that is, for authors and texts capable of shouldering the burdens of national representativeness—and a literary market that was, as Trish Loughran has argued, emergent and regionally inflected rather than fully formed and complacently national.⁴⁸ Moral authority, as it played out within the era's cultures of print, was troubled by many of the same factors that plagued the project of achieving and promoting a national culture—sectionalism and other ideological or identity-based fault lines, certainly, but also the burden of being so much to so many.⁴⁹ Moreover, if an author's moral status were undermined, that drama of decline often played out in decidedly local ways, as this book's case studies reveal—a particular volume, article, lawsuit, or speech initiated or engaged a specific set of rumors and suppositions, exacerbating existing suspicions, animosities, and resentments. An enduring moral authority, like the notion of national authorship with which it was linked, proved elusive—a nearly unoccupiable position in such a fluid and contentious cultural field. Indeed, the precariousness of moral authority speaks in multiple ways to the challenges, foreclosures, and impossibilities of literary nationalism itself.

If national authorship was a fraught and contingent affair, it was also the case that the normative status of individual, named authorship was itself very much under construction in the antebellum period. As Meredith McGill has shown, US print culture in the 1830s and 1840s comprised a matrix of reprinting practices and anonymous publication that existed alongside the now more familiar paradigm of proprietary authorship. This book suggests that authorship's moral economies operated in tension with anonymity and widespread reprinting, but also collaborated with those practices to a surprising degree. That is, while I emphasize instances of identifiable authorship, I also explore the ways in which those naming and individuating practices intersected with the formations that McGill has foregrounded. Reprinting in particular worked to amplify threads of commentary crucial to the formation and recalibration of individual authors' reputations by expanding the range of venues and audiences through which specific impressions or characterizations were repeated, endorsed, or refuted. Occasionally reprinting played a more immediate role, as when the *Liberator* facilitated Margaret Douglass's abolitionist makeover or, years earlier, when Fenimore Cooper courted ridicule by suing newspaper editors for libel over objectionable passages in material they had reprinted. Anonymity, too, figured into the construction of authorial reputation, as when authors were accused, fairly or falsely, of penning their own fawning reviews; or, to return to Cooper, when his misidentification of a pseudonymous critic fueled one of his own reputational debacles.[50] Reprinting and anonymous publication intersected with and reinforced the moral economies of authorship, even as the formations would appear to be merely parallel.

By the 1850s, reprinting and anonymous authorship were losing ground as dominant practices in US print culture, though they did not disappear. Meanwhile, as individual, named authorship gained ascendancy, Americans invested increasing energy in the elusive project of knowing their favorite authors. To that end, readers sought access to authors' personal selves through illustrated essays and collections devoted to their homes and lifestyles as well as through widely disseminated reproductions of their signatures and likenesses, the latter made possible by technological developments in photography and printing. These formations are most closely associated with the rise of celebrity culture, whose "fetish of biography," to borrow Aaron Jaffe's phrase, drove what was becoming a kind of intimacy industry by the 1850s.[51] Crucial to this development is the notion of the "public domain," a term vexed by contradiction. "Domain," that is, suggests ownership, control, centralization, and sovereignty, while "public" would seem to invoke its opposites—decentralization, risk, and exposure, but also access and transparency. A fundamental tension, then, underlies authorship's interlocking property relations—reputation is said to "belong" to the figure under discussion, but it is created through multivalent practices of assessment, recalibration, and circulation. The public element is indisputable, if imperfectly understood; the notion of "domain" is where things get complicated, especially as the era's developing technologies of celebrity promised readers the illusion of access to and intimacy with their most admired authors.

Herman Melville's *Pierre* (1852) worries these interconnections via its protagonist's ultimately disastrous authorship. Pierre is hailed, on the basis of his early writings, as "a highly respectable youth," one "blameless in morals, and harmless throughout."[52] But his intense engagement with writing in the final third of the novel parallels his "descent," to use a pervasive nineteenth-century metaphor, into sexual transgression and violence. By involving Pierre in such dissolution, Melville parodies the era's investment in authorial respectability and the literary establishment's uses of that status in the marketing of authors. This antiestablishment stance proves incomplete, however, as the novel anatomizes ways of thinking about the relationship between authorship and the market that would become entrenched, even canonical, in subsequent years. These moral and commercial compacts converge in a much-discussed moment in the chapter "Young America in Literature," an extended parody of the trappings of literary celebrity. Here an editor, thought to be modeled on Melville's one-time friend Evert Duyckinck, pressures Pierre to have his daguerreotype made so that an engraving of it can appear in the next issue of a periodical titled the "Captain Kidd Monthly."[53] Pierre refuses, taking particular offense at the suggestion that, as a published author, he is somehow "public property." The editor's violation of Pierre's notions of taste, class, and, most crucially, privacy leaves the latter incensed; that a representative of "the Captain Kidd school of literature" should so address the scion of Saddle Meadows reveals the promiscuous availability that successful authorship was coming to entail (p. 254).

Technological innovation here mediates status. Musing on the shift from the oil painting to the daguerreotype as portraiture's dominant medium, Pierre laments that "instead of, as in old times, immortalizing a genius, a portrait now only *dayalized* a dunce. Besides, when every body has his portrait published, true distinction lies in not having yours published at all" (p. 254). This passage has been read as proof of Melville's disdain for the emerging culture of celebrity in which he had played a role as a young author of South Sea adventure fiction, when he was welcomed into literary circles and praised in publications that would later dismiss him. More generally, the encounter has been taken as evidence of his disregard for conventional popularity, the esteem of those superficial skimmers of pages who were likely also collectors—or publishers—of authors' portraits. Melville's desire, as indexed in this scene, is for scarcity, for singularity, for an idiosyncratic authorial persona that, while broadly inaccessible, is nevertheless capable, as Gillian Silverman has written, of "revel[ing] in the pleasures of mutual textual sensibility"—that is, with the right kind of reader.[54]

This trope of scarcity belies the nineteenth century's developing linkage of authorship and authorial persona to notions of property and marketing. Just as the era's copyright debates sought to determine the property status of texts and, in particular, the extent to which a text's author could be considered its owner,[55] the author him- or herself began to take on a kind of property status. As the *Captain Kidd* editor suggests, representations of authors helped to sell magazines and books, even as sales spurred interest in those ancillary products, and producers, of authorial celebrity (e.g., portraits, accounts of authors' homes and haunts).[56] Most intriguing is the degree to which these developing forms were imbricated with the notion of an author's moral authority—that is, how literary celebrity emerged from, catalyzed, shored up, and sometimes undermined perceptions of authorial respectability and moral influence.

Melville lampoons such considerations in his novel's treatment of the literary establishment, whose gatekeepers declare Pierre's moral fitness on the basis of the most cursory reading of his meager published output. For Pierre, by contrast, authorship's moral authority resides in a particular version of personal as well as thematic scarcity, the ability to "deliver new, or at least miserably neglected Truth to the world" (p. 283). His folly, the narrator suggests, lies not so much in this animating wish but in his hope that "the world should hail [such a delivery] with surprise and delight" (p. 283). That is, while *Pierre* denounces the intense and devaluing public availability that authorial success seemed increasingly to entail, the novel also dramatizes a fatal contradiction: the resistant, increasingly hermetic author-protagonist nevertheless wants the approval of readers. And while the isolation (not to mention the poverty) of Pierre's studied unavailability is killing him slowly, it is his reemergence as public property—this time as a figure of scandal—that finishes him off. His flight from publicity late in the novel, as he steers Lucy and Isabel through the streets to avoid unwanted encounters, culminates in his very public murder of his cousin and his participation in a shared suicide sure to reverberate in the newspapers of this fictive world for weeks to come. *Pierre*, then, takes up a familiar tension among literary authors between an abhorrence of the notion that one's self is for sale and an equally fervent desire for recognition, for an audience, and, not least, for an income. The novel's bizarre plot, rather than distracting from this central—and, importantly, conventional—contradiction, serves instead as the means by which the author demonstrates its force.[57]

Fanny Fern's 1855 novel *Ruth Hall*, in which the protagonist—virtuous and much abused by both circumstances and callous family members—ultimately achieves success as an author, offers a more triumphant version of authorship's conflation of moral and commercial valuation. Explicitly engaging the matter of celebrity, Fern shows how Ruth's charming, accessible prose style elicits readers' bizarre attempts at achieving intimacy with her; some go so far as to offer themselves to her in marriage. The comic relief provided by these fan mail proposals notwithstanding, Ruth's celebrity within the narrative fundamentally requires her good character, insofar as the reader is invited to delight in her success because she is a good woman—and, crucially, a good mother—who has suffered adversity. *Ruth Hall* is a role model first and foremost, whose industriousness and talent happen to be rewarded with fame and its attendant wealth and influence.

Ironically, Ruth's availability vis-à-vis her fans is staged within a narrative that readers soon recognized as a roman à clef, a form that offered a tantalizing banquet of gossip within the not-so-robust privacy barrier of pseudonymous authorship.[58] Of course, Fanny Fern's identity was divined quickly enough; in some circles, as Thomas N. Baker has shown, she was already known to be Sara Payson Willis (later Parton), sister of the well-known poet and editor N. P. Willis.[59] The ensuing scandal—premised on the indecorousness of a woman criticizing her male relatives in print, not to mention the elision of the author's unhappy second marriage within this otherwise more-or-less autobiographical narrative—accelerated Fern's own celebrity while undermining her moral authority. As *Ruth Hall* and its reception suggest, readers' investment in knowing their admired authors intimately proved at odds with authorship's moral economies. Admiration typically requires a carefully calibrated distance from its object. As Emerson writes of heroes, "They are very attractive, and seem at a distance our own: but we are hindered on all sides from approach. The more we are drawn, the more we are repelled."[60] Curiosity about an author's personal, domestic, interior life risks uncovering details that might undermine his or her moral authority. Whether one begins with a desire for intimacy with or admiration for the author, this admixture of the personal and the commendable seems destined for trouble.[61] The most adaptive authorial response to this conundrum is to create an illusion of access rather than offering intimacy itself. Some of this book's key figures attempted that amiable dodge, though as I will show, it required a degree of image management that was exceedingly difficult to maintain.

The moral transactions analyzed in the following chapters took place within a nexus of informal economies of authorship that, as Leon Jackson has demonstrated, characterized the antebellum literary marketplace.[62] Like the circuits of gift and debt that Jackson examines, the traffic in authorial character shaped how individual texts were marketed and received as well as how writerly careers were represented and evaluated. Never stable, autonomous, or transcendent, moral authority was negotiated to a great degree through print conversations in a range of genres, many of them outside of what traditional scholars would call "the literary." While I am concerned with the ways in which reputation informed literary value, mid-nineteenth-century print networks were configured in such a way that any strict separation of belletristic from ostensibly instrumental texts would be artificial, even counterproductive. That is, a publisher's advertisement that positions Grace Greenwood and Fanny Forester among such solidly admired figures as Longfellow, Lowell, and Robert Browning (with the same typeface and the same amount of text devoted to each) is no less pertinent to understanding the era's structures of valuation than a long essay in the *North American Review* or an allusion within a self-consciously literary poem.[63]

The geography of print bears mentioning as well. Because cities such as New York, Boston, and Philadelphia were so central to US book publishing and to the periodicals through which books were marketed and appraised, this study necessarily gravitates toward northeastern, urban sources. That said, I draw on southern, western, and nonmetropolitan texts wherever possible in order to address the range of responses that my key authors elicited. *Moral Economies* is transatlantic as well—necessarily so, because the literary field under investigation incorporated English and other European titles, considerations, and commentaries. But because this book is primarily concerned with key moments in the formation of American literary history, I present and analyze English and continental materials insofar as they registered with US readers and commentators. Mary Prince and Thomas Pringle, the only non-US figures who receive extended attention here, matter because their collaboration illuminates so many of the tensions evident in later American slave narratives.

Nowhere is the intersection of literary, reputational, and literal (or "real") property more fraught than in the career of James Fenimore Cooper, the subject of this book's first chapter. Taking up a series of scandals that damaged the novelist's popularity in the 1830s—including his cranky defense of inherited land in the Three-Mile Point controversy, his libel suits against various hostile newspaper editors, and his publication of works perceived to be both dull and tendentious—I explore the interpenetration of class, property, and national representativeness in the establishment and reconfiguration of his reputation. Cooper's reclamation in the 1850s as a key forebear—indeed, as a founder of the American literary tradition—reveals the instability of reputation at midcentury, even as it exposes the uneasy linkage that was then emerging between national pride and literary valuation.

If the burdens of exemplarity troubled Cooper's career, they proved to be even more vexing for African American authors, as my second and third chapters explore. "Paratexts and the Making of Moral Authority" (chapter 2) begins by complicating the literary-historical commonplace that the ancillary texts of the nineteenth-century book—for example, dedications, prefaces, introductory letters, authorial and editorial footnotes, and appendices—worked primarily to establish authorial legitimacy. These paratextual gestures, I argue, are better understood as inconsistent, even contradictory, negotiations of moral currency. While they were certainly used to shore up an author's uncertain or diminished moral status, these texts also worked to trouble that authority, as when, in a move that prefigured the complexities of white sponsorship of African American authors at midcentury, the British abolitionist Thomas Pringle authenticated Mary Prince's slave narrative while simultaneously denigrating her character—or when Elizabeth Keckley, in her preface to *Behind the Scenes* (1868), identified herself as Mrs. Lincoln's friend and "confidante," but also expressed the hope that her book's disclosures might allow her to disentangle their damaged reputations. The multiple uses and resonances of paratexts within nineteenth-century African American autobiography illuminate the ways in which authors and their sponsors negotiated matters of moral authority in a context of pervasive readerly suspicion and dismissal.

Chapter 3 extends this inquiry into the moral freighting of black authorship through an analysis of Frederick Douglass's career as an autobiographer and an editor. First, I show how, in the wake of Douglass's break with William Lloyd Garrison and rampant rumors of an affair with a white coworker, *My Bondage and My Freedom*—the text itself and the means by which it was marketed— made the author's moral authority its central thesis. Douglass's editorial work, I then argue, complicated this moral repair project; within his newspaper pieces, a more combative tone and a less polished prose style offered the illusion of unmediated access to Douglass's thoughts and investments, even as his flashes of anger—less carefully calibrated here than in the autobiographies— threatened to overwhelm the circumspection that his embattled moral authority seemed to demand.

Turning to authors who were considered more mainstream—and some who were wildly popular—at midcentury, chapter 4 begins by examining the curious interdependence of advertisements and book reviews in the era's construction and rendering of authorial reputation. After establishing the intricate ways in which the question of an author's moral status suffused these forms, I pursue two case studies: first, the representation and deployment of Harriet Beecher Stowe as a potent moral-cultural force in the 1850s book market and, second, the interplay of decorum and scandal in the marketing and reception of E.D.E.N. Southworth's novels. The circulation of these two authors within the literary field reveals intriguing intersections and collaborations among popularity, literary status, and moral valuation. The immense popularity of their work (in both serial and book forms) exposed these authors to heightened scrutiny, to be sure, as potentially corrupting influences, but their success in the marketplace also relied on—and in some sense exploited—that hint of moral risk, a phenomenon that undermines any received notion that women authors were wholly and inevitably constrained by the era's moral expectations.

Moving into the postbellum period, chapter 5 analyzes the media firestorm that followed Harriet Beecher Stowe's exposé of Lord Byron's supposed incest. Noting that a significant if controversial strain of commentary on the scandal sought to separate Byron's literary genius from his personal behavior, I argue that this case prefigures the unevenness and contestation that would accompany the supposedly diminishing salience of authorial character across subsequent decades, including the curious eruptions of authorial identity and character within ostensibly text-centered critical approaches. My epilogue extends this line of inquiry, examining the critical and pedagogical tensions that authorship's reputational economies still engender both within and beyond the academy. In the field's ongoing anxiety over the meaning and the salience of moral authority, I see an opportunity to complicate and deepen our understanding of literature's premises and purposes.

In a project that seeks to establish a genealogy of authorship's moral compacts, it is impossible to avoid the matter of didacticism, that much-derided feature of nineteenth-century print culture. Textual negotiations of moral authority are inextricable from some version of the didactic, insofar as the authority at issue signals readers' investment in the trustworthiness or credibility of the author—the likelihood that the lessons and truths he or she advances will be reliable, useful, and satisfying, or at the very least not pernicious or misleading. *Moral Economies* makes the case that we substantively misunderstand didacticism when we conceive of it as simplistic or unaesthetic—as a mode that does little more than limn the boundary between the literary and the merely instructive. I suggest instead that nineteenth-century readers and commentators worried the question of authorial reputation so intensively because they apprehended the complexity and cultural potency of didacticism.[64] They habitually—almost reflexively—asked what texts might teach their readers. And, more to my point, they asked who had the authority to advance those teachings, to make them compelling as cultural, political, even spiritual, interventions. In his essay "The Poet," Ralph Waldo Emerson offers an apt, if pessimistic, take on these questions: "Man," he writes, "still watches for the arrival of a brother who can hold him steady to a truth, until he has made it his own." But human beings are "never so often deceived" as in this particular search. Its "fruition is postponed," as it becomes clear that this would-be poet/guide does not, after all, "know the way into the heavens"; he courts a degree of admiration that he does not merit and thus he fails to maintain the reader's (i.e., the poet-seeker's) attention and regard.[65] Hope, investment, disappointment, recrimination... The problematic that Emerson's elusive poet represents is what, albeit in more materialist terms, this book explores.

But if grasping after admirableness is, as Emerson suggests, a quixotic project, its abandonment seems no more promising, at least within the cultural matrix of nineteenth-century America. Hawthorne vividly renders this conundrum through the figure of Miles Coverdale, the reluctant utopian and morally impotent poet who narrates *The Blithedale Romance*. As the story progresses, it becomes painfully clear to the reader and to Coverdale himself that he does not especially matter to any other person within this fictive world. Despite being well spoken, handsome enough, and financially secure, he is socially dead to the people around him, in part because he lacks the moral authority that his rival, the reformer Hollingsworth, possesses (and misuses). The narrator's revelation in the final chapter that he has given up poetry immediately precedes his examination of the "emptiness" that has long attended his lack of purpose, his inability either to "believe in" or "aid" "human progress." As a first-person narrator, Coverdale is still in some sense a writer, but his calling as a poet, despite the "strength of [his] pretty little volume," has foundered in the face of that more general ennui, which he figures as an evacuation of the self that creative impulses and desires cannot survive.[66] And so within a text that points most obviously to the dangers and hypocrisies lurking within moral authority—the once-charismatic Zenobia is less compelling to her companions and less committed to or buoyed by her beliefs than the narrative initially promises, while Hollingsworth cannot be trusted with his enormous persuasive power—it also turns out that an abdication of moral authority, or a failure to cultivate it in the first place, proves incompatible with literary productivity. Moral authority, Hawthorne suggests, is ever a vexed proposition. It is a status not to be invested in too confidently or comprehensively—but in its absence, authorship itself threatens to collapse.

Hawthorne's anatomy of failed authorship is more interior in its configuration than the episodes and transactions that populate this study, however. *Moral Economies* concerns itself not with personal psychology (what Hawthorne called the "individual heart") or even with private character per se but rather with reputation, which might best be understood as character externalized—that is, character that has been somehow broadcast or circulated and subjected to individual and collective judgment.[67] In this regard, character aligns with Bertram Wyatt-Brown's notion of honor, which, at its "heart...lies in the evaluation of the public."[68] Reputation is more unruly and expansive, not to mention less earnest, than either character or honor, however, qualities that make it an especially slippery object of inquiry. But that very instability—premised, in my analysis, on recurring entanglements of the didactic and the salacious—makes it an element of US cultural history well worth puzzling over.

{1}

Fenimore Cooper, Property, and the Trials of National Authorship

In the 1820s and early 1830s, James Fenimore Cooper was widely identified as a literary star. Though he was not universally lauded,[1] his early novels, especially *The Spy* (1821), *The Pioneers* (1823), *The Pilot* (1823), and *The Last of the Mohicans* (1826), earned him a large and appreciative readership. Indeed, commentators on both sides of the Atlantic referred to Cooper as the American Sir Walter Scott—high praise given the latter's immense popularity and public esteem in those years—and compared him favorably to his longer-established countryman, Washington Irving.[2] "Mr Cooper," the *North American Review* noted in 1826, "has the almost singular merit of writing American novels which everybody reads."[3] Crucial to Cooper's prominence was the fact that much of his work represented what were perceived to be distinctively American sites, themes, and narrative arcs. As one US magazine noted, "His works are *national*[;] ... he has formed his narratives from our history, enacted in our own land."[4] Cooper's national representativeness was recognized abroad as well: "Mr. Cooper," an English commentator intoned, "is generally designated 'The great American Novelist.'"[5] Equally important was the fact that he was among the first US authors to be widely read and well regarded in England, not to mention elsewhere in Europe. Given Americans' oft-expressed cultural insecurities and aspirations, this combination proved energizing: Cooper promised a new kind of national authorship, both idiosyncratically American and internationally admirable—evidence that New World themes and artistic attainments might not perpetually be dismissed as inferior.

Across the next eight or ten years, however, Cooper experienced a dramatic reputational crash. While he had his defenders, the balance of public opinion—addressing not just his books but also his personal qualities—was, by the mid-to-late 1830s, remarkably negative.[6] Cooper's drift toward European topics and settings in his fiction and other writings contributed to the problem early on, insofar as it undermined the national/reputational compact on which his early fame depended. Along those lines, a review of *The Headsman*, an 1833 novel set in Switzerland, averred that "removed from the scenes and personages of his native land, the genius of Mr Cooper languishes and withers like a wildwood flower exposed to the noontide blaze of the unshadowed glade," the elaborate botanical simile betraying the extent to which the author was thought to be fundamentally connected to the land about which he had formerly written.[7] Cooper's 1835 novel *The Monikins*, considered by many, on the basis of its much-discussed dullness and convoluted, Swiftian plot, to be the worst book he ever wrote, became a kind of shorthand for what had gone wrong in his career, at least in aesthetic terms.[8] A reviewer for the *Knickerbocker* insisted that, while reading the book, "a poppied and mandragoranean influence overtook us, and we slept under a weight of somnolency such as Rip Van Winkle's could not have exceeded."[9] Perhaps the most damning assessment began with the exclamation "Alas for Cooper!" and called the novel "a monument of human delusion," while the kindest said, with remarkable understatement, that the book was "limited in its popularity."[10] Cooper's publishing disasters would continue throughout the 1830s. A reviewer of his travel narrative *Gleanings in Europe* (1837) remarked that "we can imagine a no more severe penance for our sins than we have just imposed upon ourselves in a cursory examination of this breviary of an egotist's woes" and warned that "the sands of his hour-glass, as an author, are almost run."[11] By 1838, Cooper's slump was so pronounced and so widely noticed that a piece in the *New-Yorker* referred to a newly published novel as his "latest abortion."[12]

To Cooper's seemingly boundless outrage, criticism was not limited to his books. An 1834 reviewer not only noted that the "popularity" of his novels was "apparently on the decline" (a claim, incidentally, that had been made as early as 1825), but also remarked on the author's "egregious vanity."[13] More vehemently, any number of pieces cited Cooper's vitriolic temperament, often referred to as an excess of spleen. Others imagined that an ailment had overtaken him: "From some physical defect, or some deeply seated disease which has produced mental obscuration of the most dense description, Mr. Cooper has, within these few years, found fault with all creation, excepting alone his own immaculate self."[14] Still others sought to needle Cooper rather than pathologize him: in an open letter published in the *New World* in the fall of 1840, the author's antagonists addressed him repeatedly as "Irascible Sir," a reference to his contentiousness as well as to his perceived investment in a superior class status.[15] By 1841, a commentator in the *Knickerbocker* could write with only slight exaggeration that "the name of Cooper now seldom appears in our journals, except for the purpose of censure or ridicule."[16] The author's difficulties were made all the more acute by his exquisite sensitivity to criticism: as a commentator in London's *Quarterly Review* remarked, "he winces at the very breeze."[17]

How did Cooper fall from grace so quickly and dramatically, from esteemed novelist to "superlative dolt," as the poet and editor Park Benjamin called him?[18]

And how, from these depths, could he have been sufficiently recuperated by the time of his death in 1851 that he was made the subject of a memorial publication (featuring such luminaries as William Cullen Bryant, George Bancroft, and Daniel Webster) and would appear as the honored central figure in Thomas Hicks's painting *Authors of the United States* (see Figure 2), among other marks of high status?[19] Certainly Cooper's midcareer decline owed something to overexposure: as the *North American Review* noted in 1838, "he has written not only too fast, but too much."[20] More damaging than these poorly gauged publications, however, were the various enactments of what many saw as Cooper's arrogance, including his critiques of US society and his frequent pronouncements on the idiocy of public opinion. Further, as I will explore, a newly repatriated Cooper insisted that the people of Cooperstown defer to his inherited property rights, a gesture that resulted in a heated controversy between the author and his neighbors; he then recreated the dispute and lavished praise on his apparent fictional doppelganger in the novel *Home As Found* (1838); and he initiated a series of libel suits when that volume—and the inflated self-opinion it was taken to evidence—was ridiculed in print. Perhaps most damning was the fact that Cooper was increasingly perceived to be disloyal to the United States, not just because of his many references to American folly and provincialism, but also via his (alleged) assertions of personal and ancestral superiority. Once hailed as an instantiation of "great American authorship," Cooper came to seem downright undemocratic.

Cooper's difficulties complicate recent scholarly work on American authorship in the 1830s and 1840s, a period in which debates over international

FIGURE 2 **Authors of the United States.** *This 1866 engraving by Alexander Hay Ritchie was made from Thomas Hicks's painting. Image courtesy of the Library of Congress.*

copyright intensified a perennial tension between the desire to provide readers with inexpensive access to a range of texts and the desire to protect the rights of their producers. Meredith McGill has demonstrated the degree to which authorial anonymity—and related notions of the portability and reproducibility of texts—suffused US print culture in this period. Working against the academy's tendency to privilege individual authorship, she instead emphasizes how reprinting "shifts the locus of value from textual origination to editing and arrangement, placing authorship under complex forms of occlusion."[21] While McGill has illuminated crucial elements of the literary field, Cooper's case reminds us that an investment in a singular, recognizable, and, crucially, admirable authorial identity—one that might effectively represent the nation as a fictive whole—was active at the same historical moment. The freighting of individual authorship, in other words, emerged as a signal element of literary commentary even as anonymous reprinting and its attendant decentralization of authorship proliferated. Similarly, a growing investment in the notion that an author might embody and elevate the nation existed within literary markets that were, in McGill's words, decidedly "regional in articulation."[22]

Appropriately, given his precarious status as the nation's novelist, Cooper's public persona in these years entailed a curious entanglement of reputation and property; he recognized, perhaps more acutely than most, that literary reputation circulated as a kind of property, but that awareness served him poorly. That is, Cooper's too-vigorous defense of his property, both literal and reputational, eventuated in a significant loss of public esteem. If reputation, in other words, were guarded—one might say hoarded—too closely, as seems to have been the case in Cooper's frenzy of libel suits, its value deteriorated. The historian Alan Taylor, echoing William Cullen Bryant, has rightly noted that Cooper invited criticism insofar as he treated his books too much like personal property, a stance at odds with much public sentiment in the Jacksonian era.[23] It is also the case that he treated himself—or rather, his public persona—too much like personal property, misapprehending the extent to which an individual might regulate the interpenetration of public and private identities or the terms of their circulation.

That Cooper could, late in his life and, especially, after his death, be reanointed as central to the making of American literature—a foundational figure, along with the more even-tempered Irving, whom midcentury authors could claim as forebear and inspiration—affirms how very personal his difficulties had been.[24] The idea of "James Fenimore Cooper" could better thrive after the man himself—less litigious and more cognizant of readerly tastes over time, but "irascible" still—had expired. Cooper's most controversial period predates some of the developments in literary celebrity that scholars have identified as creating an illusion of intimacy between reader and author (e.g., widely disseminated author photographs, volumes describing and illustrating the homes of literary figures). Most active professionally in an age that less routinely demanded authorial self-disclosure, Cooper nevertheless sacrificed his privacy voluntarily as a way of asserting his own righteousness—by fictionalizing his dispute with his neighbors, for example, or by contesting negative assessments via an absurd number of lawsuits. As such, he serves as an early and to some extent self-created example of the perils of authorial publicity, blurring the line between self and text even as he sought at certain moments to assert its impermeability—by avoiding public discussion of his family life, which appears to have been harmonious, and forbidding access to his personal papers after his death, a move that, as Wayne Franklin has argued, allowed his critics to shape his legacy.[25]

Cooper's case is notable, too, because his transgressions were not overtly immoral—he was not accused of adultery, nor did he publicly charge a beloved English poet with incest, as would be the case with the subjects of my third and fifth chapters, respectively. Indeed, his piety and honesty were widely acknowledged. His scandal, ultimately, was his unlikability. That a seemingly innocuous category of personal failure could elicit such vehement condemnation attests to the growing salience across the first half of the nineteenth century of an author's personhood—his character as well as his personality, temperament, and tone. Warren Susman famously called the Anglo-American nineteenth century a "culture of character," and rightly so.[26] But Cooper's reputational vagaries suggest that some notion of personality, as the term came to be understood decades later, entered the discursive field as well. Americans resented Cooper's presumptions of superiority, as responses to him in the 1830s and early 1840s attest; but his case also limns how badly Americans wanted to be able to like and admire their representative authors. In other words, Cooper's shortcomings involved not just his ill-advised lawsuits and poorly received comments on national character, but his more general failure to be personable—that is, to be an individual whom readers could want, unequivocally, to know. The promise of authorial intimacy encouraged breaches of privacy, as eager readers imposed on their favorite authors, seeking personal details and insiders' perspectives, not to mention likenesses and signatures. But the emerging vogue for knowing the author also disadvantaged those who, like Cooper, proved terribly difficult to embrace.

Property's Publics

The author's property dispute with the people of Cooperstown, New York, and a related series of lawsuits (sometimes aggregated as "The Effingham Libels," after the fictional character whom Cooper was accused of creating as his personal representative in the conflict) are, taken together, the sine qua non of Cooper's reputational crash. Without such a nexus of events and communications, that is, the author's supposed unpleasantness would not have reached scandalous proportions. Given their relevance to the story of Cooper's decline, then, these events and their associated documents merit sustained attention.

Cooper and his family returned to the United States in the fall of 1833 after a number of years in Europe, eventually settling in Cooperstown, which, as the name suggests, his father, William Cooper, had founded (in 1786) and where Cooper himself had spent much of his youth. After repurchasing and renovating Otsego Hall—sold in the early 1820s as the estate's value plummeted—the author was outraged to find that area residents were picnicking on a piece of land along the shore of Lake Otsego, which the elder Cooper had left to his descendants. In effect, the tract had been appropriated as an unofficial public park and was, according to Cooper, suffering from excessive and incautious usage. In the summer of 1837, at the height of picnic season, Cooper published the following in a local weekly:

NOTICE

The public is warned against trespassing on the three mile point, it being the intention of the subscriber rigidly to enforce the title of the estate of which he is the representative, to the same. The public has not, nor has it ever had, any right to the same, beyond what has been conceded by the liberality of the owners.

J. FENIMORE COOPER,
Executor of the estate of the late Wm. Cooper.
July 22, 1837[27]

This threat of rigid enforcement, no doubt calculated to inspire obedience, said more about the tenacity with which Cooper would pursue the matter, while the insistence that his liberality be acknowledged seems to have inspired more scorn than deference. Cooperstown residents responded to the notice by calling a public meeting, to be held that very evening, in order "to defend against the arrogant pretensions of one James Fenimore Cooper, claiming title to the 'Three Mile Point,' and denying to the citizens the right of using the same, as they have been accustomed to from time immemorial." Adopting Cooper's own language, the notice concluded with the claim that public use of the disputed land had never involved a debt "to the LIBERALITY of any one man, whether native or foreigner."[28] That final clause worked to undermine Cooper's legitimacy in at least two ways. Most obviously, the nod to foreignness alluded to the author's long residence abroad and perhaps to his investment in European themes and settings. Could he really, the notice suggested, expect to exert such rigid control over land that he had neglected, literally and thematically, for so long? The "native" reference was less straightforward. Native (that is, one born in the United States) stood in opposition to foreigner, but it may also have referred to the fact that Fenimore Cooper was not actually born in Cooperstown, or even in the state of New York, but rather in New Jersey, a fact that points to the recentness of Cooper family holdings and of Anglo settlement generally in the area, in comparison with the centuries of dominion that, say, the English peerage could claim. If Cooper sought to fashion himself as a kind of landed nobleman, his neighbors wished to remind him of his status as a relative latecomer, just like the rest of them.

The town meeting, convened as a defense against the novelist's alleged arrogance, produced a number of resolutions, the text of which Cooper published several weeks later in an attempt to embarrass his antagonists. In some sense the resolutions were absurd—especially the notion, apparently never acted on, that the village library should "remove all books, of which Cooper is the author." This suggestion, in which the town figures as a disappointed lover, discarding the letters of a no-longer-cherished suitor, reveals that Cooper's personhood and authorship were seen to be interdependent: those who could not abide him as a neighbor would not want to read his books, either. The other resolutions reinforced the degree to which Cooper had become an object of contempt in his hometown. The two most interesting took up questions of deference and status rather than the immediate matter of land use. The first, as we would expect, faulted Cooper, whose "attempts to *procure* acknowledgements [*sic*] of 'liberality,' and his attempt to force the citizens into 'asking' his permission to use the premises" resulted in his becoming "odious to a greater portion of the citizens of this community." The second, less predictably, targeted any who might comply with Cooper's demands: "Resolved,...that we will and do denounce any man as sycophant, who has, or shall, ask permission of James F. Cooper to visit the Point in question."[29] The dispute, these resolutions reveal, was less about where one might go picnicking than about who could command deference from whom.

The economic context in which the controversy emerged bears consideration as well. The year 1837 saw a severe financial panic and subsequent recession that exacerbated class tensions and destabilized economic and social hierarchies. More specifically, as Alan Taylor has shown, the Cooper family's once-immense land holdings had diminished remarkably by the mid-1830s due to William Cooper's overly confident speculations and other dubious business practices, not to mention the lavish spending (and minimal earnings) of his heirs.[30] Wayne Franklin similarly notes that the large inheritance that Fenimore Cooper had been promised in his father's will—amounting to some $50,000—for the most part never materialized, leaving him to depend on his own exertions, a fact that helps to explain his all-too-brisk pace of publication.[31] Cooper's energetic defense of this one plot of inherited land seems quixotic in the face of the larger dissolution of family wealth, especially given that he merely sought public acknowledgment of his status rather than any direct payment. Indeed, he was not even the tract's sole proprietor: Judge Cooper's will, written some thirty years prior, had "bequeath[ed]" the land in question "to all my descendants in common until the year 1850; then to be inherited by the youngest thereof bearing my name."[32] Nevertheless, like Hawthorne's Judge Pyncheon fixating on the recovery of a long-lost patrimony, Cooper endowed Three-Mile Point (or Myrtle Grove, as the tract was also called) with an ultimately self-defeating significance as a final bulwark against intergenerational dispossession. Although historians agree that Cooper acted within his legal rights when he sought to restrict access to the property, the imperiousness with which he asserted those prerogatives would cost him dearly in terms of public opinion. When he insisted, at the end of the letter in which he published the town meeting resolutions, that "the odium of this scandalous affair will infallibly fall where it ought to fall," his confidence regarding whose behavior would be perceived as odious could not have been more badly misplaced.

Literary Offenses; or, Mr. Cooper and Mr. Effingham

If Cooper had left the Three-Mile Point controversy where it lay at the end of 1837, it would likely have faded from public view relatively quickly. Instead, he initiated libel suits in response to unfavorable coverage of his role (suing one newspaper editor, for instance, for asserting that the novelist was "derided and despised" by the citizens of Cooperstown);[33] further, in a move that vastly extended the dispute's shelf life, he incorporated it the into the plot of *Home As Found*, published in November of 1838.[34] Within that narrative, a widowed landowner named Edward Effingham—identified as a descendant of Judge Temple, the fictional patriarch Cooper had made famous in *The Pioneers*—returns to Templeton with his daughter Eve and his urbane, cynical cousin John, after having spent more than a decade living in Europe. Like Cooper himself, the Effinghams find that town residents have been using and abusing a tract of family-owned land on the lakeshore; Edward Effingham publishes a notice in the local newspaper against trespassing on the disputed land; much public consternation ensues; a town meeting yields several presumptuous resolutions; and "the press," in covering the matter, "seized with avidity on anything that helped to fill its columns," without regard for the truth.[35] In Cooper's partisan retelling, Effingham is ever-temperate and righteous, while his antagonists shuttle between self-delusion and malice, a representation that led to the widely held impression that Cooper had created Edward Effingham as a fictional version of himself as aggrieved landowner. Consequently, critics interpreted every opinion that Effingham expresses (not just in *Home As Found* but also in its prequel, *Homeward Bound*, released in the spring of 1838) as Cooper's own and insisted that every quality ascribed to Effingham across hundreds of pages could be read as Cooper's self-assessment.

Home As Found, not surprisingly, elicited much critical vitriol. A reviewer in the *Gentleman's Magazine* [Philadelphia], for example, called the book "flat, stale, and miserably dull," while a reader otherwise sympathetic to Cooper noted that "neither our temper nor our digestion have been much improved by [its] perusal."³⁶ Reviewers took particular delight in ridiculing the novel's many references to Edward Effingham's good looks and exemplary character: one source, referring to a prior comment that had apparently offended Cooper deeply (thus prompting legal action), wrote:

> We charged that Mr. Cooper was "vain, weak, self-inflated and silly;" and in our extracts from the books before us, we proved that in describing Mr. Edward Effingham, intended as a portraiture of himself, he represented him as a "just," "mild," "high-minded," "quiet," "philosophical," "clear-headed," "handsome," "thoughtful," and "liberal gentleman," whose 'justice,' "courtesy," and "mild refinement," are proverbial, and who is "simple," "direct," and "full of truth." And we would simply inquire of our readers whether any person, who would thus describe himself, be not "vain, weak, self-inflated and silly?"³⁷

Reviewers seemed especially offended that Cooper's apparent self-regard coexisted in the novel with a range of negative representations of US society, both urban and rural: the *New York Review*, for example, called it "a malicious work" characterized by "the bursting out of superabundant bile," while a commentator in the *New World*, referencing Cooper's habit of initiating libel suits, wrote that both *Home As Found* and *Homeward Bound* were "despicably libellous [sic] on things and persons American."³⁸ Worse still, the novel's overlay of social disapproval seemed calculated to enshrine the author himself, via the fictional Edward Effingham, as a bemused watchman of decorum and social status. Marking the conflation of Cooper and his protagonist by means of an ambiguous personal pronoun, the *New York Review* sniffed that "we should seek in vain, among all his observations upon the various countries through which he has travelled, for any other standard of propriety, elegance, and good manners, than himself."³⁹

Cooper insisted that none of his characters, Edward Effingham included, was intended as a portrait of a real person. In fact, he devoted a great many paragraphs to the matter in a letter he published in *Brother Jonathan*, noting that Effingham was "twelve years abroad," while Cooper himself was away just over seven years; that Cooper had worked as a sailor, while Effingham had not; that Cooper was not, like Effingham, a widower, nor did he employ French servants; that Effingham was taller than his creator, with a longer nose; and so on.⁴⁰ Surely novelists, then as now, grow weary of readers' assumptions that their characters are unalloyed representations of themselves or their closest associates. And yet Cooper's protestations are as disingenuous as they are detailed. By identifying Edward Effingham as a descendant of the fictional Judge Temple, founder of Templeton, Cooper established a clear association with himself, the son of Judge Cooper, founder of Cooperstown. More obviously, the incorporation of actual documents from Cooper's own recent property dispute makes it difficult to assert credibly that Effingham is not in any sense meant as the author's representative. The distinction Cooper points out—that

Effingham is the disputed land's sole owner while he is not—seems immaterial, given the degree to which the public read Cooper's statements as an assertion of individual dominion. Indeed, the shift to direct ownership in the novel reads more like wish fulfillment than a meaningful disassociation of the author from his fictional character. In any event, a great many readers perceived Effingham to be Cooper's double. A ventriloquizing comment that appeared in the *New-York Mirror* sums up these responses: "I, Mr. Cooper, my family, my history, my books, my enemies, my squabbles with the people of Cooperstown, my prejudices, my opinions, my everything, peep through every paragraph and line of the book."[41] Others made the point more succinctly by referring to Cooper as the "'handsome Mr. Effingham,'" an epithet that the novelist explicitly resented in one of his lawsuits.[42]

This equation of Cooper with Effingham adumbrates what would emerge as the most significant element of the libel suits: the porous boundaries among a literary work, its author, and the person "behind" the author—that is, the individual in all of his dimensions other than authorship, as if such an element could be distilled and considered separately. The law held that journalists and literary critics were free to remark, however negatively, on the work itself and, by extension, on the author *in terms of* his relationship to the work and the process of its composition.[43] The courts were expected to disallow, however, negative commentary on the author as a person apart from the act of creating the literary work in question. So it was fine to say that *Home As Found* was a terrible book or that Cooper's powers of description or of plot development seemed diminished in this particular effort as compared with his prior works. To write that Cooper was an unpleasant or arrogant human being, however, opened up much trickier legal issues. As one of the presiding judges put the matter, "If the review does not allude to Mr. Cooper, except as an author, no matter whether true or false, it is not libelous; while if it does assail him as a man, it is libelous, no matter how objectionable the books."[44] Literary value and personal value were, theoretically at least, to be kept separate.

The substance of *Home As Found* did much to complicate this emerging legal standard. By appearing to write himself and his petty disputes with his neighbors as well as a raft of negative assessments of American social life into the novel's plot, Cooper enabled—even encouraged—a conflation of personhood, authorship, and fictional character. If Cooper equaled Effingham, as much textual evidence suggested, then any aspect of Cooper's personality or public self seen to be represented in Effingham (e.g., arrogance, suspicion of democracy) or any wish that Cooper seemed to be projecting onto Effingham (e.g., aristocratic lineage, vast wealth) would be fair game for critique. The volumes *Homeward Bound* and *Home As Found* were, in fact, brought into the newspaper editor James Watson Webb's first trial for criminal libel in November 1841, when his attorney insisted that they be read aloud in their entirety before judge and jury.[45] The logic underpinning this time-consuming exercise was that those deciding the case needed to understand the degree to which Cooper had injected his personal disputes into the novels, especially *Home As Found*, and thus had intermixed his personhood, protected from criticism by libel laws, with his authorship, which was subject to comment by virtue of its linkage to the works under review. (Webb's review of the novel, to which Cooper objected, had accused the author of "traduc[ing] his country for filthy lucre and from low born *spleen*" and, among other barbs, had called him "a traitor to national pride and national character" for representing American society so harshly.[46]) Apart from demonstrating the novel's courtship of critical outrage, Webb's defense counsel may have wanted to push members of the jury to a level of annoyance with Cooper—as the author of these long-winded and ponderously plotted books—that would predispose them to find against his interests regardless of the legal points at hand. (One of Cooper's enemy-editors called the readings a "grievous torture" inflicted on the court.[47]) While no record remains of jurors' responses to the Cooper read-in, this was one of the few instances in which the author did not prevail in legal terms, as the jury was unable to reach a unanimous verdict. Webb's second trial would end the same way, while the third, which took place in November of 1843, resulted in his acquittal. Interestingly, Judge John Willard, who presided over all three proceedings, disallowed full readings of Cooper's novels in the second and third outings; it is not clear whether this decision owed to his supposed bias in Cooper's favor—much discussed at the time—or to an unwillingness to endure additional reading marathons.

In any event, Webb's was the only indictment Cooper secured for criminal libel. According to Ethel Outland's exhaustive research, the author pursued civil suits against at least six other individuals between 1837 and 1845—including such well-known figures as Park Benjamin and Horace Greeley—and prevailed in nearly every instance, winning a number of retractions and over $3,000 in damages and court costs, though he had sought far more.[48] The courts found that Cooper's antagonists had gone beyond authorship and into the protected realm of personhood in their critiques, as when the editor Thurlow Weed wrote in the *Albany Evening Journal* that "the Author from whose works we used to 'distil delicious romance,' turned snarler and scold.... He libelled [sic] New York and its Citizens. He disparaged American Lakes, ridiculed American Scenery, burlesqued American Coin, and even satirized the American Flag!"[49] (Cooper successfully sued Weed for penning—and Greeley for reprinting—the piece from which I've just quoted.) The iterative quality of the lawsuits is especially noteworthy. Cooper sued individual editors multiple times, as they published negative commentary on legal initiatives already underway—including criticism of his behavior in court, which Greeley called "the reverse of honorable or magnanimous"—or reprinted material from other sources that the author found objectionable, sometimes with additional commentary.[50] The latter circumstance elicited pointed jokes about

Cooper's litigiousness, as when the editor of the *Army and Navy Chronicle*, immediately after reprinting a long extract critical of Cooper, wrote that "we hope Mr. Cooper will not sue us for a libel for copying the above choice *morceau*."[51] While editors found it downright silly that Cooper would sue over a reprint, given the practice's attenuation of individual authorship and thus, one would think, of legal culpability for libel, the courts even here tended to find in Cooper's favor, though the low monetary awards they handed down (relative to what Cooper had demanded) imply a collective impatience with his claims to injury.

As I have suggested, Cooper's victories were pyrrhic.[52] Even the author's friends acknowledged that he could not abide criticism: early on (in 1825), a prescient William Cullen Bryant declined to comment on Cooper's work in print because he feared the latter's reaction: "You tell me that I must review him, next time, myself," he wrote in a letter to R. H. Dana. "Ah, sir, he is too sensitive a creature for me to touch."[53] Cooper's enemies, who coined the term "Coopering" to refer to his aggressive pursuit of legal redress, were much harsher.[54] Among the more intriguing accusations lodged against him in the context of the Effingham suits was that Cooper had abdicated his responsibilities to authorship as a vocation: not only were his libel suits signally harming freedom of the press—a cause that an author ought to support rather than undermine—but he was in effect conceding the superiority of lawyers to authors by fighting his antagonists in the courtroom rather than on the field, so to speak, of prose. Horace Greeley advanced this critique with particular verve, at one point wondering in print why Cooper had eschewed the usual writerly protocols: "If he felt aggrieved by any thing we had published, he had only to write us, pointing out the errors, and we should have published his letter most cheerfully.... Instead of this, the first complaint we have from him reaches us in the Albany Argus, accompanied by a statement that he has directed a prosecution to be commenced against us as libelers!"[55] In another piece, Greeley challenged Cooper to a proper print war, offering "a column a day of The Tribune for ten days, promising to publish *verbatim* whatever you may write and put your name to.... We will farther agree not to write over two columns in reply to the whole," the editorial equivalent, I suppose, of fighting with one hand tied behind his back.[56] (Cooper apparently declined the offer.) Greeley's most aggressive statement along these lines notes a dig at editors in a piece that Cooper had recently published, then addresses the author directly: "Don't scatter your round shot so promiscuously, and then sue whoever throws them back again. Either stick to law or to our own mutual warfare, 'the gray goose quill,' and don't degrade the Literary profession by dodging from one to the other when a bullet strikes you. This is not the manly way."[57] While it is not clear whether, for Greeley, manliness and its requisite status inhere in consistency per se or in allegiance to authorial (rather than lawyerly) methods, the admonition clearly labels Cooper as effeminate and cowardly.

A related accusation held that Cooper's libel suits were not simply an abdication of authorship, as Greeley had charged, but a substitute for it in the wake of the former's critical and commercial disasters. Along these lines, Thurlow Weed called into question the novelist's motives as a litigant: "With him, Bookmaking has ceased to thrive, and as he has no other trade, 'the handsome Mr Effingham' has undertaken to support himself by the levy of legal 'black-mail' upon the Press."[58] Not to be outdone, Greeley joked that the settlement he owed Cooper was his way of supporting an emergent national literature: "We rather like the idea of being so munificent a patron (for our means) of American Literature; and are glad to do any thing for one of the most creditable (of old) of our authors, who are now generally reduced to any shift for a living by that grand National rascality and greater folly, the denial of International Copyright."[59]

If Cooper was a failed writer in the rhetoric of his antagonists, he was also a failed aristocrat. Four of the editors against whom he had litigated closed their scathing "open letter" to him (published in the *New World* in October of 1840) with the line "Your most defensive *Defendants*," warning Cooper "not to mistake the last word we shall write, even should it be misprinted—and thus take us for one of your Cooperstown *dependants*."[60] This bit of wordplay encapsulates many of the objections to Cooper that coalesced around the Effingham libel disputes. It would be simplistic, however, to read it as evidence of Americans' unequivocal resistance to social hierarchy. To offer one of many counterexamples, Elisa Tamarkin has shown that antebellum Americans, including journalists and editors, engaged in elaborate forms of deference and aristo-worship as means of expressing a pervasive, though far from universal or unproblematic, Anglophilia.[61] The problem with Cooper is that he came to expect a degree of deference—to his literal property rights as well as to his reputational and literary properties—that proved out of scale with his perceived status. He did not, after all, hail from an "old money" family; rather, his father had accrued a vast fortune via land speculation, some of it legally and ethically dubious, and then lost much of it, a decline compounded by the fecklessness of his heirs. Cooper himself had achieved literary prominence, but had, by 1840, published a series of critical and popular disasters. Because of these disparities between his expectations and his accomplishments, he inspired, at least among some commentators, ridicule rather than respect.

Apart from the matter of social status, Cooper's libel suits invite a number of questions relevant to our understanding of authorship and the celebrity that increasingly attended it: What kind of property does reputation—both literary and personal—constitute? How can something that necessarily depends on exposure to the public and on the nature of that public's responses simultaneously operate as something private to be defended by recourse to the law? If reputation cannot be literally possessed or purchased, like land or jewelry, how might its loss be compensated? And what risks inhere in demanding that an entity so intangible—and so fragile—be quantified? As a piece in the *New*

World (admittedly a partisan source, as Cooper had sued one of its editors) remarked, Cooper's suits were "in vile taste" insofar as "a public appeal to a jury to assess the pecuniary value of one's literary and intellectual qualities, is a sort of *last resort*, to which none but a desperate man could have recourse."[62] When Cooper was awarded $400 in his suit against Thurlow Weed, the latter used the fact of a specific monetary settlement to ridicule the plaintiff: "The value of Mr Cooper's character... has been judicially ascertained. It is worth exactly four hundred dollars."[63] Indeed, Cooper's "character" appears to have cheapened over time; when Greeley lost his case a year later, he was required to pay the author just $200. Elsewhere, Greeley referred to Cooper's reputation as a "worthless commodity."[64]

The Effingham suits also ask us to consider to whom an author's reputation properly belongs, whatever its value. Cooper behaved as though he were the sole owner, a position that his monetary awards would seem to reinforce. But other points of view were percolating. In a legal opinion that emerged from one of Webb's criminal libel proceedings, Judge Hiram Kinne wrote that "an author, who attains celebrity as such, gets a reputation which becomes a sort of public property, in which his fellow-citizens take a lively interest, and they feel any unwarrantable attack upon it acutely."[65] Literary reputation here is not Cooper's private property but operates instead as something that his "fellow-citizens" possess in common, so an attack on Cooper is an attack, by extension, on the reading public that cherishes him (to the extent that such a thing still existed in 1840). This reversal makes a certain kind of sense in a criminal proceeding, wherein the state, representing its citizens as a whole, seeks recompense in the form of incarceration and fines rather than retractions and civil damages. And yet Kinne's rendering of the stakes upends the original relationship of self to property with which Cooper began his legal quest. That is, the judge's representation of Cooper's reputation makes it analogous to the public-use picnic ground that the latter had attempted to wrest back into private ownership; the author's reputation matters, in other words, not because he feels personally diminished by journalistic evisceration, but because some amorphous notion of the "public" cares about him and therefore loses something when he is denigrated.

Fiction's Properties

This vexed relationship between property and the public suffuses *Home As Found*, though the Three-Mile Point controversy figures into just three of its twenty-nine chapters. Of course much nineteenth-century fiction treats the transfer of wealth through marriage or inheritance, the complications of which drive any number of plots. What distinguishes this particular novel are, first, its remarkably hermetic take on inheritance and, second, its incongruous references to literary property that invoke Cooper's more successful creative past—as if the novel itself were marking, and protesting, its author's decline.[66]

Home As Found is premised on the immensity and curious division of Effingham wealth, delineated early in *Homeward Bound* and referenced throughout the second novel. Edward Effingham, the narrative's stable patriarch, holds the land ("a large hereditary property, that brought a good income"), while John Effingham, his nomadic, Europeanized, and ostensibly childless cousin, possesses the cash ("a large commercial fortune").[67] Their heirs—Edward's beloved only child Eve and whomever she marries—stand to inherit both elements, a much-remarked fact that seems calculated to build suspense vis-à-vis Eve's eventual choice of a husband. When she rejects the pleasant if bland English aristocrat Sir George Templemore in favor of Paul Powis, a charismatic former sailor with a mysterious past, she seems to be taking a tremendous risk. Could he be a deceiver, a fortune-seeker, a cad? Not at all. To the surprise and delight of the novel's central characters, he turns out to be...an Effingham. The narrative arc that brings us to this revelation is as convoluted as it is improbable. The cousins Edward and John, we discover early on, had "both passionately loved" the same woman, Eve's excellent though short-lived mother, also named Eve.[68] When the elder Eve chose Edward as her husband over John, the latter fled all his familiar associations, changed his name for a time, and, as Cooper reveals near the end of *Home As Found*, made "a sudden marriage" to a young, beautiful southerner in order to "supplant the old passion, which was so near destroying [him]" (p. 402). This unlucky consolation prize of a bride, upon discovering that her husband's "heart [was] still yearning toward another," declared herself "unwilling to continue the wife of any man on such terms" (p. 404); in one of the novel's few references to the frontier lifestyle its author was famous for representing, John subsequently "plunged into the prairies," living "in the company of hunters and trappers," unaware that his estranged wife was pregnant. Eventually informed of her death, but not of his son's birth, John "thought all the ties, all the obligations, all the traces of [his] ill-judged marriage were extinct" and decided "to pass as a bachelor" (living in Europe for the most part) under his original name, without disclosing even to his closest relations that he was in fact a widower. Meanwhile, his wife's family, deceived by the assumed name, confused his identity with that of an already-married man and assumed therefore that the child (who would eventually adopt a guardian's surname) was the illegitimate offspring of a bigamous marriage. This backstory—which, if fully dramatized, would likely have made for a more popular novel—serves primarily to explain how it is that John Effingham could reach his fifties without knowing that he had a legitimate son, while the son could reach adulthood without knowing his father's legal name. Crucially, the father is free of guilt, the son untainted by bastardy.

Most significantly, this all-Effingham union reinforces the novel's insistent enclosure of both sociability and wealth. As Paul says to Eve, in contemplation of their overlapping and reflexive property claims, "we are each other's natural heirs. Of the name and blood of Effingham, neither has a relative nearer than the other, for though but cousins in the third degree, our family is so small as to render the husband, in this case, the natural heir of the wife, and the wife the natural heir of the husband" (p. 444). Though they are literally cousins (second rather than third, as the quotation has it), the two are structurally more like long-lost siblings; Eve is the daughter and namesake of her new father-in-law's first and greatest love, while Paul turns out to be the son of Eve's mother's surrogate. The insularity continues as Eve later gives birth to "a miniature Eve," representing a third generation so like the first and second that she has no need even of a new name; the only significant difference is that her mother, unlike both grandmothers, survives the child's infancy (p. 435). If Cooper's marriage plot reads as a milquetoast House of Usher (Poe's story would appear in *Burton's Gentleman's Magazine* almost a year later), it is important to note that the gothic possibilities of the Effinghams' quasi-incestuous isolation are sanitized by their aggressive admirableness (or so the novel would have it). Further, as creepy as this all-in-the-family courtship may seem, it is ultimately more about property than transgressive sexuality, as the Effinghams achieve marriage, reproduction, and the transfer and consolidation of immense wealth without recourse to outsiders, to any version of a public—an entity much maligned within the narrative—that might threaten their monolithic dominion.[69] To the extent that the novel can be read biographically, obviously a matter of much contestation, this conclusion works to rectify the missteps and miscalculations of the author's own inheritance drama. That is, contra the messy working out of the Cooper estate, with siblings—not to mention their scheming spouses—working at cross-purposes and old rivals buying up property at firesale prices, the Effingham legacy is secure and indivisible.[70]

If heritable property could be neatly managed, at least within Cooper's novel, literary property proved more unwieldy. Having established that Edward Effingham is "a descendant of a family of the same name that we have had occasion to introduce into another work [i.e., *The Pioneers*]" (p. 111), Cooper relocates his ensemble from New York City to Templeton and peppers the narrative with references to the earlier novel and, in particular, to its most famous character, Natty Bumppo. When John Effingham leads the group along a steep wooded trail overlooking the village, Eve remarks, "I cannot yet imagine why we are led into this forest, unless it be to visit some spot hallowed by a deed of Natty Bumppo's!" (p. 124). On a lake excursion, Eve points out the location where once "stood the hut of Natty Bumppo, one known throughout all these mountains as a renowned hunter; a man who had the simplicity of a woodsman, the heroism of a savage, the faith of a Christian, and the feelings of a poet" (p. 196). Natty is not simply a remarkable individual; he represents the values that Templeton and its environs have abandoned. As John Effingham laments, "I see few remains of his character in a region where speculation is more rife than moralizing, and emigrants are plentier than hunters" (p. 197). Lake Otsego's seventy-year-old commodore, whom the group encounters several times, notes that "the Leather-Stocking used to talk for hours at a time with the animals of the forest" (p. 199) and ranks him with George Washington "as the two only really great men of my time" (p. 200). "Some people maintain," says the commodore, that the lake's famous echoes are instead sounds made by "the spirit of the Leather-Stocking, which keeps about its old haunts, and repeats everything we say, in mockery of the invasion of the woods" (p. 200). John Effingham soon reiterates the sentiment, calling Leatherstocking a "mocking spirit" (p. 204).

These reappearances of the Leatherstocking, I would suggest, serve most pointedly to mock his creator. *Home As Found* represents Natty Bumppo as an actual historical personage and as a legend, a figure both real and ghostly who is referenced repeatedly—for a while, every time the novel's characters venture any distance into "nature"—within a narrative that has little to do with the plots in which the fictional Natty had heretofore appeared.[71] The Leatherstocking references most obviously work to situate *Home As Found* within the author's oeuvre as a novel about the same place and the same family, loosely speaking, as *The Pioneers*, thus giving its setting and characters a widely recognized backstory. But these gestures of affiliation come to haunt the narrative, as Cooper's best-loved fictional creation lurks as a reminder and residue of past success, and of past claims to national authorship, even as the novel's active, living characters—disasters, as it turned out, in terms of audience appeal—do all the talking and take all the action. And so this book, a watershed in Cooper's midcareer slump, carries within it traces of his reputational property as a beloved author. Elements that seem intended to establish the book's lineage instead serve to index its author's decline.

Frederick Jackson's 1841 parody of *Home As Found* (titled *The Effinghams, or Home As I Found It*), a two-volume narrative nearly as detailed as Cooper's original, reformulates this curious preoccupation with Natty as an emblem of the author's illustrious past, transforming him from recurring referent to active character. The Leatherstocking figure first appears in a reenactment of the famous scene from *The Pioneers* in which Natty shoots and kills a panther that menaces Elizabeth Temple, Judge Temple's daughter, and her companion Louisa; here, predictably, the old hunter's kill shot saves Eve Effingham and her entourage, who marvel at the minute calculations that have ensured his success. The story then moves into more surreal territory, as James Effingham (Jackson's conflation of James Fenimore Cooper and Edward Effingham) "nearly smothered the old man with his kisses on his rough, time worn, and weatherbeaten cheek," exclaiming "'my old friend, my much loved friend.'"[72] Natty, nearing the end of his life (despite the fact that Cooper had already killed him off in *The Prairie* [1827]), spends his last days with Effingham as his near-constant companion, telling stories of his early life as a woodsman. After Natty dies peacefully in his hut—the very dwelling that he burns to the ground late in *The*

Pioneers—Effingham performs "the last offices for him, with his own hands" and then gives "his early life to the world in the character of 'The Deer-slayer,'" a novel that Cooper had published to relatively positive reviews by the time Jackson wrote *The Effinghams*.[73] If Natty presides over *Home As Found* as an admonishing spirit, he serves in Jackson's parody as a kind of deus ex machina— or, more appropriately, a god from the woods—returning the misguided author to affective wholeness (affectionate kisses, salubrious grief) and to "a species of composition [i.e., the frontier tale] in which he stands unrivalled."[74] This image of a chastened author returning to his proper field of representation accords to an extent with Cooper's postslump trajectory, though as I will argue, his efforts to inhabit the role of national author would remain more fraught than this woodsman's rescue admits of.

(Trans)national Disappointments

In an 1831 profile of Cooper, London's *New Monthly Magazine* insisted that national authorship, once achieved, is entirely secure: "When the name of a writer becomes identified...with that of his country, he may feel sufficiently assured of the permanency of his reputation. He may, with perfect safety, leave his fame to take care of itself."[75] For Cooper, this reassurance proved false, as his negotiations of the terms and expectations of national representativeness grew ever more awkward and self-defeating. Things had gone relatively smoothly early on: held up as a great American novelist—prominent in a not-so-crowded field of competitors—he gained ground at home in part as a result of his positive reception in England, an ironclad endorsement that reflected back across the Atlantic as an approbation not just of Cooper-the-novelist but of America itself as an apt subject for and producer of literary works.[76] This crucial intersection of the national and the transatlantic is evident in the oft-repeated claim, invoked in this chapter's introduction, that Cooper was the American Sir Walter Scott, an author whose overwhelming international popularity in the first half of the nineteenth century was predicated on the perceived excellence of novels that treated decidedly local themes.[77] The comparison to Scott announces Cooper's importance in registers both national and transnational, but it also asserts, by analogy, that his relevance to the centers of literary and cultural taste-making depended on his potent association with and access to the periphery. Just as Scott mattered in London—and by extension in New York and Boston—because of his representational purchase on an imagined, quasi-historical Scotland, Cooper mattered because of his skill at rendering the forests, natives, and pioneers of North America (and to some extent the sea, insofar as his experience in the navy was hailed as having provided him special access to representational fidelity). Also noteworthy is the unidirectionality of the Scott/Cooper comparison. Scott is demonstrably not the United Kingdom's Cooper.

In the nineteenth century, cultural accolades, like the course of empire, were thought to move from east to west. Granted, Scott had established himself as an author earlier than did Cooper, but his geocultural siting overshadowed any temporal advantage.

That Cooper's difficulties in enacting the role of national author over time extended beyond his libel suits and off-putting novels is made clear in his mismanagement of this crucial reputational tie to Scott. Cooper violated the hierarchical terms of that linkage when, in October of 1838, he published a long piece in the *Knickerbocker* that was highly critical of the by-then-deceased Scott. Ostensibly a review of John G. Lockhart's *Memoirs of the Life of Sir Walter Scott*, the article sought to disabuse the public of its credulous veneration of the novelist. In a detailed takedown, Cooper represents Scott as charming but unprincipled, a superficial social climber who "feigned" simplicity and habitually sacrificed his integrity in the interest of popularity and status: "The effort which has been made to set him up as a model character," Cooper insisted, "is abundantly absurd." Even Scott's much-touted literary abilities were overrated, in Cooper's assessment. He describes Scott as a talented embellisher of preexisting stories and contexts, but no master of invention and certainly no conveyer of great moral truths: "His sole object was to direct the imagination of the reader, or perhaps it were still truer to say, that he gave vent to the workings of his own fertile imagination, ... without other thought of any moral consequences, than a proper care not to offend."[78]

Cooper did not possess his target's penchant for avoiding offense. One respondent, writing in the *New-Yorker*, accused Cooper of malice in "attempt[ing] to vilify the object of his impotent and contemptible hatred,"[79] while a contributor to the *Knickerbocker* took issue with his hubris in criticizing a superior author: Cooper has "come before the world...with ostentatious pretensions to superior virtue, honor, truth, etc. etc. and, under such high impulses, has assailed...the moral character of one of the greatest men of any age or country."[80] An English source (*Fraser's Magazine*) combined these avenues of critique, characterizing Cooper's "materials" as "spite, envy, hatred of order, and of all deservedly exalted characters; hatred, too, of the best efforts of successful genius; and the whole production brought out for effect, under a pretended zeal for 'principle.'" Lampooning Cooper's attempt to serve as a "transatlantic moralist," this author likened him instead to "a paltry insect trying his best (or worst) to undermine an oak-tree."[81] The futility of Cooper's attack was a commonly expressed sentiment: as the *New-York Mirror* put the matter, "we believe that the great novelist's fame is as safe from the censure, as from the envy or *competition!* of his critick [sic]."[82]

These responses—and the dearth of articles defending Cooper's take on Scott—suggest that Cooper fundamentally misunderstood how deference functioned in antebellum culture.[83] As Scott's upstart American analogue, Cooper was expected to evidence his respect for the greater man. Instead, the *Knickerbocker* article made Cooper seem both indecorous (because he spoke ill of the dead) and ungrateful (because he denigrated an author widely identified as a model and inspiration for his own work).[84] As the *New-York Mirror* put it, the review was "an outrage upon courtesy, propriety and taste."[85] It did not help matters that many of Cooper's grievances against Scott were so petty (e.g., he made much of Scott's supposed dishonesty in suggesting to his brother that they use a code in order to signal how the famous author should interpret the latter's letters of introduction) or that Cooper's own ego seemed implicated in the affair—not only had he had taken issue in print with the dismissive way Scott had represented their encounters in his diaries, but his own work had been lambasted in the *Quarterly Review*, of which Lockhart, Scott's biographer and son-in-law, was editor. Perhaps more damaging was the fact that Cooper's attack on Scott came under discussion at a point when his own sensitivity to criticism was attracting public notice. While there was surely a degree of editorial piling on in the responses to Cooper's review, the piece undermined both his credibility and his appeal as a representative national author. As one offended reader commented, "the grave, and especially the resting spot of genius should be sacred from intrusion; and who has not seen with deepest regret, the great novelist of one hemisphere troubling the ashes of him who was the glory of another."[86] Instead of playing the role of Scott's gracious heir, Cooper came across as waspish and self-serving.

As the Scott controversy suggests, the transatlanticism that had catalyzed Cooper's early success came to rank among his signal public relations disasters, as he weighed in on international political conflicts, commented endlessly on national character, and, in general, compared Europe and America in ways that annoyed both sides. He was accused of an unpatriotic Anglophilia and a disdain for his native land on the one hand and of a parochial loyalty to the United States on the other.[87] To make matters worse, he often combined his political interventions and national commentary with personal grievances, not just in his fiction, as we have seen, but also in polemics like *A Letter to His Countrymen* (1834), a text that James Franklin Beard has called "a masterpiece of miscalculation."[88] In part an argument against Americans' excessive "deference to foreign opinion," the *Letter* attracted notice more for its obsessive attention to negative reviews the author had received and for its petulant, not to mention premature, announcement of his retirement ("I lay aside the pen").[89]

Alongside publications like the much-derided *Letter*, the very fact of Cooper's long residence abroad occasioned some suspicion that his tastes, not to mention his self-concept, had surpassed his origins. One reviewer opined that living in Europe had undermined his talent as a writer, suggesting that *Homeward Bound*'s aesthetic shortcomings owed to Cooper's ever-increasing estimation of his own status: "Whether it is, that the merchant service [a key element in the novel's plot] is not congenial to one of his lofty bearing, or that his taste has become too fastidious, by the refinements of Europe, for a faithful narrator of nautical adventures, it is unnecessary to decide:—whatever may be the cause, the result is certain—the trident has fallen from his hand."⁹⁰ *Home As Found* compounded the problem: representing neither sea nor wilderness, the novel's disquisitions on Americans' flaws offended a range of readers, including those with no obvious link to the Effingham libel suits. And yet the book's Anglo/Europhilia is far from pure or straightforward. The heroine Eve, for example, despite expressing her disappointment at the state of US fashion, architecture, and social conversation, is delighted to discover that her mysterious, multilingual suitor is American rather than European. And Templeton's foremost Anglophile, a fifty-year-old named Tom Howel, is lampooned for his single-minded attachment to a country he has never visited and for his summary dismissal not only of the United States, but of the rest of Europe as well. Alongside the novel's many references to American inferiority, these intimations of patriotism would seem to defend Cooper from charges of a mindless hostility to his native country. That said, the terms on which the novel critiques Howel's disposition toward England are themselves open to the charge of elitism, as the narrator and other characters ridicule his narrow knowledge base and his reluctance to travel, to see in person the wonders he idolizes. These passages ultimately critique the wrong kind of Anglophilia (naive, provincial, prolix) rather than the sentiment itself. Further, the Americans whom the narrative praises are those who have spent the most time abroad.

If, within the logic of Cooper's novel, the best Americans are those who have been least "at home," the available evidence suggests that for US readers Cooper himself had become, by the mid-1830s, insufficiently American in his tastes and political sensibilities. A circumspect (that is, performatively humble) reentry into US society might have ameliorated the problem, but instead, Cooper's homecoming was both awkward and impolitic, not least because it involved a rejection of local hospitality. Upon his return in the fall of 1833, Cooper received the following invitation, signed by such prominent New Yorkers as Peter Jay and Fitz-Greene Halleck, among others:

> Sir—A number of your old friends, pleased with your return among them, are desirous of testifying to you the continuance of their friendship. Your distinguished talents and manly defence of the institutions of our country while abroad, have won our esteem and affection, and we, therefore, beg your acceptance of a dinner, at such time as shall be most agreeable and convenient to you.⁹¹

Cooper replied that he was "compelled by circumstances to deny [him]self the pleasure" and went on to rehearse in vague terms some of the controversies that he would later detail in *A Letter to His Countrymen*: "I have particular satisfaction in learning that so respectable a portion of my fellow-citizens approve of my course, in reference to our common character and national institutions; for some pains have been taken to persuade foreigners that, in this respect, I am opposed by the intelligence and virtue of the community to which I belong."

Noting that his interventions had "been loudly censured by some among ourselves," Cooper expressed "the highest gratification in now learning that so many gentlemen, whom I have long known and respected, have viewed the matter differently."[92] It is not clear why Cooper declined this invitation, even as he belabored his recent controversies. His private letters suggest that he was not averse to social engagements in general; further, to judge from his travel writings and other evidence, he relished public demonstrations of his literary and social importance. James Franklin Beard notes that Cooper had attended a similar dinner in honor of Commodore Isaac Chauncey "just four days after his return" from Europe, where he was disappointed in the welcome he received. As Cooper later wrote, "those of his acquaintances who did speak to him, (two-thirds did not,) addressed him as if they had seen him the week before, and so cold and constrained did every man's manner seem, that he had great difficulty in persuading himself that there was not something wrong.... the chill was so thorough, that he found it impossible to sit out the dinner."[93] Whether Cooper's displeasure owed to actual ostracism or to outsized expectations, his newfound distaste for such events only exacerbated his reputational difficulties.

A piece that appeared in the *New-York Mirror*, commenting on Cooper's rejection of the invitation, begins with a long discussion of how a well-wrought public dinner can help to dissipate resentment and fractiousness:

> By promoting a pleasant intercourse of refined wit and exuberant fancy, and causing a genial effervescence of the kindliest sympathies of our nature, [the public dinner] contributes to remove many a prejudice, which, originating we know not whence, has tinged our feelings with a hue of personal aversion; and, by showing to us the man whose portrait we had drawn from a jaundiced imagination, divested of his supposed attributes, and all smiles and affability, it tends by the mere force of contrast, to rivet our attachment when least anticipated.[94]

Though Cooper goes unnamed until the final third of the piece, he is clearly its referent—the one who has refused this opportunity to be reimagined by and reattached to his countrymen. Significantly, the article later compares Cooper to Washington Irving, who had welcomed a public dinner in his honor upon his return from Europe the previous year—and whose time abroad seems not to have saddled him with a snobbish reputation.

The public dinner dust-up, though a minor episode in Cooper's most controversial decade, foreshadows matters that would reemerge in the ensuing years: the perception that he lacked humility, most obviously, but also his habit of rejecting the terms on which the public sought to embrace him, whether through a social invitation or through its preference for certain of his writings over others. National authorship placed demands on Cooper that he often failed—or refused—to meet. Nevertheless, Cooper was not unequivocally banished in the 1830s from the status of "great American author"; indeed, there were ongoing attempts to reclaim him as a representative figure. But even these ensconcing documents—typically biographical sketches and career overviews—betrayed hints of trouble. Some tried to minimize Cooper's difficulties, framing them as hiccups in an otherwise exemplary career. A generally positive piece that appeared in the *Southern Literary Messenger*, for example, conceded that some of his works had "elicited severe and often merited criticism," but ended with the prediction that Cooper "will doubtless yield to the renewed inspiration of the native American muse, and entwine himself for many succeeding years around our hearts."[95] Others enacted an almost gymnastic self-distancing within some version of a reputational rescue: a feature in the *Hartford Pearl*, for example, offered (within a single sentence) a critical preface—"Whatever weaknesses, or overweening confidence in his own talents, may have been manifested by Mr Cooper—however splenetic may have seemed the last effusion from his pen"—then a double negative ("still, we cannot but acknowledge"); and finally praise ("the hand of a master is visible in his first works").[96] The same piece included a note detailing the editor's difficulties in commissioning the piece: he had first asked two "friends of Mr Cooper" to suggest someone who might write it, but they did not respond, so he was left to secure his own contributor, whose article was "prepared in great haste" and whose expressed "sentiments" (he does not say which) the editor did not fully share. The article itself then half-heartedly defended Cooper against his various critics and ended with the following tentative endorsement: "We believe that the present chilling blast of criticism will pass away, that our countrymen will awake to the masterly power of American genius—describing American scenes."[97] As these examples attest, it was difficult, by the late 1830s, to offer Cooper unmitigated praise.

The wide range of responses to Cooper's missteps—both transatlantic and domestic—reinforces my sense that scholars (and some antebellum commentators) have overstated the extent to which his reputational troubles owed to political rivalries that, if not entirely local, were mostly regional in scope. The charge of a political vendetta against Cooper was sufficiently active in the early 1840s that Horace Greeley felt the need to respond to it in print. Insisting that the attacks were not politically motivated, he noted that other authors aligned with the Democratic Party (e.g., Bryant, Hawthorne, Bancroft) had received favorable treatment: "Where have the merits of these gifted Americans—against us in politics, but not less admired for their genius and their Literary achievements, and proudly regarded as country-men—been more heartily acknowledged and steadily commended than in the columns of the Whig Press?"[98] The claims of political ill will would persist, however. The most vehement is Dorothy Waples's 1938 study *The Whig Myth of James Fenimore Cooper*, in which the novelist emerges as the innocent victim of a malicious "Whig tornado."[99] More recently, Wayne Franklin, in his preface to *James Fenimore Cooper: The Early Years* (2007), emphasizes the damage that Whig editors caused to Cooper's reputation, though he acknowledges the author's "complicity" in his fate.[100]

That Cooper's immediate antagonists in the Effingham libels were associated with Whig Party politics is indisputable. Too, a number of Cooper's most controversial, criticism-attracting publications addressed political issues, typically from an anti-Whig position. But the author's reputational crises extended well beyond politics, even when his immediate topical investments were ostensibly partisan; for one thing, it was Cooper's habit of mixing politics and personal grievances, as Beard has suggested, rather than his politics alone, that elicited the most outrage.[101] And, even if Whig editors were motivated by politics when they derided Cooper, as many have charged, it is important to note that the author's comportment and his books were also criticized in venues that had no consistent or overt political affiliation (e.g., the *New-York Mirror*, Sarah J. Hale's *Ladies' Magazine*) and in those that originated well beyond New York state, ground zero for Cooper's lawsuits and for the negative responses they most immediately elicited (e.g., the *Southern Literary Messenger*, various British journals). Further, Cooper was criticized in periodicals to which he had at several points contributed (e.g., the *Knickerbocker*, *Graham's*), suggesting that he was not ever and always an outsider vis-à-vis those venues.[102] Perhaps most telling is the fact that organs affiliated with the Democratic Party did not come to Cooper's defense as vigorously as one would expect, were his conflicts essentially partisan. Even the *Democratic Review*, with its dual investments in politics and literary nationalism, did not defend Cooper with any enthusiasm in the late 1830s and early 1840s when he was most under fire, choosing not to review *Home As Found* and avoiding direct commentary on the author's land dispute.[103] The *Review* printed remarks favorable to Cooper at various points, especially late in his career, but it offered no consistent point of view regarding his entanglements with the press. Though a commentator remarked in 1849 that "perhaps [no one]...has...been pursued with a more vindictive and untiring malice by a portion of the public press, than this pure-minded man," a negative review of *The Crater* (1847) took issue with Cooper's "savage flings against the newspapers, with which he has been at war so many years": "There are, no doubt, many great abuses in the management of our newspapers, but what would we be without them?...if the press has annoyed [Cooper], it has also given him his standing as an author. Without its aid he could never have earned his bread by writing novels."[104] The press, this reviewer suggested, did Cooper at least as much good as harm. Whether that accounting is entirely accurate, I would argue that Cooper's midcareer troubles were less about politics than personality—and the intriguing ways in which it was coming to matter within the literary field.

Recuperation

As any number of commentators had urged, Cooper did indeed return to "American scenes" in the 1840s, jump-starting the Leatherstocking franchise with *The Pathfinder* (1840) and *The Deerslayer* (1841). And he reengaged the sea novel genre, the source of much of his erstwhile popularity, with *The Two Admirals* and *The Wing-and-Wing*, both published in 1842. But Cooper's restoration was neither immediate nor unequivocal. One review of *The Pathfinder*, for example, expressed relief that Cooper had "at length desisted" from his attacks on his critics, but offered a tepid assessment of the novel itself: "His success, if not brilliant in this instance, is at least respectable."[105] Even in more positive reviews, references to the novelist's recent troubles abounded: the *Casket* [Philadelphia] welcomed *The Pathfinder* "as an omen that Mr. Cooper will hereafter forego his satires and be, as he once was, the lord of prairie, storm, and sea," while a review in the *Knickerbocker* effectively put Cooper on notice that the reading public's patience was limited: "So long as Mr. Cooper shall continue to lay before the public works like 'The Deerslayer,' just so long will he find no lack of readers to reward his endeavors to entertain them."[106] The *Ladies' Companion* made a similar point in more positive terms: "We are happy to meet Mr. Cooper once more in his proper sphere[,] delighting and instructing by his beautiful delineations of the characters and scenery of his own 'free land.'"[107] The *Southern Literary Messenger*, too, mingled praise and relief in its review of *The Two Admirals*: "Cooper's forte is the sea, and we welcome him back to an element, upon which he has spent a considerable portion of his life, and upon which he is evidently so much at home."[108] The *New World* called the book "delightful" (apart from its preface, which the reader is advised to skip "if he wishes to be in good humor with the author") and sought to erase any residue of readerly alienation: "We hope that no one will deny himself, on account of any former unpleasant thoughts of the author, the pleasure of reading this capital novel."[109] One of the most positive assessments in this recuperative period appeared in *Graham's*: "Mr. Cooper, in the book before us [*The Two Admirals*], has re-asserted his right to the rank of the first living American novelist."[110] While Cooper's fictional offerings elicited the warmest reviews, his *History of the Navy* (1839) garnered praise as well: the book provides "evidence of the final triumph of his kindlier and more manly feelings over the promptings of Satan and the spleen. The very preface is redolent of a returning good humor—of a recovered modesty—of a resuscitated common sense."[111] Remarks on Cooper's return to a path of authorial righteousness became, in this period, a kind of reflex.

Despite these developments, some remained skeptical: the *North American Review*, for example, insisted in 1850 that Cooper had "committed literary suicide at least ten years ago; and the volume now before us [*The Ways of the*

Hour]...certainly affords no proof of his resurrection, or the restoration of his faculties."[112] But the author's recuperation was sufficiently robust that publishers felt confident, by the late 1840s, in releasing uniform editions and thematic groupings of his works. Two firms, G. P. Putnam and Stringer and Townsend, brought out editions of Cooper's novels—Putnam's offerings, beginning with *The Spy*, featured revised and corrected texts in hardbound volumes "uniform with the New Edition of 'Irving's Works,'" while Stringer and Townsend produced cheaper books (75 cents per volume, versus $1.25 for the Putnam editions) aimed at a wide readership.[113] Stringer and Townsend published a range of titles, including such unpopular offerings as *The Monikins* and *Home As Found*, but Putnam avoided reissuing works that seemed unlikely to attract new buyers. Accordingly, the latter firm's announcement for the new series sought a delicate balance. It insisted on Cooper's high status (calling him "the American novelist" and citing a review that grouped Cooper with Irving as an originator of "American classics"), but also conceded his missteps: "To refer to the censures and counter-censures which have been connected with some of Mr. Cooper's later writings is a thankless, and perhaps, in this place, an impertinent task." The advertisement then turned the attention of potential buyers to Cooper's "earlier volumes[, which] must live freshly in the memories of thousands of the present generation."[114] Both publishers capitalized on Cooper's most popular offerings, advertising the "Sea Novels" or "Sea Tales" and the "Leatherstocking Tales" as ready-made groupings.[115] Reviewers tended to endorse this reification of Cooper's prominence via focused attention to his best-loved books. The *Democratic Review*'s brief notice of the collected Leatherstocking Tales, for example, insisted that "this series...constitut[es] a standard work, which must ever be to the race now nearly passed away, what Shakespeare and Scott have been to the History of England, and the manners of the middle ages. To say that no library is complete without [it]...is but to repeat a truism."[116] The reviewer's point is clear: Cooper's best work, organized and labeled as such by a respectable publisher, constitutes classic American literature. Across the next fifty years, numerous publishing houses, both English (Bentley, Routledge) and American (W. A. Townsend, Appleton, Collier, and Putnam again) would release uniform or collected editions of Cooper's works.

Michael Anesko has argued that the history of an author's collected editions "reveals to us the complex process by which an author and his works become invested with cultural authority."[117] In Cooper's case, this process featured temporal contradictions—a newly released series comprising his earliest works; premature assertions of a long-standing centrality to American letters—and elaborate gestures of selection, insofar as few publishers attempted a complete catalog. In packaging Cooper, comprehensiveness posed a risk. Further, the author's long midcareer slump defied the more obvious developmental narratives (e.g., an ever-improving novelist representing an ascendant national literature) that were available to publishers and other participants in the literary scene. Selling Cooper required a cagier pitch—one that emphasized his centrality without defending his worst qualities (or his worst books) and that made a case for his midcentury relevance on the basis of early works, most written in the 1820s, that represented an even more remote American past.

The valedictories that followed Cooper's death in September of 1851, especially those included in the *Memorial of James Fenimore Cooper* (1852), further illuminate the thematics of his recuperation. William Cullen Bryant, whose speech at an event held in honor of the deceased was among the materials reproduced in the *Memorial*, remarked that "in the general grief for [Cooper's] loss, his virtues only were remembered, and his failings forgotten."[118] That was not actually the case, even among the relatively friendly group that contributed to the volume. Edward Everett, for example, mentioned the uneven quality of Cooper's literary output—"He wrote too much to write every thing equally well"—and suggested that "had he been longer spared to us," the author himself might have wished "to recall" (that is, retract) some of his works, while Bryant himself conceded the limitations of Cooper's prose style, which "attained no special felicity, variety, or compass of expression."[119] Neither did Cooper's contentious reputation go unmentioned: Herman Melville referred decorously to the fact that the author's "fame at home ... received a slight, temporary clouding," but figured his disputes as "very paltry accidents, incident more or less to the general career of letters."[120] Bryant, despite his assertion of collective amnesia, rehearsed Cooper's controversies in greater detail: *A Letter to His Countrymen*, he noted, "awaken[ed] in certain quarters a kind of resentment that a successful writer of fiction should presume to give lessons in politics," while *Homeward Bound* and *Home As Found* failed in part because "Cooper did not, and, because he was too deeply in earnest, perhaps would not, infuse into his satirical works that gayety without which satire becomes wearisome."[121] For Bryant, Cooper's eventual literary restoration overshadowed these miscalculations. By 1840, he remarked, "people had begun to think of [Cooper] as a controversialist, acute, keen, and persevering, occupied with his personal wrongs and schemes of attack and defense."[122] But his publication of *The Pathfinder* materially altered this perception, as the reading public was "startled from this estimate of his character by the moral beauty of that glorious work"; Cooper's return to Leatherstocking not only reaffirmed his literary greatness but also restored his personal reputation. To prove the point, Bryant quoted an anonymous commentator whose personal relationship with Cooper had been characterized "for some years" by "an unhappy coolness": "'They may say what they will of Cooper; the man who wrote this book is not only a great man, but a good man.'"[123]

Much of the praise included in the *Memorial* emphasized Cooper's national relevance. Bryant called him "one of the permanent ornaments" of the country's literature; C. J. Ingersoll, an author and retired congressman, referred to the Leatherstocking character as "entirely American"; Everett noted that "much about [Cooper]... was intensely national"; the New York Historical Society (a record of its October 7, 1851 meeting was reproduced in the *Memorial*) resolved that "in [Cooper's] contributions to our literature, he displayed eminent genius and a truly national spirit"; and the historian William H. Prescott insisted that "there is no one, I am sure, in this country... who does not look on the fame of Cooper as the property of the nation."[124] This national prominence had much to do with the widespread perception (which William Charvat's scholarship would eventually confirm) that Cooper was the United States' first professional author. A letter from George Bancroft, printed in the *Memorial*, stated that Cooper was "the first to devote himself exclusively to letters" and served as "the pioneer" of his country's "literary independence."[125] Bancroft's speech reiterated this notion: calling Cooper "the first great American man of letters who has passed from amongst us" (perhaps the author had enhanced his status by dying before Irving?), he went on to hail the novelist as "a forerunner,—one of the very few who, at long distances from one another, went before us."[126] The notion of scarcity informed another of Bancroft's comparisons: "The men of letters of the coming generations, and the men of letters who now live, must consent to stand close together, like trees in the densest forest; but Cooper dwelt, as it were, alone on one of his own prairies."[127]

This image of Cooper alone on his prairie is more apt than perhaps Bancroft intended. Cooper was recuperated so energetically in the early 1850s in large part because American literature's practitioners and champions were keen on establishing for it a sense of history, of lineage.[128] And Cooper, of all the "forerunner" candidates, served better at midcentury as a representative of American literature's past than he could, in the 1830s, as its present. Bryant noted that Cooper's "character was like the bark of the cinnamon, a rough and astringent rind without, and an intense sweetness within" and insisted that he "was one of those who, to be loved, must be intimately known."[129] For those beyond this privileged inner circle, Cooper was also one of those who, to be loved, must be held at a significant distance. If his authorial career was successful in terms of name recognition, status, and, not least, book sales, it was also riddled with controversy and, I have argued, with an admixture of self-sabotage. But I also wish to emphasize the degree to which national representativeness, from its very inception, entailed a set of expectations, challenges, and obligations that perhaps no one, even a writer better suited to public scrutiny than Cooper, could entirely satisfy.

In the chapter that follows, I turn my attention to authors who lacked Cooper's purchase on national significance or representativeness; that is, by virtue of their race or class status or positioning within literary markets, national iconicity was never theirs to lose. And yet their attempts at navigating reputational economies were every bit as complex and illuminating as Cooper's. Analyzing the uses to which such figures (and their variously positioned advocates, editors, and "handlers") put the era's ubiquitous paratexts—including prefaces, appendices, dedication pages, and headnotes—I make the case that moral authority mattered well beyond the nation's emerging, if embattled, literary elite, informing not just sales and textual valuation but also such fundamental matters as credibility, legitimacy, and the attribution of both authorship and blame.

{ 2 }

Paratexts and the Making of Moral Authority

Gérard Genette has famously defined the paratext as "a zone not only of transition but of *transaction*: a privileged place of a pragmatics and a strategy, of an influence on the public, an influence that—whether well or poorly understood and achieved—is at the service of a better reception for the text and a more pertinent reading of it."[1] Within nineteenth-century American print culture, these zones of transaction—including prefaces, introductions, dedications, footnotes, and appendices, to name the most prominent—emerged as crucial sites for constructing, reclaiming, and sometimes undermining an author's moral status. Whether they advertised his or her connections to the literary elite or defended the main text's apparent transgressions, these framing documents invited readers to perceive texts and authors in the context of (and sometimes in opposition to) particular moral frameworks. Following Genette, I address this heterogeneous genre largely in terms of functionality—how, that is, do these varied framing, previewing, and commenting devices work to steer readers toward particular conceptions of and affects with regard to the text and its creator? However, against Genette's notion of the paratext as a kind of airlock that facilitates, with varying degrees of economy or proficiency, the reader's movement into and out of the main text, I conceive of these adjunct genres as contentious and porous, often operating in tension with the main text as they introduce details and perspectives at odds with its author's ostensible purposes.[2] Indeed, some of the era's more elaborate paratexts eschew even an internally cohesive message or agenda, much less a pointed and univocal commentary on the texts they purport to frame. As Beth A. McCoy has noted in reference to African American cultural documents, paratexts are best conceived as "territory important, fraught, and contested."[3] Their structural subordination, in other words, belies the degree to which paratexts and their creators struggled with the text itself for dominance, both thematic and ideological.

The paratexts that accompanied Frank J. Webb's 1857 novel *The Garies and Their Friends* hint at these contradictions. In keeping with the common practice of an author publicizing his affiliation with an individual of greater status and influence, Webb dedicates the book to "Lady Noel Byron," the British abolitionist and widow of the poet Byron, "by her kind permission," he is careful to note. In doing so, Webb asserts his deference and gratitude even as he links both his authorial identity and his novel with a morally righteous figure of aristocratic lineage, and, indirectly, with the literary status of her (albeit estranged and deceased) spouse. The book's front matter also includes a letter from Lord Brougham, another upper-class English abolitionist, who admits that he is writing as a last-minute substitute for Harriet Beecher Stowe, who had intended "to introduce this work to the British public" but was delayed by "a severe domestic affliction."[4] Lord Brougham goes on to cite Stowe's faint praise of the book, derived from "a letter to one of her friends": "There are points in the book of which I think very highly. The style is simple and unambitious—the characters, most of them faithfully drawn from real life, are quite fresh, and the incident... is often deeply interesting." Stowe considers the book "of worth *in itself*," Brougham's document continues, because "it shows what I [i.e., Stowe] long have wanted to show; what the *free people of color do attain*, and what they can do in spite of all social obstacles."[5] In other words, the book matters to Stowe insofar as it proves her point within an ongoing sociocultural debate; in her framing, Webb is an example of the potential of "the race" rather than an autonomous creator of a literary text.

Stowe's own preface, a footnote explains, unexpectedly arrived in time for publication and, confusingly, appears in the book's front matter immediately before Lord Brougham's apology for its absence. In this late-arriving document, Stowe refers to the novelist only as "a coloured young man, born and reared in the city of Philadelphia" and again links the novel to questions of racial progress and potential: "The book... may be of interest in relation to a question which the late agitation of the subject of slavery has raised in many thoughtful minds; viz.—Are the race at present held as slaves capable of freedom, self-government, and progress?"[6] Through this chain of associations (the unnamed Webb, though born free in Philadelphia, represents "the race at present held as slaves" and, by writing a novel, helps to prove their fitness for liberty), Stowe commends the book to the same public that had made her own novel a bestseller—and herself a celebrity—in England, even as she embeds its author within an undifferentiated mass of potential achievers. Cementing this erasure of Webb's subjectivity, Stowe's final sentence uses the term *author* to refer to herself rather than to the novelist she purports to introduce: "The author takes pleasure in recommending this simple and truthfully-told story to the attention and interest of the friends of progress and humanity in England."[7] Insofar as the preface stages a transaction between Stowe-as-celebrity and the English public—or rather, the portion of that public identifiable as "friends of progress and humanity"—it asserts the moral authority of the text's sponsor and audience at the expense of its creator. Where Webb reemerges, albeit faintly, is in his fulfillment of moderate expectations—his "simple and truthfully-told story" testifies to the potential of "the race," without any unseemly aesthetic overreaching.

The paratexts introducing *The Garies*, then, enact a series of endorsements and substitutions. They associate Frank Webb with high-status and morally respectable figures—most notably Lady Byron and Stowe, whose conjoined reputational crash some twelve years later I address in chapter 5—who matter to a book-buying English public. But they also reassure that public that Webb represents no threat to the established order of things. The appearance of his name on the title page notwithstanding, Stowe's preface reduces him to an anonymous example, one who tells simple truths without challenging anyone's conceptions of narrative form on the one hand or racial hierarchy on the other. And so a novel that is itself very much about African American self-sufficiency is framed within a regime of white appropriation, made possible by the exigencies of a book market in which Stowe's name sold copies and Webb's did not. Webb's moral authority, meanwhile, remains dormant in these preliminary texts; those who read his narrative would encounter an implicit case for it in his candid protest against Philadelphia's notorious white-on-black violence, but those who encountered only Stowe's and Lord Brougham's remarks would be encouraged to credit their moral status rather than his.

In keeping with this mélange of marketing, earnest endorsement, and self-serving counterpurposes, the chapter that follows takes up midcentury paratexts as vexed and contradictory gestures within the literary field's larger moral economies. First I consider the ways in which prefaces, perhaps the era's most commonly deployed paratextual form, asserted—but also parodied and in some cases rejected—moral authority as a requisite of authorship. I then offer an extended analysis of African American life writing as a genre whose paratexts exemplify some of the form's most intriguing and most egregious possibilities.

Prefacing Reputation

In contrast to Stowe's elision of Webb in the preface to *The Garies*, nineteenth-century prefaces more typically worked to proclaim or restore an author's moral legitimacy.[8] While aestheticist and antibiographical positions with regard to literary valuation erupted here and there—and gained momentum late in the century—at midcentury authors, editors, and publishers presumed that an author's moral status mattered to most readers and that assertions of such status were apt uses of paratextual space.

A brief taxonomy may prove useful. Many prefaces, of course, were penned by the book's author, though some referred to themselves in the third person.

Others were written by sponsoring figures, typically better known or of higher status than the author, who sought to frame and justify the work at hand; many of these external authors signed their prefaces, lending the weight of their identities to the legitimating project. But paratextual authorship was often murky, with many of the era's anonymous prefaces remaining unattributed to this day. In terms of their tone, nineteenth-century prefaces ranged from earnest to ironic, from grave to playful. On the earnest end of the spectrum, consider Louisa May Alcott's adaptation of a poem from John Bunyan's *Pilgrim's Progress* in the preface to *Little Women*, a strategy that asserts the didactic potency of her novel while aligning its author with an eminently respectable predecessor. Catharine Sedgwick's preface to *Married or Single?*, by way of contrast, begins more facetiously. Instead of linking her authorial identity with some unassailable moral or literary figure, Sedgwick calls into question the value of the entire authorial enterprise: "The want of an innocent occupation may be reason enough why one should write, but some better reason or a plausible apology should be rendered for inflicting the writing upon the public." Light-hearted self-deprecation soon gives way, however, to an expressed hope that readers will take in her book "with some profit; and possibly there are those who will relish better a glass of water from our own fountains, than a draught of French concoction, whose enticing flavor but disguises its insidious poison."[9] In an era known for its temperance fervor, what better way for Sedgwick to assert her moral authority than by comparing herself and her book to fresh water from a native fountain, as opposed to an "insidious" foreign cocktail?

In any number of midcentury prefaces, moral justification appeared as a straightforward assertion. The preface to *Sparing to Spend* (1853), for example, one of T. S. Arthur's many offerings, aligns the author explicitly with the figure of the "moral teacher" who rests his hope in those readers (to be found "in all classes") "who need only the clear presentation of a truth, to lead to its adoption."[10] Similarly, the publisher's preface accompanying Mary Denison's *Nobody's Child* (1857) calls its author "a closely reasoning moralist" and "an earnest teacher of truth for the truth's sake"; the preface to F. Colburn Adams's *Justice in the By-Ways* (1856), meanwhile, avers that the author's "purpose...was a high moral one," though that declaration is sandwiched between an opening remark on readers' distaste for prefaces and a long account of the capriciousness of American publishers.[11] Sedgwick's preface to the second edition of *A New England Tale* strikes a more defensive pose, affirming that the book "was written under a sincere conviction of its beneficial tendency" such that "the objections which have been made to [its] moral and religious character... the writer cannot comprehend."[12]

Prefaces sometimes took on an overtly commercial valence. For instance, the publisher's preface to Emerson Bennett's *Intriguing for a Princess* (1859) blurs the line between introductory remarks and advertisement; quoting at length "from a distinguished critic," the preface assures readers that Bennett's "reputation is the common property of all lovers of the noble maxims which he inculcates, the morality which he teaches, and the virtue which he adorns, in a style at once the purest and most fascinating."[13] Authorial reputation, in other words, was the property of readers and book-buyers rather than of the work's creator or promoter. Others linked reputation more directly to personal advancement, though profit-seeking had to be framed so as to preserve the author's respectability and propriety: Sarah J. Hale's preface to a new edition of *Northwood*—titled, chummily, "A Word with the Reader"—constructs the author as a suffering widow who wrote the book not "to win fame, but a support for my little children." "Northwood," she continues, "was written literally with my baby in my arms." This emblem of maternal sorrow soon morphs, however, into a savvy professional, as Hale informs readers that her "literary life" has proven sufficiently successful that she has been able "to educate my children liberally, as their father would have done."[14]

Other prefaces commented on the author's worth only indirectly, foregrounding instead the moral value of the text as a kind of proxy. A brief preface "by the author" of the anonymous novel *Alice Granger, A Tale of the West* (1852) is representative on this score. The book's "merit," readers are assured, lies not in its success as a "tale of love" but rather in its "moral sentiment"; the author "sincerely desires that its meaning and use, may be received by some youthful minds, as a *way* leading to the 'good, and the *true*.'"[15] T. S. Arthur's *Leaves from the Book of Human Life* (1855) offers a similar endorsement of the volume's salubrious tendencies: "While we offer, in these pages, a pleasant recreation for leisure hours, it is such a recreation as will, we trust, leave the mind active with good purposes and kindly sympathies."[16]

Even authors who resisted such conventions nevertheless made self-justifying and self-legitimating gestures. In "The Custom-House," for instance, Hawthorne responds obliquely to the scandal that attended his dismissal from a government post by dramatizing the severity of his treatment (his firing is figured as the stroke of a guillotine) even as he minimizes the degree to which he had actually fought to retain the role. Reinforcing this nonchalance, he takes leave of his "old native town" of Salem, declaring himself "a citizen of somewhere else" and, by implication, an author impervious to the judgments of his reader-neighbors. And yet in the preface's final paragraph, he owns up to the "transporting and triumphant thought... that the great-grandchildren of the present race may sometimes think kindly of the scribbler of bygone days."[17] If his current reputation, at least among Salem residents, lies beneath or beyond his notice, he cannot help but register higher hopes for his legacy. The preface to *The House of the Seven Gables* evinces a similar ambivalence with regard to mid-century fiction's moral imperatives. Here Hawthorne resists laying claim to an overt moral purpose: "The author has considered it hardly worth his while... relentlessly to impale the story with its moral, as with an iron rod,—or, rather, as by sticking a pin through a butterfly,—thus at once depriving it of life, and causing it to stiffen in an ungainly and unnatural attitude." But provide a moral he does, with the gloss that a moral agenda works best when wedded to aesthetics: "A high truth, indeed, fairly, finely, and skillfully wrought out, brightening at every step, and crowning the final development of a work of fiction, may add an artistic glory, but is never any truer, and seldom any more evident, at the last page than at the first."[18]

Plenty of midcentury books, to be sure, appeared without prefaces—indeed, without any introductory materials at all, apart from a title page—and any number of authors and publishers released some of their works with prefaces and others without. Even without a friendly or officious or self-promotional preface, books offered their readers certain signposts: the author's name, especially if he or she were famous; the publisher's reputation; the form and cost of the book; the other titles advertised between its covers; and so on. In many cases the absence of a preface surely signified nothing in particular, though some authors (most obviously Stowe) included a preface when the work in question promised to invite controversy (e.g., *Uncle Tom's Cabin* or *Dred*), but omitted it when the volume seemed poised for a more benign reception (e.g., *The Minister's Wooing*). In some cases, however, the absence of a preface is more fraught, especially when considered within a particular author's career trajectory. The case of Herman Melville, whose 1857 novel *The Confidence-Man* appeared without a preface, a dedication page, or an introduction, merits consideration. Given the overlay of moral righteousness that permeated the era's typical introductory matter, and given *The Confidence-Man*'s preoccupation with the vagaries of trust, this unprefaced text suggests its author's rejection of—or at the very least a waning faith in—such investments in authorial reputation.

Melville's first novel *Typee* (1846) included a thoroughly conventional preface. Referring to himself in the third person, the author touches on some well-worn themes: his nod to humility, for instance—"No one," he writes, "can be more sensible than the author of his deficiencies"—could have graced any number of contemporaneous texts. And his reliance on experience (his time spent "tossing about on the wide ocean") as a guarantor of credibility breaks no new ground.[19] But Melville's preface nevertheless does important public relations work. Anticipating the criticism that his book unfairly lambastes Christian missionaries, Melville disavows any animosity toward the faith or its ministers—that "glorious cause which has not always been served by the proceedings of some of its advocates." Like Frederick Douglass's appendix to his first narrative, published a year before *Typee*, this preface figures Melville as pro-Christianity but antihypocrisy. His negative representations are based on "facts admitting of no contradiction, and which have come immediately under the writer's cognizance."[20] He is a faithful reporter, not some atheistic partisan. *Omoo*'s preface, appearing the following year, offers similar assurances. "A strict adherence to facts," the author insists, "has been scrupulously observed" with respect to the "missionary operations" referenced in the text; indeed, Melville tells us, "nothing but an earnest desire for truth and good has led him to touch upon this subject at all."²¹ Following several self-justifying paragraphs touching on his research into "the history and ancient customs of Tahiti," his rendering of native dialects, and his inability to provide exact dates for the events narrated, Melville closes the preface with an assertion, written in the third person, of his fidelity to what he has witnessed: "He has merely described what he has seen; and if reflections are occasionally indulged in, they are spontaneous, and such as would, very probably, suggest themselves to the most casual observer."²² Credibility here seems contingent on typicality.

Melville began to drift away from the conventions of earnest prefacing in *Mardi*, which begins with a mildly acerbic chiastic joke: because his first two books were received "in many quarters... with incredulity," he claims to have decided to write "a romance of Polynesian adventure... to see whether, the fiction might not, possibly, be received for a verity."²³ *Moby-Dick*'s introductory materials moved further into a facetious mode. The author, rather than putting himself forward as a trustworthy guide to the material within, instead lurks as a gentle satirist. His twinned prefaces, labeled "Etymology" and "Extracts," construct minor, ironic figures (a "Late Consumptive Usher to a Grammar School" and "a Sub-Sub-Librarian," respectively) who supply the reader with arcane introductory information relating to word and whale.²⁴ *Pierre*, published the following year, went further afield, featuring a long dedication to a geological formation—Mt. Greylock, from which the author claims to have "received... most bounteous and unstinted fertilizations"—but no preface.²⁵ And then in 1857 Melville published *The Confidence-Man* with no prefatory material whatsoever. Did he consider his ethos, as far as the reading public perceived it, to be too far gone by that point to be paratextually redeemed? That is, in the wake of the aesthetic and personal scandals attending the publication of *Pierre*, was there any way to reclaim the image of the trustworthy, upstanding author?²⁶ Or might *The Confidence-Man*'s layered ironies and moral dodges have rendered it incompatible with the kinds of gestures that mid-nineteenth-century prefaces seemed to make available?

Melville returned to the earnest preface in *Battle-Pieces*, the collection of Civil War poems he published in 1866. Here he makes some conventional introductory moves: he identifies the event that precipitated most of the included work—the Fall of Richmond—and notes that that the individual poems "were composed without reference to collective arrangement." This straightforward, understated exposition gives way to a curious disavowal of authorial volition. In writing these poems, the author "yield[ed] instinctively... to feelings" inspired by a number of disparate sources. Describing himself as "unmindful, without purposing to be, of consistency," Melville removes himself utterly from a position of agency. "I seem," he concludes, "in most of these verses, to have but placed a harp in a window, and noted the contrasted airs which wayward winds have played upon the strings."[27] The author barely seems present, much less self-promoting. Melville does not use this space to shore up his moral authority—indeed, he claims no authority at all.

The Confidence-Man's absent preface, by contrast, is curiously assertive as silences go, suggesting that the author resides in a place beyond making excuses or attempting self-promotion in the guise of self-deprecating charm. The reader's initial encounter is not with a friendly author-as-guide, but rather with a "mute" in "cream-colors," who boards the steamboat with "neither trunk, valise, carpet-bag, nor parcel. No porter followed him. He was unaccompanied by friends. From the shrugged shoulders, titters, whispers, wonderings of the crowd, it was plain that he was, in the extremest sense of the word, a stranger."[28] It is tempting to see this rootless being, whom most readers subsequently identify as the confidence-man's first iteration, as a metaphor for the author himself, whose alienation from his audience mirrors the mute's cool reception on the *Fidèle*. Indeed, one contemporary reviewer, writing in London's *Literary Gazette*, identified Melville as an authorial confidence man who delighted in confusing and frustrating an earnest reading public.[29] But I would suggest that this quiet stranger is just as aptly a figure for the reader, whose entry into an unprefaced text seems analogous to the character's embarkation without luggage or companion. Whether that unencumbered entrance signifies interpretive freedom or destitution ranks among the book's many ambiguities.

To the extent that *The Confidence-Man*'s absent preface both echoes and reinforces the novel's notorious inaccessibility, the ways in which it undermines the reader's faith and engagement, its complement appears in chapter 42, in the form of the barber's "gilt notification swinging among colored fly-papers from the ceiling" announcing "No Trust."[30] The fact that the barber is persuaded to set aside his sign, at least temporarily, and is then bilked out of the cost of the shave he has just provided, invites readers to meditate on the elusiveness not just of trust but of trustworthiness in narrative as well as commercial transactions. Melville's refusal to provide a preface that asks for the reader's trust, if read in light of this late episode, can be interpreted as a gesture of respect rather than dismissal, insofar as the rest of the book calls into question the very reasonableness of trust—or, for that matter, mistrust—as a reliable interpersonal register. As this retreat suggests, *The Confidence-Man*'s address to its readers is finally more ambivalent than hostile, a claim congruent with James Machor's assertion that the "master narrative" of Melville's career, according to which he "grew increasingly antagonistic toward his contemporary readership," is an oversimplification.[31] For instance, the very fact that *The Confidence-Man* poses such daunting interpretive challenges implies Melville's acknowledgment of an at least potentially astute reader, one equipped to puzzle out the relationships among and significance of a complex sequence of episodes and to make sense of a shifting cast of characters, none of whom especially invites readerly identification. And yet the narrative evidences an unmistakable chill toward its readers—it does not greet them or flatter them or solicit their approval in any easily recognizable way. The book's more obvious departures from midcentury narrative conventions—its rejection of the usual expectations regarding plot, characterization, and moral edification—echo this foundational revision of the era's expected compact between author and reader.[32]

In this as in many matters, Melville positioned himself—and was situated by readers and critics—outside the literary mainstream, which continued to invest in prefaces as key sites for shaping an audience's perceptions and evaluations. Despite midcentury authors' worries (articulated, oddly enough, within their prefaces) that prefaces were losing influence—they lamented that readers no longer paid any attention to prefatory remarks or that they had gone out of style—they continued to write them. On the whole, the era's prefaces registered a fundamental regard for the reader's judgment (or a recognition that such a regard ought to be performed if not felt), not to mention a faith that such judgment could be shaped by the claims of the author or his or her sponsor. The fact that so many prefaces sought to reassure or appease their readers—to forestall negative assessments, either of book or author—attests to this faith. But as the rest of this chapter will demonstrate, the relations between authors and readers that these paratexts mediated often fell short of happy communion. Nineteenth-century prefaces worked so energetically to establish trust because, for most authors, a stable and compelling moral authority was so elusive to begin with.

Abolition's Scandals: The Case of Mary Prince

Nineteenth-century African American life writing—a category that includes slave narratives, both self-authored and otherwise, alongside other forms—offered especially complex interactions between texts and their paratexts. The prefaces, dedications, footnotes, and appendices that accompanied these publications worked to construct or repair (and in some cases to undermine) the credibility and moral status of authors and narrators, as we might expect, but also, indirectly, of editors and amanuenses. Scholars have had a great deal to say about these legitimating gestures, asserting that they not only responded to audiences' presumed prejudices and reservations, but also worked to reinforce those very structures of inequality.[33] These claims are borne out in much of the material I analyze here, though I question the premise, put forward most directly in William Andrews's groundbreaking work on the slave narrative as a genre, that "white autobiographers," by contrast, "could assume their readership would grant them the status of peer and would assume their sincerity unless they contradicted themselves or transgressed important moral norms in their narration."[34] As this book's examples and analyses demonstrate, white authors did not typically enjoy such reputational security. Some earned it over time, but it was not an a priori entitlement of white authorship to be maintained or lost. I would argue instead that the uses of paratexts within African American life writing should be considered in the context of a larger print culture wherein the vast majority of authors were confronting the uncertainties of moral authority and reputation.[35] That is, African American authors and their sponsors foregrounded and intensified widely used paratextual practices of authentication and self-promotion, refining them in response to specific social and material exigencies—racial prejudice and the ongoing fact of slavery, obviously, but also African Americans' limited access to literacy, to publication, and to various forms of economic gain. As a result, even as these gestures served the vexed project of legitimating black authorship and in some sense reified in the process the very injustices that made such efforts necessary, they also aligned with broader practices of authorial self-justification.

The extensive paratexts that accompanied *The History of Mary Prince* (1831) provide an intriguing, if unusually stark, case study along these lines, though including Prince's narrative in a book about US cultures of print initially seems counterintuitive. Prince was born in Bermuda and lived as a slave there and in various West Indian locales; her narrative was composed in London and published in both London and Edinburgh with the assistance of UK-based abolitionists; and the book was not, as far as I have been able to discern, reviewed or discussed in antebellum US periodicals, though it may well have been purchased (or borrowed) and read by Americans. Indeed, the narrative was not published in the United States until 1987, when it emerged as a key text within a broader recovery of the slave narrative as a genre. Nevertheless, Prince's book has, over the last thirty years or so, become part of Americanist scholarly and pedagogical conversations: articles and chapters analyzing it have appeared in US—and, more broadly, North American-oriented publications (e.g., *Early American Literature*, *African American Review*, a monograph in the University of Pennsylvania Press's "Rethinking the Americas" series, and Greenwood Press's reference volume *African American Authors, 1745–1945*).[36] Meanwhile, the narrative itself has been republished in venues largely devoted to US concerns, including *Documenting the American South* (a digital project sponsored by the University of North Carolina) and such widely available course texts as the Schomburg Library's *Six Women's Slave Narratives* and Dover Press's *Three Narratives of Slavery*.[37] Of course Prince's narrative fits into other academic constellations as well—Caribbean, Black Atlantic, British, and Commonwealth literatures; feminist literary studies; and biography studies, to name the most obvious. Her narrative and its accompanying paratexts matter to my inquiry because they prefigure the interplay of suspicion and legitimation that would characterize later US slave narratives as publishing events and as textual artifacts. Within a decidedly transatlantic abolitionist print culture, *The History of Mary Prince* lays bare some of the ways in which racial identity and a personal history of enslavement worked to complicate authorship's moral economies.

Compared with later narratives by Frederick Douglass, William Wells Brown, or Harriet Jacobs, however, Prince's agency in creating this text is attenuated, to say the least. Not only did an amanuensis (Susanna Strickland, a young Englishwoman recently converted to the antislavery cause) compose the text based on Prince's oral account, but the abolitionist Thomas Pringle, who was also Prince's London employer, served as its editor, contributing a preface, explanatory notes interleaved with the main narrative, and an extensive supplement that commented on and attempted to corroborate the work's more controversial elements.[38] A letter appended to the third edition took this work of validation to an absurdly literal endpoint; here Pringle's wife detailed two separate "inspection[s]" of Prince's scarred body, carried out by herself, Strickland, and two other white women, in an attempt to prove the veracity of the narrative's abuse claims.[39] The presence of so much scrutiny and mediation on the part of white activists threatened to overwhelm Prince's own voice and undermine her dignity, even as it marked her prior marginalization—made most obvious by her lack of access to print literacy—and her vulnerability, the degree to which she stood in need of whites' assistance and protection but was also subject to their well-intentioned overreaching. And yet specific elements of these framing texts, especially Pringle's engagement with the accusations and countercharges with which Prince was entangled, implied that her voice and her story were all too powerful—capable, at the very least, of catalyzing animosity and libel suits among elite white men. Pringle, it seems, was as preoccupied with taming and regulating Mary Prince as he was with advancing her specific claims and the abolitionist cause writ large.

If, as I have argued, paratexts played a key role in the establishment and circulation of moral authority, they also sometimes engaged its complement: scandal. This phenomenon was especially evident within abolitionist print culture, which derived much of its energy and persuasive force from the strategic deployment of shock value. Using sensational stories of horrific punishment, coercive sex, and family separation, abolitionists sought to convince their readers that the practice of slavery was morally abhorrent but also curiously absorbing. Proslavery forces, of course, countered with their own uses of scandal, insisting that abolitionist writers (including novelists, polemicists, and slave narrators) were trading in outright lies that not only besmirched individual and regional reputations but that also functioned as a kind of pornography. Not surprisingly, then, abolitionists explicitly argued for the credibility of their texts, providing extensive documentation and, in the case of many black authors, offering some sort of white imprimatur to guarantee the narrator's veracity. William Lloyd Garrison's preface to Frederick Douglass's 1845 *Narrative* is perhaps the most widely cited of these authenticating gestures, notable for its well-meaning condescension and its complicity with white audiences' devaluation of black authorship.

Here Douglass's ubiquity in Americanist scholarship skews as much as it illuminates, however. *The History of Mary Prince* evidences abolition's far less subtle negotiations of credibility, authorship, and scandal. Taking up such dicey matters as Prince's sexual and religious purity, endlessly questioned by her detractors, and the presence or absence of bodily scars that might corroborate her tales of violence, this history's paratexts tell as complex and fraught a story as does its central narrative. Thomas Pringle's faint praise of Mary Prince—who emerges in his prose as an honest witness, though a poor housekeeper with a bad temper—may reorient readers toward Garrison as a comparatively supportive patron, at least before Douglass's return from England in 1847. More pressingly, Pringle's detailed parsing of the salacious details that Prince's life story both alleged and elicited illuminates the era's print battles over national and racial character, as well as over the more immediate matter of slavery. His framing of Prince/Strickland's collaborative text allows us to consider how scandal and the responses it generated worked to mediate moral status within—and perhaps beyond—the discursive field of abolition.

In a narrative that details any number of abuses at the hands of Prince's masters—including physically debilitating work assignments, vicious and degrading punishments, and extreme forms of what we would now call sexual harassment—it's worth noting where the text identifies her antagonists by name and where it does not. Two of Prince's tormenters, the most overtly violent of the lot, are tagged only by an honorific and an initial ("Captain I—" and "Mr. D—") while her final owner is identified not just by name (Mr. John Wood), but by his hometown in Antigua. This differential treatment may index Prince's fears of retaliation—though these unnamed former owners were themselves deceased, she may have had friends or relatives still living under the control of their heirs—but it also owes to the fact that Wood and Prince, at the point of the narrative's publication, were already engaged in a kind of paper war.[40] Prince's narrative represents just one intervention within that larger conflict, which would eventually comprise published letters, articles in various periodicals, at least two subsequent editions of the narrative itself with added editorial materials, and two libel suits, with attendant newspaper coverage. These texts and their multiple authors reveal a fierce competition over moral capital, extending not just to individuals but to entire political factions and indeed to England itself, which is figured as the colonies' moral superior, but also, by its inaction on emancipation, as their partner in crime.[41]

Prince's conflicts with Mr. and Mrs. Wood occurred at a liminal moment in the history of English abolition. The courts had already declared that slaves brought to England were free while on English soil; their owners could not compel them to return to the colonies, where slaveholding remained legal.[42] Thus slaves in England—those who were aware of the law, that is—faced a wrenching dilemma. They could walk away from their masters without fear of legal reprisal (extralegal retaliation was of course another matter) but could not return to their homes and families without being consigned to slavery once again. Further, their prospects for employment and social acceptance in England were uncertain at best. Mary Prince's experiences dramatize this conundrum. She left the Woods' London residence in 1828 burdened with a negative letter of introduction from John Wood (attesting that she "does not evince a disposition to make herself useful"), which sorely limited her employment prospects. Destitute, Prince sought the assistance of the Anti-Slavery Society, not just to resolve her immediate economic crisis but to engage its members' assistance in finding a legal means by which she might return to her husband and home in Antigua. Her white advocates first attempted to negotiate with Wood for her freedom; when that effort failed, they prepared (and eventually presented) a petition to Parliament on her behalf, using the threat of publicity to try to force Wood to relent. Instead Wood went on the offensive, accusing Prince of a litany of moral lapses including dishonesty, ingratitude, and sexual promiscuity both before and during her marriage. In response, Pringle published the first edition of Prince's narrative, which detailed Wood's cruelty and further fueled the conflict.[43]

A series of subsequent interventions by James Macqueen, the proslavery editor of the Glasgow *Courier*, made Wood's accusations seem mild.[44] In a widely noticed article that appeared in the November 1831 issue of *Blackwood's* (and that led to one of the libel suits just mentioned), Macqueen called Prince a "despicable tool" of England's "anti-colonial" faction and reproduced the allegations of one Martha Wilcox, a "free woman of colour" whom Prince had known in Antigua, that the latter had slept with another woman's husband and had engaged in prostitution. Adumbrating the tactics of proslavery Americans who, across the next few decades, would accuse abolitionists of amalgamationist desires, Macqueen extended the charges of sexual misconduct to Pringle himself, implying that his "secret closetings and labours with Mary" were more sexual than narrative and alleging, more generally, that his political activism had undermined the "delicacy, modesty, [and] morality" of his female relatives, insofar as it brought them into contact with licentious former slaves and exposed them to his own unsavory preoccupation with "colonial immorality and uncleanness."[45]

Tawdry accusations, these. Though they appeared after Pringle's editorial supplement was published, and so could not have directly influenced its strategies, they suggest how toxic the conversation regarding colonial slavery had become by the early 1830s. In this context, it is not surprising that Thomas Pringle would pen an editorial supplement nearly as long as Prince's narrative, in which he reproduces and refutes a range of scandalous charges. Some of Pringle's moves are precisely what one would expect: he calls on a resident of Antigua to provide a positive assessment of Prince's history and character; he rehearses at length the bad behavior of her detractors; and he points out the many contradictions in her former owner's claims. In making his case, Pringle dwells on the accusations themselves, reproducing Wood's initial accusatory letter, though he omits what he identifies as the worst charge against Prince, noting that "it is too indecent to appear in a publication likely to be perused by females" (p. 27). Whether propriety constitutes his only motivation here is arguable, as the omission, marked by eleven asterisks, would seem to evoke more prurient interest than would a concise statement of the allegation.

Even more incongruous are Pringle's recurring meditations on Prince's possible guilt. At several points in the supplement his defense of her character seems half-hearted—he remarks, for example, that this unnamed charge against her is "*in all probability*, a vile calumny" (p. 27; italics added) and notes elsewhere that her version of events "is at least as credible as Mr. Wood's" (p. 29). But Pringle also explicitly asks, what if Prince were guilty as charged? According to him, it would not especially matter: "Mary's character, important though its exculpation be to her, is not really the point of chief practical interest in this case" (p. 35). In Pringle's rendering, Wood is guilty and slavery is wrong, regardless of Prince's particular moral disposition. Though he spends page after page shoring up her credibility, he ultimately claims that her character is irrelevant to "the main facts" (p. 35). Why, then, does he engage the scandal at all?

In a 2001 *Callaloo* article, Barbara Baumgartner asks precisely this question: "Why reprint questionable material about Prince that suggests moral turpitude in a society obsessed with female propriety?" The answer, she claims, has to do with Pringle's "obsessive concern with Prince's sexualized body," his attention to which "undermines Prince's interpretation of her own body as a site of resistance." Pringle, Baumgartner argues, "sacrifices Prince's body and character to the antislavery cause."[46] The charge is in some sense warranted: Pringle emerges in his editorial supplement as the apotheosis of the condescending, self-serving white patron who purports to legitimize a black author's narrative, all the while looking after his own—and the movement's—interests. Nevertheless, Baumgartner's critical outrage relies on a historical blind spot. Pringle's ambivalent defenses of Prince in his framing documents are indeed the first (and perhaps only) exposure for most twenty-first-century readers to the invasive and degrading questions that Prince endured about her sexual history. But Prince's contemporaries—the judgmental audience Baumgartner invokes—would have had ample access to the details of the scandal regardless of whether Pringle chose to rehearse them. The sexual reticence of Prince's own narrative, that is, was undermined via Wood's letter and eventually in court testimony, which was itself covered in the London newspapers.[47] Adapting a key line in Pringle's supplement, Baumgartner suggests that the charges against Prince "'would probably never have appeared' had Pringle not reproduced them."[48] But the original text is worth highlighting here, as Pringle claimed that Prince's

History and his supplement "would probably never have appeared" if Wood had not first impugned Prince's character in his widely circulated letter (p. 31). That Pringle's editorial supplement represented one node in an ongoing conversation reminds us of the social and political embeddedness of the slave narrative as a genre—one that intervened in immediate controversies (e.g., the British Parliament's debates over colonial slavery), not to mention scandals. Pringle's chief concerns were ending slavery in the British colonies and shoring up his own reputation, which his advocacy of Prince's cause had undermined. As he readily admits, Prince's reputation and legacy are not his signal concerns. Indeed, he treats Prince's story as instrumental, with little regard for her privacy or agency. But it is important to acknowledge that Prince's body and character were put on trial in a range of venues and genres; Pringle's supplement participated in, but did not initiate, those impositions.

Mary Prince was not as powerless as this account of her sexual shaming might suggest, however. By publicly accusing Prince of scandalous behavior in an attempt to undermine her credibility, the Woods indirectly acknowledged her ability to attract an audience and, consequently, to do them reputational harm. Their recourse to such accusations, in other words, both emerges from and indexes her rise in status from a slave known only to small, local colonial communities to a cause célèbre among English abolitionists, the subject of a petition to the House of Commons and the narrator of a published account that went through at least three editions within the year. Pringle's interventions seem gauged to wrest control over Prince's status as well. In writing to an audience predisposed to expect little from those of African descent, Pringle presents Prince as a woman imperfect enough to be credible. He registers his own complaints about her character and temperament, noting that she has "a somewhat violent and hasty temper, and a considerable share of natural pride and self-importance." Further, her "religious knowledge ... is still but very limited, and her views of Christianity indistinct" (p. 35). In reference to John Wood's accusations, Pringle invites readers more than once to consider the possibility that she is guilty as charged. And he includes the testimony of a Mr. Joseph Phillips of Antigua, who defends Prince as a respectable servant "in whose integrity" the Woods had "placed unlimited confidence," but who also confirms the charge that Prince had had a sexual relationship with a white man. "Such connexions," Phillips remarks in her defense, "are so common, I might almost say universal, in our slave colonies," that they are considered "if faults at all, so very venial as scarcely to deserve the name of immorality" (p. 32). Prince, in other words, is no worse than her surroundings.

Moral authority intersects with marketing in a number of ways here, as is the case, I would argue, throughout abolitionist print culture.[49] Pringle's supplement invokes—indeed, obsesses on—the scandal over Prince's sexuality in an attempt to repair his own reputation while gaining some control over hers. At the same time, Pringle capitalizes on the scandal in order to sell more books, not just to disseminate the abolitionist message but also to broadcast various critiques of Mr. and Mrs. Wood (who would sue him for libel in 1832). Throughout, Pringle is marketing Prince's supposed character flaws. He reassures his readers that the ascendancy that, I have argued, got Prince embroiled in the scandal in the first place is incomplete. She is decidedly not, in his rendering, a moral exemplar. She is simply better than her owners—and, as one of Pringle's many footnotes remarks, she is better than her history of victimization would lead one to expect. "It is indeed wonderful," he writes, "to find her such as she now is" (p. 35). Pringle manages to excoriate Prince's masters while maintaining his investment in white racial and moral superiority. Rehearsing the scandal, then, guarantees that it will continue to keep Prince in her place, so to speak, even as her ongoing labor as a domestic servant (now employed rather than enslaved) marks the limits of her socioeconomic mobility. Scandal does a great deal more than sell books; in this case it stabilizes—and constrains—its subject's moral and social status.

Authorship, Evidence, and Art

The History of Mary Prince prefigured, albeit in hyperbolic form, much of what was to come, as slave narratives and other forms of African American life writing became crucial elements of the antislavery movement's persuasive strategies. While the rumors and accusations that circulated around Prince and her former owners were perhaps more salacious than was typical, they provide a fitting backdrop for analyzing a textual form that, for many Euro-American readers, was inherently scandalous, insofar as black authorship challenged pervasive notions of the inferiority of the race, even as frank talk of slavery's abuses elicited not only denials but appeals to some lost sense of decorum, to the notion that such things could not be true, but even if they were, they should not have been committed to print. The questions of credibility, legitimacy, and status that suffused Prince's text and its paratexts would continue to matter across the next thirty-plus years.

One way in which African American authors asserted their moral authority within this matrix of suspicion and dismissal was to disavow any impulse toward authorship for its own sake, which might expose them to charges of arrogance or an unseemly pursuit of fame. Narrators routinely insisted that they were "urged," "request[ed]," "encouraged," or "induced" to tell their stories,[50] or they claimed that they wrote with a larger moral purpose in mind—a desire to aid those remaining in slavery or to disabuse northern whites of the notion that slaveholders were benevolent caretakers.[51] We see this reflex in white-authored texts as well—note, for example, the second paragraph of *Walden*, in which Thoreau writes: "I should not obtrude my affairs so much on the notice of my readers if very particular inquiries had not been made by my townsmen concerning my mode of life."⁵² Responding to neighbors' queries seems reasonable, if also somewhat contentious in Thoreau's rendering, while an unsolicited narration of one's "affairs" suggests an unattractive penchant for self-disclosure. Even so, it was especially crucial for African American authors to forestall charges of vanity or presumptuousness. Moreover, given the disturbing content included in many narratives of enslavement and escape, their authors and narrators were at pains to demonstrate that they would not have put such matters into print without external pressure or some higher purpose, lest they be accused of sensationalism as well as self-regard.

Some antebellum narratives written or dictated by African Americans articulated the explicit goal of raising funds for a worthy purpose, thus deflecting any impression that the individual wrote in pursuit of fame, status, or gratuitous personal gain. The Reverend Noah Davis, for example, published his narrative in the hope that it might enable him to "RAISE SUFFICIENT MEANS TO FREE HIS LAST TWO CHILDREN FROM SLAVERY"; lest the reader think Davis relied solely on such charitable assistance, the "Notice" asserts that he had "already, within twelve years past, purchased himself, his wife, and five of his children, at a cost, altogether, of over *four thousand dollars*," an accomplishment that may explain why he looks so weary in the accompanying portrait.⁵³ The preface to *The Memoirs of Elleanor Eldridge* indicates that the work has been produced "for the express purpose of giving a helping hand to suffering and persecuted merit" in the person of Eldridge herself, while the preface to *The Story of Mattie J. Jackson* (1866) implores the public "to buy my little book to aid me in obtaining an education, that I may be enabled to do some good in behalf of the elevation of my emancipated brothers and sisters."⁵⁴ As fraught as charitable appeals could be when they crossed lines of racial and economic privilege, they were perceived to be less disruptive than was assertive, autonomous authorship; these authors and their sponsors calculated that readers, even those sympathetic to the antislavery cause, were more at ease with African Americans as supplicants than as creative agents.

In at least one instance, an African American author combined seemingly disparate modes of disavowing authorial agency when he explicitly linked his fundraising goals to the intervention of a higher power. Desperate to purchase the freedom of three still-enslaved offspring, Israel Campbell asked in the preface to his 1861 narrative "What wilt Thou have me to do, Lord?" The response, which came in the form of a "thought, convincing, while it was consoling," urged authorship: "Cannot you, from experience, tell a tale which will place the truth uppermost, and enable both friends and the public to judge impartially of the great question of the age?"⁵⁵ Both his narrative and his charitable appeal were, according to this account, divinely ordained. Most narrators, though, relied on more mundane forms of approbation, typically testimonials from well-regarded white acquaintances and sponsors that were written explicitly for the publication at hand or that appeared as reprinted letters of introduction. The

Reverend Charles See, for example, in his preface to Francis Fedric's narrative, called the latter "an honest man, and a good Christian"; William Lloyd Garrison's testimonial on behalf of the fugitive Thomas Jones described him as "exemplary in life—a servant and minister of Jesus Christ"; and Thomas Church Brownell, a Connecticut clergyman, wrote that James Watkins, whom he had known "for the last five years," had throughout that time "sustained an excellent character for sobriety, industry, and integrity."[56] As these examples suggest, recommenders tended to keep their praise succinct and generic—Garrison's preface to Douglass's 1845 narrative, it's worth noting, is unusually voluble with regard to the latter's character, demeanor, and talents. More typically, the point was not to relate elaborate anecdotes as evidence of the narrator's trustworthiness, but rather to rely on the respectability of the white sponsor as guarantor. The fact that a former slave had attracted such patronage was advanced as proof of his (and sometimes her) good character, a respectability-by-association that also demonstrated the narrator's interpersonal savvy—his or her ability to be, or to appear, grateful for whites' guidance rather than vengeful or dangerously self-asserting.[57] *A Narrative of the Life and Labors of the Rev. G. W. Offley* affirmed the importance of this associative strategy, electing simply to list the names of eleven "gentlemen who speak in high terms of [Offley's] moral worth" without including specific testimonials.[58] Such gestures of affiliation and approval aided white authors, too, especially those who were relatively unknown or were somehow geographically or socially marginalized. In a culture that was increasingly preoccupied with the problem of moral legibility, some kind of recommendation from or affiliation with the known and trusted was crucial.[59] But African American authors depended especially on these associations, having more to overcome in terms of public suspicion and often lacking other proofs of social acceptability.

As we saw in *The History of Mary Prince*, assertions of narrative credibility went well beyond such personal endorsements. Like their Euro-American counterparts who wrote on controversial topics, African American authors and their sponsors went to great lengths to corroborate the details related in their texts. That is, the pressure to provide evidence to support one's claims transcended racial categories, at least within the era's debates over slavery, though the specific strategies employed were racially inflected. White authors, that is, tended to present documentary and transcribed eyewitness evidence directly, as Stowe did in her *Key to Uncle Tom's Cabin* (1853). Such efforts were not invariably persuasive—*A Key* was as soundly disbelieved and reviled among proslavery readers as the novel itself—but they entailed no foundational insult to the author's credibility. Texts authored or narrated by African Americans, by contrast, typically routed their corroborating evidence through an authenticating white figure—an editor or other sponsor thought capable of parsing and verifying the available material. Within this schema, evidence and identity emerged as mutually constitutive and mutually complicating formations within what Robert Stepto has called the narrative's "authenticating machinery."⁶⁰ Textual evidence and personal testimony established the facts of the case—in some instances they were called upon to confirm even the most basic assertion that a particular narrator was who he claimed to be (that is, a former slave, a fugitive from a particular town or state or plantation, etc.). And yet even literate former slaves were not generally trusted to serve as the conduits of such testimony or the sole authenticators of corroborating documents, as if text and testimony themselves were somehow the special property of whiteness, a premise that the publication of these narratives specifically worked to undermine.

The provenance, so to speak, of the narrative and its teller were critical to this regime of legitimation. J. C. Lovejoy's preface to the *Narrative of the Sufferings of Lewis Clarke*, for instance, reassured readers that Clarke had "been repeatedly recognized in the Free States by persons [including the antislavery activist Cassius Clay] who knew him in Kentucky, when a slave" and noted that "persons of discriminating minds have heard [his narrative] repeatedly, under a great variety of circumstances, and the story, in all substantial respects, has been always the same."⁶¹ If the narrative's consistency across retellings mattered, so too did the terms of its transmission when an amanuensis or editor was involved. Lovejoy noted, for example, that "much of [Clarke's story] is in his own language, and all of it according to his own dictation."⁶² While the distinction between "language" and "dictation" remains murky here, Lovejoy's stake in articulating a direct correspondence between teller and text is clear. Such reassurances were common enough, as when an amanuensis began his preface with the assurance that "the following Narrative was taken entirely from the lips of Peter Wheeler. I have in all instances given his own language, and faithfully recorded his story as he told it, *without any change whatever*."⁶³ Occasionally, however, this attention to the narrative's transmission obscures more than it reveals, as when the Reverend Charles Thompson thanked William H. Rhodes "for his valuable assistance in the preparation of my manuscript for the printer. He has re-written the whole of it for me." Thompson's phrasing leaves open the question of whether rewriting meant revising or simply transcribing the original.⁶⁴ In other instances the editorial apparatus articulates precisely the kinds of changes, deletions, or insertions that have been introduced. James Watkins's narrative, its editor (identified by the initials "H. R.") assures readers, was "written down as the words dropped from the lips" of the fugitive, though the story was "afterwards arranged for the press by the writer, with a few [inserted] remarks bearing on this monstrous iniquity—Slavery."⁶⁵

The Life and Sufferings of Leonard Black admits of more direct intervention, though the work's subtitle includes the phrase "written by himself": as A. M. Macy puts the matter in an introductory notice, "the book was written substantially by Mr. Black himself, but, in consequence of his deficiency of education... it needed considerable correction to fit it for the press." The "friend" who took on these editorial duties, however, was "very careful to preserve the narrative as nearly unchanged as possible—confining himself mostly to punctuating, correcting the orthography, striking out unnecessary words and sentences, &c. &c."[66] The need to reassure readers of the text's authenticity and the need to be explicit about editorial interventions are at odds here, as the list of changes and emendations suggests something other than a "nearly unchanged" story. Charles Ball's narrative, by contrast, appeared without even the pretense of fidelity to the fugitive's story. The book's introduction identifies a "Mr. Fisher" as the work's author, though his name does not appear on the title page, and emphasizes his distance (social and linguistic) from the fugitive whose story he tells: it is "sufficiently obvious from the felicity of [Fisher's] style, that the *language* of the book is not that of the unlettered slave, whose adventures he records." Further, this author's "various profound and interesting reflections [are] interspersed throughout the work" and "many of the anecdotes in the book illustrative of southern society were not obtained from Ball, but from other and creditable sources." In a subsequent preface, Fisher insists that "the narrative is taken from the mouth of the adventurer." but notes that "many of [Ball's] opinions have been cautiously omitted, or carefully suppressed, as being of no value to the reader." In other words, this is and is not Ball's story, a paradox reinforced by the fact that in the narrative's first chapter, the pronoun "I" initially refers to Fisher, but soon shifts to represent Ball instead—or rather, Fisher's rendering of Ball, unmoored from the latter's bothersome "opinions" and "sentiments."[67]

The genre's preoccupation with verifiable facts free from the taint of opinion or invention emerged in conjunction with the antislavery movement's broader strategies. As Philip Gould has written, "the antebellum slave narrative came of age in the context of the abolitionist obsession with 'evidence' and the new documentary compendia meant to fill that role."[68] Nowhere is this evidentiary turn more obvious than in the materials that introduced Henry Bibb's 1849 narrative, a collection of texts that, as Stepto has noted, "may be the most elaborate guarantee of authenticity found in the slave narrative canon."[69] Here Lucius Matlack, a white Methodist minister and author of the narrative's introduction, assures readers that he is "well acquainted with [Bibb's] handwriting and style" and that he personally witnessed Bibb in the act of writing the "closing pages" of the manuscript, which Matlack has "preserved for inspection" should anyone doubt the claim that his editorial interventions involved matters "of orthography and punctuation merely, an arrangement of the chapters, and a table of contents."[70] This much amounts to an especially punctilious version of paratextual boilerplate. What follows, however, warrants more attention, as the introduction incorporates the report of a "committee appointed by the Detroit Liberty Association to investigate the truth of the narrative of Henry Bibb." Bibb, the report indicates, appeared before the committee and "was subjected to a rigorous examination. Facts—dates—persons—and localities were demanded and cheerfully furnished." Further, the committee made "proper inquiry—either by letter, or personally, or through the medium of friends... from *every* person, and in *every* quarter likely to elucidate the truth." The resulting testimony, from "slave owners, slave dealers, fugitives from slavery, political friends and political foes," is excerpted in the committee's report (with explanatory footnotes); these witnesses, many of them hostile to Bibb's cause, "corroborated beyond all question," the report avers, "the main facts of [Bibb's] narrative and many of the minor ones."[71] Marshaling a range of evidence that would seem more appropriate to a high-stakes lawsuit than to the publication of a personal narrative, Matlack and the members of the investigating committee demonstrate in extremis the fraught position of the slave narrator, who cannot, it seems, be taken at his word on any matter of significance. The now debunked (but oft-repeated and curiously powerful) story of Phillis Wheatley's face-to-face examination before Boston's white elite more than sixty years earlier morphs into Bibb's grilling by a panel of white abolitionists keen to establish not so much his literal authorship—though Matlack briefly worries that question—but rather his credibility as a conveyer of politically potent truths.[72]

This echo of Wheatley's apocryphal interview, in which her intellectual and poetic capacities were supposedly put on trial, invites attention to the matter of writerly aesthetics as they intersected with these vexed questions of credibility. Indeed, mid-nineteenth-century African American life writing bore a complex relationship to aesthetics, insofar as good writing, however defined, promised an enjoyable reading experience and signaled the intellectual attainments and potential of the race as a whole, even as it threatened to destabilize the genre's orientation toward verifiable testimony. Artfulness, in other words, because it was associated with invention rather than documentation—and because readers expected it of well-educated, privileged authors, but not of fugitive narrators—might undermine credibility. And so we encounter in these narratives' paratexts a range of assurances that the former slave's engaging speaking style and storytelling ability promised a good, engaging read: testimonials that prefaced J. D. Green's narrative, for example, foregrounded the "capabilities which he seemed to possess to interest an audience" and the "able and efficient lecture" that he had recently given. Similarly, two pastors who endorsed Thomas H. Jones's narrative attested to "the unanimous sentiments" of their congregations that his lectures evidenced a life story "of thrilling interest, calculated to secure the attention of any audience."[73] But readers also encountered myriad disavowals of literariness: Henry Bibb wrote in his author's preface that he made "no pretension to literature," having instead "been educated in the school of adversity, whips, and chains"; the fugitive Levin Tilmon noted in the preface to his personal narrative that the work was "hastily thrown together" and "a humble effort"; Charles Thompson's preface insisted that he made "no pretensions to literary attainments," claiming for his book only "truthfulness and honesty of purpose"; and John Andrew Jackson called his narrative "unvarnished"—a key term in antebellum print culture, signifying both truthfulness and plainness of style—in the first sentence of his prefatory remarks.[74] Along similar lines, Samuel Ringgold Ward asserted in the preface to his 1855 autobiography that the "work is not a literary one, for it is not written by a literary man; it is no more than its humble title indicates—the Autobiography of a Fugitive Negro." Ward was cognizant, however, of humility's risks: "I hope," he wrote, "that this Book will not be looked upon as a specimen of what a well educated Negro could do, nor as a fair representation of what Negro talent can produce."[75] Artlessness, in other words, might bolster credibility at the expense of status.

A similar tension suffuses the paratexts that accompanied Frederick Douglass's *My Bondage and My Freedom*, published in the same year as Ward's narrative. By this point in his career, Douglass had wrested a great deal of control over his own life story, though I maintain that he was still on the defensive—still justifying and legitimating himself—in ways consonant with antebellum authorship's moral economies. A number of scholars have commented on the fact that Douglass's 1845 narrative began with a preface by William Lloyd Garrison followed by a letter from the white abolitionist Wendell Phillips, while his 1855 offering featured instead an introduction by James McCune Smith, an African American abolitionist and physician known to be hostile to Garrisonian strategies. This shift, from foregrounding the imprimaturs of white patrons and mentors to featuring that of an African American peer, has been read as evidence of Douglass's growing self-confidence on the one hand and his growing resentment of the white antislavery establishment on the other.[76] Less often remarked on is the 1855 book's nested preface, which features a letter from Douglass himself embedded within and addressed to the anonymous author of what is labeled the "Editor's Preface." This bracketing strategy suggests that Douglass does not wish to seem presumptuous; he frames his letter—and indeed the entire book—as a response to his editor's request rather than an autonomously generated project, a move that aligns him with his less famous fellow autobiographers, who worked to obscure or disavow their will to authorship.

Gerald Fulkerson, textual editor of the Yale University Press edition of *My Bondage and My Freedom*, has asserted that this unnamed editor was "almost certainly" Julia Griffiths, a white English abolitionist who had for some time played a significant role in the production of *Frederick Douglass' Paper*.[77] If that supposition is accurate, the fact that her name does not appear in these pages signals something other than a womanly abhorrence of publicity, given that Griffiths seems to have been perfectly at ease with her name (and sometimes her initials) appearing in print elsewhere. As Douglass scholars are well aware, Griffiths was a scandalous figure in abolitionist circles: rumors had circulated in the early 1850s that she and Douglass were adulterous lovers (he was married; she was not), a matter to which I will return in chapter 3. Though she had returned to England—permanently, as it turned out—by the time the book was released, her name in the prefatory materials would have invoked transgression rather than authorial legitimacy, at least for movement insiders.

What intrigues me about this preface—apart from the tantalizing lacuna just noted—is the fact that it energetically disavows the aesthetic, either as the volume's reason for being or as the grounds on which it ought to be evaluated, a move that embeds Douglass's life writing within a broader discourse of the "unvarnished," contra the scholarly impulse to isolate it as an unusually autonomous—and self-consciously literary—narrative. The editor's opening claims are worth quoting at length:

> If the volume now presented to the public were a mere work of Art, the history of its misfortune might be written in two very simple words—TOO LATE. The nature and character of slavery have been subjects of an almost endless variety of artistic representation; and after the brilliant achievements in that field...he who would add another to the legion, must possess the charm of transcendent excellence, or apologize for something worse than rashness. The reader is, therefore, assured...that his attention is not invited to a work of Art, but to a work of Facts.[78]

The market, Douglass's editor suggests, for well-written antislavery material is glutted; his only chance of selling the book is to promote it as unmediated testimony. Douglass's own segment takes the matter further. Facts of the kind he offers in *My Bondage and My Freedom*, which are "calculated to enlighten the public mind, by revealing the true nature...of the slave system,...can scarcely be innocently withheld."[79] The author emerges here as a witness under subpoena, obliged to divulge what he has seen and heard.

This sense of obligation notwithstanding, Douglass expresses an acute discomfort with the narration of personal experience. He refers to his "somewhat positive repugnance to writing or speaking anything for the public" that would open him to the accusation that he seeks "personal notoriety, for its own sake." On those grounds, he writes, "I have often refused to narrate my personal experience...when urged to do so by friends" and "have generally aimed to discuss the question of Slavery in the light of fundamental principles, and upon facts, notorious and open to all."[80] Later in the book, and elsewhere, Douglass reveals that he often felt relegated to the realm of the personal and the experiential in his time as a Garrisonian lecturer. Experience, it seems, operates as both the grounds of his authority and as a particularly frustrating delimiter.

The question of aesthetics reemerges at the end of Douglass's letter, seemingly in defiance of the editor's opening volley. Douglass avers that he has agreed to write this book because he wishes to disprove the widely held belief that "the enslaved people" are, "naturally, inferior"—"*so low* in the scale of humanity, and so utterly stupid, that they are unconscious of their wrongs, and do not apprehend their rights."[81] And so the "facts" of his experience are more powerful if he is able to narrate them effectively himself. He is doing good, in other words, by writing well. For at least one reader, this gambit worked. An anonymous reviewer in the *Christian Advocate* used the literary value of the book to judge its author: "This volume," he writes, "besides its many moving and thrilling details, affords evidence of a most remarkable man."[82]

My Bondage and My Freedom sold well, a fact trumpeted within the many advertisements for the book that ran in *Frederick Douglass' Paper* and elsewhere. While it is impossible to say to what extent the preface contributed to that success, these few introductory paragraphs reveal a great deal about Douglass's tenuous relationship to the literary market as a whole and to his imagined readers. Within the preface he is, by turns, a man on trial and a witness at the trials of others; a purveyor of straightforward facts and a renegade artist out to demonstrate the capacity of the race; an admirable man and a figure accused of arrogance, dishonesty, and myriad other transgressions. The many burdens of proof outlined here weigh on him—and must be addressed—before the narrative itself can begin.

The Status of Secrets

Matters of proof, legitimacy, and authorial reputation would continue to preoccupy African American autobiographers after slavery's official demise. Elizabeth Keckley's *Behind the Scenes* (1868), an unlikely hybrid of the slave narrative and the celebrity tell-all, demonstrates the persistence of these concerns within the shifting exigencies of postbellum print culture. *Behind the Scenes* has often been characterized as a conservative book in terms of its racial and class politics; the narrator extends to some of her white southern acquaintances and former owners a measured affection, for example, that seems to excuse her past subjugation. And, in contrast with the slave narrative genre's sensationalist antecedents, Keckley's text understates and abbreviates the cruelties of slavery—most notably, her sexual victimization by a white man is related in a single paragraph, whereas an analogous sequence of events in Harriet Jacobs's *Incidents* plays out across several chapters. Further, as Frances Smith Foster has written, the narrative's emphasis on Keckley's time in the White House and her success as a businesswoman accords with a postbellum ethos of individual economic uplift that would reach its zenith in Booker T. Washington's *Up from Slavery*.[83]

Granted, when read against the strategic outrage evident in an antebellum text like *My Bondage and My Freedom*, Keckley's narrative seems apolitical, even complacent, with presidential hagiography standing in for Douglass's restless critique of northern failures and half-measures. But that impression obscures a number of ways in which *Behind the Scenes* is oppositional rather than simply opportunistic with respect to northern social and racial expectations.[84] For instance, the text, like Douglass's 1855 offering, eschews the antebellum slave narrative's most obvious authenticating and legitimating gestures: a white-authored preface, introduction, and letters of sponsorship. Instead, it begins with a preface that immediately introduces the narrator herself, speaking in the first person. While she invokes the well-worn trope of the elicited story ("I have often been asked to write my life"; "at last I have acceded to the importunities of my friends") and offers a conventional disavowal of artistry ("[I] have *hastily sketched* some of the striking incidents that go to make up my history"), this narrative persona also presumes to speak for herself, addressing and attempting to answer in her opening paragraph the criticism she anticipates from readers, who might take issue with her representations of slavery ("If I have portrayed the dark side of slavery, I also have painted the bright side") or with her disclosure of intimate details regarding the former First Lady, Mary Todd Lincoln.[85] Keckley's text replaces the antebellum slave narrative's white (and usually male) authenticators with an alternative regime of legitimation that turns on satisfied white female customers—whose endorsement of and dependence on Keckley as a "modiste" affirms her talent as well as her character—and on forms of patronage that prove to be far more intimate and complex than the measured, self-distancing gestures of approval we see in the paratexts of more typical slave narratives.

I have referred to the voice in this preface as the "narrator" or "narrative persona" rather than as Keckley herself because the precise authorship of *Behind the Scenes* remains unclear. Foster writes that Elizabeth Keckley's "penchant for perfection...no doubt influenced her to rely heavily upon her publisher and other professionals for advice and editing"; Susan S. Williams envisions rather more intervention, noting that Keckley frequently met with the editor James Redpath "to collaborate on the manuscript"; and Barbara Ryan phrases the matter even more forcefully, asserting that "it is routinely acknowledged that [*Behind the Scenes*] was ghost-written."[86] Whether this is a collaborative or a ghostwritten text (the latter term sounds much more underhanded) or a largely self-authored narrative that underwent some degree of editing and arranging, scholars agree that Keckley's text was almost certainly shaped by the interventions of another figure, most likely a white man with authorial and editorial experience. What intrigues me, in light of the slave narrative genre's energetic advertisement of white intervention and sponsorship, is the fact that Keckley and her supposed collaborator chose to elide any mention of the latter's contributions within the text itself. What had served in previous decades as a guarantee of an African American narrator's legitimacy appears to have become a liability. The preface, indeed, offers a version of the genre's by-then-ritualized assertion of the narrative's fidelity to truth ("My life...may sound like a dream to the matter-of-fact reader, nevertheless everything I have written is strictly true; much has been omitted, but nothing has been exaggerated" [p. 3]), but in doing so it avoids all mention of the narrator's collaborator/amanuensis/

editor/ghostwriter, the very figure who, in so many earlier texts, articulated his or her methods, emphases, and erasures as a way of reassuring readers that the text could be trusted.

Why might Keckley and/or her collaborator have chosen to obscure these editorial and perhaps compositional interventions? To a great extent, the decision owes to the fact that *Behind the Scenes* belongs to competing and in some sense incommensurate genres. Slave narratives traditionally relied on overt assertions of white involvement and approval, but the genre's immediate reason for being—that is, recounting past suffering in the interest of abolishing slavery—had shifted after emancipation. The emerging genre of the celebrity tell-all, by contrast, promised unmediated eyewitness testimony. Keckley, in other words, presents herself less as a former slave whose tales of subjection require external validation (á la Henry Bibb) than as a White House insider uniquely positioned to testify to the experiences and motivations of figures far more famous and more socially prominent than she. That Keckley offered herself as proof and guarantor of key observations and secrets about the Lincolns' family life and Mary Todd Lincoln's widowhood attests to her boldness and her awareness of crucial shifts in the print marketplace. By securing access to the Lincolns in the first place, and then by presuming to disclose their actions and conversations, she lays claim to a kind of authority vis-à-vis both her subjects and her readers. But as the book's harsh reception and mixed critical history demonstrate, that authority—and the moral and social status it purported to assert—would prove precarious indeed.

The matter of Keckley's status is, fittingly enough, her book's overriding theme and problematic. The journey from slavery to the White House, underscored by her subtitle, suggests a unidirectional ascent that belies the complications inherent in her relationship to Mrs. Lincoln, the narrator's main object of inquiry. Ostensibly, Keckley is a successful businesswoman and Mrs. Lincoln is her client, albeit a much-sought-after and demanding one. But the duties that the former assumes go well beyond dressmaking: on the one hand, she literally dresses the First Lady and arranges her hair, tasks that would typically be assigned to a domestic servant (and, in much of the divided nation, to a slave); on the other hand, Keckley emerges in the narrative as Mary Lincoln's trusted friend, confidante, and advisor, roles that would seem reserved for a social equal or even a superior. Mary Lincoln "outranks" Elizabeth Keckley according to nineteenth-century Americans' most obvious status metrics, and yet Keckley possesses certain advantages over her employer/pseudo-mistress/friend. She has marketable skills and a profitable business, after all, whereas Mary Lincoln has neither. Lincoln is deeply in debt, with a dubious reputation in terms of common sense and even basic sanity, while Keckley, at least in her self-presentation, is eminently sensible, one whose benevolence serves her community and whose counsel is well worth seeking.[87]

Keckley's preface highlights these tensions, even as it anticipates and attempts to forestall the criticism that the narrative would soon elicit. "It may be charged," she writes, "that I have written too freely on some questions, especially in regard to Mrs. Lincoln. I do not think so; at least I have been prompted by the purest motive"—namely, the herculean project of repairing Mary Lincoln's reputation and, by extension, her own (p. 4). The former First Lady, Keckley insists, "forced herself into notoriety. She stepped beyond the formal lines which hedge about a private life, and invited public criticism" (p. 4). The text's violations of established privacy codes, then, are merely attempts to rescue Mrs. Lincoln from her own missteps. By revealing the good intentions undergirding those unwise actions—especially the much-derided attempt in 1867 to sell off her White House-era dresses and accessories—Keckley hopes to put Mary Lincoln "in a better light before the world" (p. 5). These motivations seem high minded and disinterested, a matter of correcting public misperceptions, until Keckley reveals that her own reputation is at stake as well: "I have been intimately associated with that lady in the most eventful periods of her life. I have been her confidante, and if evil charges are laid at her door, they must also be laid at mine, since I have been a party to all her movements" (p. 5). If Keckley appears here as Lincoln's codefendant rather than her benevolent superior, that moment of equivalence is short-lived, as the very next sentence repositions her as the first lady's humble retainer: "To defend myself I must defend the lady that I have served" (p. 5).

As these contradictions suggest, *Behind the Scenes* enacts a series of hierarchical realignments and strategic reversals. Instead of relying on a white editor to endorse her story publicly, Keckley obscures his very existence. Instead of routing documentary evidence through trusted white patrons, she asserts the legitimacy of her possession and disclosure of evidence—most controversially, in the form of Mary Lincoln's letters. Noting that she has "excluded everything of a personal character from [Lincoln's] letters," Keckley goes on to assert that their worth derives from their very privacy: the letters "were not written for publication, for which reason they are all the more valuable; they are the frank overflowings of the heart, the outcropping of impulse, the key to genuine motives" (p. 5). The letters, and the secrets (impersonal yet heartfelt?) that they impart, function as a kind of property and, in their dissemination, as currency. Keckley trades on Mary Lincoln's secrets—dispossesses her of them—as a means of selling the book and, in her rendering, as a means of renovating the two women's linked reputational properties, which have suffered via the mismanagement and bungled marketing of a third kind of property: the garments (labeled in the press, contradictorily, as both "old clothes" and "finery") that Keckley literally created and for which Lincoln (in part) incurred her outsized debts.

The interdependent property relations at issue here only exacerbate the status confusion that Keckley both deploys and glosses over in her narrative.

One of the book's more controversial chapters, titled "Candid Opinions," foregrounds that instability. By way of introducing her discussion of Mary Lincoln's mistrust of various key figures in her husband's administration (e.g., Salmon Chase, William Seward), Keckley writes that the Lincolns "often...discussed the relations of Cabinet officers, and gentlemen prominent in politics, in my presence" (p. 57). This claim has multiple valences: it suggests, most obviously, that the Lincolns trusted her so thoroughly that they felt free to speak their minds in her presence, though the fact that the claim immediately precedes a violation of that trust would seem to prove their faith misplaced. At the same time, the Lincolns' conversational freedom could be taken to mean that they considered Keckley to be an insensible presence—one unlikely to absorb or comprehend, much less repeat, their "candid" political opinions. In that case her disclosures serve as proof of her political awareness rather than of a propensity for personal betrayal.

This tension between a betrayal of trust and a vindication of dismissal suffuses the matter of Lincoln's letters as well. Keckley was criticized, not just in the press but by Mary Lincoln and her son Robert, for reproducing the First Lady's letters in her text's appendix. One has to wonder, though, why Mary Lincoln might have thought her epistolary disclosures private in the first place. Was her trust in Keckley's friendship and discretion so secure that she failed to anticipate this outcome? Or had she considered Keckley, by virtue of her race and history of enslavement, to be incapable of doing her harm regardless of intention? When Lincoln referred to Keckley derisively as "*the colored* historian" after the book's publication, she was using the latter's identity to discredit her project, playing on *colored*'s dual uses as a racial descriptor and a reference to bias.[88] But the First Lady's annoyance also suggests that something she had thought impossible has somehow come to pass, as her dressmaker and sometimes-paid comforter has transformed herself into a historian and, worse, a critic. And yet Keckley's agency here may itself be an illusion. A number of scholars have suggested that James Redpath published the letters—or some portion of them—without Keckley's approval, a possibility that, if true, repositions her as a naïve figure whose violation of Lincoln's trust was, more properly, an instance of trusting others too far.[89]

Whatever the reality underlying the letters controversy, *Behind the Scenes* stands as a performance of agency that asserts Keckley's moral authority in novel, if risky, ways. To judge by the work's initial reception, this gambit was largely unsuccessful.[90] Not only did Keckley's business suffer in the wake of the book's publication, according to her biographer Jennifer Fleischner, but the work inspired a vicious parody titled *Behind the Seams: By a Nigger Woman Who Took in Work from Mrs. Lincoln and Mrs. Davis* (1869) and elicited any number of outraged reviews, including one in the *New-York Citizen* that called it "grossly and shamelessly indecent...an offence of the same grade as the opening of other people's letters, the listening at keyholes, or the mean system of espionage which unearths family secrets with a view to blackmailing the unfortunate victims." Indeed, this reviewer declared that Keckley's book was "hardly less offensive" than the era's print pornography, those "illustrated papers" and "shameless sheets that are displayed on every news-stand, and whose existence is a reproach to our laws and to the police authorities of the city."[91] Keckley's supposed status as a disloyal servant amplified her indecency, as a review in the *Atlantic Monthly* suggested: an editor, the reviewer sarcastically asserted, "need never want inspiration while there are cooks, lady's maids, coachmen, and footmen about, who have lived in families of eminent persons."[92] The *New-York Citizen* review alleged, further, that Keckley must have "had some difficulty with Mrs. Lincoln—probably on the subject of wages—and having left her service, takes this method of revenging herself on her former mistress." *Godey's*, meanwhile, reinforced the "disgruntled former employee" theory with a note of privileged-class solidarity: "We do not approve of servants publishing books about their employers, for who will be safe. We may have our own private lives served up by Mary Jane or Susan Sophia."[93] These characterizations of the book as servant's gossip reveal that it was not simply the fact of Keckley's disclosures that troubled readers, but her broader suggestion within the narrative that intimacy trumped, or at least mitigated, inequality of status in a postemancipation context.

Keckley's ability as an author was questioned as well. *Putnam's*, for example, complained that her book's "contents are as flat as a Dutch landscape..., [relating] the direst trivialities of Mr. Lincoln's family life, and the humiliating details of Mrs. Lincoln's conduct subsequent to leaving the White House."[94] The *New-York Citizen*, for its part, discounted Keckley's authorship entirely in a piece that appeared a week after its initial review: "The facts—or falsehoods—which [Keckley] furnished have been thrown together by some literary hack, and the result is the present volume of vulgar, illiterate, ungrammatical twaddle." The same issue published Keckley's own response to the earlier critique of her book, in which she called out the paper's editor for participating in the press's vicious criticism of Mary Todd Lincoln and then hypocritically defending the First Lady's outraged privacy. The paper then countered with another attack on the book's authorship: "The writer of the foregoing letter...seems to have identified himself so completely with the woman in whose name he writes, as to be unable to comprehend the existence of any higher standard of decency than that which one would naturally expect to find among the slaves on a southern plantation." For this commentator, Keckley's history of enslavement has rendered her incapable not just of authorship but of a proper understanding of social decorum; the "unscrupulous Bohemian" who penned her story, meanwhile, ought to have known better.[95]

Amid these recriminations, at least one reviewer found Keckley's claims to good intentions—and her book's narrative style—to be compelling.[96] An unsigned notice in *Hours at Home* begins with the expected nod to outraged propriety, asserting that "[*Behind the Scenes*] belongs to a class of writings which deserve reprobation rather than encouragement." But the reviewer goes on to acknowledge Keckley's "honest and praiseworthy motive," asserting that the book emerged "less from a desire to gratify a vulgar curiosity and minister to the love of scandal, than from a desire to vindicate the reputation of the widow of our late venerated President." Not only does the reviewer assert that the book's readers will "be forced to commiserate and throw over the unfortunate and maligned woman [i.e., Mrs. Lincoln], the mantle of charity," but he or she ends the piece with praise for the author herself: "Mrs. Keckley writes with a straightforwardness, a propriety, good sense, and grace and force of diction, that is not a little surprising, and which proves her true womanhood, notwithstanding she was born in slavery."[97] Despite the admixture of condescension, these remarks suggest that Keckley's elaborate paratextual staging of her moral authority and respectability was not rejected as universally as scholars have claimed. Indeed, her history of enslavement, which her critics often used to delegitimize her text and character, in this instance testifies to her ability to overcome adversity. While a single sympathetic review hardly overturns the scholarly consensus that Keckley's reputation suffered as a result of her book's publication, it does serve as an apt reminder that nineteenth-century authorship's moral economies were complex and polysemous, offering up few unequivocal successes or failures.

In the chapters that follow, contemporary reception figures prominently as a means of gauging the success of authors' and editors' varied reputational gambits. These inquiries abundantly demonstrate the ways in which claims to moral authority could go awry, as appeals to sympathy or understanding instead met with scorn. But mid-nineteenth-century Americans' elaborate print conversations about books and authors—carried out in reviews, advertisements, and letters to the editor, as well as in parodies and allusions—also demonstrate the degree to which moral authority was malleable and almost infinitely susceptible to reclamation, especially when the authors in question had articles of interest—be they secrets, stirring plots, or clever turns of phrase—to sell.

{3}

Frederick Douglass's Marketing of Moral Repair

Frederick Douglass was a controversial figure following the publication of his 1845 *Narrative*, a text whose rhetorical sophistication fueled proslavery suspicions that it was an elaborate fake and whose naming of specific sites and individuals elicited a range of defensive retorts. But in the early 1850s Douglass became embroiled in conflicts much closer to his ideological home, as his break with William Lloyd Garrison (and the latter's allies) sparked a contentious back-and-forth, carried on at conventions and in abolitionist papers, that lasted for years. Within the maelstrom of criticism leveled at Douglass, much of which focused on the scandal of his "ingratitude" toward his early mentors, there emerged a prurient subscandal involving Douglass's relationship with the white English abolitionist Julia Griffiths, who moved to Rochester in 1849, worked closely with Douglass on his paper, and, for a time, lived in his home.[1]

Gossip is largely ephemeral, a matter of whispered comments, knowing looks, and social snubs, and thus much of the viciousness surrounding the Douglass/Griffiths relationship has been lost. What remains are remarks and allusions in private correspondence—enough that William S. McFeely describes "the decibel range among antislavery people" regarding the matter as reaching "the level of a screech"[2]—and a series of barely coded exchanges in reform periodicals, most notably Garrison's *Liberator* and Douglass's own paper. Garrison committed the widespread rumors to print in the November 18, 1853 issue of the *Liberator*, writing that "for several years past, [Douglass] has had one of the worst advisers in his printing-office, whose influence over him has not only caused much unhappiness in his household, but perniciously biassed [sic] his own judgment."[3] Douglass responded with outrage: "He [Garrison] has seen fit to invade my house-hold, despise the sacredness of my home, break through the just limits of public controversy, and has sought to blast me in the name of my family." Many paragraphs later he defended Griffiths against the claim that she was a poor advisor, but refused to respond directly to the suggestion of a romantic entanglement: "The charge of 'unhappiness in my household,' is one which I refuse to answer in this place, or in any public journal, unless required to do so by some proper and competent tribunal, known to the laws of the land." Douglass appended an eight-point justification for this refusal, including the observation that no one "who was before dissatisfied" would be convinced by a public denial and the assertion that "a man's wife and children should be spared the mortification involved in a public discussion of matter so entirely private, and which can come to no issue in such a court."[4] Garrison fired back a week later, stating at first that his comment about "unhappiness" in Douglass's "household" was not "intended to imply any thing [sic] immoral," but then rendering Douglass as an unwitting Samson, "slumbering in the lap of a prejudiced, sectarian Delilah."[5] So much for conciliation.

Insofar as "household unhappiness" emerged as the euphemism of choice for Douglass's alleged affair and the violation of his and his family's privacy provided the grounds for his self-defense, perhaps the most poignant of the printed responses to the accusation was a short note addressed to Garrison directly, ostensibly from Anna Douglass: "Sir—It is not true, that the presence of a certain person in the office of Frederick Douglass causes unhappiness in his family. Please insert this in your next paper."[6] Garrison did print the statement (and Douglass would soon reprint it), with a preface insisting that the note "is evasive in its language, as our charge had reference to the past, and not to the present. It is not possible that Mrs. D. means deliberately to affirm, that there has been no unhappiness created in her family, in regard to the person alluded to."[7] Not content with having undermined Anna Douglass's privacy and dignity, Garrison questioned her honesty as well.[8]

The outlines of the Douglass/Griffiths scandal, and of the internecine battles that formed its backdrop, are well known.[9] Less obvious is the extent to which *My Bondage and My Freedom* (1855), published some two months after Julia Griffiths returned to England, is a book about scandal, one that emerges from and responds to the shadows cast on its author's moral character.[10] Although *My Bondage and My Freedom* comments (albeit with more judicious phrasing than Douglass employed in other venues) on the author's conflicts with the Garrisonians, it does not respond directly to the Griffiths rumors. Nevertheless, scandal animates the narrative, fueling the author's relentless assertion and enactment of his own admirableness. While the text challenges the mid-nineteenth century's racialization of both authorship and character, it never abandons the notion that writing and publishing are signal means of laying claim to moral status. Indeed, an assertion of Douglass's moral authority is in some sense the book's thesis.

If, as I am suggesting, *My Bondage and My Freedom* can be read as an extended meditation on and a critical intervention into the relationship between authorship and moral authority, the book's embrace of the market, of its (and its author's) status as a commodity, bears thinking about in ethical terms.

Douglass advances and elaborates a version of his own property status in this text, submitting to the market in ways this chapter will analyze. But he also exerts significant control within the market insofar as he launches a brilliant cross-platform promotional scheme, whereby *My Bondage and My Freedom*, *Frederick Douglass' Paper*, and the author himself effectively sell one another. That is, the autobiography sells Douglass's public persona (as self-liberator, public intellectual, abolitionist, and, of course, as author and editor); meanwhile, the newspaper sells *My Bondage and My Freedom* (carries advertisements for it and prints favorable commentary on it), even as the book publicizes and legitimizes the newspaper. And Douglass as a publicly available figure—staring out from the image in the frontispiece of *My Bondage and My Freedom* and appearing as a speaker in lecture halls and at antislavery conventions—sells both texts.[11] But all of this self-marketing, Douglass insists, amounts to more than lining the author's pockets and keeping his self-titled periodical afloat. Selling Douglass's persona and his texts involves promoting not only antislavery and antiracist principles but the very idea of an intellectually independent, morally upstanding, and rhetorically astute black man.

Moral Properties

Douglass, in his autobiographical and editorial writings, makes strategic use of his status as property, both literal and literary. Saidiya Hartman argues in *Scenes of Subjection* (1997) that slavery and freedom cannot be conceived of as a neat binary, two separate territories whose border one crossed permanently and unequivocally—a thesis that *My Bondage and My Freedom*, with its attention to the racial injustices of the antebellum North, supports.[12] In a similar vein, Douglass's book suggests that the notion of the self-as-property and the notion of autonomous personhood are not entirely separable, either. Moral authority, in the way Douglass pursues it here, entails a great deal of submission—to public scrutiny generally and, more precisely, to his own commodification and circulation—even as it simultaneously requires assertive, even contentious, gestures toward autonomy and self-possession.[13] The very boldness of *My Bondage and My Freedom*, its critique of northern racism and white abolitionist myopia, is premised on such canny forms of submission.

Douglass's book ranks among American literature's most energetic exercises in self-promotion, but I don't mean that as pejoratively as it sounds. The text engages in a kind of self-promotion that has crucial sociopolitical implications—Douglass narrates himself in the service of such reform projects as abolition and civil rights. And, in keeping with his practice of presenting himself as both representative and exceptional, Douglass promotes himself as an independent author, editor, and intellectual whose successes attest to the capacity of the race as a whole. In defending his decision to write his own life story (for a second time), a move that he admits exposes him to "the imputation of weakness, vanity, and egotism," Douglass suggests that his autobiography serves as a defense of "the enslaved people" as a whole, who are alleged to be both insensible of their low status and incapable of improving it.[14]

Scholars have noted that *My Bondage and My Freedom* attends to its narrator's embeddedness within communities of color, at least in comparison with the 1845 narrative, in which Douglass represents his personal development largely in solitary and self-created terms. Certainly many of the second narrative's details—especially Douglass's rendering of his life in Baltimore—represent him as engaged by and benefiting from intraracial friendships and informal organizations. But the theme of personal exceptionalism recurs in *My Bondage and My Freedom*, as Douglass's account of his life in slavery repeatedly asserts his superiority to—or his ability to transcend—his circumstances. For instance, his description of the plantation where his beloved grandmother reluctantly, if deceptively, leaves him as a boy emphasizes the limitations of the spoken language he encounters: "There is not, probably, in the whole south, a plantation where the English language is more imperfectly spoken than on Col. Lloyd's," he writes in the midst of his own eloquently phrased narrative (p. 45). In reference to the slaves there "who had been brought from the coast of Africa," he notes that he "could scarcely understand them when I first went among them, so broken was their speech; and I am persuaded that I could not have been dropped anywhere on the globe, where I could reap less, in the way of knowledge, from my immediate associates, than on this plantation" (p. 45). Imperfect command of English here signals the slaves' lack of access to knowledge itself. The language that surrounds Douglass is morally corrupt as well. As he writes in reference to Captain Anthony's beating of Esther, "her piercing cries seemed only to increase his fury. His answers to them are too coarse and blasphemous to be produced here" (p. 51). Further, the region's linguistic poverty and immorality mirror its sluggish economy. When Douglass ends up in the "village" of St. Michael's as an adolescent he finds "a few comfortable dwellings in it," but remarks that "the place, as a whole, wore a dull, slovenly, enterprise-forsaken aspect" (p. 106). The lack of industry that the broader culture so often attributed to slaves is here ascribed to the entire community, including its white landowners.

Douglass's emphasis on his unpromising early surroundings contrasts with his eventual rise—not just to freedom but to public speaking, authorship, and editorship. In recounting his removal to Baltimore, a "high privilege" that made available the advantages and opportunities that eventually facilitated his escape, the author shuttles between crediting luck and acknowledging a belief in his own chosenness. "There was a wide margin from which to select," he notes, including "boys younger, boys older, and boys of the same age, belonging to my old master," a rendering that makes his selection seem random. And yet despite the fear of being "deemed superstitious and egotistical," he admits that, at least as a child, he "regard[ed] this event as a special interposition of Divine Providence in my favor"—a moment of election, if you will. Douglass's self-construction in this passage requires a careful distancing of the adult narrator from the child protagonist: "The thought [that God had ordained his relocation] is a part of my history, and I should be false to the earliest and most cherished sentiments of my soul, if I suppressed, or hesitated to avow that opinion, although it may be characterized as irrational by the wise, and ridiculous by the scoffer" (p. 80).

Elsewhere the narrator abandons this frame of distanced reassessment, assuming instead a near-messianic tone.[15] When Douglass takes refuge with Sandy, a fellow slave, and his wife prior to his violent showdown with Covey, he remarks on their extraordinary kindness toward him: "Both seemed to esteem it a privilege to succor me; for, although I was hated by Covey and by my master, I was loved by the colored people, because *they* thought I was hated for my knowledge, and persecuted because I was feared. I was the *only* slave *now* in that region who could read and write." "My knowledge," he added, "was now the pride of my brother slaves" (p. 135). Douglass's literacy fuels his persecution, but it also makes him a treasure within his community—a being both rare and (potentially) powerful. Once the fight with Covey allows him to realize that physical, active potency, Douglass's singularity is reinforced: "The report got abroad, that I was hard to whip; that I was guilty of kicking back." These rumors, he avers, "distinguished me among my servile brethren" (p. 142).

Douglass's relationship to those "servile" others is vexed to say the least. As readers of his autobiographies have long remarked, Douglass's figuration of violence as the crucible through which he achieves full adulthood (*manhood* in his lexicon) and, ultimately, freedom implies that those who did not or could not fight back so directly somehow merited their subjugation. In a passage that resonates with Emerson's most famous essays from the previous decade, Douglass remarks that "a man, without force, is without the essential dignity of humanity. Human nature is so constituted, that it cannot *honor* a helpless man, although it can *pity* him; and even this it cannot do long, if the signs of power do not arise" (p. 141). And yet Douglass's self-presentation intermixes this aggressive individualism with an emphasis on his ability to influence and aid others: "I was a bad sheep. I hated slavery, slaveholders, and all pertaining to them; and I did not fail to inspire others with the same feeling, wherever and whenever opportunity was presented. This made me a marked lad among the slaves, and a suspected one among the slaveholders" (p. 143). Of his role in a failed group escape attempt, he writes: "If any one is to blame for disturbing the quiet of the slaves and slave-masters of the neighborhood of St. Michael's, *I am the man*," phrasing that intertwines his masculinity with his singularity (p. 159). Literacy, too, figures prominently in this secular evangelism. In reflecting on the clandestine teaching he had done while still in slavery, he remarks on having "met several slaves from Maryland, who were once my scholars; and who obtained their freedom, I doubt not, partly in consequence of the ideas imparted to them in that school" (p. 152). Throughout, self-sacrifice tempers (that is, both moderates and strengthens) Douglass's self-assertion, even after he has achieved freedom. Commenting on the longevity of his newspaper, he writes: "I rejoice in having engaged in the enterprise, and count it joy to have been able to suffer, in many ways, for its success, and for the success of the cause to which it has been faithfully devoted" (p. 227).

Printed responses to *My Bondage and My Freedom* suggest that at least some readers accepted the text's convergence of authorship and moral status. For the author of a lengthy review in the Edinburgh *Daily Scotsman*, Douglass's intellect, as proven via his text, heightened the injustice of his experiences in slavery. Applauding the narrative's exclusion of "tawdry ornament, inflated declamation, unsound reasoning, ... [and] an African viciousness of taste," the reviewer touts Douglass's writing ability as evidence of an extraordinary mind, which in turn makes his enslavement all the more reprehensible: "If ... superiority of intellect gave one human being a right to treat another as a brute, which of the defenders of slavery in America or in Britain, male or female, would be entitled to hold Frederick Douglass in bondage?"[16] A review in the *Independent* put the matter more succinctly, remarking that Douglass "is in his own person one of the most emphatic arguments against slavery."[17] Even a reviewer who attempted to maintain neutrality on the slavery question commended Douglass's achievements: "Whatever may be our opinions of slavery, or of the best means of acting upon it, we cannot but admire the force and integrity of character which has enabled Frederick Douglass to attain his present unique position."[18] Others commented directly on the degree to which Douglass's personal qualities promoted his book: "This is a splendid work. The personal worth of the author, the deserved popularity he has secured throughout this nation, and the universal desire that prevails to have a momento [sic] of one of nature's noblemen, will conspire to create an unprecedented demand for this book."[19] An anonymous reviewer in the *Christian Advocate* reversed the equation, using the value of the book to judge its author: "This volume, besides its many moving and thrilling details, affords evidence of a most remarkable man. Mr. Douglass has emphatically made himself."[20] The author's personal qualities render the book desirable, even as the book's value serves as proxy for and proof of its creator's moral, intellectual, and personal status.

Integral to Douglass's complex self-promotion is the particular use he makes of his status as public property. The first edition of *My Bondage and My Freedom*, for example, displays the author's portrait in the front matter of the book. This move insists on Douglass's particularity—he is a specific person who has suffered and succeeded in specific ways—even as it invokes his racial identity in order to debunk the widespread association of authorship with whiteness. The use of the portrait, too, capitalizes on Douglass's popularity as a public speaker in both England and the northern United States; for readers who had attended a lecture by Douglass in the past, the image would serve as a reminder of his extraordinary personal presence. And, as Douglass's biographers remind us, the author's exceptional physical attractiveness was much remarked on by his contemporaries.[21] As in our own times, an author's good looks would almost certainly have aided in the marketing of his book.

My Bondage and My Freedom's engagement with the question of property also works retrospectively, trading on and reconfiguring Douglass's prior status as chattel, as in his elaborate description of the posthumous valuation of Captain Anthony's property: "What an assemblage! Men and women, young and old, married and single; moral and intellectual beings, in open contempt of their humanity, leveled at a blow with horses, sheep, horned cattle and swine" (p. 100). Douglass's outrage at being equated with livestock energizes his narrative of literal self-claiming—how a slave was made a man, in his words. And yet that plot trajectory is embedded within the larger frame of a marketable selfhood. Granted, any autobiographer has to accept some notion of a commodified self—the self as a story to be bought and sold, retold and repackaged. But given Douglass's personal history, that accession is especially dicey. *My Bondage and My Freedom*'s title page includes an intriguing epigraph from Coleridge: "By a principle essential to christianity, a PERSON is eternally differenced from a THING; so that the idea of a HUMAN BEING, necessarily excludes the idea of PROPERTY IN THAT BEING." But this pronouncement belies the extent to which the narrative struggles to rearticulate rather than negate the relation of selfhood to property. If, as Michael Newbury has argued, American authors at midcentury used the figure of the slave as an analogue for their own disempowerment within an emergent and increasingly aggressive culture of celebrity, Douglass's book performs a critical inversion: it uses the author's literal history of enslavement as a vehicle for legitimation (that is, experience has qualified him to speak against the institution of slavery) and self-assertion, insofar as his original act of self-claiming makes possible the very conditions of his authorship.[22]

Nineteenth-century Americans admitted of a range of notions of the self as property apart from the practice of chattel slavery. Independent adulthood was often figured as self-possession, a state to which African Americans, as Douglass was acutely aware, were thought to have little access. Wives and children were classified as property at certain moments and for certain purposes, while, as Brook Thomas and others have shown, legal constructions of privacy and reputation were much entangled with the concept of property.[23] At the end of the century, Albion Tourgée would argue before the Supreme Court that segregation laws had robbed Homer Plessy of his "reputation of being white"—a tricky kind of property indeed for a man of mixed racial heritage in the postbellum South. Douglass's investment in reputation likewise renders the self as property, and so his moral authority, which intersects at every turn with his authorship, becomes the linchpin of this delicate negotiation. The final third of *My*

Bondage and My Freedom, especially, is rife with assertions of the author's good character. Douglass takes care to mention, for example, that he "had never given up, in reality, [his] religious faith," answering long-standing charges that, because he excoriated Christian slaveholders for their hypocrisy, he was himself anti-Christian (p. 202).[24] His decision to break with two northern congregations, he asserts, has resulted from their ideological shortcomings rather than any apostasy on his part: the first, a predominantly white Methodist church, practiced racial segregation, while the second, a "small body of colored Methodists," Douglass chose to abandon when he "found that it consented to the same spirit which held my brethren in chains" (p. 203). And moral authority infuses Douglass's decision to return to the United States after his successful tour of the British Isles: "I felt that I had a duty to perform—and that was, to labor and suffer with the oppressed in my native land" (p. 216–17). The personal cost of this choice—a return to the racial injustices of his homeland—is made clear in the narrator's description of his treatment on the *Cambria*, where the cabin Douglass has paid for is given to a white passenger and he is "forbidden" to enter the ship's "saloon" (p. 225).

The most striking alignment of authorship and reputation occurs in the final chapter, when Douglass describes his accession to the role of editor. "The paper has been successful," he declares, despite the prediction of skeptics that it would fail, and despite the suggestion on the part of "friends in Boston" (i.e., Garrison and his cohort) that Douglass was "better fitted to speak than to write" (pp. 227, 226). Linking explicitly his own development as an author and editor with the condition of the race as a whole, Douglass writes: "I look upon the time, money, and labor bestowed upon [the newspaper], as being amply rewarded, in the development of my own mental and moral energies, and in the corresponding development of my deeply injured and oppressed people" (pp. 227–28). Douglass's reputation, his status as a public figure, suffuses the circulating property of his paper, which by this point includes his name in its title, even as the paper, the product of so much time, labor, and money, works to "develop" the race.[25]

Significantly, Douglass pairs "mental" and "moral" development in his assessment of the paper's value. Certainly such a move echoes conventional reformist rhetoric about the need to improve both the intellectual and moral status of slaves and free blacks—but instead of foregrounding the attainment of basic literacy and good work habits, outcomes that such discourse typically encouraged, Douglass emphasizes his achievements as the editor of a widely circulating paper. More immediately, this convergence matters because Julia Griffiths worked so closely with Douglass on that project. Given that some of his critics viewed the offices of his newspaper as a transgressive, erotic space within which his adulterous desires festered, Douglass counters with the assertion that working on the paper—and by extension working with Griffiths—has improved both his mind and his morals. Douglass's compulsion to wed intellectual to moral status was, to some extent, of a piece with his era—many of his contemporaries laid claim to moral legitimacy as a component of their intellectual or artistic authority. But the gesture is even more crucial within a culture so dramatically invested in the notion of an insuperable mental and moral weakness among those of African descent. At stake in Douglass's denial of moral corruption at his newspaper is the matter of black intellect (the ability not only to write well but, as editor, to manage, organize, and select the writings of others) as well as self-control (the ability to work closely with a white woman without becoming her lover).

Despite the aggressive forms of self-promotion delineated here, Douglass's text evinces some misgivings about the authorial availability that his project entails. He writes in his preface of his "positive repugnance to writing or speaking anything for the public, which could...make me liable to the imputation of seeking personal notoriety, for its own sake" (p. 5). But unlike Melville's Pierre, who greeted the prospect of public availability with a kind of horror, Douglass's narrative persona accepts it as an opportunity—not simply to make a point forcefully before the reading public, but to establish the terms and limits of his own property status. This reading of *My Bondage and My Freedom* coheres with Douglass's more overt pragmatism with respect to his status as chattel. That is, one of his early points of contention with the Garrisonians had to do with his choice to allow his freedom to be bought—a move that his opponents characterized as complicit with the institution of slavery. For Douglass, this "commercial transaction" (p. 216), as he terms it, is not capitulation but strategy. Accordingly, he draws an explicit connection between his public status as author and his decision to allow English abolitionists to purchase his freedom: "Had I been a private person," he writes, "I should never have consented to the payment of so large a sum for the privilege of living securely under our glorious republican form of government. I could have remained in England, or have gone to some other country; and perhaps I could even have lived unobserved in this" (pp. 229–30). But authorship, he notes in reference to his 1845 narrative, has made him "notorious" (p. 230), a public figure especially susceptible to recapture as literal property. And so it is precisely his status as public property that necessitates his no longer being legally defined as one white American's *particular* property. Were he simply an anonymous, autonomous "private person," he suggests, his own forceful assertion of property-in-himself would have been sufficient to offset the claims of an individual slaveholder. Even as celebrity strengthens Douglass's hand—insofar as it renders him a more potent catalyst for social change—it weakens his ability to protect himself in concrete terms.

Marketing Reputation

Douglass's self-promotional strategies, the ways in which his authorial/public personae refer to and promote one another, can be read as operating within a kind of entrepreneurial ethics, a strategy of putting marketing to work toward principled activist ends. In making that claim, I don't discount the possibility that egotism fueled these initiatives to some degree, but it seems clear that Douglass's cross-platform marketing, however much it may have served his personal interests, also promoted a larger abolitionist and antiracist agenda. The business world of the twentieth and twenty-first centuries calls these strategies "branding," an eerily resonant term given Douglass's subject matter. Branding, in this case, comprises a matrix of promotions and reinforcements, with Douglass providing (as author and lecturer) or controlling (as editor) the content within mutually reinforcing genres. The following examples reveal the extent to which Douglass sought to shape his own commodification—to brand, so to speak, these multiple versions of himself as an upstanding, authoritative, credible, and not least, intriguing set of purchases.

Advertisements for *My Bondage and My Freedom* ran in a number of publications—including the *Liberator*—but they figured especially prominently in *Frederick Douglass' Paper*. In keeping with widely used marketing practices in the antebellum period, notices printed in advance of the book's publication sought to spark early interest. One of these promises, as midcentury notices frequently did, that the book will include a "Steel Portrait" of the author and comments on his "fine genius, and...rapidly developing powers";[26] another, which paired *My Bondage and My Freedom* with a new edition of Richard Hildreth's *The White Slave* (here titled *Archy Moore, The White Slave*), invited all to "READ THE STORY OF HIS [Douglass's] WRONGS!" beginning on August 15, the book's expected release date.[27] Later advertisements foregrounded the book's impressive early sales. One announced "5,000 COPIES SOLD IN TWO DAYS!" and included a quasi-poetic response to the question "WHY SO POPULAR!":

> It is the Work of an American Slave,
> Therefore excites American Sympathy!
> Every line and letter are his own,
> And it is a Volume of Truth and Power!
> It tells the earnest—startling truth
> Without ranting or madness!
> It addresses the intellect and the heart!
> Every free Press chants its praise,
> Every free voter will read it,
> And every Bookseller supply it![28]

The piece accommodates the prejudices of white readers (e.g., the expectation that "ranting" and "madness" would characterize the prose of a former slave), but it also invites those who refuse to read the narrative to reckon with the possibility that they are *not* free. And, intriguingly, the pitch specifically mentions "voters," suggesting that the book's target audience consists of politically active white men. Other advertisements incorporated more direct evidence of the book's favorable reception. One that ran in the August 31, 1855 issue (two weeks after the book's release) reprinted endorsements from sources as well known as the *New York Tribune* or as obscure as the *Yates Co. Whig* or the *Oswego Times*. This advertisement also indulged in some in-crowd wordplay: "Read it," the publisher promised potential buyers, "and you cannot Resist it"—a joke that represents the book as the public's enchanter, but that also invokes warring abolitionist factions by referencing Garrisonian nonresistance.[29] The *National Era* ran this advertisement as well, inserting it within a narrow column of text between two other examples of moral righteousness for sale: above it is an advertisement for a newly published "collection of church music"; immediately below, there appears a notice of "free labor goods" for sale in Philadelphia "at market rates."[30] Those likely to buy and read Douglass's book, this placement suggests, would not wish to do so while clothed in slave-harvested cotton.

These advertisements made the case that *My Bondage and My Freedom* was a significant event in abolitionist—and American—publishing.[31] To reinforce the point, *Frederick Douglass' Paper* also printed a number of commentaries on the book, the tone and diction of which approach the levels of enthusiasm recorded in the era's parodies of literary approbation.[32] Under the heading "New Publications," for example, the following endorsement appeared: "We have read nothing since Uncle Tom's Cabin, which so thrilled every fibre of the soul and awoke such intense sympathy for the slave as this touching autobiography.... My Bondage and My Freedom is a remarkable book. We could not but wonder, as we read, at the terseness, vigor and polish of the style, which would do credit to the ripest scholar and most practiced writer in our country."[33] A letter from the Reverend J. W. Loguen, who was selling copies of the book on Douglass's behalf, states that "the manner in which [*My Bondage and My Freedom*] sells, shows that the people are awakening to an appreciation of black men's talents for bookmaking."[34] Another piece, reprinted from the *Northern Christian Advocate*, forecasts that Douglass's book "will be read by tens of thousands, if not by hundreds of thousands of our American people; it is just one of that class of books needed for the times."[35] Celebrity testimony appeared as well: Fanny Fern's praise of the book—she calls it "thrillingly fascinating" and commends its "fair, frank, just spirit"—appears under a headnote indicating that the paper's staff has "take[n] the liberty of inserting" her comments during one of Douglass's absences from Rochester, thus absolving him of any direct role in capitalizing on the famous writer's endorsement.[36] As a practical adjunct to this energetic promotion of the volume, the newspaper offices took orders for it and offered copies as "incentive[s] for abolitionists to recruit new subscribers."[37]

An upsurge of scholarly interest in *My Bondage and My Freedom* across the last two decades has resulted in astute comparisons of the 1845 and 1855 autobiographies, texts that, when read against each other, do much to illuminate the author's intellectual and rhetorical development. The marketing synergy and cross-referencing I have outlined suggest that *My Bondage and My Freedom* and *Frederick Douglass' Paper* form another revealing diptych, one that speaks to the tensions within Douglass's growing cultural and political influence. No regular reader of *Frederick Douglass' Paper* in 1855 or 1856 could have remained unaware of *My Bondage and My Freedom*, just as anyone who finished the autobiography would have found it impossible to ignore the salience of Douglass's founding of his own newspaper.[38] That event and the author's return to the United States from England stand as the twinned apices of his narrative's teleology. And Douglass's early 1850s scandals only added to this momentum—just as his newspaper might, in any issue, include another volley aimed at the Garrisonians or another instance of impassioned self-defense, his autobiography might reveal to purchasers some new account of his political conversion or hint regarding his alleged transgressions. Even bad publicity, Douglass surely realized, sold books.

Douglass's entrepreneurial verve may have served other purposes as well. As William McFeely has pointed out, he was acutely sensitive when it came to the matter of his business sense and particularly resented the fact that many white abolitionists seemed unwilling to trust African Americans with money—on Douglass's English lecture tour, for example, Maria Weston Chapman directed his white traveling companion, the abolitionist James Buffum, to handle the finances.[39] And so the demonstration of marketing savvy became an end in itself, a way of asserting Douglass's own financial/commercial adulthood, and, by extension, the potential of the race to "manage" itself.

The Tribulation of an Editor

The moral freighting of editorial work, to which Douglass alludes in the final segments of *My Bondage and My Freedom*, emerges as a central preoccupation within his newspaper. The prospectus for the *North Star*, released in the fall of 1847, sets the tone, promising that the paper will "exalt the standard of Public Morality" and "promote the Moral and Intellectual Improvement of the COLORED PEOPLE," while a piece in the first issue "solemnly dedicate[s] the 'North Star' to the cause of our long oppressed and plundered fellow countrymen."[40] The moral purpose of the paper melds with that of its editor, as Douglass calls editorial work his "duty to God and man" and emphasizes the stakes of the enterprise: "That others have failed, is a reason for our earnestly endeavoring to succeed. Our race must be vindicated from the embarrassing imputations resulting from former non-success."[41] A year later, Douglass puts the matter in even stronger terms: "Should [the *North Star*] fall from the moral sky, it would be missed and regretted by many dear friends...; while on the other hand, the enemies of human brotherhood—the haters of human freedom—the slanderers of our race, might well take courage, and cry, Aha! aha! aha! we told you so!—these 'negroes are after all an inferior people and that inferiority will show itself even when they are surrounded by the most favorable influences for improvement.' We tremble at the reproach which would fall upon us, should this effort fail."[42] The newspaper is a city upon a hill, with Douglass as its creator, defender, and liable party.

For Douglass, editorship's burdens and possibilities take on a distinctly identitarian valence. "It has long been our anxious wish to see," he writes, "in this slave-holding, slave-trading, and negro-hating land, a printing-press and paper, permanently established, under the complete control and direction of the immediate victims of slavery and oppression." An individual who has actually experienced slavery, in other words, must lead the campaign against it in print. It makes sense, then, that Douglass emphasizes his own former status as chattel in the paper's first issue, noting in the first-person plural of editorial authority that "nine years ago... we were held as a slave, shrouded in the midnight ignorance of that infernal system." As a way of inaugurating his new role, Douglass reprints documents related to his own manumission (under the title "Free Papers," which I'm tempted to read as an intentional pun) on the same page as his declarations of past and purpose. These materials, insofar as they prove Douglass's prior enslavement and achievement of freedom, work to authorize the newspaper, marking its first issue as a kind of liminal space—a sense that Douglass reinforces in "Our Paper and Its Prospects," the column that introduces his project, when he claims to be on the "threshold" of "obtaining" the long desired object of editing his own paper. By contrast, Douglass's prospectus to the paper's eighth volume, published in December of 1854 (when he was in the midst of intense intramovement conflict), evidences no such hesitation or consciousness of an identity under construction, but rather asserts an already-achieved dominion: "This paper, as its name imports, is Frederick Douglass' paper, in the fullest sense. He is its Editor, and Proprietor. It is under the control of no sect or party; but is conducted according to the best judgment of its Editor and Proprietor, without reference to boards, cliques, or committees." Not only does Douglass insist on his complete and solitary control over the paper, but he asserts its singularity and representativeness within US print culture: "As there is no other paper, in this country, conducted by a colored man, it claims now to be peculiarly the exponent of the views and wishes of the colored people." Ownership of the paper morphs into a broader proprietorship over black public opinion and collective interest, an amalgam of "views and wishes" that Douglass purports to be able to discern and then disseminate.[43]

Though Douglass only occasionally demonstrated the expansive sense of personal authority evident in that 1854 prospectus, he printed (or reprinted) a great deal of material praising his own abilities and attainments. The January 7,

1848 issue of the *North Star*, for example, included glowing letters of appreciation from readers who had admired the paper's debut issue: Samuel J. May, a white abolitionist and Unitarian minister, wrote that he "read it all with entire satisfaction—much of it with delight"; J.W.C. Pennington—like Douglass, an escaped slave and man of letters—noted that he "like[d] the paper very much" and commended the choice of name; the Rhode Island merchant and abolitionist Isaac C. Kenyon called the paper a "truly laudable undertaking"; and Abner H. Francis, a successful black businessman based in Buffalo, New York, asserted that "the principles there set forth, strictly adhered to, will effect more to accomplish the end designed than any similar organ ever commenced in this country."[44] Despite Douglass's promise that "far less will be said about ourself in future numbers, than appears in this week's paper," he and his editorial associates continued to publish approving commentary, both in the *North Star* and in its sequel, *Frederick Douglass' Paper*. In 1849, for instance, Douglass reprinted a statement from the editor of the *Pennsylvania Freeman* that "there are few papers in our land whose editorials are written with more clearness and force than Mr. Douglass's."[45] A reprint from the *Chicago Daily Tribune*, published in November of 1854, called Douglass "the great colored orator of America" and noted, in reference to a recent lecture, that "there were not less than *fifteen hundred people* in the Hall, and nearly as many more went away unable to obtain admittance." Douglass's "speech," the piece continued, "was received with the greatest enthusiasm."[46] Subsequent issues included "A Gratifying Testimonial" from a group of antislavery activists in Philadelphia, who "recognize [in *Frederick Douglass' Paper*] a powerful engine to our elevation" and who called the editor himself "a firm and able champion of Human Rights...whom we delight to honor"; an excerpted letter from "a friend in Chicago" that named Douglass "the great leader of reform among the colored people of this country," one who ought to be sustained as "soldiers [are] under obligations to sustain their General on the battle field"; and a reference to Douglass as "probably the most talented colored man in the land" whom "very few of any race or country can equal."[47]

As the foregoing commendations suggest, the praise heaped on Douglass often referred explicitly to his role as a lecturer. Indeed, his newspaper served as a venue for commenting on and in some cases reproducing his speeches. Many issues included accounts of Douglass's lecture tours—sometimes these are reports (or reprints of reports) by audience members or event organizers, but more often they are penned by the editor himself, taking the form of a retrospective account of his recent activities or an extended letter to the paper written during and sent from a lecture tour. Some emphasize the importance of antislavery lecturing or the timeliness of Douglass's appearances: in May of 1848, for example, he writes that "the interesting events transpiring at home and abroad, makes this a most happy moment for enforcing, from the platform, the great principles of justice and human brotherhood against slavery."[48]

In other instances, Douglass's reports from the field echo the era's travel narratives, as in the following description of Ithaca, New York: "The site of the village is quite romantic and picturesque. Few places are more charmingly situated. It is perfectly girt about with lofty hills, many of which are covered with trees of the richest foliage."[49] In contrast with this tone of leisurely appreciation, other dispatches emphasize the hardships that attend the life he has chosen. In the winter of 1849, for example, he closes a piece with an overt plea for sympathy: "My poor old horse and shattered old sleigh are at the door, ready to take me through the snow storm on my mission of freedom and humanity."[50]

Douglass occasionally betrayed some discomfort with the extent of his self-chronicling, worrying that his lengthy missives from this or that town might make him appear "egotistical and ridiculous."[51] "It is true," he wrote, "that minute accounts of my own public movements have appeared in the columns of the North Star; and it is also true that I have pretty nearly abandoned the practice of inserting them—but certainly not before it had become thoroughly distasteful to me, and perhaps equally so to my readers." Despite this disavowal, he proceeded to publish just such details, recounting his ongoing lecturing and advocacy work in Toronto. Douglass may have reduced the frequency of his first-hand reports over time (though they did not disappear entirely), but he continued to use the paper as a way to publicize his work as a lecturer. Indeed, in the summer and fall of 1854 *Frederick Douglass' Paper* included extensive coverage of two speeches—one delivered as part of Western Reserve College's commencement ceremonies and the other a well-attended lecture in Chicago, the text of which was reprinted, albeit imperfectly, in the November 10 issue.[52] Throughout, his growing prominence and influence (as an invited speaker at an institution of higher learning, as a figure able to command the attention of hundreds) are foregrounded.

The synergy here is significant not just in marketing terms, as I have argued, but also in terms of Douglass's development of a broader identity as a key—if controversial—presence within the antislavery movement. That said, for Douglass lecturing and writing/editing were also in conflict. Interestingly, Garrison had warned of this very problem: as Robert S. Levine has noted, in the summer of 1847 Garrison applauded Douglass's (short-lived) decision to give up on the plan of starting his own paper, writing that "it is quite impracticable to combine the editor with the lecturer, without either causing the paper to be more or less neglected, or the sphere of lecturing to be severely circumscribed."[53] Douglass would worry this question in the pages of his newspaper for years to come. Early on he notes that "the two positions are so dissimilar, that to be proficient in the one, is to be almost necessarily deficient in the other." Six years later the balancing act seems just as difficult: "The pen is a bore to the speaker," he wrote, "and the writer generally would be excused from speech-making. He who has to work in both departments, must not be held to a very strict account, either as to the matter or manner of his work." Near the end of 1854 he would lament that "it is not easy...to fling off the extemporaneous habit of the platform, and to assume that which is fitting the editorial chair, after seven weeks of exciting labors in the lecturing field. There is that in the former which measurably unfits one for the duties of the latter."[54] This combination of activities may have intensified Douglass's effectiveness as an activist, but it also proved exhausting and to some degree, he suggests, self-defeating.

Douglass's ranking of the two enterprises bears consideration as well. He occasionally elevates speech over writing as the more arresting medium for pursuing social change:

> The pen is not to be despised, but who that knows anything of the might and electricity of speech as it bursts from hearts of fire, glowing with light and life, will not acknowledge the superiority over the pen for immediate effect.... Ink and paper have no sense of shame—they cannot blush under exposure, nor smart under rebuke and indignation.[55]

Speech is not only more effective in this rendering, but it's more emotionally honest as well. Elsewhere, though, Douglass frames his lecture tours as unwelcome distractions from his editorial work: "I should like to write at length," he notes at one point, "but talk is the order of the day, amd [sic] I must be off."[56] The typographical error seems only to underscore his point (though in fact he could not have been the one setting the type, as he was writing from out of town). Across multiple issues of the newspaper, it becomes clear why Douglass lectures so frenetically, despite the fact that his travels leave him exhausted and unable to attend as assiduously as he would like to his editorial role. Lecturing, he makes clear, enables him to secure additional subscriptions for the newspaper, which are essential to its survival, as the following excerpts attest:

> You will sympathize with me when I tell you that I find it necessary to go abroad in person to secure the number of subscribers requisite to the support of our paper.[57]

> Our readers must not be dissatisfied with continued absence from our editorial chair.... We find it absolutely necessary to travel and lecture in order to extend the circulation of the "North Star," and otherwise advance the cause.[58]

> The urgent demands upon us to attend and address public meetings, and the absolute necessity of increasing our subscription list, and the fact that we can do much towards the latter result by attending public meetings, will, we fear, for the present, make it our duty to travel much more than we contemplated, at the establishment of the North Star.[59]

> All who really desire the North Star to be sustained, will bear my absence with indulgent patience, since the paper can be sustained only by giving

it a good subscription list, and this can be done only by presenting its claims to the public, and soliciting subscribers to it.[60]

Occasionally Douglass's tone veers from apologetic to annoyed, as the following lines, apparently written in response to readers' criticism, demonstrate:

> If our readers would have us more at our post, they have only to exert themselves in order to secure a sufficient number of subscribers to support the paper, and we shall joyfully confine our energies to our editorial duties. Our readers must not expect us to make bricks without straw. It is impossible to produce a first rate paper from week to week while travelling every day and lecturing every night.[61]

These statements are just a sampling of the many that appeared in the paper, especially in its early years when the size of the subscription list was a matter of near-constant concern.[62] I have cited them at length in order to suggest the frequency with which Douglass-as-editor comes across less as a political firebrand or leader of the race than as a beleaguered businessman, one whose more detailed pleas tap artfully into the guilt economy of social activism. In the editorial marking the end of the *North Star*'s second volume, for instance, Douglass admits to feeling "apprehension and discouragement," with subscriptions failing to cover expenses—indeed, those subscribers whom Douglass worked so hard to secure often failed to pay—and the paper relying on donations to make up the difference: "Friends, do you desire this? Do the think it best that the North Star should be allowed to languish? Is it of so little service to the cause of freedom that it can even be entirely dispensed with? We think not. We know that it has done good, and that it is every week increasing in usefulness."[63]

Financial anxiety was a recurring theme in both the *North Star* and *Frederick Douglass' Paper*, taking the form not just of apologies for the editor's many absences but of outright—indeed, sometimes comically frank—dunning notices aimed at delinquent subscribers. As Leon Jackson has shown, the dun was a ubiquitous subgenre in antebellum periodicals, one that mediated between "competing necessities: on the one hand to honor and sustain a sense of community... and on the other to ensure the sort of cash flow necessary for trade at a distance."[64] Douglass, as the editor of a paper promoting a movement that required collective action, must have felt that tension sharply, insofar as alienating subscribers might entail driving them away from the larger abolitionist project. While he flattered and cajoled remiss subscribers in some of his appeals (as when he referred to those who are "honest and who mean to pay"), elsewhere the editor's frustration with his debtors is obvious.[65] A piece that ran in January of 1850, for instance, admonished subscribers to "Pay up! Pay up!! Pay up!!!," with accumulating exclamation marks and an insistence that money be sent "at once" betraying Douglass's irritation.[66] Compliance was apparently little better some five years later, when Douglass wrote (under the headline "To Our Subscribers—Bills! Bills! Bills!!") that "we cannot afford to publish this paper gratuitously, and it requires the strictest economy, combined with unyielding perseverance, to publish it at all. Of this, our friends must, certainly, be aware."[67] A longer piece alluded to the "humiliating history" of black American newspaper publishing and identified as the "chief cause" of these failures an "amazing disparity, painfully visible to Editors in general, and black Editors in particular, between the disposition to *read* and the disposition to *pay*."[68]

Postage was another point of contention, as Douglass repeatedly asked correspondents to "*pre-pay* the letters with which they favor us."[69] According to Jackson, an "elaborate but rarely stated etiquette" imperfectly regulated the matter of who paid to send letters through the 1840s: generally speaking, the recipient paid postage on a "familiar" letter, while the sender was expected to prepay when mailing a business letter, though the boundary between the two was murky.[70] By the early 1850s prepayment was becoming increasingly common for all correspondence—and would become a legal requirement by 1855—but vestiges of the earlier protocol remained.[71] For Douglass, whose correspondents were often personal friends as well as colaborers in the antislavery field, the matter was especially dicey, as is evident in the volume of letters he received that required payment. His insistence on prepayment is one of many efforts to keep the newspaper solvent, but it also registers as an attempt to formalize the business, so to speak, of antislavery work. Shared goals and experiences—even shared travels on the lecture circuit—might eventuate in a degree of interpersonal warmth, but they did not change the fact that for Douglass, editing the newspaper was a form of work more than an exercise of sociability or even of philanthropy. To that point, he sought in an 1854 piece to disabuse his "colored brethren" of the notion that he had "become wealthy enough to edit and publish a paper for gratuitous distribution, for the good of mankind, and our own amusement!"[72]

Despite Douglass's stated dislike of "anything like *whining*," his editorials, like his appeals for prompt payment, often lamented the hardships of newspaper editing.[73] Announcing the completion of the *North Star*'s first volume, for instance, Douglass wrote that "persons unacquainted with the expense, difficulties and hardships to be encountered and endured by one who undertakes to establish a large weekly periodical, devoted to an unpopular cause, with few friends, small capital, and smaller experience, can but poorly appreciate the satisfaction which we feel in even the limited success implied" in reaching this milestone.[74] Though the point here is his triumph over adversity, the weight of the sentence is on obstacles and frustrations. Three years later, Douglass wrote that "the atmosphere into which we ushered our new paper, [was] chilly, cold and unfriendly."[75] The mistrust with which others, including free African Americans, perceived his role exacerbated these difficulties: "Tell them that a well conducted press in the hands of colored men is essential to the progress and elevation of the colored man, and they will regard you as one merely seeking a living at the public expense 'to get along without work.'"[76] By 1852, he was able to approach his critics with more levity; in a facetious piece on the travails of editorship—especially as it involved dealing with the complaints and disappointments of would-be contributors—Douglass asked his "kind reader" to "picture to himself a man constantly beset by creditors, with bills for paper, bills for printing, bills for light and fuel, and *bad* bills, and no bills from subscribers to meet these dunning *bills*, and will add to this, the aforementioned perplexities, we think he will sympathize with the tribulation of an editor."[77] Other meditations on the vagaries of editing contrast Douglass's ironclad good intentions with the obstacles he has encountered. Having taken on the editorial role "impressed by a conscientious conviction of duty [and] impelled by unwavering confidence in the omnipotence of Truth," Douglass nevertheless encountered "the virulent opposition of determined enemies," including those from within the antislavery movement.[78]

Contending with these antagonists occupied tremendous time and energy. Indeed, Douglass's controversies and paper wars with other antislavery figures emerge as a constitutive element of his editorial voice, in marked contrast with the narrative persona of *My Bondage and My Freedom*. Certainly that volume touches on its author's disillusionment with Garrison and other figures—made evident not just in the prose but in their notable absence as framing or legitimating voices—but overall the tone is restrained, even decorous. Douglass's moral authority as an autobiographer in some sense relies on this understated self-assertion and individuation from his former mentors and associates; the story he wishes to tell is too momentous—and too grave—to be given over to the settling of political scores. In his newspapers, however, the gloves come off.[79] Douglass as editor, at least at certain junctures, registers as a contentious figure, one whose heated prose occasionally edges into pettiness or, worse, petulance, as when he suggests that the delayed arrival of Henry Bibb's narrative might owe to its author's having "felt it proper to serve a black editor last" or when he denounces (under the headline "Slanderers") the "guilty and base reptile who can sneak through the community, with a bland smile upon the cheek, and a lie upon the lip," but then coyly leaves the offenders unnamed, saying only that "there are some such within the range of our acquaintance."[80] As these examples suggest, Douglass's tendency toward division began well ahead of his famous defection from the Garrisonian camp—which he dates precisely to May of 1851—on the matter of the US Constitution.[81] Earlier conflicts involved, among others, Samuel Ringgold Ward, Martin Delany, and Henry Highland Garnet, whose remark in the summer of 1849 that Douglass was "unstable" elicited an especially pointed response.[82]

The break with Garrison and the antagonisms that followed intensified Douglass's impulse to defend himself in print, to the point where the December 9, 1853 issue of the newspaper was almost entirely given over to the enterprise;

on page one Douglass reprinted various attacks on him that had appeared in other abolitionist papers, then devoted the second and third pages (of a four-page publication) to his extended response, which included a long preamble delineating the various reasons why silence might be advisable (in order to maintain "the peace and the harmony of our great national, anti-slavery family" and to avoid appearing "querulous"), followed by his rationale for choosing to speak out anyway: "The impunity allowed to my adversaries by my silence, like all other submission to wrong, has failed to soften the hearts of the wrong doers. My seeming retreat has occasioned an additional advance on their part.... Their assaults are now unbearable. Every apology for honorable silence has been wrenched from me."[83] What follows is a point-by-point refutation of the charges against him, culminating in a refusal to answer the most incendiary among them—that of adultery—with which this chapter opened.

The sentence that begins this disquisition reveals much of what is at stake: "I am now entering upon a work personal to myself," Douglass writes, "and shall therefore, dispense with the we, and speak in the pronoun singular."[84] The attacks on his personal morality and antislavery ideology have wrested from him, at least temporarily, the dignity and distance of the editorial role, the authoritative "we" that he has worked so hard to achieve and maintain, forcing him back into individual personhood, into the aggrieved "I" of the autobiographer. But this time his antagonists are not the Auld family or proslavery ministers, but rather his erstwhile friends and colaborers, a fact that undermines his role as self-styled representative of the cause—or of the race. The newspaper's serial form allowed the pace of the conflict to accelerate as well, though if reprinting-and-refutation figured as a key strategy in Douglass's campaign of self-justification, it was not his alone; Garrison would use the same tools against him, reproducing and ridiculing his remarks in the *Liberator*. Not surprisingly, the virulence of Douglass's rhetoric itself became an object of critique in this period, which he felt the need to answer in print: "While we are not conscious that an innate proclivity to 'scatter, tear, and slay,' is a component element of our being," he wrote in December of 1854, "still we have ever endeavored to present a bold, determined front to opposition, irrespective of the form it might assume, regardless of the source whence it might emanate."[85]

My point is not that Douglass was harsher in terms of his rhetoric or his tone than were his antagonists—he patently was not. In fact, Garrison was far more snide, and more personally insulting, in his attacks than was Douglass. Nevertheless, the latter's contentiousness, especially as expressed in his newspaper, at times threatened the larger project of moral repair that the publication was ostensibly calculated to support. In defending himself, that is, Douglass courted the very qualities he was accused of possessing, most notably arrogance and self-absorption. His effectiveness as a social and political activist—predicated as it was on the maintenance of a prodigious moral authority—had long required a careful calibration and deployment of righteous anger. The outrage that erupted in his newspaper editorials, and especially in the long blast of December 1853, exposed the movement to public ridicule and shifted attention from the plight of the slave to the rivalries and resentments among activists, just as Douglass had feared it might. And it undermined the carefully built collaboration by which Douglass's moral and experiential authority authorized the newspaper, while the paper served to endorse him as an influential and representative figure, insofar as the public airing of grievances substituted Douglass as personal antagonist for Douglass as editor. This disruption would prove temporary and partial—the paper remained in circulation for years to come and would, as I have argued, play a key role in promoting the 1855 autobiography, even as its forays into intramovement bickering would render the release and circulation of that volume ever more pressing.

If Douglass emerged within the newspaper as a querulous figure, to use his term—one whose sensitivity to criticism hardly approached the extremities of a predecessor like Fenimore Cooper, but nevertheless entailed a degree of self-sabotage within his particular context—this sharper tone might also strike a twenty-first-century reader as refreshingly candid. Douglass's newspaper articles and editorials—because of their rapidity of production and response—offer us a less polished and less carefully orchestrated persona than those we encounter in the autobiographies, which were, scholars tell us, labored over and heavily revised. The care with which Douglass crafted *My Bondage and My Freedom* is made evident in a letter to Gerrit Smith, in which the former wrote that his process of composition was "more of a job than at first I supposed it would be and I am beginning to be weary of it," an admission that suggests a degree of painstaking well beyond what this prolific writer and lecturer ordinarily had time for.[86] In his newspaper pieces, by contrast, Douglass often remarks on the haste with which he has written them, offering to continue a particular thread in a subsequent editorial or apologizing for a lack of thoroughness. It is not that Douglass's editorial voice is somehow unmediated—briskness of production does not magically produce authenticity or direct access to an author's interior self—but rather that the voice is differently mediated, subject to more pressing deadlines and more immediate exigencies (recent events, obstacles, or conflicts) than he encountered when dealing with the long horizon of life writing in monograph form.

Personal Property

Whatever their tonal differences, Douglass's books and his newspaper pieces both registered a keen awareness of the complications of authorship and property, especially as they colluded, and at times collided, with notions of moral authority. While his contemporary Herman Melville chose to dramatize the untenable and paradoxical quality of an author's desire for both privacy and audience, as I discussed in this book's introduction, Douglass embraced the contradictions, putting himself out there, so to speak, in myriad ways. As an African American author passionately engaged in struggles for freedom, he risked a great deal in making himself public property—and in giving that circulating persona a moral valence—but the potential payoff was significant as well. Douglass's accession to public availability meant literally risking his well-being: even after his freedom was purchased, the level of racist vitriol directed at him suggested that physical attack remained a possibility. And for Douglass, the self as property and the self on display always referenced the slave market to some degree, an association that must have been a source of pain. Further, his position as racial representative meant that his successes or failures (in the matter of self-promotion, as in all matters) would be magnified.[87] So an autobiography that failed to attract a readership or a newspaper that folded for lack of subscribers, as he often warned, would be read as a pronouncement on the prospects, literary and otherwise, of the race.[88] By the same token, his successful self-promotion would prove to the Garrisonians and to the broader public that an independent black man could hold his own within, and beyond, the antislavery publishing scene, even as his texts pressed for such social revolutions as abolition and racial equality.

Finally, it's important to acknowledge that Douglass's engagement with structures of publicity and property had its limits. In his newspapers he offered some access to his personal and family life: though he refused to speak directly to the charge of an extramarital affair, he did at times disclose the details of less explosive matters, relating, for example, his young daughter's distress at being separated from other students at an otherwise all-white school and the details of his own and his children's illnesses (e.g., a son's bout with typhus, Douglass's own "attack of bilious fever" while traveling in Illinois).[89] *My Bondage and My Freedom,* by contrast, maintains a near-complete silence with respect to domestic matters. While his published response to Garrison's infidelity accusation indulged in some fiery rhetoric about outraged privacy, and by extension outraged property, the narrative itself studiously avoids the matter, even as it elides Douglass's family life almost entirely. The text does describe some intimate friendships, but only from the past—for example, Douglass's devotion to Henry and John Harris, two of the young men who participated in his failed escape attempt, is quite intense: toward them, he writes, "I felt a friendship as strong as one man can feel for another; for I could have died with and for them" (p. 156). And Douglass characterizes his early feelings toward Garrison as a combination of "love and reverence" (p. 204). But the author mentions his wife only briefly and his children not at all.[90] An authorial persona may be for sale in Douglass's texts, but the keys to his house are kept secure. Or rather, those keys are resecured following the domestic exposures and invasions that the Griffiths scandal entailed. Even a selfhood as public as Frederick Douglass's struggled to keep something in reserve.

In the chapter that follows, I consider the reception and circulation of authors who (once established) did not face the kinds of financial exigencies that kept Douglass perpetually on the lecture circuit. In fact, my two principle objects of inquiry—Harriet Beecher Stowe and E.D.E.N. Southworth—attracted media attention for their immense sales and significant earning power. But popularity—and its sometime-complement, prosperity—made available an array of moral risks and opportunities that required especially astute strategies, and perhaps some luck, to navigate.

{4}

The Currency of Reputation

The famously prolific writer T. S. Arthur enjoyed a remarkable reputational security in the middle decades of the nineteenth century. His authorship essentially became a brand, as marketers would later come to use the term, such that his very name was thought to guarantee a morally salubrious product.[1] Despite occasional forays into the fraught arena of sensationalism—the eye-gouging incident from *Ten Nights in a Bar-Room* is perhaps the best-known example—Arthur's works elicited such uniform praise for their didactic fitness that the intervention of the reviewer came to seem superfluous, as the following comment from *Godey's Lady's Book* attests: "Mr. Arthur is already so universally known as a writer of the most excellent moral and instructive tales that the simple announcement of a new book from his pen is sufficient, without adding a word in comment."[2] Reviews of Arthur's works tended to be brief, even by the standards of the day—he was endlessly noticed in "Editor's Table" and "Books Received" sections, but was not featured in the long reviews and author profiles that ran in many prominent publications (e.g., the *North American Review*, *Putnam's*, the *Southern Literary Messenger*).[3] For some, the strength of the Arthur brand obviated the need even to read, much less offer a critical judgment on, his work. As a commentator noted in 1845, "we are not afraid to recommend, unread, anything from the warm heart and sound judgment of Mr. Arthur."[4]

T. S. Arthur was an outlier, however, within the nineteenth-century literary field insofar as his moral authority, as received and promulgated in print conversations about books and authorship, was unusually stable. As a reviewer noted in *Peterson's*, "the fictions of this author are always unexceptionable in their morality," a sentiment that any number of commentators echoed.[5] Even on the few occasions when his work elicited a response other than praise, its morality was not the target, as when the *Union Magazine* noted that "Mr. Arthur's stories always have an excellent aim; but this one [*Insubordination*] lacks the usual refinement of his delineations."[6] Though a few of Arthur's contemporaries enjoyed a similar reputational stability, the moral authority of authors was more typically a matter of ongoing debate and recalibration, shifting with the social and ideological investments of readers and morphing from one publication to the next. Further, the degree to which Arthur was applauded for his moral vigor, with little reference to literary-aesthetic achievement, belied the fact that, for many authors of the period, moral authority and literary value were conceived as interdependent and mutually reinforcing—or mutually unraveling—phenomena.[7]

If it was unusual for an author's name to guarantee his book in the straightforward manner that Arthur's reviewers claimed, there was nevertheless widespread agreement that authorial character—however unstable or difficult to discern—formed and legitimated the lessons that emerged within individual works. Conversely, the work was thought to reveal or, more pejoratively, to expose its author, as Barbara Hochman and others have shown.[8] As Caroline Kirkland, one of the era's most astute commentators on authorship, wrote in her *Book for the Home Circle* (1853), "No man can write a book without letting his real self peep out, whatever be the style he chooses to assume, or the sentiments he endeavours to adopt for the time. The reader catches glimpses of his face behind a mask."[9] The *Southern Literary Messenger*'s 1842 defense of the controversial English novelist Edward Bulwer, meanwhile, asserted that objectionable passages in his work were "the fault of the artist, [rather] than the man; for no where will you find a loftier and purer morality inculcated, than in those very novels in which the objectionable passages occur"; the novel as a whole, in other words, reveals the morals of the man, even if his aesthetic judgment and execution occasionally fail him.[10] Even Edgar Allan Poe, though he expressed discomfort elsewhere with the widespread assumption that moral assessment was an obligatory (or even an apt) literary-critical project, wrote in "The Literati of New York City" that a work both represents and reveals its author: "The supposition that the book of an author is a thing apart from the author's self, is, I think, ill-founded."[11] For many commentators an author's influence—his or her ability to shape the reader's impressions, judgments, and sentiments—was a key element within this paradigm of revelation: as editor Alfred Guernsey ventured in the July 1857 issue of *Harper's New Monthly Magazine*, "every author...who really influences the mind, who plants in it thoughts and sentiments which take root and grow, communicates his character. Error and immorality...escape *from* him if they are *in* him, and pass into the recipient mind through subtle avenues invisible to consciousness."[12] This quasi-mesmeric conception of authorial influence argues for the importance of the literary critic or reviewer, who might warn unsuspecting readers if an author's "communications" threaten to do harm.

A novelist's conception and delineation of fictional characters was one key means by which these transmissions occurred. As James L. Machor writes, "the type of characters presented, the way in which they were developed, and the sympathy (or lack) with which they were treated could be read—and were read by reviewers—as revealing signs of an author's own character."[13] An article on Charles Dickens that appeared in the March 1855 issue of *Putnam's* is one of many that exemplify Machor's claim: "No man can write as frankly as Dickens has done, without revealing the hue and quality of his own spirit." No author, the piece concluded, could create such "rare" and "sweet" characters as Dickens had "without being himself kindred in soul to the characters he describes."[14] A brief notice of Catharine Maria Sedgwick's *Home* used a familial metaphor to reinforce the point, noting that "Miss Sedgwick's favorite characters seem to inherit" their "sunny nature" from the author herself.[15]

Authorial biography also shaped the reception of a book's moral messages: as one reviewer noted, William North's *The Slave of the Lamp* (1855) would be "dangerous" in moral terms, had it not included "its own antidote in the short biography of the author prefixed to it," which follows him "from a privileged youth through a wretched manhood to a dishonored death."[16] The author's extratextual life provides a cautionary tale that pervades and conditions, for this reviewer, any competent reception of his work. But lest we imagine that these critical gestures were unremittingly earnest, it's worth noting that mid-century reviewers sometimes demonstrated a sense of humor with regard to their moral/authorial investments: in praising a new volume (*The Knight of Gwynne*) by the Irish novelist Charles Lever, a reviewer in *Godey's* joked that despite the book's "rollicking and frolicking by sea and land," "nothing can come amiss" because the author in question is a *"moral lever."*[17]

This emphasis on the author's self-revelation or emergence via his or her work dovetailed with a marked preoccupation among mid-nineteenth-century book reviewers with the "moral tendency," to use one of the era's recurring phrases, of both authors and individual works. Scholars have long noted the centrality of these concerns. Nina Baym, for example, in her landmark study *Novels, Readers, and Reviewers* (1984), writes that "talk about morality is so characteristic of and so widely prevalent in novel reviewing of the 1840s and 1850s as to indicate that it was taken as part of the reviewer's job"; in fact, her survey of some two thousand antebellum reviews yields just one critic (Poe, unsurprisingly) who explicitly remarked "that in principle the morality of the books he wrote about was not his business." Further, to the extent that the reviewer's gender can be discerned, Baym's research suggests that male and female reviewers were more or less equally invested in morality as an evaluative criterion.[18] More recently, Machor has argued that antebellum book reviewers saw fiction "as an inherently didactic discourse" and conceived of readers as "susceptible to and in need of instruction from novels and tales."[19]

The chapter that follows builds on these findings, but shifts the focus in a couple of significant ways. First, unlike these predecessors, I am not exclusively interested in responses to fictional texts; my research into mid-nineteenth-century print culture suggests that concerns about the moral fitness of books and authors extended well beyond fiction as a genre. Granted, novels figured prominently in these conversations—in part because they so compellingly dramatized moral decision-making and in part because some still considered the form to be morally risky—but other modes of authorship attracted relevant scrutiny as well.[20] Second, and more crucially, my analysis embeds these reputational considerations within a conception of authorship as a matrix of economies, both formal and informal. That is, I am interested in reception as it intersected with assessments, claims, and attributions made evident not just in book reviews but in advertisements and other forms of printed commentary. Moral reputation possessed and became, within this network, a kind of currency not just in the temporal sense of the term (i.e., reputation was not fixed or transcendent but rather contingent on the circumstances of a particular cultural moment), but in its economic meanings as well. That is, reputation, like money, could be spent, diminished, borrowed, and exchanged. Nowhere is this homology more resonant than in the careers of Harriet Beecher Stowe and E.D.E.N. Southworth, the subjects of this chapter's extended case studies. Widely acknowledged during their lifetimes for their popularity and prodigious earnings, both weathered and by some measures prevailed within controversies over their moral "fitness" as producers of widely read literature. In an era in which readers insisted on the relevance of an author's moral tone—but also eagerly consumed sensational and scandalous texts—the relationship between popularity and moral authority was under a great deal of pressure, a matter to be negotiated rather than presumed.

Interdependencies

Mid-nineteenth-century cultures of print abundantly disprove the notion that advertisements belong exclusively to the world of marketing while reviews adhere unproblematically to the sphere of reception, though both are key sources for analyzing authorial economies. Advertisements and reviews from this period are best understood as mutually reinforcing and to some extent mutually constitutive genres.[21] The era's widespread practice of "puffery"—the dissemination of glowing reviews sometimes provided anonymously by the author of the work under consideration, but more often written by an associate who stood to benefit from the author's or publisher's good will—is but one form that their interpenetration took.[22] Even ostensibly objective reviews worked to publicize the text in question, and some were so insubstantial that they served more properly as advertisements than as critical evaluations; indeed, a number of publications called their book sections "Literary Notices," a heading that blurred the distinction between reviews and advertisements, as the ensuing content announced the release of various titles—and sometimes noted where they might be purchased—with minimal commentary. And critical, even harsh, reviews still gave an author and his or her work "play"—notoriety if not endorsement—within the literary field, which surely increased sales and readership in some instances.

Occasionally the interdependence of reviewers and publishers was overtly referenced: the December 1852 issue of *Godey's*, for example, noted with evident irritation that "our copy [of J. Thornton Randolph's *The Cabin and the Parlor*], unfortunately, was not received until it was too late to give the work more than a cursory examination, even had the leaves been cut or separated, as should always be the case when a patient investigation and a 'good notice' are expected."[23] Apart from instructing publishers and authors in proper etiquette vis-à-vis book preparation and delivery, *Godey's* reveals the degree to which book reviewing was understood to be a professional courtesy within a larger regime of production and marketing rather than a discrete, independent critical gesture. That *Godey's* published the admonishment rather than relaying it privately suggests, further, that missteps within this informal economy were common enough to warrant a public reprimand, such that other publishers who sought the magazine's editorial favor might take note.[24]

The economic interdependence of magazines and publishers took more direct forms as well. In some instances a single entity published both books and magazines. Harper and Brothers is perhaps the most obvious example—not only was there common ownership but, predictably, *Harper's New Monthly Magazine* and *Harper's Weekly* "noticed" and advertised works published by their parent press.[25] More generally, serial publications that ran book advertisements had a clear financial stake in the solvency and longevity of publishing houses, especially given that the era's subscribers paid irregularly, if at all, for the magazines and newspapers they received.[26] Even serials that did not print publishers' advertisements often featured essays, poems, and stories contributed by the very authors whose books they were asked to review. And in the broadest sense newspaper and magazine editors shared with book publishers an interest in promoting the habit of purchasing printed material in whatever form. Advertisements and book reviews, moreover, were profoundly cross-referential. Publishers, then as now, often quoted from favorable reviews within their advertisements, as Ronald J. Zboray and others have shown.[27] A promotion for Frederick Douglass's *My Bondage and My Freedom*, for example, which appeared in the August 31, 1855 issue of *Frederick Douglass' Paper*, quotes from nineteen separate reviews, introducing each with a pithy heading in all capital letters; the advertisement adopts the technique so energetically, in fact, that one wonders if it was intended as a parody—not just of marketing practices within the trade generally but also of the expectation that African American authors needed white approbation in order to sell their books (see Figure 3).[28] Less frequently reviewers commented on publishers' promotional

THE GREAT PLEA FOR FREEDOM.

Read it and you cannot Resist it.

MY BONDAGE
AND
MY FREEDOM,
BY FREDERICK DOUGLASS.
One Vol., 12mo. 464 pp., Illustrated, Price $1 25.

IT WILL BE READ WITH AVIDITY.
It cannot fail to be read with avidity, as one of the most striking illustrations of American Slavery, which either fact or fiction has presented to the public.—*N. Y. Tribune.*

A WORK OF INTRINSIC MERIT.
It is a work of intrinsic merit, and speaks volumes in praise of the man, his intellect and culture. The incidents of his life, woven up in the web of narrative by his polished and classical mind, and graceful pen, are full of interest.—*Buffalo Express.*

A MASTER AUTHOR AND ORATOR.
Frederick Douglass is a remarkable man. As a writer and speaker, he ranks with the most effective and natural—after our master authors and orators.—*Utica Herald.*

TRUE, AND OF ABSORBING INTEREST.
The story of Frederick Douglass' life as detailed in this volume, possesses an interest which is really absorbing. The truthfulness of the narrative which he gives of his bondage will be generally conceded, and certainly realizes the truth of the old adage—"truth is strange—stranger than fiction."—*Boston Journal.*

EXPOSES THE BANE OF THE REPUBLIC.
It reveals the miseries of servile life with an intense vividness and impressiveness, that can but fasten its facts and arguments upon the reader's mind as with a pen of iron and with the point of a diamond.—*Vt. Journal.*

NO ROMANCE MORE EXCITING.
No romance can be more exciting to the reader than this truthful narrative. The work is having a wide circulation.—*Yates Co. Whig.*

IT STIRS THE FEELINGS.
We have not read a work which has stirred our feelings to a greater extent for some years, and we are glad that Mr. SLOSSON intends to keep a good stock on hand. We think he will need it. The book is a powerful, vivid picture of a slave's life, and effectually removes the gloss which pro-slavery men attempt to throw over the beatitudes of this aid to the "highest state of human existence!"—*Oswego Times.*

A SELF-MADE MAN.
This volume, besides its many moving and thrilling details, affords evidence of a most remarkable man. Mr. Douglass has emphatically made himself. As a writer and speaker, he has but few equals in the country. His book is readable and interesting.—*Christian Advocate.*

AN INTERESTING AND REMARKABLE WORK.
The book is one of the most interesting and remarkable ever published—a well written work on Slavery, by one who was born and bred a slave.—*Vt. Watchman.*

NERVOUS, CLEAR, AND TELLING.
It presents a clear and graphic picture of his slave-life from his earliest recollections: his escape and his life since, including his experiences in this country and Europe. No one will deny Mr. Douglass the possession of genius and character of a high order. He writes in a nervous, clear and most telling manner, clothing his narrative with intense interest, and conveying his moral impressions with a vividness that leaves the reader scarcely any escape. The subject is deeply tragic, and, in his masterly handling possesses an engrossing interest.—*N. Y. Evangelist.*

WORTH A HUNDRED VOLUMES OF ROMANCE.
We recommend the book as worth a hundred volumes of the trashy literature of the day.—*Pittsburgh Herald.*

HOW IT DIFFERS FROM OTHER WORKS.
We have before listened to the homely tale of the liberated slave, but it did not impress us as does this narrative of Douglass, for the reason that we were left to supply the commentary which is here pressed upon us by one who has both seen and felt what he relates. The story bears throughout the impress of truth, and the manner in which it is told stamps the writer as a man of genius, and a high order of talent.—*Ohio State Journal.*

CIRCULATE IT WIDELY.
The encroachments and usurpations of Slavery are becoming more flagrant every day, and a work animating the public mind, enlightening it upon this bane of the American Republic, and from the high source whence this emanates, ought to be very extensively read in the Free States.—*Whitehall Chronicle.*

HOW WRITTEN—ITS CHARACTER.
The book is written with the happiest descriptive power, with nerve and vigor of expression, and with richness of style. It has an ample resource in phrase, great perspicuity, and a musical, resonating, and half rhythmatic style, which reminds the reader of the author's origin, and of the native melodies of his race. The book manifests a high, and, to us, unexpected polish. The interest aroused and kept up by a perusal of this book is of a high order, and rarely degenerates.—*Detroit Daily Advertiser.*

IT IS PECULIARLY ATTRACTIVE.
We need not say that the volume possesses extraordinary attractions. The life of such a man cannot fail to excite an interest in the public mind seldom equaled, even in this book-making age.—*Christian Ambassador.*

THE AUTHOR POPULAR—HIS BOOK IN DEMAND.
This is a splendid work. The personal worth of the author, the deserved popularity he has secured throughout this nation, and the universal desire that prevails, to have a memento of one of nature's noblemen, will conspire to create an unprecedented demand for this book.—*Wesleyan.*

THE EVILS OF SLAVERY CALMLY UNFOLDED.
There are no lines of ranting madness here.—Calmly, dispassionately he unfolds to us all the evils of the bondage system in its varied aspects, and must thus commend his disclosures to all true Americans, south as well as north. The entire work is of a high intellectual order, and intensely interesting from its beginning to its close.—*American Spectator.*

THOUGHT AND REASON IN WHAT HE SAYS.
Mr. Douglass is a spirited and pointed writer, and his oratory will bear favorable comparison with any of our public speakers. There is thought and reason in all he says, and though his language is sometimes bitter, it is usually calm, dignified, and earnest.—*Buffalo Courier.*

WE WONDER HOW HE DID IT.
As an orator, the public here and elsewhere have had abundant opportunity to judge; and we suppose that none have ever listened to his graceful elocution, his cutting satire, and his frequent bursts of eloquence, without wonder that a man who emerged from the dense darkness of slavery, after reaching his manhood, who in fact learned his alphabet after coming to maturity, could deservedly rank among the first orators of the day.—*Rock American.*

☞ For sale by all booksellers and News Agents and also at this Office.
☞ Single copies sent by mail, post paid, on receipt of price.

MILLER, ORTON & MULLIGAN,
Publishers, 25 Park Row, New York, and 107 Genesee st., Auburn.

FIGURE 3 *Advertisement for* My Bondage and My Freedom, *Frederick Douglass' Paper, August 31, 1855, p. 3. Image courtesy of the Library of Congress.*

efforts, sometimes mentioning print advertisements, but more typically noting their boasts of extraordinary sales and their sometimes-aggressive dissemination of positive reviews or blurbs, which publishers often sent out bundled with the books they wanted noticed. In the mid-nineteenth century, both critical and promotional genres participated in authorship's moral economies, though reviews were more voluble on the matter—and consequently figure more prominently in the discussion that follows—if only because their format allowed more space for such commentary.

Moral Printscapes

To be fair, any number of mid-nineteenth-century reviews—and an even greater proportion of advertisements—did not address the moral register of either book or author, even when such commentary would have been considered timely or appropriate. *Godey's*, for example, in noticing a collection of N. P. Willis's magazine articles, called his style "pleasant," but made no mention of his moral status despite—or perhaps because of—his recent scandalous identification as the model for the protagonist's vain, callous brother in the popular novel *Ruth Hall*.[29] (That Willis had been an occasional contributor to the magazine may have motivated this reticence, though it may also have owed to the magazine's expressed distaste for *Ruth Hall*'s airing of family grievances.[30]) Even Susan Warner's *Wide, Wide World*, a novel whose moral soundness was widely extolled, was noticed in *Sartain's* with reference only to the work's literary value—its "surpassing beauty and power" and its author's "title to the true nobility of genius."[31]

If attention to the link between authorship and moral status was not universal, however, it was certainly widespread. The author and visual artist Charles Lanman, writing in the April 1840 issue of the *Southern Literary Messenger*, went so far as to claim that the literary life was itself conducive to moral improvement:

> I do not mean to say, that all literary men are of necessity good—for such is not the case; but I do say, that there are few professions more innocent, or better calculated to form the Christian character. The literary man mostly lives in company with the mighty spirits of the past, and the beings of his own mind. True, he studies the human heart in his daily walks, but the greater part of his knowledge is gathered from the past, and from thence his mind reaches forward into futurity, so that the field over which his soul may roam in search of wisdom is boundless as the universe.[32]

Lanman's idealization of the writer's vocation—especially its leisurely communion with past and future—contrasts starkly with the literary field's imbrication of commercial and moral matters within a relentless immediacy. Nowhere is the latter disposition more obvious than in publishers' advertisements, which used the moral fitness of authors and their works as a marketing ploy. An 1858 advertisement for Lydia Sigourney's *Lucy Howard's Journal*, for example, cited a review that commended the author's "pure and prolific pen."[33] A promotional moral authority could operate in the aggregate as well: an advertisement that appeared in *Harper's Weekly* in 1857 asserted that the "sketches, poetry, domestic stories, &c., &c., [featured in *Peterson's*] ... *always inculcate morality and virtue.* On this account, [the magazine] is recommended by clergymen."[34] Another promotion from *Harper's Weekly* reassured readers that "the stories in Godey [i.e., *Godey's Lady's Book*] are strictly of a moral nature, and you may search in vain through the 54 volumes for a single profane word."[35] In these cases the editor stood in for the author as moral monitor, selecting and arranging a magazine's praiseworthy offerings.

Commentary on an individual author's moral status was often linked to the aesthetic value of the work rather than simply to its "safety" or appropriateness for impressionable readers. A piece in the October 1837 issue of the *North American Review*, for instance, noted that "in speaking of the great worth of Miss [Catharine Maria] Sedgwick's writings, in a moral and political point of view, ... we have implied our sense of their high literary excellence; since if her pictures were not radiantly true and vivid, they would not charm and move readers as they do."[36] For another contributor, the obverse held true: in a work of literature, "moral obliquity ever indicates an intellectual defect"—or, as a scathing review of Elizabeth Stoddard's *The Morgesons* put the matter, "there are things in morals and taste so deformed that no true artist will select them."[37] The failure to gravitate toward moral themes evidenced a fundamental aesthetic lack, as the *North American Review* asserted in reference to Poe: "[He] seems ... to have been led into the error of excluding moral and spiritual themes from poetry, by a lack of susceptibility in his nature, which blinded him to their intrinsic beauty."[38] In some cases, the relationship between the aesthetic and the moral was figured as complementary rather than causal or indicative. "A new novel by Mrs. [Anne] Marsh is always welcome," wrote a reviewer in *Peterson's*: "To much intellectual power, she unites morality and religion, so that her fictions are not only deeply interesting, but instructive in the highest sense."[39] Another *Peterson's* review called Alexander Dumas "the least exceptionable, as well as the most talented of the French novelists," while a third asserted that the novel "'Kate Weston' has not only decided literary merit, but is eminently moral."[40] Whatever the syntactical variations, literature's moral-aesthetic compact was sufficiently powerful that reviewers could remark on a work's "moral charms" or "the beauty of [an author's] moral courage" without evident concern that the logic undergirding that linkage would be questioned.[41]

Mid-nineteenth-century literary culture invites us to rethink the critical commonplace, operating at least since early-twentieth-century modernism, that moral purpose—or, to use an even more derided term, didacticism—bears an inverse relationship to aesthetic or literary value. For nineteenth-century commentators, moral purpose operated within aesthetic registers: that is, it could be enacted well or badly, but its mere presence did not cast a work or its author outside the realm of literary achievement. Occasionally reviewers acknowledged that textual moralism could become tedious, but then worked to rescue a particular author from the charge, as in the following notice from *Godey's*: "[Mrs. Haven] is plain and sensible in her style, and her writings have a high and sound moral tone, which, instead of causing the slightest approach to dulness [sic], is perhaps, their greatest charm."[42] A Professor Alden attempted a similar recuperation in reference to the English poet Jane Taylor: "In all her works there is a high moral and religious aim.... Religion did not cramp her imagination, or render dull the operations of her reason, or chill the ardor of her affections. On the contrary, all her powers were strengthened and purified by its hallowed influence."[43] And "Browne's Roman Literature," the *Literary World* reassured its readers, "is eminently instructive and didactic, without ceasing to be interesting."[44]

Midcentury uses of the term *didactic* complicate this conversation, however. Many commentators used it pejoratively, much as the next century's critics would, to describe a tedious or ham-handed approach to moral instruction. The *Union Magazine* noted, for example, that "moral truth, presented in a well-wrought story, is more likely to find access to the young heart, than more didactic instruction," while *Peterson's* commended *The Courtesies of Wedded Life* as a book "free ... from the fault of being too didactic: the moral is inculcated without wearying the reader."[45] In other published commentary, "didactic" stood in stolid opposition to more conventionally literary adjectives like "fanciful," "lyrical," or "imaginative." That said, any number of commentators used the term neutrally or even positively. *Godey's*, for example, praised the essays included in the book *Springs of Action* as "didactic and moral, without either dogmatism or cant," while the *Eclectic Magazine of Foreign Literature* noted that Emerson's *English Traits* possessed both "literary attraction and didactic value."[46] More importantly, when reviewers and other commentators used the term *didactic* to signal aesthetic failure, the overarching project to which they referred—that is, employing literature to teach moral lessons—not only remained culturally sanctioned but was framed as a potential contributor to a work's aesthetic achievement.[47] Later critics, especially those working from the mid-twentieth century onward, have taken the negative, dismissive, and antiliterary meanings associated with didacticism in the prior century to stand in for the larger cultural project of literary/textual moralism, an overgeneralization that elides many of the mid-nineteenth-century literary field's most intriguing complications.

I wish to recuperate some of those nuances. Nineteenth-century commentators treated the matter of effective or aesthetically pleasing didacticism as a key element of literary criticism. Foremost was the question of how an author with a serious moral purpose might best hold his or her reader's interest, with the result that didacticism was put into conversation with matters of style, tone, pacing, and plot. For instance, while didacticism was often framed as sensationalism's opposite—as when a *Peterson's* reviewer sniffed that the author of *Mary Brandegee* (1865) "may become a writer of merit" if she "curbs the extravagances and improves the morals of her novels"—sometimes the two modes were said to coexist more or less harmoniously. A review of George Lippard's *Paul Ardenheim, the Monk of Wissahikon* (1848), for example, acknowledged that the book was "written in his peculiar style, full of nervous thoughts and strong imaginings," but conceded that these sensational elements concealed "morals of deep import under a vein of wild and strange rhapsody."[48] If a heated style helped to hold the reader's interest, so too did brevity: as the *North American Review* advised, "all experience speaks against the attempt to enforce a single moral of any kind by a fiction extended to any great length."[49]

Subtlety, even indirection, were considered vital as well: the moral, one *Godey's* review noted, should be "brought out by events and conversations, not by the direct teachings of the authoress," while a piece in the *Atlantic Monthly* advised that an author's moral purpose should be executed through "the apparently natural development of the story itself."[50] A reviewer in the *Ladies' Repository* remarked, in a similar vein, that "the didactic purpose of the novel … should be only incidental," but insisted that it should "not, therefore, [be] subordinate or secondary."[51] To be effective, in other words, didacticism had to be central to the work, yet unobtrusive. As the *North American Review* complained at length, the novelist G.P.R. James failed to achieve that standard: "Mr. James follows the progress of the plot, catechism in hand, and reads a homily from it whenever the necessities of morality require."[52] Characterizing this vein of complaint, Nina Baym notes that for most mid-nineteenth-century reviewers "lumps of moral were bad, but a pedagogical tone was worse still."[53] The subtlety that eluded James could be taken too far, however, as commentary on Caroline Chesebro's novel *Isa: A Pilgrimage* (1852) attests: "Considered as a work of Art, the highest praise will be conceded to 'Isa,'" but "the moral aspect of the book may not be so universally agreed upon." The main character is not one to imitate, nor is she striking as a cautionary tale. Still, the piece ends with an affirmation: "We apprehend that all thinking and earnest readers will perceive the lofty aim of the author, and understand the moral intended, without having it tacked on to the end in the form of a homily." After worrying over the book's moral clarity, the reviewer ultimately decides that the best readers, those who are "thinking" and "earnest," will apprehend its lessons without the aesthetically damaging inclusion of an overt sermon.[54] This reluctant acknowledgment that subtlety, however artful, could imperil moral messaging is overridden by an investment in the challenges inherent in achieving a proper balance. Instead of signaling a retreat from the aesthetic as a project or a category of value, literary didacticism calls for a higher standard, one that many authors lacked the sophistication to achieve—and if achieved, some readers lacked the discernment properly to comprehend. To judge from a number of the period's reviews and essays, literary didacticism was at least potentially a site of compositional virtuosity rather than evidence of its absence.

An intriguing tension pervades these examinations of literature's moral purposes. Commentators routinely remarked that a good moral enhanced a book's sales, thus registering their faith that readers would recognize and gravitate toward works that effectively inculcated moral lessons. A review of Lydia Sigourney's *Poems*, for example, linked popularity with moral effect: "When we reflect on the thousands of hearts, all over this wide land, on which the poetry of Mrs. Sigourney has shed its holy influence, we feel assured that the demand for this book will far transcend that of any former numbers of the series," which included works by such prominent figures as Longfellow, Bryant, and N. P. Willis.[55] Similarly, *Godey's Lady's Book* praised Mrs. [Hannah] Lee, author of *Three Experiments in Living* and a contributor to the magazine: "The sale of some hundred thousands of [her] little book showed that the moral was felt and applied."[56] The equation of morality and popularity was advanced with particular energy vis-à-vis juvenile literature: a notice in *Godey's* remarked, for example, that the children's author Mrs. Anna Bache was "extremely popular on account of the admirable tendency of her writings."[57]

But alongside this much-vaunted faith in the appeal of edifying literature lurked a worry that readers might gravitate instead toward morally dangerous books. The popularity of French novels, for instance—whose authors, according to *Peterson's*, "have been aptly called...high-priests of disorder"— occasioned a great deal of concern.[58] British fiction was considered less objectionable, with some notable exceptions. The novelist Edward Bulwer was an especially worrisome case, according to a long piece in the July 1838 issue of the *Southern Literary Messenger* contributed "By a Native of Petersburg, Va." Identifying Bulwer as a kind of pernicious genius, the author calls him "the most gifted and the most remorseless, the most imaginative and the most seductive of novelists." Bulwer is bad, the article goes on to assert, precisely because his felicitous style obscures his depravity: "Strip the narratives of Mr. Bulwer of the splendor of his style and imagery, and nothing will be found but a loathsome desecration of all the observances so vitally connected, in the opinion of every moral being, with the welfare of society."[59] This is strong rhetoric, to be sure, and readers may well have received it skeptically. Nevertheless, the fact that the author felt such vehemence to be warranted suggests at least the perception of a pressing moral hazard.

Some thirteen years later the *Southern Literary Messenger* acknowledged book reviewers' complicity in perpetuating literature's less salubrious influences: "We are aware that in speaking thus plainly of 'Alban' [*Alban: A Tale of the New World*], we run the risk of inducing many persons of prurient fancy to buy and read the volume who might not otherwise have their attention drawn to it." Such exposure was justifiable, however, insofar as the criticism included might "guard many innocent minds against [the work's] contamination." Despite this wholesale attack on the book's objectionable morals—including the stated regret that "Mr. Putnam" had chosen to publish it—the review closes with a note indicating where interested readers might purchase the volume, a gesture that foregrounds the interdependence of literary reviewing and book marketing, even as it calls into question the sincerity of the reviewer's righteous hand-wringing.[60]

If commentators sometimes offered the tonic that time would sort moral wheat from chaff—"No work tending to corrupt public morals," one sanguine observer noted, "will meet with admiration in after ages, if the mind is left unfettered"—it was nevertheless the case that literature's moral valences compelled careful attention in the immediate moment, a circumstance that reviewers used to assert their own cultural significance. The difficulty, as the two case studies that follow will demonstrate, was that many of the era's most popular and influential authors elicited widely varying responses, such that the work of monitoring and evaluating moral authority proved more fraught than reassuring.

Stowe's Emergence

As the century's most polarizing work of American fiction, eliciting both giddy praise and vehement condemnation, *Uncle Tom's Cabin* is an apt test case for examining the circulation of reputational currency at midcentury.[61] Americans in the 1850s recognized the book's publication as a watershed, whatever their disposition toward it. Stowe's novel set a new standard, many noted, for what could be considered a popular or bestselling work. One commentator went so far as to claim that "hereafter, the book which does not circulate to the extent of a million copies, will be regarded as a failure."[62] Owing in large part to its prodigious sales figures, the novel seems to have accelerated a trend in American publishing toward reformist narratives in general and fiction about slavery in particular. A hostile assessment of this development appeared in an 1853 issue of *Graham's Magazine* under the title "Black Letters; or Uncle Tom-Foolery in Literature": "The shelves of booksellers groan," the author complained, "under the weight of Sambo's woes, done up in covers!"[63] This facetious displacement of slaves' suffering onto booksellers' overburdened shelves lamented the collateral damage that, for this author, attended the commercial exploitation of readerly sentiment. A later piece in *Graham's* would assert, along these lines, that antislavery novelists possessed an "almost infernal rage for making money out of moral questions," a quality that made them "fully as much the children of Satan as any they rebuke."[64]

Alongside the texts invoked in these complaints, the 1850s and early 1860s saw the publication of at least thirty so-called anti-Tom narratives designed to counter the transformations that Stowe advocated.[65] The much-remarked power of Stowe's novel no doubt prompted both imitators and antagonists to weigh in, but we should not assume that their motives were entirely political, ideological, or even aesthetic. That is, Stowe's remarkable sales figures must have suggested to authors and publishers alike that similar books—or counterarguments that referenced the original novel—might also sell.[66] One author of an unpublished manuscript, according to a piece in *Putnam's*, approached a publisher with the claim that, because "every reader [of *Uncle Tom's Cabin*] ... would be anxious to hear the other side of the story of domestic slavery," she could guarantee the sale of 150,000 copies of her book (approximately the number Stowe was thought to have sold by that point).[67]

The *Uncle Tom's Cabin* phenomenon—including the figure of Stowe as a suddenly iconic author—informed the literary scene at a cultural moment in which the literary and the ideological were in especially close commerce. Book reviews and other printed commentary on the publishing world that specifically referenced Stowe suggested that her fame intensified and catalyzed existing cultural formations, bringing race, gender, and region ever more forcefully into Americans' conversations about authorship and books. I have argued that mid-nineteenth-century Americans had profound and often contradictory investments in the moral status and moral authority of the authors they read, reviewed, praised, and reviled. Within that context Stowe became a kind of cultural keyword, malleable and resistant by turns, an object of fascination as well as a lightning rod for sectional, political, and gender-based conflicts. Using her as a point of comparison or cautionary tale or exemplar, these texts attempted to reify or undermine her status, both moral and literary. But as a cultural signifier, Stowe proved more complex and multivalent than individual commentators might have wished, raising key questions about the imbrication of celebrity, moral authority, and book marketing at midcentury.

The extraordinary popularity of *Uncle Tom's Cabin* was an effect as well as a cause, according to some observers. That is, the book's phenomenal sales—and the media attention trained on it, which sparked still more sales—depended on the new printing technologies and enhanced distribution networks available by the early 1850s. As *Putnam's* noted, "it required all the aid of our new machinery to produce the phenomenon; our steam-presses, steam-ships, steam-carriages, iron roads, electric telegraphs, and universal peace among the reading nations of the earth. But beyond all, it required the readers to consume the books, and these have never before been so numerous."[68] Some ventured the opinion, too, that Stowe published her book at the precise moment when northern readers were most open to its messages: "No story with equal power," one commentator wrote some twelve years after the novel's initial release, "could have attained its eminence at a later stage of the revolutionary feelings of the North."⁶⁹ Stowe's much-remarked powers of persuasion, in other words, relied on this already-receptive audience.

Stowe's presence in 1850s print conversations about books and reading begins, of course, with the disparate and impassioned responses that *Uncle Tom's Cabin* elicited. Some, to be sure, hailed the author as a kind of modern saint. A piece in the April 22, 1852 issue of the *National Era*, where the novel had first appeared in serialized form, approached hagiography: "So great and good a thing has Mrs. Stowe here accomplished for humanity, for freedom, for God, that we cannot refrain from applying to her sacred words, and exclaiming, 'Blessed art thou among women!'" Another commentator, taking to heart Stowe's claim that a higher power had written the book, intoned that "God has…made great use of Mrs. Stowe's fiction to wake up a good spirit" and claimed, on what evidence I cannot say, that the book "has excited a taste for the Bible in France."⁷⁰ The book's capacity to instruct and improve readers was, for some, so self-evident that at least one schoolmaster made it required reading for upper-level students.⁷¹

Other antislavery responses entailed considerably less fawning. As Robert S. Levine has shown, discussions of the book in *Frederick Douglass' Paper* revealed crucial divisions among African American abolitionists over the role of whites in the antislavery movement and over the importance of what we might term ideological purity.⁷² Was the novel's Liberian ending, which was so offensive to ardent abolitionists, both black and white, a deal-killer, so to speak, rendering this forceful (if problematic) antislavery narrative useless to the cause? Douglass held that Stowe's persuasive abilities outweighed her unfortunate choice of narrative resolutions. For Martin Delany, however, no promise of converting previously unenlightened white readers to the cause could outweigh Stowe's arrogance and misrepresentation of slave experience. The author and her text were bankrupt, in Delany's view, not only because they embraced colonization but because they evinced a fundamentally paternalistic—not to mention ill-informed—orientation toward African Americans. The *Provincial Freeman*, a Canadian paper edited by African American expatriates, took a middle course, referencing Stowe's novel positively in a number of instances, even as it railed against her Liberian conclusion: "The manner in which Mrs. Stowe disposes of [George Harris]…always struck us as a piece of needless and hurtful encouragement of the vile spirit of Yankee Colonizationism. We never could reconcile it with an anti-slavery tale."⁷³

In proslavery discourse, too, Stowe was figured as misguided and presumptuous, though here the responses to her and her work were far more venomous. A piece in *DeBow's*, for example, likened her to Hollingsworth, the monomaniacal and, crucially, gold-digging reformer featured in *The Blithedale Romance*, published the same year. This comparison to Hawthorne's coarse, über-manly creation gestures toward a broader preoccupation with Stowe's gender identity, insofar as many hostile reviewers accused her of having left woman's proper sphere in writing this novel. Authorship itself was not, for these observers, unwomanly; on the contrary, they praised the many women who later penned novels in opposition to Stowe's. Further, some of the harshest published comments on the author and her book were written by women, who clearly saw no problem with appearing in print per se. Rather, the proslavery camp's accusations of gender transgression had to do with the perception that Stowe's book was, first, overtly political, and second, extremist in orientation. A piece from the *New Orleans Picayune* remarked that Stowe "has proved herself false to her womanly mission—a stirrer up of strife, rather than a 'peace maker.'"[74] A long commentary on *Uncle Tom's Cabin* that appeared in the *Southern Literary Messenger* went to great lengths to justify what might be perceived as an ungallant attack on a lady: "If [Stowe] deliberately steps beyond the hallowed precincts—the enchanted circle [that is, of proper femininity]—which encompasses her as with the halo of divinity, she has wantonly forfeited her privilege of immunity..., and the harshness which she may provoke is invited by her own folly and impropriety."[75] If conventional femininity was sacred ground—as longstanding codes of masculine honor insisted—then Stowe's supposed violation of its terms pushed her beyond the realm not just of propriety but of piety as well. The charge that Stowe's authorship amounted to a religious transgression also appeared in northern periodicals. An anonymous piece in New York's *Literary World* calls Stowe's plot "odorous" and excoriates her for supposedly betraying her responsibilities as a female member of a well-known clerical family:

> Slavery is bad enough, but for Heaven's sake, Mrs. Stowe! wife of one clergyman, daughter of another, and sister to half a dozen, respect the cloud of black cloth with which you are surrounded, and if you *will* write of such matters, give us plain unvarnished truth, and strive to advise us in our trouble—not to preach up bloodshed and massacre.[76]

The claim that Stowe was a traitor to pious womanhood referenced her sexuality as well. So much commentary appeared with regard to her supposed prurience, in fact, that a parodic poem that ventriloquized proslavery sentiment referred to her as "naughty Mrs. Stowe,"[77] an epithet that Ishmael Reed would echo in *Flight to Canada* (1976) when he calls her "Naughty Harriet." Louisa McCord's assessment of Stowe, for example, published in the January 1853 issue of the *Southern Quarterly Review*, lamented not just her "malignant bitterness" but "the foul imagination which could invent such scenes."[78] Another female commentator called Stowe "deficient in the delicacy and purity of a woman, inasmuch as she has painted from her own libidinous imagination, scenes which no modest woman could conceive of."[79] Stowe's only merit, in this author's view, is that she teaches right-minded women the perils of excessive independence. Especially irksome to southern reviewers was the possibility that women might read and be corrupted by the novel's foulness. Not only was it "a horrible thought that a woman should write... [such] scenes of license and impurity," but it was "intolerable that Southern women should defile themselves by bringing the putrid waters to their lips."[80] The theme of gender disruption continued in responses to Stowe's later antislavery novel *Dred* (1856). The *Southern Literary Messenger* published a long condemnation of the book's moral failures, written, the editor claimed, by a New England woman who concluded her attack on Stowe with the following quip: "Were she a woman, we should blush for the sex—luckily she is only a Beecher."[81]

References to Stowe abounded in reviews of the many novels written in response to *Uncle Tom's Cabin*. Proslavery reviewers invoked her not just as a provocateur but as the very antithesis of the authors—often women—whom they championed. A short review of Caroline Hentz's proslavery novel *The Planter's Northern Bride*, which appeared in the *Southern Quarterly Review*, is an apt example. Though admitting that "Mrs. Hentz has not the power of Mrs. Stowe," the reviewer remarked that the former "is more truthful, more pure, and imbued with a more becoming Christian spirit."[82] In most such reviews, Stowe's honesty was directly called into question. An 1859 notice in the *Southern Literary Messenger* referenced "the inventions of Mrs. Stowe" in contrast to the heartfelt truths represented in the novel under discussion (*The Tenant-House, or Embers from Poverty's Hearth-Stone*), which treated the suffering of poverty-stricken New Yorkers.[83] As late as 1869, one southern newspaper still referred to Stowe as "the notorious and mendacious authoress of 'Uncle Tom's Cabin,'" while another piece from the same year ranked Stowe among those "who live in the world for no purpose but evil."[84]

In the southern press, then, Stowe's name became shorthand for a range of transgressions—dishonesty, arrogance, meddling, betrayal of gender norms, and the penning of pornography.[85] Curiously, though, her narrative talents were frequently acknowledged—sometimes overtly, if grudgingly, as when *DeBow's* referenced her novel's "brilliant imagination"—but more often by implication.[86] Proslavery commentators could not stop talking about her and her book, suggesting that they read and were engaged by this work that nevertheless infuriated them.[87] The threat that Stowe posed, apart from the obvious possibility that she might undermine the proslavery cause in the sociopolitical realm, was that she divorced narrative engagement from writerly ethos. In other words, her ability to compel the attention of readers, even southern readers, far exceeded her moral authority, in their eyes, as a commentator on slavery, a disarticulation of aesthetics and morals that was perhaps more broadly threatening than the specific contents of her book.

The publishing world in the 1850s registered a fascination with Stowe's popularity quite apart from this conundrum, however. Magazines and newspapers paid a great deal of attention to the book's unprecedented sales figures—and obsessed on Stowe's resulting profits—with much consideration of how the *Uncle Tom's Cabin* phenomenon might reshape American publishing and book marketing. In any number of reviews and advertisements Stowe served as an icon of popularity or success, a publishing star against whom other authors might be measured. Mentioning a title that had just reached its tenth edition, one commentator then discounted the accomplishment: "A tenth edition with us seems insignificant beside the three or four hundred thousand copies that 'Uncle Tom' has circulated."[88] Excitement over new releases, too, was indexed via comparison to Stowe's novel. For example, in reference to a new work by Charlotte Brontë (named here only as "the author of 'Jane Eyre'"), a short notice in *Putnam's* affirmed the book's appeal: "A new 'Uncle Tom's Cabin,' could not produce more sensation in the literary world."[89] Similarly, an 1853 advertisement for the now-forgotten novel *Beatrice: or, the Unknown Relatives* boasted that the "book bids fair to rival the famed 'Uncle Tom,' in the immensity of its sale" and quoted a review averring that "what 'Uncle Tom,'... is in one field, BEATRICE... promises to be in another."[90] The 1854 antislavery novel *Ida May*—which many initially attributed to Stowe herself—was lauded as a book "destined to make a sensation in the circles of literature and philanthropy second only to that of its peerless predecessor, 'Uncle Tom's Cabin'"; another notice ventured that *Ida May* "would probably have never seen the light but for the prodigious success" of Stowe's novel.[91] Combining a recognition of Stowe's ability to sell books with an image of her as a kind of excoriator-in-chief, one advocate for women's education wrote that anyone who doubts that women can write books "deserves... to be classed among slave-catchers in Mrs. Stowe's next edition of Uncle Tom's Cabin."[92] Stowe's name appeared within newly published texts, too, as a kind of imprimatur: Solomon Northup dedicated his 1853 narrative *Twelve Years a Slave* to her; a few years later, Stowe's preface to Frank Webb's *The Garies and Their Friends* (1857) was announced on the novel's title page, with her name in the same size font as the author's.[93] If Stowe's reception among African American activists was mixed, her endorsement was nevertheless perceived as a potential boon to the sales of black authors' works.

The height of Stowe's popularity might be most aptly marked by a moment in which she became literally iconic. The *Liberator*, which covered Stowe's 1853 tour of England in detail, included in its June 10 issue details from a London antislavery event at which Stowe had appeared as guest of honor: "The assembly filed past Mrs. Stowe, exchanging courtesies," the article noted, "and afterwards adjourned to supper, where a marble bust of Mrs. Stowe, by Bernard, was exhibited."[94] It had to be unusual for a woman (or a man, for that matter) and her marble likeness to appear at the same gathering. The sheer oddity of these guests encountering Stowe and her statue in rapid succession intensifies the contrast between the cool, white marble of the bust—suggestive of remoteness, authority, purity, status—and the live, conversant, dare I say mildly frumpy middle-aged author before them. This juxtaposition collapses time, preempting the long process of canonization that would ordinarily precede the commissioning of an author's bust, a static object calculated to signify his or her timelessness. Their coexistence also undermines the customary distance between presence and reputation, the bust reminding guests of Stowe's preeminence in the world of letters and of social reform, even as her literal self dines among them.

This marble rendering, exhibited by and for English abolitionists, both indexes and asserts the synergy between Stowe's popularity and her moral authority. But the terms of that linkage are far from transparent. To what extent did Stowe's popularity derive from her moral righteousness? That is, how many of the hundreds of thousands who bought her book wanted to read it not simply because they had heard that it offered a well-told narrative but because it tapped into their own preexisting sense of slavery's injustice? For some—including, I would guess, many of Stowe's upper-class English admirers—such was the case. But the converse is also possible: that is, in some sense the novel's very popularity may have endowed its author with a degree of moral authority, an ability to influence the beliefs and actions of others, that she did not have at the outset. If, for proslavery authors, Stowe's talents as a storyteller belied her fundamental corruption, for other readers, the novel's effectiveness, its ability to engage readers, evidenced its underlying righteousness. But we must not lose sight of the fact that many read and enjoyed this book without acknowledging its moral force and certainly without being converted by it. Some reviewers explicitly separated their aesthetic assessment of the novel from its political content. As Robert Scholnick has noted, the *Boston Post* criticized *Uncle Tom's Cabin* for "grossly...exaggerat[ing] the actual evils of negro slavery in this country," but lavished praise on its dialogue and character development, calling it "one of the most remarkable literary productions of the time."[95] Similarly, a Mrs. M'Kee wrote in the *Christian Parlor Magazine* that "a work which can thus force admiration from the indifferent, and compel respect even from opposers, must have most extraordinary power," but then sought to neutralize that power by claiming to "speak...only of its merit as a literary work, and without reference to its moral bearings on slavery."[96] The immense appeal of stage plays and songs based on the novel, many of which traded more in minstrelsy than in social reform, attests to the ease with which the story could be extricated from those "moral bearings."

The third term energizing this conversation is literary status, a category that Stowe's marble bust silently references. What strikes me most forcefully in midcentury commentary on Stowe (bracketing, for a moment, the many proslavery screeds) is the relative esteem in which she was held as an author—a status that extended beyond the Civil War, though it would not survive the one-two punch of late-nineteenth-century realism and twentieth-century modernism. A reviewer in the *New Englander*, for example, wrote in 1852 that *Uncle Tom's Cabin*'s "literary merits...are as legitimate a subject of critical discussion, as the merits of Waverley or Hamlet."[97] Other commentators compared Stowe to Dickens, among the most widely read and admired authors in the United States at the time. An 1854 piece in *Putnam's* ranked her with Hawthorne and Cooper as well as a pantheon of esteemed English novelists, including Defoe and Thackeray.[98] Ten years later the *Round Table*, a New York City-based weekly, offered a similar assessment, situating Stowe among a group of "distinguished authors" that included Longfellow, Emerson, and Hawthorne.[99] She was the only woman on the list.

I do not mean to suggest that Stowe was universally esteemed at midcentury, only to fall precipitously from grace by century's end. Plenty of readers in the 1850s and 1860s thought her fiction uneven, or overly sensational, or otherwise deficient. And still others classed her not with the era's most eminent authors but rather with popular offerings that occupied a kind of middle space between Hawthorne and George Eliot on an upper rung and a largely formulaic novelist like Emerson Bennett on a lower. My point, rather, is that Stowe emerged at a cultural moment when literary status, moral authority, and popularity could be complementary—even mutually constituting—elements. The reception and redeployment of *Uncle Tom's Cabin* underscores that confluence, even as individual reviewers and commentators argued over and sought to control its terms.

E.D.E.N. Southworth's Balancing Act

Stowe's emergence as a controversial figure was sudden and dramatic, sparked by the publication of a narrative in whose wake she would find herself living and writing ever after. The novelist E.D.E.N. Southworth, meanwhile, engaged in much more diffuse reputational negotiations; no single bombshell publication or biographical event stands out as formative in the way that *Uncle Tom's Cabin* proved to be for Stowe. Even so, Southworth's moral authority—her very respectability—was remarkably precarious at midcentury, as a range of reviews and other commentary suggests. Intriguingly, the author and her advocates were able to shape and manage her reputation over time, enabling her works to remain both publishable and profitable. Southworth's much-cited sensationalism—marked in the era's discourse by terms like *passion* and *extravagance*—seemed at times to threaten her status within the literary field, but ultimately she was able to turn those elements to her advantage, appearing transgressive enough to be intriguing, but not so bad as to be exiled.[100] Her moral ambiguity, in other words, fueled her popularity.

To be sure, some reviewers lavished unmixed praise on Southworth's books. The *Home Journal* commended *The Mother-in-Law* for its "fine scenic episodes" and "rich domestic atmosphere," while *Graham's* noted that "her plots... frequently abound in well constructed dramatic positions and incidents."[101] Moreover, she was at times deemed a "moral" author, in seeming contradiction to the reputational instability I will explore. *Godey's* insisted that *The Lost*

Heiress's "impressions...upon the mind of the well-disposed reader will have no other than a truly moral, religious, and elevating tendency"; a notice in the *Flag of Our Union*, meanwhile, remarked that the author "has strongly endeared herself to the better class of readers in this country, by the excellent moral she invariably weaves into her romances," a judgment that *Graham's* affirmed, reassuring readers that Southworth's fiction "invariably tends to a pleasing moral."[102] Other assessments of her fiction's moral tendency were less approving, however. A notice in *Holden's Dollar Magazine* conceded that the novel *Retribution* had a discernible moral—"that every sin has its punishment"—but added that this morsel was so self-evident as to be meaningless: "It would be quite as sensible," the reviewer complained, "to write a tale to prove that two parallel lines can never come together."[103] Though the piece acknowledged the narrative's capacity to engage readers, it cast the author's moral sense as obtuse at best. A *Godey's* notice of *The Curse of Clifton* similarly emphasized the book's absorbing qualities, but in moral terms affirmed only that it would do no harm.[104]

Southworth's capacity to absorb, even entrance, her readers was remarked on endlessly as the source of her immense popularity, though often in concert with some stated anxiety about the overarching value of her writing. A review from *Peterson's*, for instance, called *The Curse of Clifton* "thrilling," "engrossing," and "difficult to lay down," but also noted its "serious faults of style" and identifies "exaggeration" as its author's chief narrative "vice," while a piece in the *Literary World* commended the "dramatic power" and "vigor and aptitude of the dialogue" in *The Deserted Wife*, but decried its departures from probability and its overly complicated plot.[105] A "JGW" (probably John Greenleaf Whittier), reviewing *Retribution* in the *National Era*, praised the book's "searching analysis of character, intensity of passion, and power of description," but worried that its "scenes are overdrawn."[106] Another piece, after referencing Southworth's "passion" and "dramatic force," sought to downgrade her literary abilities, noting that she could not be ranked "above many of her contemporaries" and granting her only "a rough sort of eloquence" that was "slightly refreshing," at least when compared with the "flaccid sentimentalities of the day."[107] The ambivalence evident in this faintest of praise was even more marked when reviewers addressed Southworth's moral authority. The *Home Magazine*, for example, praised *The Missing Bride* as one of her "powerfully written, highly dramatic stories," but expressed the wish that "the author, with her fine talents, would develop in some of her characters a higher moral purpose."[108] A notice in Rufus Griswold's short-lived *International Monthly Magazine of Literature, Science and Art* [New York] identified Southworth as "the most popular of our female novelists, notwithstanding the doubtful morality of her works."[109] Perhaps the most damning was a remark that appeared in *Frederick Douglass' Paper* in reference to *The Deserted Wife*: "While we admire [Southworth's] power and enjoy to the full her truly wonderful skill at description, we confess to thinking her works justly deserve the ban written against them...by our staid Quaker friends, under the head of 'pernicious books.'"[110] This habit of turning an initially positive statement toward the negative recurred in critics' responses to her work. A review in the *Albion* summed up the general sentiment: "If strong writing be Mrs. Southworth's forte, we prefer something weaker and better."[111]

Southworth's fiction, deemed insufficiently didactic by many, itself inspired a monitory tone in reviewers, many of whom seemed intent on regulating or taming, if not also shaming, the author. A mostly positive assessment of *Retribution*, for example, nevertheless admonished the author against returning to the tenor of her prior works, in which "impure fancies, stimulants to already over-excited passions...have been sent forth on their errands of evil."[112] Another piece on the same novel worries that Southworth "lets her pen go out in untamed exuberance of language; and though all this may...produce excited interest in many readers, it is injurious to the moral power and permanent influence of her works." Advising the author to "select some better development of character, treat it more calmly, [and] chasten down her language," the critic promises that "a richer product of salutary influence would be the result."[113] Reviewers' condescension extended as well to matters of literary form and style. *Graham's*, for instance, concluded its long, hostile review of *The Curse of Clifton* with the suggestion that Southworth ought to receive the foregoing criticism with gratitude: "All this is doubtless very different from the good-natured, meaningless puffery which the lady probably has already received from those who have noticed her works. But we speak in a spirit of the truest friendship, in warning her...against 'that fatal facility' of writing and publishing which has betrayed so many."[114] The *Southern Quarterly Review*, commenting on the same novel, acknowledged that Southworth "possesses many unquestionable powers," but warned of her "great need to tame her disposition to exaggerate monstrously the features which she attempts to delineate." Her readers, the piece continued, were "made to sleep on surprises, to sup on horrors, and to sit down at the board with some of the most unmitigated social monsters."[115] The very language of this critique invokes Southworth's ability to engage readers, who come to feel that they are sleeping and dining with, even consuming, her fictional creations. That power to absorb is figured as coercive rather than simply attractive, however, as readers are "made to" experience this horrific immersion as the unwitting objects—even victims—of the author's machinations.

The intimation that Southworth wielded too much power over a naïve, pliant readership operated in tension with another recurring theme in the reviews: that she was at various points in decline—at least in formal, stylistic terms—as an author. A review of *Shannondale*, for instance, remarked that "Mrs. Southworth has not been true to her own talent in [the book's] preparation. It is crudely conceived, and clumsily wrought out to its conclusion," not to mention being "offensive to good taste and conversational propriety." In a tone more appropriate to a headmaster scolding a recalcitrant student, the reviewer added that "she is now at the perilous moment in her career. The indulgence of the reader will scarcely be extended to another volume like the present."[116] Within a literary field that so intimately linked moral and compositional success, the use of the term *perilous* was especially apt—Southworth's career was said to be at risk because her plotting and characterization had gotten sloppy, but also and perhaps more crucially because she was perceived to be flouting the rules of "good taste" and "propriety."

Reviewers often leveled the charge that Southworth wrote too quickly, and in some sense she did—certainly her personal finances depended on the rapid production of new works. But what's intriguing is how often this alleged carelessness was linked, thematically and syntactically, to her supposed breaches of decorum. A piece in the *Southern Quarterly Review*—one of the publications whose contributors seemed most intent on disciplining her—offered a characteristic blend of the two charges: "She has written too rapidly, with too little preparation and design, and much too little regard to the propriety of her characterization." A work's moral respectability, in this rendering, required as much authorial attention as did the creation of dialogue or plot: Southworth, the reviewer intoned, "must labour, more than she does, at the proprieties."[117] Attentional lapses, it seems, led to moral lapses, as if some indecorous beast were ever waiting for the opportunity to pounce.

Some reviews dispensed with these attempts at instructing or improving Southworth and instead denounced one or another of her novels outright. A brief notice of *The Deserted Wife*, for instance, decried its sibling incest plot as "unnatural" and "monstrous," clear evidence that the book "should not [have been] printed."[118] But even a reviewer convinced of her work's wholesale immorality might struggle to identify its precise elements. A piece on *The Mother-in-Law* that appeared in the *Southern Literary Messenger* addressed this question at length. Admitting that her writings contained "no positively immoral *passages*," the reviewer noted that "it is rather in the tone, the coloring, the general moulding of character and feeling that this lady's strong, unfeminine, thoroughly *French* organization betrays itself." The identification of this amorphous immorality, the piece continued, might itself pose a danger—"God forbid…that [Southworth's work] should be bought and read to verify our remarks! There could be few greater evils in our estimation."[119] Tellingly, even the most hostile reviews, this one included, generally conceded that she had talent, even if they insisted that she was bent on using her powers for evil rather than for good.

Southworth's reception in the periodical press—often mixed and sometimes downright scathing—did not prevent her from becoming one of the most widely read and best-compensated American authors of her time. One possible or partial explanation for her resilience in the marketplace is that book and magazine buyers continued to want her offerings despite being warned of their moral and stylistic vagaries, thus demonstrating that reviewers' concerns about the attractions of immorality had some merit. No doubt some readers sought out her work because it was considered suspect, just as commentators feared they would. Southworth's publishers and magazine editors perceived and to some extent capitalized on this possibility, as I will discuss in detail. But I first want to propose an alternative more congruent with dominant cultural attitudes about salubrious reading. That is, I am suggesting that Southworth's advocates—her editors, publishers, and friendly reviewers—worked with some success to reframe and temper her mixed reception, helping to establish her as both respectable and marketable.

Southworth's book publishers and the editors who serialized her novels worked, as one would expect, to cast her in a positive light. Appleton's publishing house, in its efforts to promote *The Deserted Wife*, emphasized the novel's "moral," which "conveys a healthful lesson to all who have at heart the reality of domestic bliss."[120] While it is difficult to say what "the reality of domestic bliss" might mean in the context of Southworth's semiautobiographical plot, which featured more turmoil than harmony, the statement at least made the book sound respectable. Other advertisements capitalized instead on the author's established popularity, calling her "celebrated," or emphasized her "genius," "gifted[ness]", and "originality." As was typical of the era, advertisements for her novels quoted extensively from the most positive published reviews—some of which had appeared in fairly obscure venues (e.g., the *Wheeling Times and Gazette*), but others of which hailed from widely circulating papers. Among the more detailed promotions are advertisements for the *Saturday Evening Post*, which foregrounded Southworth's serialized fiction as one of the magazine's chief selling points, all the while emphasizing how expensive it was to retain her as a contributor. Her ability to command significant payment for her work serves here as a proxy for her literary value, even as the crassness of the pronouncement would seem to undermine the respectability of both the paper and its shrewd negotiator/contributor.

Though the *Post* seemed most keen to emphasize Southworth's status, it also asserted, indirectly at least, her morality. A lengthy advertisement that ran in 1850 devoted approximately half of its text to promoting her fictional contributions, including a "new story" to debut early the following year (see Figure 4). Then, after a brief detour into the reprints and "reports of lectures" on offer within the magazine, the piece declared the *Post* to be "A MORAL PAPER":

> We shall maintain for the Post the character it has acquired of being a strictly moral paper; one that a parent may allow to go freely before his innocent sons and daughters. We need hardly repeat here, that the Post has done more to prevent the publication and sale of immoral works, than any half-a-dozen other papers in the land.[121]

THE SATURDAY EVENING POST.

THE LEADING AND LARGEST WEEKLY IN THE UNION.

THE SATURDAY EVENING POST is now, beyond all denial, the leading as well as the largest Weekly Paper in the United States. Its circulation is undeniably greater than that of any other paper, of the same kind, in the Union; while its literary contents are allowed, by the best judges, to be unsurpassed. Such tales as "The Deserted Wife," "Shannondale," &c., &c., have placed "The Post," by almost universal admission, a "head and shoulders" above its contemporaries.

We now have the pleasure of announcing to the American public, that we have made arrangements with one of the

FIRST NOVELISTS IN AMERICA,

MRS. EMMA D. E. N. SOUTHWORTH, author of "RETRIBUTION," "THE DESERTED WIFE," "SHANNONDALE," etc., by which the productions of her gifted pen will be secured hereafter (with the exception of an occasional story in a Washington paper)

EXCLUSIVELY FOR THE POST.

Mrs. Southworth, as an American novelist of great power—a rising Star in the West—has been hailed with acclamation by all those who can recognize genius as well in a native as in a foreign author. We design to commence a

NEW STORY BY MRS. SOUTHWORTH,

about the beginning of the year. How many stories she will be able to furnish during 1851, will depend upon the state of her health, etc.

In the intervals of Mrs. Southworth's Novelets, we design publishing other and shorter Novelets from authors of admitted celebrity. We have two now on hand, which we shall publish as soon as possible:

THE IRON HAND, by T. S. ARTHUR, ESQ.
THE TEXAN HUNTRESS, by C. W. WEBBER, Author of "Old Hicks, the Guide," "The Shot in the Eye," etc.

And mark this! What the proprietors of the Post promise, they perform—or do better. They do not announce a long list of distinguished contributors with whom they have made no arrangement, and whose stories never appear. Such a system may delude an intelligent public *one* year, but it will not answer a *second* time. If the public are humbugged *once*, it is the fault of the humbugger; if *twice*, it is their own.

In addition to such choice ORIGINAL articles, involving a large outlay of money, the columns of the Post will contain a great amount of Miscellaneous reading—such as the

CREAM OF THE FOREIGN PERIODICALS,

Witty and Humorous articles, Selections from the Agricultural Journals, Riddles and Conundrums, etc., etc.

REPORTS OF LECTURES—during the past year we gave the celebrated Lectures on Shakspeare by Mr. Dana; and the instructive and interesting ones of Dr. Baird upon Europe—LETTERS FROM ABROAD—GENERAL NEWS—Reports of the Markets—a Bank Note and Stock List, etc., etc.

One or more PORTRAITS of remarkable persons, or PICTURES OF REMARKABLE PLACES are also weekly given.

A MORAL PAPER.

In conclusion, we may say—that we shall maintain for the Post the character it has acquired of being a strictly moral paper; one that a parent may allow to go freely before his innocent sons and daughters. We need hardly repeat here, that the POST has done more to prevent the publication and sale of immoral works, than any half-a-dozen other papers in the land. *A careful guard shall also be kept, as heretofore, over our* ADVERTISING COLUMNS, *that nothing of an improper character may obtain admittance.*

In short, whatever is calculated to refine, instruct, amuse, or gratify, shall find its appropriate place in the POST; and let the reader mark one thing, whatever others may *promise*, we will not be behind in the *performance*. A paper that has stood for twenty-nine years, steadily progressing all that time, and which has now the *largest* list of subscribers of any paper of the same class, in the United States, is not to be left behind in the race by *any* rival.

TERMS.

The terms of the POST are Two Dollars if paid in advance, Three Dollars if not paid in advance. For Five Dollars one copy is sent three years. We continue the following low terms to Clubs, to be sent, in the city, to one address, and, in the country, to one post-office.

4 Copies, - - - - - - - - - - - $5.00	Per Annum.
8 " (And one to Agent, or the getter up of the Club,) $10.00	"
13 " (And one to agent, or the getter up of the Club,) $15.00	"
20 " (And one to Agent, or the getter up of the Club,) $20.00	"

The Money for Clubs must always be sent in advance. Subscriptions may be sent at our risk. When the sum is large, a draft should be procured if possible—the cost of which may be deducted from the amount. Address, *always post-paid*,

DEACON & PETERSON, NO. 66 SOUTH THIRD STREET, PHILADELPHIA.

N. B.—Any person desirous of receiving a copy of the POST *as a sample*, can be accommodated by notifying the Publishers by letter, *post paid*.

FIGURE 4 *Advertisement,* Saturday Evening Post, *November 23, 1850, p. 2. Image courtesy of the Library of Congress.*

Whether this insertion was meant specifically to counter negative assessments of Southworth's moral authority, its proximity to a long discussion of the novelist's presence in the magazine is intriguing, especially in light of editor Henry Peterson's habit of scolding her in private letters for what he perceived to be her fiction's moral lapses.[122] At the very least the assertions of righteousness so evident in this notice sought to reassure readers that the magazine's quest for popularity via exciting, even sensational offerings—exemplified by the contract with Southworth—would not come at the price of moral compromise. *Peterson's* used a similar, though less typographically striking, strategy: an advertisement inviting readers to "Subscribe for 1857!!" opened its second paragraph with the heading "Its [i.e., the magazine's] Healthy Literature." The text that followed insisted that the "sketches, poetry, domestic stories, &c., &c., are the best written for any lady's or family magazine, and they *always inculcate morality and virtue.*" Southworth is then named, alongside the popular novelist Mrs. Ann S. Stephens, as a prized contributor.[123]

A now-obscure Washington, DC-based paper called the *Huntress* took the project of shoring up Southworth's reputation in a more personal direction. The piece opened predictably enough, with brief mentions of two of the author's serialized novels, which were then running in the *National Era* and the *Saturday Evening Post*. It went on to repeat the *Post* editor's claim that he was offering his readers "a splendid story and that last week's number is the best yet published." This mention was no doubt what Southworth's editors sought—positive references that took their word for the quality of her work. And the piece adds some praise of its own, remarking "with what astonishing rapidity she moves her pen, and how bright her imagination—surely some superhuman agent must have dropped its mantle over her." But then the article veers off course, recounting a local investigation into the novelist's family background: "Hearing this lady, Mrs. Southworth, was a native of Washington…we have been making inquiry [sic] about her." Happily, the reviewer notes, "she proves to be the daughter of Mrs. Wales, deceased, a widow lady of this city, of the first respectability." The rest of the article dwells on the benevolence of the novelist's mother: not only was she "gentle," with charming manners, but "she was an angel of mercy to the poor and distressed, unwearied in her attendance upon the sick and afflicted." So we arrive at a kind of respectability by association: if the paper cannot directly attest to the author's personal righteousness, it can at least associate her with an admirable parent, a move that was unusual within its own cultural moment and nearly inconceivable in ours.[124]

More recognizable from a twenty-first-century standpoint is a reviewer's annoyance at being lobbied by one of Southworth's publishers. A long paragraph on *The Wife's Victory*, which appeared in the *Albion*, a long-running New York weekly, began with the following comment:

"The enterprising publisher" (we think that's the common phrase) "of the above valuable work" is really a very obliging man; for he not only sends us his books, but in most cases a printed leaf in each, crammed with favourable notices. If we should happen to have no mind of our own, we might be impressed by the great authorities brought to bear upon us.... If we happen to have no time to read the book or books in question... it is so easy to pick out a few thrilling adjectives from Mr. Peterson's gratuitous stock, and manufacture "a first-rate notice" off hand.[125]

As this cranky opening implies, the reviewer chose not to avail himself of these ready-made accolades and instead offered an assessment of the work that ranged from tepid to hostile. But if T. B. Peterson's promotional apparatus failed in this instance, it and similar efforts by other publishers succeeded elsewhere. Reviews of Southworth's novels—like reviews of works by her contemporaries—often cited endorsements that had appeared in other papers. While some of these encomiums may well have been selected by the editor or reviewer him- or herself in keeping with the era's broader practices of exchange and reprinting, many were no doubt lifted directly from the "printed leaf" supplied by an "enterprising publisher."

The promotional strategies I have cited were widespread in the nineteenth-century book trade. Indeed, reviewers sometimes admitted that they were quoting from reviews by other critics because they had not yet read the book in question. The Southworth case matters not because the practices themselves were exclusive to her promotion and reception, but because she was a figure whose work elicited especially ambivalent responses, at least among those that appeared in print. As a result, the selection of positive blurbs and the careful framing of promotional materials (e.g., placing a discussion of her contribution above an assertion of the paper's moral tone) took on particular importance. I do not mean to suggest that readers were duped wholesale by these efforts: surely some took critical notices to heart and avoided Southworth's writings, while others chose to judge for themselves. But the reframing of Southworth that took place in advertisements and among friendly—or lazy or overextended—reviewers was part of an elaborate balancing act that tempered and diluted the pronouncements of her harshest critics. The risks that she took as a novelist—by flirting, so to speak, with sensationalism and sin, among other alleged improprieties—made these accommodations all the more crucial, though they also earned her a readership sufficiently riveted by her work that they were willing to overlook any taint that remained.

A final pair of examples further complicates this consideration of Southworth's marketing and reception. The *Saturday Evening Post*, just fifteen months before it ran the "MORAL PAPER" advertisement just discussed, took a riskier approach to promoting her contributions. A short piece titled "Criticism" cites a review from the *Washington Intelligencer* that reassures readers of Southworth's tame, respectable prose, insisting that her stories "*are without thrilling incidents, or strong and powerful developments of passion; they run on to the conclusion smoothly and evenly*, and possess a fine moral tone." In keeping with the efforts at moral insulation cited above one would expect the *Post* to endorse this assessment, but it does not. Instead, the next paragraph works to overturn that benign judgment: "We do not know when we have seen a criticism…so very wide of the mark.—Mrs. Southworth's 'Retribution' and 'The Deserted Wife,' which we are now publishing, are both *full of* 'thrilling incidents and strong and powerful developments of passion,' and they do any thing else but 'run on to the conclusion smoothly and evenly.'" The only part of the *Intelligencer* blurb that goes uncontested is the claim that Southworth's work "possess[es] a fine moral tone." Surely this gambit is partly facetious—the *Post* is having a little fun with the pieties of the day. But it is also a version-in-miniature of the marketing strategies that helped to make Southworth so successful, as the *Post* makes certain to assert her respectability, if in ventriloquized form, but then allows the promise of raciness and "passion" to trump those reassurances without ever explicitly abandoning the high ground of "moral tone." The strategy recurs on the same page of the paper, just a couple of columns to the left, where the *Post* offers the following with regard to *The Deserted Wife*, which it was then serializing:

> If any of our readers should feel a little shocked by some of the sentiments expressed by "Hagar" this week, we would advise them not to prejudge her or the story on that account. Hagar's opinions are in consonance with her character, unhappy circumstances, and want of proper guidance in youth. She is to be pitied more than blamed. Wait in the patience, dear reader, and have faith in the author, as we have.[126]

Again, the *Post* reassured readers that Southworth's fiction was morally sound, even while highlighting its potentially "shock[ing]" elements. As this strategy implies, the novelist succeeded in some sense because of her dubious reputation, rather than in spite of it.

Southworth's moral authority sometimes wobbled, but it never collapsed—in part, I have claimed, because she and her (economically interested) advocates were savvy in their negotiations of the era's moral economies. Stowe, meanwhile, survived the political tumult of the 1850s with her immense, albeit sectionally inflected, popularity intact, largely because she had managed to create characters and narrative trajectories that captivated—but did not necessarily convert—a broad swath of readers. Some years later, as the next chapter explores, Stowe would become embroiled in another controversy, one that reveals a crucial, if subtle, postbellum shift in the relationship between authorial reputation and literary value.

{5}

Stowe, Byron, and the Art of Scandal

In the late summer of 1869, one of the Victorian era's most salacious literary scandals erupted. Harriet Beecher Stowe, in an article published simultaneously in the *Atlantic Monthly* and the British *MacMillan's Magazine*, asserted that Lord Byron—by this point dead more than forty years—had, as a young man, fallen "into the depths of a secret adulterous intrigue with a blood relation," his half-sister Augusta Leigh.[1] Claiming that she had the story from Byron's by-then-deceased wife, who had long maintained a public silence on the cause of the famous couple's separation, Stowe sought to clear Lady Byron of the charge, lodged most recently in an 1868 book by Byron's Italian mistress, that she had been heartless and exacting in her dealings with her husband.[2] While Byron's intemperance and licentiousness, to use two favorite nineteenth-century terms, were well known, his partisans had charged that the wife was to blame—that she was an inadequate moral laundress, if you will, unwilling to brook his imperfections in the interest of redeeming him. "The True Story of Lady Byron's Life," as Stowe titled the article, sought to reveal a crime so heinous that the wife's departure would be justified and Byron's dangerous popularity—his seductive effect on young, morally unformed readers—arrested. Stowe miscalculated on both counts: following her article's publication, Lady Byron's character and credibility were questioned to an unprecedented degree, while commentators remarked on a dramatic increase in the sale of Byron's works.

Although Stowe's article revived an old rumor rather than alleging some heretofore unimagined outrage, it elicited extraordinarily vehement responses—many, though by no means all, critical of Stowe herself, who was called an "assassin of reputations" and a "libeller of the dead."[3] Even those inclined to believe the incest claim typically expressed the view that Stowe should never have committed it to print. But accompanying these exhortations to decorum and reticence was an astonishing volume of commentary on the matter.[4] The result is an unusually extensive transatlantic record of readers' responses to a periodical publication, including letters to the editors of newspapers, magazine articles (both originals and reprints), parodies, cartoons, acrostics, and entire volumes compiling a range of interventions or purporting to tell the *true* true story.[5] Among the lighter offerings are *Lord Byron's Defence*, described as "a smartly written squib in which the poet is supposed to answer his traducer in the Don Juan metre," and *The True Story of Mrs. Shakespeare's Life*, a parody featuring an anonymous author whose "venerable ancestor," Mrs. H—B. Cherstow, has learned from Shakespeare's wife that the revered dramatist was in fact a serial murderer (of his "fellow-playwrights," no less).[6] The highlight of the volume is a series of quotations from Shakespeare relating to murder, blood, or guilt, which, in imitation of Stowe's attempts to read Byron's poems as evidence of his crimes, are presented as mock proof of the playwright's villainy.

If the scandal produced a kind of logorrhea, no one contributed more than Stowe herself, who responded to the controversy by publishing *Lady Byron Vindicated* (1870), a 482-page volume that seeks to exonerate both its author and its subject. At the core of this iterative gesture lies Stowe's faith in her own moral authority, her capacity to push others toward certain figurations of "the good" by means of her personal example and persuasive abilities. More broadly, the volume registers her stake in a particular version of authorship's moral compacts. But the Byron controversy, as some called it, revealed that readers' investments in an author's moral authority were more complex and contradictory than Stowe had anticipated. In response, *Lady Byron Vindicated* works to instantiate and legitimate a form of that authority that might shore up Stowe's by-then battered reputation. The author's own immersion in scandal both haunts and animates her text.

This chapter reads the Stowe/Byron scandal as a rich and contentious conversation about authorship, credibility, and transgression, one that incorporates Stowe's past authorial selves, but that also marks a departure from the dominant moral economies of the previous decades, during which the relevance of authorial character to the question of literary value was rarely questioned.[7] Echoes of the 1850s abound in the controversy over Stowe's accusations against Byron: most obviously, perceptions of Stowe's credibility were shaped by her involvement in the antislavery movement, certainly through her authorship of *Uncle Tom's Cabin* and to a lesser extent *Dred*, but also through her contacts with prominent English abolitionists. Her friendship with Lady Byron, in fact, began when Stowe toured England in the 1850s as an antislavery author-celebrity. In the widely disseminated critiques of Stowe that followed her publication of the "True Story," references to her antislavery efforts figured prominently—her poor judgment, some alleged, led her to champion unworthy victims in both contexts: slaves who were happy enough as they were and a misguided, possibly mentally unstable, widow. If, for some readers,

Stowe's record as a novelist railing against injustice legitimized her mediation of Lady Byron's story, for others, that same history helped to prove her wrong, especially insofar as the transgressive sexuality permeating both interventions (masters' sexual abuse of enslaved women; Byron's incest) allowed her critics to position her outside the sphere of social acceptability.

Many of the responses to Stowe, however, evinced less concern for what she had advocated in the past than for whom she was attacking. The intensity of some readers' investments in Lord Byron's reputation—literary and personal— invites a number of questions: how and why did the medium of poetry allow individuals to care so deeply about someone long dead, whom they did not personally know? The interventions of Lord and Lady Byron's friends and associates make sense—they had an obvious stake in how those figures were represented and perceived. But what about those who were "just" readers? What were they trying to preserve or defeat? And what did it mean to commit "a crime against literature," as one of Stowe's critics alleged?[8]

As this accusation suggests, competing notions of literary value—and, indeed, of literature's prerogatives—undergirded and complicated the debates over Byron's and Stowe's supposed transgressions. What emerged in this paper war was not just a clash over evidence, credibility, and propriety, but also over the proper relationship between aesthetic and moral judgments. While many of the angriest commentators were sure that Byron could not have done the deed, others were saying, in more temperate tones, so what if he did? He wrote such wonderful poetry.... Byron's literary style and status—imbricated with notions of genre, self-presentation, and gender—could, at this cultural moment, be used to exempt him from the usual moral standards, though no one seemed quite ready to discard the standards themselves—that is, to say that incest was not so bad. Meanwhile, Stowe's prose style in the "True Story" was called uneven and sensational, serving for her critics as further evidence of her bankruptcy, both moral and artistic.

In an era in which many readers remained deeply invested in didacticism as a guarantor of the legitimacy of both author and text, it is worth paying attention to where and on what terms it is disavowed.[9] The Byron case, in fact, contrasts intriguingly with the recuperation of Walt Whitman, whose postbellum transformation from a "disgraceful" (to cite Dickinson) poet of the body to a respectable national icon has garnered a great deal of critical attention.[10] As scholars such as David Haven Blake and William Pannapacker have shown, Whitman created a literary-reputational synergy in the mid- to late-1860s and 1870s, linking himself to the by-then-heroic figure of a martyred president Lincoln by means of self-consciously decorous poems (e.g., "When Lilacs Last..." and "O Captain, My Captain") and his oft-repeated "Lincoln lecture."[11] As Blake writes, Whitman "used Lincoln's image to ratify himself and his book."[12] Although it surely matters that Whitman was alive at this point and able to orchestrate his reputational makeover, while Byron was long dead, it is nevertheless telling that the defenses this chapter relates—of Byron's poetic works over and against their author's alleged moral turpitude—emerged at precisely the same cultural moment in which Whitman was so bent on achieving literary status through personal respectability.

As the contrasting cases of Byron and Whitman suggest, attitudes toward literary value and especially toward authors—as artists, celebrities, and moral guides—were under especially intense pressure in the second half of the nineteenth century.[13] Across this period a relatively detached or disembodied notion of the primacy of literary aesthetics began to displace the earlier salience of authorial character, and with it authorial intention, a development that would reach its zenith in the next century's New Criticism. This so-called retreat of the author was hardly monolithic: Americans remained interested in authors as celebrities; no less prominent a figure than William Dean Howells would continue to argue for some degree of confluence between authorial character and literary value; and the increasing importance of the journalistic byline suggests an ongoing investment in an author's name as a guarantor of credibility. Nevertheless, it has been identified as a key feature of the US literary field from the 1880s onward.[14] The Stowe/Byron scandal, I wish to claim, situates the declining relevance of authorial character in matters of literary valuation rather earlier than this critical consensus would suggest, but it also prefigures the unevenness and contestation that would accompany that development as well as the degree to which it would be complicated by the very identity categories and political investments that such a text-centered approach seems intent on eliding. Indeed, this tension continues to vex literary studies, as a preoccupation with authorial character reemerges at unexpected moments, however energetically academics and others may disavow it.

Intimacy, Evidence, and Narrative

Lady Byron Vindicated, though released late in the controversy that this chapter reconstructs, represents Stowe's most elaborate defense of authorial character as the cornerstone of literary value. That said, the book has largely been dismissed (or derided) in its own time and in ours. Stowe's contemporaries wrote that it added little to her original claims against Byron—a Boston paper remarked that the volume consisted of her *Atlantic* article "hammered out thin," while *Putnam's* labeled it "a loose, inconsequent summary" and an "unutterably dull" book, holding "no interest for any mortal, unless he be a special student of the Byron controversy, or of Mrs. Stowe's own state of mind."[15] Others saw the book in a more pernicious light: reversing Stowe's claims that Byron's poetry had the potential to corrupt young readers, Boston's *Universalist Quarterly* charged that *Lady Byron Vindicated* posed a similar risk: "Thousands of young people, reading this book, will probably for the first time have this loathsome crime [i.e., incest] suggested to them as a thing possible, a horrible reality, instead of the dream of a corrupt imagination."[16]

With a few exceptions, scholars have treated the book as little more than an embarrassing footnote.[17] Against this dismissal, I contend that *Lady Byron Vindicated* matters because it offers an extended meditation on questions of authorship, moral authority, celebrity, and transgression, an endeavor made all the more potent by Stowe's own relationship to scandal at the moment of the book's composition. When she wrote the original "True Story" she was no doubt thinking about Byron's scandalousness and to some extent Lady Byron's, but by the time she composed *Lady Byron Vindicated*, she had to be thinking about her own, an investment that intensifies the book's multiple vindications. Too, its blending of disparate genres—for example, historical report, apologia, sentimental narrative, temperance tract, legal brief—and its mix of rhetorical strategies render it an intriguing object of study. Stowe to some degree adopts in this text, as Jennifer Cognard-Black has argued, the emerging standards of professional literary realism, privileging such evidentiary forms as quotations, documents, and dates—representational strategies that have much in common with contemporaneous developments in American journalism. But *Lady Byron Vindicated* also insists on affect (both expressed and elicited) as a central persuasive and evidentiary force.[18] Indeed, the book weds affect to evidence in ways consonant with any number of widely circulating moral reform texts, from midcentury antislavery almanacs to Jacob Riis's *How the Other Half Lives* (1890).

Stowe had attempted this kind of self-defense before: in the midst of the national debate over the truth value of *Uncle Tom's Cabin*, she published *A Key to Uncle Tom's Cabin* (1853), a compendium of anecdotes, newspaper articles, and other elaborations on the cruelties of slavery. But Stowe's ongoing investment in the legitimating power of such documents—that is, of print as evidence—resonates beyond the specific controversies in which she engaged. In some sense, these defensive texts worked to distance and de-gender the author, to transfer the audience's locus of trust from a specific person—the author who claims a thing to be true—to the printed page. That said, the documents Stowe assembled in *Lady Byron Vindicated* could not erase the vicious attacks she had endured, nor did they lessen the intensity of many readers' investments in Lord Byron's reputation and in the broader principle of female silence with regard to sexual matters. Moreover, Stowe herself was not willing to jettison the centrality of the writer as a moral authority, a personal guarantor of textual truths. Her use of evidence, in fact, seems calculated to complement rather than replace that authority, though her defensive tone throughout the volume seems to acknowledge the fact that she has chosen an especially dicey test case for such a collaboration.

For Stowe, the act of writing is more than an artifact of or a means of expressing her moral authority—it is integral to that authority's construction. In keeping with this notion that writing has the power to confer or catalyze such status, Stowe's book extends to Lady Byron a kind of authorship by proxy. Although the latter's studied silence on the question of her separation, as well as her many good deeds, had won her some admirers, Stowe maintains that, "for a virtuous life to bear testimony to the world, its details must be *told*."[19] Further, Stowe asserted that outside of England, where Lady Byron's personal character was less well known, she "stood judged and condemned on the testimony of her brilliant husband" (*LBV*, p. 159); his potent, if morally debased, authorship overwrote and overwhelmed her life well lived. Stowe implies that in the absence of a published "Memoir" (*LBV*, pp. 157, 158) of Lady Byron, featuring her own letters and private writings, the "True Story" and *Lady Byron Vindicated* are the best opportunities available for the kind of posthumous print circulation that Stowe felt would repair the Englishwoman's damaged reputation.

Lady Byron Vindicated combines this ventriloquism of Lady Byron—based on Stowe's conversations and correspondence with her as well as on a certain amount of speculation—with long disquisitions on Byron's life and especially his debauchery; a detailed analysis of the poet's literary and personal reputation, both before and after his death; and a spirited defense of Stowe's own authorial legitimacy.[20] The last of these projects proceeds along several axes. Not surprisingly, Stowe attempts to defend herself against the charge that she has broken Lady Byron's confidence by publishing her story. Here she uses the book's most overtly sentimental rhetoric, inviting readers to imagine Lady Byron as their own daughter and thus "to make the case their own" (*LBV*, p. 283). More specifically, Stowe asks female readers to weigh her dilemma for themselves: "You, my sisters, are to judge whether the accusation laid against Lady Byron by the 'Blackwood,' in 1869 [which rehearsed and endorsed the Countess Guiccioli's contentions], was not of so barbarous a nature as to justify my producing the truth I held in my hands in reply" (*LBV*, p. 404).[21]

A good deal more space is given, however, to Stowe's evidentiary self-defense. Although she concedes that the most solid proof of her claims—"the statement prepared by Lady Byron, and the proof by which she expected to sustain it"—remains unavailable ("in the hands of her trustees," who have chosen inexplicably to keep it hidden), Stowe nevertheless produces page after page of assertions and quotations in support of her original article, along with a number of remarks on the ways in which evidence has been used and perceived in the scandal overall (*LBV*, p. 369). For instance, she details Byron's many dishonesties in an effort to undermine the credibility of his claims about his wife and criticizes the ways in which her detractors have used evidence from personal letters, quoting portions without making complete documents available and concealing their provenance and chain of possession, details that might enhance or undermine the credibility of printed evidence. "As it is now too late to have the securities of a legal trial," she writes, "certainly the rules of historical evidence should be strictly observed" (*LBV*, p. 322). And beyond the legitimacy of particular texts, she decries the evidentiary double standard at work in much commentary on the scandal—Byron's claims, that is, tend to be accepted at face value, while Lady Byron's are said to require proof (*LBV*, pp. 310, 315).

Proof remains a vexed matter in this book, as it was in the larger periodical culture to which Stowe was responding. Even the missing documents, so often invoked in press coverage of the scandal, were themselves only Lady Byron's own testimony, subject to the same doubts and questions as her other reported statements. No Byron sex tape, in other words, would circulate, just as no DNA test would establish his scandalous paternity of Elizabeth Medora Leigh—at least not in Stowe's lifetime. In response to this evidentiary void, *Lady Byron Vindicated* both uses and disavows the language of the legal system that so pervaded the printed critiques directed at Stowe in the previous months. At times she adopts the rhetorical style of a prosecutor in court, beginning more than one sentence with the phrase "I claim, and shall prove," and promising to show "*who did do it*" (that is, who, rather than herself, was responsible for "stirr[ing] up" the Byron controversy) (*LBV*, p. 2). She refers to individuals as "witnesses" and to printed statements as "testimony" (*LBV*, pp. 299, 301). But Stowe also asserts that she received Lady Byron's story as truth, not as testimony to be verified and corroborated, thus putting the discourse of legal proceedings in conflict with an ethos of friendship and sisterly confidences. Moreover, she refers to her book as a kind of legal testimony ("It has been my object...to place myself just where I should stand were I giving evidence under oath" [*LBV*, p. 258]), but later states that the controversy "cannot be managed with the accuracy of a legal trial" (*LBV*, p. 262). She wants it both ways: the cool logic of lawyerly argumentation, but also the fervor of a temperance tale, with wronged womanhood and sexual transgression at its core. And so the testimony of "witnesses" competes in this book with a long account of Byron's alcohol-fueled degeneracy, which led him not only to a hideous sin but to the abuse of a good woman. Stowe's conclusion reinforces this ambivalence, mapping it onto her own status as figurative defendant. After having spent hundreds of pages attempting to convince readers that the evidence and rationales she has presented are credible and compelling, she writes that her own role in the controversy can be judged by "God alone" (*LBV*, p. 406).

As we might expect of a novelist, Stowe deploys narrative as the book's most compelling form of evidence. Indeed, a chapter titled "Lady Byron's Story As Told Me" serves as the book's affective and evidentiary core. Here Stowe narrates the setting and occasion of her fateful interview with Lady Byron, and in a story-within-a-story that would seem at home in the era's sensational novels, she relates, in the third person, Lady Byron's tumultuous courtship and marriage, her discovery of her husband's crime, and her upstanding behavior in its aftermath. This retelling embeds the details of the marriage and its dissolution (or, rather, Stowe's version of Lady Byron's version of those details) within a larger story of feminine suffering—of abuse, rejection, and a self-imposed sentence of principled renunciation. And by dramatizing the intimacy between Stowe and Lady Byron—much of the narrative proceeds as a dialogue between them—Stowe seeks to reassure skeptical readers of her full access to the story and of her good conduct as its custodian. As Stowe writes in an earlier chapter, "the credibility of a history depends greatly on the character of its narrator" (*LBV*, p. 204). The story embedded in *Lady Byron Vindicated* works to reestablish the good character of both narrators—Stowe and Lady Byron—whose reputations were, by 1870, very much in need of repair. In the process, however, Stowe's text reduces the complexities of authorship to the relatively narrow registers of credibility and moral legitimacy, while her contemporaries seemed increasingly invested in the role's more capacious possibilities.

The Byron Whirlwind

The public conversations that Stowe's writings on Byron prompted reveal intriguing fissures in postbellum attitudes toward authorship and, indeed, toward reputational economies more broadly conceived.[22] In December of 1869, a few months before *Lady Byron Vindicated* was released, Philip Quilibet (pseudonym of the author George Edward Pond) characterized the mainstream response to the Byron controversy in an article aptly titled "The Great Moral Drama." New York City's Tammany Theatre, according to this report, had been displaying "a collection of portraits" to the audience following the evening's regular program: "First comes Lady Byron's, which is greeted with slight hisses; then Mrs. Stowe's, with Bowery execrations; then Mrs. Leigh's, with hearty cheers; then Lord Byron's, with tumultuous applause."[23] This inversion of the moral hierarchy that Stowe posits in the "True Story" and, later, in *Lady Byron Vindicated* demonstrates not only the extent to which public perceptions were spinning out of her control, but also the depth of her unpopularity, presuming that the audience was not entirely made up of Romantic poetry aficionados, who might be especially troubled by an attack on Byron. But the vignette obscures as much as it reveals. That is, while this account of boisterous audience response reifies the intensity and viciousness of that season's anti-Stowe rhetoric, it also glosses over the range of positions that commentators took.

Most obviously missing from this anecdote are the voices of Stowe's supporters, most of whom were unlikely to attend productions at the Tammany Theater in any case. Among her most ardent defenders, as Joan Hedrick has noted, were woman's rights advocates.[24] Elizabeth Cady Stanton, for example, wrote that Stowe's statements were doubtless true "because she is too cautious and conscientious to venture such publications without abundant proof to substantiate them." Assuring readers that Stowe's motives in publishing the article were "worthy and pure," Stanton asserted that, "when a person has a noble motive for performing an ungracious task[,] a question of taste must be subservient to the public good." But for Stanton, the Byron controversy was less about Stowe's reputation or decorum than about the broader injustices of marriage, which she described as "the hideous, disgusting slavery in which the women of every class and clime ever have been and are held to-day."[25] Stowe's fellow antislavery author Lydia Maria Child came to her defense as well, expressing her conviction that "Lady Byron has been deeply wronged..., and that noble motives impelled Mrs. Stowe to seek to right the wrong."[26] The October 1869 issue of *Harper's Magazine* also included a lengthy defense of the "True Story" in its "Editor's Easy Chair" column, though it focused more on Lady Byron than on Stowe. After critiquing those who denied the article's veracity, the author asserted that a "blameless" Lady Byron had "not in anger nor in revenge, but from a sober conviction of duty, told her story and left the world to judge its truth."[27] Some defended Stowe on similar grounds. An editorial published in the *Buffalo Express* stated that, "receiving the facts as she did, in the manner she did, from Lady Byron, it was her duty to make them public."[28]

The English press included some favorable notices as well, despite the fact that at least one commentator called its condemnation of Stowe "unanimous."[29] A piece that appeared in the *Times* [London] noted that, although Stowe's article "will owe much of its universal interest to the fact that it gratifies the lowest kind of curiosity," in reality "it was not written and ought not to be read with this end in view. It is a late and necessary act of justice."[30] A *Daily News* [London] article called Stowe's piece "a fair and valuable contribution to the veracity and exactitude of history," while a letter to the editor of the *Times*, penned by Sampson Low, Jr., testified to Stowe's "truthfulness and freedom from all selfish motive" in writing her article: citing "many years' personal intimacy with Mrs. Stowe," Low added that "a more genuine, true-hearted, and truth-loving character does not exist."[31] Reversing the usual tendency to blame the scandal on Stowe, one commentator, writing in London's *Pall Mall Gazette*, instead excoriated Lord Byron's partisans: "The question [regarding the cause of Byron's separation from his wife]... might willingly have been let die but for the indiscretion of the poet's admirers, who could not refrain from spreading cruel insinuations and imputations against others in their eagerness to vindicate his character."[32]

Despite these defenses and countercharges, it is fair to say that the majority of responses to Stowe's accusation, both English and American, were negative. In addition to breaking with generally accepted rules of behavior (one should not speak ill of the dead; one ought not reveal another person's long-kept secret without express permission), Stowe was accused of a range of ulterior motives. Some charged her with crass profit-seeking: London's *Echo*, for example, published the amount she had earned for her article (250 pounds from each magazine), presumably in order to impugn her motives, while a contributor to the *Daily Telegraph* noted more vaguely that, "commercially speaking, the result has doubtless been satisfactory to all concerned."[33] Others claimed that Stowe's article was a pathetic attempt to revive a waning career or, more simply, to be "the first to tell a horrible story."[34] Perhaps the most snide of these attacks was the suggestion that she was a crass social climber whose primary goal in publishing the "True Story" was to advertise her intimate friendship with a member of England's upper class.[35] Predictably, the English backlash against Stowe included ardent invocations of nationalism, literary and otherwise, with respondents expressing outrage that this American "authoress" had dared to malign one of the nation's greatest poets. Stowe, for her part, reversed that nationalist argument, claiming that, because no English citizen had done his or her duty to Lady Byron's memory, it was left to a forthright American to set the record straight.

Within this general disapprobation, variations and disjunctions emerged that attest to authorship's instability vis-à-vis the matter of readerly trust. Stowe's credibility, especially her use (or lack) of evidence, came under particular scrutiny. Among Stowe's critics, a significant contingent refused outright to believe the charges against Byron—or thought them so improbable as to be unworthy of serious consideration. While some simply proclaimed their disbelief, others demonstrated a great deal more precision, attacking Stowe's accuracy and logic. Her casual approach to dates and timelines provided them with ammunition: Stowe misstated the length of Lord and Lady Byron's cohabitation (it was just over a year, though Stowe claimed it was two). Moreover, a letter to the London *Telegraph* asserted that "Lord Byron did not meet Mrs. Leigh from a period before his marriage until after the separation from Lady Byron," while Stowe's article had detailed a dramatic confrontation involving the scandal's three principals prior to Lady Byron's departure.[36] Most surprising is the fact that editors gave ink and space to detailed discussions of these matters—the number of months a now-dead couple had lived together several decades previously would not generally be considered interesting or marketable commentary. But the Byron scandal inspired such investment in minutiae; a number of commentators even cited Stowe's misspelling of Lady Byron's maiden name (Millbank versus the correct Milbanke) as proof that she could not be trusted.[37]

The evidentiary attack on Stowe went beyond quibbling over dates and spelling, as commentators sought to undermine her claims by presenting competing evidence. A former servant of Lady Byron, for example, was quoted as saying that her employer spoke of Augusta Leigh "'always in terms of the deepest affection, often designating her as her best friend.'"[38] More persuasive were Lady Byron's own letters to her sister-in-law, reprinted in both the English and American press, which convey an affection and regard for Mrs. Leigh that would seem incompatible with the incest charge.[39] A letter dated shortly after Lady Byron left her husband, for example, begins

"My Dearest Augusta: Shall I be still your sister? I must resign my rights to be so considered; but I don't think that will make any difference in the kindness I have so uniformly experienced from you."[40] These apparent inconsistencies gave way to much arguing over Lady Byron's cognitive, emotional, and psychological states: What did she know and when did she know it? In whom might she reasonably have confided? And from whom would she have kept her secret?

More imaginative commentators proposed alternative explanations for the Byron break-up. "If–then" statements and conditional phrasing ("would," "might," "could") abound in these texts, as those who excoriated Stowe for relying on conjecture engaged in some guesswork of their own. A contributor to the *Nation* suggested that Byron had invented the incest story himself. Claiming that he was in the habit of trying to "make people think him worse even than he was," the author asks, "may he not have first hinted this horror, or plainly told it to [his wife], to try his power over her, to see the effect it would have on her nerves, and to gratify whatever morbid instinct it might be which prompted him to his other blackenings of himself?"[41] Other counternarratives departed entirely from the incest controversy. A particularly strident one charged that "the true cause" of the couple's separation was that Lady Byron, in a fit of resentment, taunted her husband about his physical deformity, the clubfoot he referred to as "his 'curse of life.'"[42]

Far more damaging were the many attacks on Lady Byron's sanity. A piece that appeared in the London *Times* early in the controversy defended Stowe's veracity, but added that "we think it perfectly possible—and, indeed, probable—that Lady Byron was herself the victim of a delusion."[43] Stowe was so perturbed by such suggestions that she confronted them directly in *Lady Byron Vindicated*, citing a long letter from a Dr. Forbes Winslow to the London *Times* in which he argued that Lady Byron's disclosure of her secret bore no relationship to a hallucination or delusion as medical science understood those phenomena (*LBV*, pp. 352–53). Implicit in this marshaling of expert testimony, of course, is Stowe's refutation of the charge that she lacked discernment in having accepted the truth value of Lady Byron's claim. She did not wish to be identified as one of those with "credulous minds," to quote a *Putnam's* "Table-Talk" column, on whom a delusional Lady Byron supposedly "work[ed]" her "vile imaginations."[44]

Stowe's own identity—as a woman, an abolitionist, a Beecher, and an American—emerged as a crucial feature of this transatlantic backlash. To a great extent, the attacks on her character were gendered. In some publications, the scandal took on a war-between-the-sexes tone overall, with Stowe representing a meddling, even ruthless, femininity that sought to undermine Byron's masculine genius. The London-based weekly *Fun*, for example, which commented extensively on the scandal, combined harsh and sometimes comical critiques of Stowe with a settled opposition to woman's rights. Railing against the "unfeminine goings-on of 'Woman's Rights' advocates, and unsexed females of that kind," a March 1870 piece noted that "Thanks to the attitude assumed by these persons, we find women discussing... subjects which either they ought to know nothing about, or knowing should be too decent to talk about. We have two damsels, scarcely out of their teens, turning the horrors of the Byron scandal to after-dinner talk with creatures of the opposite sex."[45] Keen female interest in a recent scandalous divorce case is then linked to this general dismantling of feminine propriety. An accompanying illustration further critiques the unholy alliance of divorce courts, woman's rights advocates, and scandalmongering; here throngs of women eagerly seek divorce-related gossip, while an innocent-looking pair is persuaded to support divorce by an especially unattractive woman's rights campaigner (see Figure 5). All the while a little girl sits on the floor unnoticed, reading a book about the Byron scandal. Although Stowe does not appear in the illustration, she lurks as its animating force, one of many "unsexed" women threatening the stability and well-being of families.

The gendering of the Byron scandal persisted even when criticism of Stowe was comparatively mild. The American editor Theodore Tilton, for example, writing in the *Independent* in August of 1869, defended Stowe's character (as we might expect, given his professional and personal ties to the Beecher family at that juncture): "Whatever has been her misstep in the present instance, she cannot thereby lose her standing among the best and greatest women of her country." Tilton went on to say, however, that "Mrs. Stowe, in penning her late paper, seems to have repressed her better judgment and nobler self. An offense against Christian charity is more ungentle in a woman than in a man."[46] Conversely, Stowe had seen her foray into Byron's life story as a way of doing her duty as a woman by defending a maligned sister who had proven unwilling or unable to speak for herself.

If recourse to gender was inevitable in a nineteenth-century controversy over marriage and sexuality, the interjection of Stowe's abolitionist past seems incongruous, given that the Byron break-up ostensibly had nothing to do with racial oppression except by analogy, insofar as woman's right's activists often compared the wife's subjection within marriage to the plight of the slave. That said, abolition had, in the postbellum period, taken on a quaint, archaic quality (cf. Henry James's Miss Birdseye in *The Bostonians*), as the work of national reunion came to displace more pointed calls for racial and social justice. Thus Stowe's authorship of *Uncle Tom's Cabin* could be used to position her as simultaneously a troublemaker and an anachronism.[47] Not all references to the novel were negative—one English commentator noted that "in common with most of our countrymen, we have long had a very genuine admiration of the peculiar genius of Mrs. Harriet Beecher Stowe," whose book made her "the spokeswoman of a holy cause."[48] And some authors simply

FIGURE 5 *"Ladies! Ladies! (The Mystery of Modern Modesty),"* Fun, March 12, 1870, pp. 8–9. *Image courtesy of the Library of Congress.*

invoked the work as the source of Stowe's fame, especially in England, where the Beecher family was not so well known as in the United States. But Stowe's abolitionism was more often used to undermine her authority, both moral and evidentiary. A quip that appeared in *Fun* is more or less representative: "Mrs. Beecher Stowe made her first success by white-washing the black. She is now trying to revive an expiring popularity by blackening a white [i.e., Lord Byron]." A later offering, titled "The Stowe-ry Teller," used a similar reversal in a bit of anti-Stowe wordplay: "As the authoress of Topsy she was once famous for her coloured female, now she will be notorious for her black mail."[49] A contributor to the *Saturday Review* put the matter in more straightforward terms, assuring readers that he or she placed little confidence in "a writer so inaccurate, and in other ways so positively repellant, as the authoress of 'Uncle Tom's Cabin.'"[50] And, linking anti-Stowe sentiment to resentment of England's role in the abolitionist movement, an American congressman writing to the London *Times* blamed the English for Stowe's early popularity, asserting that "the great notice which a certain class of English philanthropists gave that book at the time gave her the only literary reputation she ever had with us." The Byron scandal, for him, amounts to a kind of payback: "We are not grieved that [Stowe] should now turn ungratefully on all England by calumniating the private character of her greatest modern poetic genius."[51]

As Jennifer Cognard-Black has shown, *Uncle Tom's Cabin* figured into anti-Stowe cartoons as well. One has Uncle Tom bemoaning Stowe's cruelty in "paint[ing] one of her own brethren so *black*," while another has a grotesquely caricatured Topsy greeting Byron in "Spirit Land" with the assertion that according to Stowe, he is even more wicked than she. This racialization of attacks on Stowe, Cognard-Black argues, "is a throwback to the media contention surrounding *Uncle Tom's Cabin* but also a typical nineteenth-century elision, collapsing gender with racial degeneracy and, in so doing, threatening Stowe's most powerful claim to social power: her whiteness."[52] One crucial nexus here, as Cognard-Black notes, is sexuality—Stowe's representation of black women's sexual exploitation in her fiction was transformed, in the ensuing attacks on her, into a representation of her own prurience, her unladylike preoccupation with and candor regarding sex. Similarly, the post-Byron attacks on Stowe emphasized her lack of sexual decorum—a proper woman, to paraphrase one of her detractors, would not know about such things, or if knowing, would not discuss them.

Stowe's long-standing interest in social reform projects informs one of the milder sexualized critiques leveled against her. An English commentator wrote in the *Standard* [London] that Stowe, by publishing her article, was "endeavouring, with frantic ardour, as though engaged in a task of benevolence, to fasten upon one of the greatest…men that ever lived…the most indelible of stigmas."[53]

Benevolence was associated in the nineteenth century with such sentiments as love and duty, but not typically with "frantic ardour," a description that suggests that Stowe's benevolent efforts were as libidinal as they were misguided. A more daring attack, which appeared in the San Francisco-based *Overland Monthly*, figures Stowe's sexuality as homoerotic and incestuous, if also reproductive. "In an evil hour," the unsigned article intoned, "Lady Byron was visited in her retirement by Mrs. Harriet Beecher Stowe. A fatal intimacy—degrading to the hitherto unblemished reputation of both parties—took place. The offspring of that intimacy—an intimacy unhallowed and forbidden by consanguinity of intellect and taste—was born in London, on the first of September, in the pages of *MacMillan's*."[54] Surely the author is parodying Stowe's own heated prose, not to mention her incest accusation against Byron, but the choice to render her as Lady Byron's lover and as the parent of a "monstrous" child is especially pointed, given Stowe's narrative preoccupation with (chaste) sisterly sentiment and mother-child bonds.

The most striking invocation of Stowe's sexuality represented it as grotesque and ridiculous, the impulses and proclivities of an aging and notably perverted bluestocking.[55] A cartoon featured in the September 18, 1869, issue of *Fun* (see Figure 6) features a beak-nosed Stowe, rendered in dark, heavily cross-hatched lines, climbing a statue of Lord Byron. Having left black hand- and footprints all over its previously unblemished surface, the Stowe figure hooks the sharp handle of her umbrella over the marble poet's shoulder in a final, desperate attempt to reach the top of this larger-than-life figure. Scholars have taken note of this cartoon, emphasizing the illustrator's strategy of collapsing ink into filth and opposing Byron's nobility to Stowe's foolishness.[56] But what strikes me most forcefully about this piece is its suggestion that Stowe is, to use an indecorous term myself, humping Byron's statue. The bystander's comment, printed below the image in the original, reinforces this reading: "Now then, old gal, if you want to make yourself conspicuous, you had better go elsewhere and not leave your dirty marks there!" She is a dog in heat or a masturbating vagrant, in marked contrast to Byron's cool, impassive intellectualism. The rude joke animating this image exemplifies a crucial element of the Stowe/Byron scandal: the degree to which the charge of misdirected sexuality was turned against her. But the image also, more subtly, comments on the literary judgments and hierarchies structuring the debate. Byron's representation as a statue insists on his high cultural status—only a literary icon would merit such commemoration. Further, it suggests his timelessness, a purity of literary achievement that cannot be (permanently) altered by a petty, self-gratifying attack. Stowe, meanwhile, is figured as a literary bag lady, leaving behind inky handprints but no lasting achievement that would warrant her own memorialization in stone.

FIGURE 6 *"Stowe It!"* Fun, *September 18, 1869, pp. 18–19. Image courtesy of the Library of Congress.*

Literary Status

As the "Stowe It!" cartoon suggests, the Stowe/Byron scandal engaged an elaborate discourse on the links between moral authority and literary value. In much of this print conversation, Stowe's own never-quite-secure status as an author of respectable or high-quality literature was denigrated. Her prose style came under particular attack: indeed, one of the most frequently appearing comments on the "True Story" was that it was badly written. The editor of *The Stowe-Byron Controversy* (1869), a volume comprising mostly English commentary on the scandal, asserted that Stowe's article was written "in her very worst style, being throughout rambling and confused to a most unsatisfactory degree."[57] Apart from the implication that she had several bad writing styles, among which this was the most egregious, the foregoing remark suggests that an imperfect style undermined the credibility of the entire piece. If the author is "rambling and confused" at the level of composition, how confused must she be about the facts?

Two other elements of Stowe's writing suffused the debate: the fact that she was best known as a novelist and the fact that many perceived her writing to be sensational. While the novel as a genre had gained respectability across the previous decades, it still bore, for some, the taint of frivolity, even immorality, that had dogged its early existence. Such disdain could be deployed as another means of attacking Stowe, especially when she claimed to write truth rather than fiction. Some suggested that Stowe did not know the difference between the two or purposefully disguised one as the other. Along these lines, a headline in the *Independent* referred to the "True Story" as "Mrs. Stowe's Last Romance" and *Fun* called it her "last fiction," while a piece in the *New York Times* asserted that she had "lost the power to discriminate between truth and fiction."[58] *Lady Byron Vindicated* elicited similar criticism. Calling the book a "cheap novel—that disgusts as often as it excites," an American reviewer remarked that it provided "the singular example of a novelist applying the rules and license of fiction to matters of fact."[59] Others claimed that Stowe ought to stick to what she did well: "No reader can doubt the talents of Mrs. Stowe as a fiction writer . . . but she has now eclipsed herself by this atrocious libel."[60]

Fiction, moreover, continued to rank lower than poetry in many nineteenth-century readers' notions of literary hierarchy, though the latter's prominence in the marketplace would diminish across the next few decades.[61] If Stowe's move to publicize her relationship with Lady Byron was a form of social climbing, her attack on the poet could be read as literary class warfare. For one English commentator, Stowe's article both ensured and justified her exclusion from the literary elite: "High literary society in all countries taboos the human vultures who feed upon the reputations of the dead; and the morality of our common civilization denounces the cannibalism which occasionally disgraces the brotherhood of the pen."[62] "Civilization" had closed ranks, leaving Stowe outside its borders, the literary equivalent of a scavenging bird or a man-eating "savage."

Another observer added Stowe's Americanness to the catalog of her inadequacies: "If Posterity deigns to preserve the memory of this foul fable in connection with [Byron's] name, it will be only to remember that it was penned by an American writer of romances,... but after due scrutiny and just reflection entirely repudiated by the definitive voice of an offended people."[63]

Literary hierarchies also figured into the charge that Stowe was a "sensationalist," one likely to dredge up or invent a scandal in order to have some shocking material to publish. The term *sensation* and its variants, in fact, appeared often in reference to Stowe's writings on Byron and to her authorship overall. One article referred to the "True Story" as "the gushing of a professional sensation-monger," while another of Stowe's antagonists remarked that "in America the Beechers are known as mere 'sensationalists,' without true merit or substantial talents."[64] By opposing sensation to both truth and substance, Stowe's detractor undermines the validity of her claims against Byron, even as he places her on the lower echelons of literary and intellectual life generally. In the nineteenth century (as in the twenty-first), sensational texts were both devoured and disavowed, enough so to render superfluous the adjective "mere" in the quotation above. Intriguingly, Stowe's sentimentalism, a crucial feature of her work for twentieth- and twenty-first-century critics, was not a notable target in most of the printed responses to her article.[65] Indeed, a series of newspaper editorials defending Stowe, which were later attributed to Mark Twain, instead called her critics sentimental for their overweening emotional attachment to Byron.[66]

Lord Byron's literary style emerged as a key feature of these debates as well. Of course not all commentators esteemed his poetry highly. One English author remarked that "the admiration felt for Lord Byron's poetry is a youthful passion" and was thus more appropriate to readers in the United States, a nation "in the first flush of exuberant energy."[67] A contributor to the *Times*, meanwhile, noted that although interest remained high in Byron's life and iconic status as a poet, "forty-five years have worn out the spell which once belonged to Byron's verse" and "criticism has dealt coldly and calmly with it, rejecting its meretricious sentiment and determining its sterling qualities."[68] More commonly, however, those who responded to Stowe's accusations against Byron extolled his literary genius, in many cases aligning his status as a poet with England's national identity and cultural pride. A contributor to the *Standard* referred to English-authored defenses of Stowe's article as "treason," while an especially enthusiastic reader of Byron claimed that his name rivaled Shakespeare's and averred that "every competent critic" would agree with Goethe's assertion that "'the nation which boasts so many great names will class Byron among the first of those through whom she has acquired such glory.'"[69] Another lent Byron a more universal status: "To the end of time Byron and his verse will be among the most cherished possessions of mankind."[70] For many of Byron's most ardent fans, the accusation of incest was too dreadful to accept. One commentator, "painfully hesitating to fix a blot so frightful on the name of the brightest genius of the century," consigned the matter to "Eternity," which might eventually resolve the mystery.[71] Meanwhile, a

Saturday Evening Post article closed with the following harangue: "Why did [Lady Byron] put it into the power of any indiscreet friend to discharge this terrible accusation at the memory and reputation of one who not only had been her husband, but the greatest poet, perhaps, with one exception, that ever glorified the English tongue?" Francis Blandford, writing from London to the *American Literary Gazette*, put the matter more succinctly, calling Stowe's accusations "libels on departed genius."[72]

As the citations above suggest, *genius* emerged as a keyword within the Stowe-Byron crisis, though its repetition cloaks a marked instability. As Gustavus Stadler has written, the nineteenth century's discourse of genius comprised a number of overlapping forms:

> That of the "great" man whose life and words were seen to crystallize a nation or period of history; that of the innate, unlearned talents of an artist, performer, writer, or orator; that of the irreducible originality of an idea, work of art, or collective self-conception; that of the irreducible essence of an idea, work of art, or collective self-conception.[73]

In keeping with this proliferation of meanings, Stadler notes that figures as diverse as Jenny Lind, Jean-Jacques Rousseau, and Toussaint L'Ouverture were all referred to as geniuses; meanwhile, the category they occupied came to do elaborate forms of ideological and emotional work, from reifying notions of national pride and identity to "fortify[ing] middle-class men and women by taking upon their [i.e., the geniuses'] own minds and bodies the troubling, potentially shattering phenomena associated with modernity."[74] Byron's partisans assigned him a number of the roles that Stadler has enumerated—Byron was said to embody and represent English literary greatness, even as he was identified as a figure of innate, natural poetic talent; he was an inimitable original who nevertheless stood in for the nation as a whole; and, crucially, for those who greeted the woman's rights movement with a mixture of horror and disdain, he served as a figure whose memory and reputation had to be protected from the alarming new ideas that Stowe was taken to represent.

Despite the energy with which Byron was defended, his status as genius was not invariably offered as a justification for denying (or endlessly deferring the question of) his sexual guilt. Some used the Byron controversy instead as an occasion to meditate on the relationship, actual or ideal, between literary genius and moral status. For an anonymous contributor to England's *Daily News*, characterological truth always mattered more than literary status: "The public has an interest in knowing what the gods of its idolatry are, and when admiration is claimed for geniuses like that of Lord Byron, it is a duty which supersedes questions of taste and feeling to let us know the truth about them."[75] Admiration in the absence of hard moral truths, this author suggested, risked a false and dangerous "idolatry." Another English commentator sought to separate literary genius from personal admiration, even as he or she maintained the importance of character: "It is by no means creditable to us as a nation that such a man as Byron should so long have been one of its favourite heroes; and though his genius must command admiration while the English language lasts, his character will...come, before long, to be regarded with feelings very different from those with which nine out of ten Englishmen regard it now."[76] Heroism and genius, in this schema, could and ought to be judged separately, with genius exerting the more limited influence.

The foregoing sentiments accord with conventional understandings of Victorian cultures of reading, which identify the prominence, at least through the middle third of the century, of a moralistic paradigm through which authors were evaluated and interpreted. Authors and their works, that is, were typically (though not exclusively) considered in light of their effects—salubrious or pernicious—on readers, an evaluative mode that M. H. Abrams called "pragmatic criticism." Abrams's landmark study *The Mirror and the Lamp* foregrounded a self-conscious literary-critical elite for whom this mode gave way in the early decades of the nineteenth century to an ascendant interest in "the poet himself, and his own mental powers and emotional needs, as the predominant cause and even the end and test of art."[77] For more mainstream Anglo-American book reviewers and commentators, however, this Romantic reorientation toward the mind of the artist coexisted with—and indeed was often overshadowed by—an ongoing preoccupation with literature's moral effects. And yet we see within the Byron controversy a thread that emphasizes not so much the mind of the literary creator per se but rather his or her text as a freestanding, autonomous object of analysis. Anticipating a later era's privileging of text over authorial character, one English author claimed that a majority of readers "had lost the remembrance of [Byron's] possible domestic errors in the brilliancy of his poetical career, and had been ready to accept his glorious contributions to English literature as some atonement for the reputed sins of his private life, or at least as something which tended to make one less ready to scrutinise that life and more lenient in our judgment upon it."[78] John Morley, editor of England's *Fortnightly Review*, made a more general case—one that depended less on temporal distance from the author's bad behavior: though he acknowledged that personal character mattered a great deal when choosing friends or public officials, it was irrelevant to literary evaluation: "The work is before us, its own warranty."[79]

This position had its advocates in the United States as well. In a piece titled "Mrs. Stowe's Mistake," a contributor to the New York-based *Appletons' Journal of Literature, Science and Art* identified Byron's escape from moral condemnation as part of a general societal tendency: "By the law that humanity is more and more, and the individual less and less, and by the still deeper law that evil is evanescent,...there was being a gradual loss of interest in the faulty details of Byron's life, and a narrowing of public attention to his intellectual work. It was by no means any reversal of moral judgment concerning the poet's personal character, but a slow and silent crumbling into oblivion of all concerning him that was least worthy to be remembered." Stowe's error, according to the author, lay in her failure to recognize this fundamental shift. In a claim apparently calculated to defy Stowe's deep investment in reform, he or she intoned: "It is useless to lament the state of the public mind; it was [Stowe's] business to know that before, and act accordingly."[80]

If a significant proportion of readers were thoroughly oriented toward Byron's poetic achievements, why did the reintroduction of his behavioral shortcomings so enthrall and outrage Stowe's audience? The notion of literary genius itself embodies this contradiction, insofar as the act of naming a particular author a genius—alternative usages referred to the author as possessing genius, not being one—purports to train our attention on his (and sometimes her) texts, the products of that extraordinary mind, while at the same time invoking a Romantic notion of the artist as outlier, rebel, enfant terrible, sacrificial lamb, force of nature, and so on. That is, the discourse of genius emerging in this period smuggles in a preoccupation with authorial identity even as it privileges, perhaps sacralizes, the literary text. In that sense the Byron controversy bridges Romantic and New Critical paradigms, attempting a renegotiation of authorship's moral economies that allowed the figure of the artist to continue to matter while cordoning off unsavory behavior as somehow beside the point. Textual brilliance, in other words, allows us to excuse—or bracket—an author's moral shortcomings without having to jettison biography entirely. A February 1870 piece in the *Saturday Evening Post* crystallizes this position: "Certain allowances must be made in judging men of genius. It is not well, or even sensible, to treat the deviations from the common rules of thought and action of such men as Shakspeare [sic], Milton, Burns, and Byron, as if they were the grovelling errors of natures esssentially [sic] vulgar and profligate." Interestingly, this exemption is represented as a matter of sentiment rather than reasoned judgment: "The instinct of mankind has been truer than its reason in regard to the short-comings of the gifted sons of song.... The great heart of the world has always been true to its poets and its prophets, and has covered with the mantle of its undying love the defects and weaknesses which marred the brightness of their appearing."[81] However strenuously the discourse of genius relies on some notion of isolation and exceptionalism, it is nevertheless the case that Byron's genius, as described in responses to Stowe's article and book, is figured as antagonistic rather than endogenous; that is, within this print conversation the poet emerges as a genius most starkly vis-à-vis his hectoring accuser. It is Stowe's refusal to concur with the world's "great heart," after all, that occasions these declarations.[82]

It's worth noting, however, that Stowe herself was not immune to Byron's literary and personal power. She confesses a youthful fascination with Byron's persona as well as an ongoing regard for his poetic abilities; further, nineteenth-century commentators and contemporary scholars alike have identified any number of Byronic traces in her fiction.[83] Byron's magnetism, in fact, is what worries Stowe the most—that is, in the absence of her principled accusations,

Byron's seductions might continue, albeit posthumously, to undermine the moral well-being of the reading public. In a telling selection, Stowe cites a letter from Lady Byron to a friend, in which she remarks that Byron "is the absolute monarch of words, and uses them, as Bonaparte did lives, for conquest."[84] Outraged by the extent to which Byron had been excused from the usual moral standards of the age, Stowe claims that Thomas Moore, the editor of Byron's memoirs, managed to turn the poet into "a perfected idol for a world longing for one." In Moore's rendering, Byron's "admitted faults [were to be] spoken of as peculiarities of sacred origin,—and the world given to understand that no common rule...could apply to such an undoubtedly divine production; and so the hearts of men were to be wrung with pity for his sorrows...and with anger at his injuries as sacrilege on the sacredness of genius" (*LBV*, p. 100). This fascination with Byron, Stowe suggests, takes on a decidedly sexual cast: Moore, she claims, was "as much bewitched by [Byron] as ever man has been by woman" (*LBV*, p. 99). In addition to his other transgressions, then, Stowe charged Byron with the charm that dare not speak its name: "He led [sic] captive Moore and Murray by being beautiful, a genius, and a lord;....He first insulted Sir Walter Scott, and then witched his heart out of him by ingenuous confessions and poetical compliments; he took Wilson's heart by flattering messages and a beautifully-written letter," and so on (*LBV*, pp. 84–85).[85] This homoerotic literary clique, Stowe implies, threatens to undermine the legitimacy of authorship itself. In *Lady Byron Vindicated* especially, she sets out to dismantle what Moore's text, and Byron's own poetry and letters, have built—that is, the moral insulation of genius. In its place, Stowe proposes a kind of intellectual-moral egalitarianism, whereby all authors, whatever their literary status, are held accountable for their behavior. For Stowe, in other words, genius is decidedly not a moral blank check. For her contemporaries, however, the matter was increasingly up for debate.

Marketing Scandal

At every level, the Stowe/Byron scandal engaged the structures and vagaries of the literary marketplace, as the following screed from the *Independent* laments:

> An authoress of reputation gets hold of a disgusting story about Byron—a story which, true or false, is revolting and obscene. She sells it to a publisher; and for weeks before its appearance the press is inundated with little preliminary puffs, whetting and goading on the meanest curiosity on the part of the public. The coming disclosures are advertised, announced, heralded, trumpeted everywhere; and, of course, the result is a splendid success. A story which would have suited and delighted the taste of a Borgia family-circle is sent into every household in the United States; and the circulation of the magazine is thereby made enormous.[86]

Regardless of whether the scandal marked a general cultural decline as this commentator claimed, it affected the sales and marketing of printed material in fascinating ways. For instance, in contrast to the *Independent*'s assertion, the scandal seems actually to have hurt the *Atlantic*'s sales, as the public came to associate the magazine with inappropriate sexual content.[87] But evidence suggests that the controversy increased Byron's popularity and marketability. As one of Stowe's critics put the matter, her accusation against Byron "provoked the very consequences it was designed to prevent."[88] "From comparative neglect," the *Newcastle Daily Chronicle* asserted, "the writings of Byron have sprung into such request, that if the copyright were still in force, surmises as to pecuniary motives would not be unnatural. We have...entered into all the ardours of a Byronic revival."[89] A notice in the *Saturday Evening Post* insisted that not only was there "a largely increased demand for his poems," but "close observers say the demand comes mainly from a class of persons that never read them before."[90] While these declarations of brisk sales were not supported by solid figures—and indeed, some came so quickly on the heels of Stowe's "True Story" that it is difficult to invest much in their accuracy—many perceived the scandal to have increased Byron's popularity among the book-buying public.[91]

Book advertisements further support the notion that the scandal increased Byron's popularity—or at least the perception among publishers that his poems were marketable commodities. Judging from the wide range of sources indexed in the *American Periodicals* online database, advertisements featuring Byron's works—offered at various price points—increased by approximately 50 percent (that is, when comparing the two-year period prior to the scandal's eruption in August 1869 to the two-year period that followed).[92] And it was not just Byron's own books but books about him that garnered increased attention. Indeed, an impressive range of Byron-related texts were advertised in US periodicals in late 1869 and 1870, including Moore's *Life of Byron*, sheet music for a song titled "Byron to His Sister" (which drew on Byron's own verse for its lyrics, but whose publisher surely sought to capitalize on the recent controversy), and an illustrated volume titled *Gallery of Byron Beauties*, "Containing Portraits of the Female Characters in Lord Byron's Poems."[93] While the last of these offerings had been available for some time, its American publisher (D. Appleton & Co.) chose the late fall of 1869 to advertise the book (at a pricey $12) among its "splendid gift-books for the holiday season."[94] And the recently launched book-trade periodical titled the *American Bibliopolist* considered Byron to be a sufficiently timely topic that it devoted four pages of its December 1869 issue to listing "editions of Byron and Byronana."[95] The Countess Guiccioli's *Recollections of Lord Byron*, the volume whose representations had so troubled Stowe that she introduced her "True Story" as a response to its allegations, seems to have lost ground in the wake of the scandal, however. Though heavily advertised in the spring of 1869, it faded from view that fall. A commentator's claim that, as of late November, "new and cheap editions" of the book were coming on the market appears to have been incorrect.[96]

The scandal sparked commentary not just on the literary fortunes of its principals but on the US book market writ large, as an article in the *Nation* attests:

> If it could be proved of any author, however uninteresting and obscure—a maker of algebras—that he had had a hand in the commission of any great crime or any great folly—that he had sold his grandmother into slavery, or frozen his twin children, or sawed off his feet—the booksellers would at once lay in a stock of his writings, and feel sure of turning a good many honest pennies by the sale of them.[97]

According to this observer, the Stowe/Byron controversy exemplified, even as it accelerated, a pervasive degeneracy in the literary marketplace. For all the claims of scandal's profitability, however, Stowe's literary reputation appears to have suffered, though it is difficult to recover the extent to which this circumstance resulted in any actual loss of sales. Certainly the public perceived her to have lost ground as a literary or public figure. As *Putnam's* intoned, in reference to *Lady Byron Vindicated*, "few will doubt that Mrs. Stowe has hurt her literary reputation by a most illogical and useless piece of special pleading."[98] Another commentator declared "Mrs. Stowe's own influence" to have been "shaken" by the scandal.[99] Further, any association with her Byron accusation seemed to carry a taint: Stowe's publisher (Fields, Osgood, and Co.) was criticized for attempting to use the notoriety of the scandal to launch an inexpensive edition of Godwin's *Caleb Williams*, which Stowe references in *Lady Byron Vindicated* (and which the publisher advertises in the front matter of the latter book, with page numbers keyed to Stowe's mentions of the novel). According to commentary reprinted in the *American Bibliopolist*, Godwin's novel "is a story rather to be admired and wondered at than to be liked; and the fact that it is now, so to speak, picked out of the filth of the Byron discussion does not make it any less disagreeable."[100] Perhaps in response to the backlash against Stowe in the press, Fields, Osgood & Co. did relatively little to promote *Lady Byron Vindicated*—advertisements for the book appeared in just six issues of *Every Saturday*, a weekly published by the same house, though the company's usual practice was to advertise in a broader range of periodicals.[101]

However harshly Stowe was criticized for her role in the Byron controversy—and however negatively *Lady Byron Vindicated* was reviewed—the claims of her contemporaries that the scandal had ruined her reputation appear to have been overstated.[102] According to Evert and George Duyckinck's *Cyclopaedia of American Literature* (1875 edition), *Lady Byron Vindicated* sold a respectable 8,000 copies in six months—hardly a publishing debacle.[103] And a wealth of evidence suggests that the literary world did not treat Stowe as a pariah in the wake of the scandal—her works, including books for young readers, continued to be advertised widely, belying the suggestion that she had somehow become too transgressive for mainstream audiences. She continued to place her writing in prominent venues (including the *Atlantic Monthly*, *Harper's Bazaar*, and the *Saturday Evening Post*); her works still received mentions in the era's many "literary notices" and "books received" columns; and she was often listed as a contributor in advertisements for particular titles (e.g., the *Youth's Companion*, *Old and New*, the *Christian Union*), implying that editors still perceived her to be a commercial draw. Further, as Joan Hedrick notes, whatever decline in popularity Stowe experienced across those years cannot be blamed entirely on the Byron scandal—her displacement had to do with larger trends on the literary scene, including the declining popularity of literary sentimentalism.[104]

It is the case, nevertheless, that the scandal failed to give Stowe the reputational or commercial boost that it seems to have given Byron. In the nineteenth-century literary marketplace, it was apparently better to have done the deed than to have written about it. The gendering of both authorship and conduct plays a role here—much of the backlash against Stowe used her femaleness as a way to dismiss or excoriate her. That said, it would be specious to claim that Stowe's gender, in some simple or direct way, sealed her fate as the victim of the Byron backlash when, just seventeen years earlier, the scandals that erupted over her publication of *Uncle Tom's Cabin* increased both her sales and her public profile. The marketing success of a book like *Ruth Hall* (1854) further undermines the gender argument—Fanny Fern (a.k.a. Sara Willis Parton) was lambasted in the press for her unladylike exposure of intimate family conflicts, but readers bought the book in droves.[105] Perhaps *Lady Byron Vindicated*'s length and sometimes-exhausting generic code-switching failed to provide the kind of sustained, engaging narrative—or the new revelations—that might have made for more robust sales. And clearly Stowe overestimated her own moral authority, and the centrality of moral authority to emerging conceptions of authorship, both in her original article and in its long sequel. Stowe's overreaching, though, is only part of the story: I have argued that literary genius as a cultural construct was in the process of acquiring a kind of protected status, as some of Stowe's respondents attest. Nevertheless, such exemptions had to be argued for with vigor. That a broad book-buying public could find Stowe's accusations so unpalatable and yet somehow worth talking about, contesting, or lamenting, speaks to the instability of authorship's moral economies and to the risks inherent in presuming to understand or control their implications.

It's tempting to look back on this crisis with a touch of smugness, insofar as the incest accusation that catalyzed it fails to scandalize us much now. While incest itself has hardly achieved social respectability, talking about it is no longer quite so objectionable, to judge by the popularity of talk-therapy television programs, memoirs, and news stories that detail dysfunctional family relations. Those prim Victorians seem too easily, even inexplicably, outraged.

But in fact the Stowe/Byron scandal raises questions about authorship that are still very much in contention. Public commentary on scandalous authorship may be more subdued than in 1869–1870, but authors' personal and moral shortcomings still make good copy—and still inform scholarly discourse—as my epilogue will explore.

Epilogue

REPUTATION REDUX

Much has changed since the mid-nineteenth century in terms of moral authority's circulation within the literary field. Mainstream book reviewers no longer offer reflexive, near-obligatory commentary on a text's moral tendencies, nor are contemporary authors commended for their purity. Perhaps most strikingly, an author's frank treatment of sexuality, including its many nonmarital and nonheteronormative forms, no longer compels Whitmanian feats of reputational repair. Literary reception would appear to have arrived at a kind of postmoralism. And yet authorship's moral economies routinely reemerge, often in ways strangely conversant with the nineteenth-century cultures of print that this book has investigated. In keeping with a prior era's evidentiary preoccupations, for example, any number of writers have elicited vehement media criticism for including exaggerated or invented episodes in their putative memoirs. While James Frey's missteps garnered unusually widespread attention, eventuating in a public grilling on the Oprah Winfrey show in 2006, outraged reports of memoirists' fabrications—with the inevitable laments of readerly trust betrayed—crop up frequently. In other cases, an author's private life is the problem, as when *Vanity Fair* and other outlets alleged that the playwright Arthur Miller, that paragon of Cold War moral rectitude and chronicler of father-child angst, had effectively disowned his cognitively disabled son.[1]

Contemporary mass culture invests in various kinds of celebrities as role models (athletes and actors, most energetically), even as commentators repeatedly, ritualistically, point out the absurdities inherent in the practice. In that sense it's unsurprising that the same wishes and burdens attach to literary authors with significant name recognition and wide readership. Some of the most heated debates over authorial character, however—replete with biographical and textual analyses that seem remarkably congruent with mid-nineteenth-century author scandals—have taken place within the academy, among those who would likely disdain an analogous investment in the latest Oscar recipient's personal comportment. As Thomas Mitchell has written in the context of an 1880s controversy, "in the rhetorical extremes with which the participants in the feud defended their chosen idols [in this case, Nathaniel Hawthorne and Margaret Fuller], we see also just how fitting is literature's appropriation of the concept of canonization to describe the need to create and defend a faith in unblemished cultural saints."[2] While Mitchell's phrasing is a bit too extreme to apply to the twenty-first-century academy—even the most ardent defender of a particular author can usually admit of a blemish or two—a version of the habit of mind he describes, a kind of secular beatification, inflects our scholarly practices.

These residues and reformulations of an earlier era's modes of valuation take a number of forms, as the New Critical impetus to separate textual from biographical evidence has given way to a marked uncertainty within literary studies about the moral status of authorship. For instance, late twentieth- and twenty-first-century academics may be unperturbed by Harriet Beecher Stowe's decision to level a charge of incest in print, but we are troubled by her racial representations and appropriations, as myriad publications attest. Too, the interconnections between reputational and literary properties, so active in the case studies this book has taken up, assume new forms in the contemporary academy, as scholars' sense of ownership over particular authors, texts, and literary movements eventuates, in many cases, in an impulse to defend them against perceived attacks. Author society panels at academic conferences have been the sites of many such conflicts, as expertise morphs into a kind of guardianship over the reputation (literary and/or personal) of the writer in question and scholars' intellectual and professional identities in some sense merge with those of their objects of study. That someone might still be referred to as a Dickinson scholar or a Douglass scholar or, better yet, a Melvillean, which sounds like some exotic creature, is proof of our field's ongoing penchant for blurring these boundaries.

Attempts to recuperate authorial reputations range from frankly odd rationalizations of questionable behavior to carefully evidenced studies that have meaningfully altered the field's perceptions of particular figures. In terms of the former, I would point to a now-superseded author headnote from the *Heath Anthology of American Literature*. Anticipating students' shock upon learning that Edgar Allan Poe had married his thirteen-year-old cousin, William Goldhurst frames the event as Poe's attempt "to establish some permanence" for the "improvised family" (that is, his aunt and her child-bride daughter) with whom he had been living.[3] Apart from the dubious suggestion that a move now widely deemed child abuse might reasonably have been, in the antebellum period, a means of ensuring domestic stability, one has to wonder why he commented on Poe's marriage at all. That Goldhurst put the anthology's critical apparatus in the service of sanitizing an author's personal behavior suggests that these concerns are pedagogical as well as scholarly—students, that is, needed a less immoral Poe, at least in his estimation. Recuperative gestures are often far more substantive than this example might suggest, however. Consider Len Gougeon's carefully evidenced argument that Emerson was an earlier and more ardent proponent of abolition than many had claimed, work that contributed to the field's gradual, if still incomplete, deconstruction of the supposed antagonism between literary aesthetics and political activism.[4] Gougeon's very title, *Virtue's Hero*, attests to the ongoing salience of nineteenth-century authorship's moral economies, even as the work itself intervened in its own critical moment, when scholars were approaching the literatures of slavery with a new urgency. Indeed, the field's heightened interest in politically and socially engaged literature generally (since the mid-1980s, more or less) has made it difficult to ignore authorship's moral valences, as attention has turned to the ways in which a given text, and by extension its creator, might have shaped—and sought to improve conditions within—a particular historical moment.

Authorship's moral economies have structured the field's critical practices in other ways as well, a phenomenon I will explore briefly through two at least superficially unrelated paradigms: the recovery of lost or forgotten American women's writing (work that was most active in the 1970s and 1980s, but that is ongoing) and the more recent interest in ecocriticism. What these modes of inquiry share, for my purposes, is a deep investment in righting wrongs—the dismissal of key literary figures because of their gender; the thoughtless or self-serving destruction of the environment—which expands into a consideration of authors' moral authority, though the term *moral* itself is frequently disavowed, giving way to alternatives (such as *ethical* or *progressive*) that seem less tainted by self-righteousness and rigidity.

Recovery work, which contributed hugely to late twentieth-century revisions of the American literary canon, involves mutually reinforcing acts of moral repair. That is, in the search for lost, forgotten, dismissed, and demoted authors, the scholar takes on a quasi-heroic identity as rescuer (of texts, of reputations, of lost histories) and truth-teller, working to reclaim the field at large from its past oversights and acts of injustice. At the same time, the author being rediscovered is often figured as a prescient voice or wise forebear or role model, contra the pejorative associations that had heretofore consigned her to irrelevance. And within those recovery practices, there has been a tendency to frame the authors and texts under consideration in ways that seem congruent with currently held values, lines of inquiry that are often emphasized in scholarly introductions to reissued works. Granted, scholars' introductions are typically complimentary toward the author whose work is being previewed—the scholar chooses (or is chosen for) the project on the basis of a significant investment in the text and author under discussion, which, for most, involves a degree of admiration; meanwhile, the sponsoring press has a stake in putting forward an introduction that tells readers why the book is worth purchasing or assigning. Introductions to recovered texts by nineteenth-century women authors are clearly participating in that broader mode, but their praise of the author so often accords with notions of admirable womanhood in the moment of the book's reissue that a more palpable transhistorical moral economy comes into play. Carolyn Karcher's 1986 introduction to *Hobomok*, for example, foregrounds Lydia Maria Child's "strength," "rebelliousness," and "feminist consciousness"; further, Karcher notes, her novel "conspicuously flout[ed] patriarchal authority and revis[ed] patriarchal script." She "succeeded in infiltrating radical ideas into her writings" and, in keeping with the field's search for literary forebears, Child is said to have "founded both a female countertradition of American literature and an alternative vision of race and gender relations."[5] Thus Child's moral authority is established for the introduction's late twentieth-century readers on terms very different from those that won the praise of her contemporaries. Joyce Warren's introduction to *Ruth Hall*, also reissued in 1986 as part of Rutgers University Press's American Women Writers series, proceeds along similar lines: "The career of Ruth Hall—and incidentally of Fanny Fern herself—provided a rare role model for nineteenth-century women: the example of a woman who had achieved financial independence solely on her own." Fern, Warren continues, "unlike less sensitive writers who made minority groups and the uneducated classes the butt of their humor, always directed her satire at pretentiousness and pomp. Her sympathy is with decent people, whatever their race, religion, or social status."[6] Fanny Fern matters in this rendering because she transcended the prejudices of her own cultural moment.[7] Augusta Jane Evans, the southern novelist and ardent supporter of the Confederacy, is more difficult to rehabilitate for a contemporary readership—in addition to her proslavery and secessionist politics, her novels recur to conventional notions of feminine domesticity and self-effacement. "Her heroines," Rebecca Grant Sexton notes in the introduction to a 2002 edition of Evans's correspondence, "after having worked hard...to establish their independence, frequently marry domineering men who demand their submission." But Sexton adds some key compensatory details, emphasizing that Evans "went further than her contemporary authors" in "stress[ing] the importance of a good education" for women and noting instances in which her female characters dedicate themselves to careers and public service rather than to marriage.[8] Even a deeply conservative nineteenth-century author must be shown to have some ideological common ground with would-be readers in the contemporary academy and its classrooms. Beyond these specific gestures the very critical practices that developed alongside the recovery of forgotten or occluded works, most obviously Jane Tompkins's influential charge to examine the cultural work that texts do (rather than what they transcendently "are"), have trained our attention on the uses—and usefulness—of literary texts and, by extension, on the effectiveness of the author in social, political, and, I would argue, moral terms.

Ecocriticism has also refashioned nineteenth-century authors to fit late twentieth- and twenty-first-century concerns and moral paradigms. Henry David Thoreau, most notably, has emerged as a key figure in the development of the field based on his exquisitely observed writings about nature, to be sure, but also on the anticonsumerist rethinking of modernity that structures *Walden*. A range of ecocritical interventions invoke Thoreau, sometimes as a central object of inquiry (most recently within food studies), but also as a kind of presiding figure, brought into the conversation to evidence a longstanding American tradition of environmental consciousness.[9] As a result, Thoreau takes on a new kind of moral authority—not his first such reimagining, as scholars and general readers had already claimed him as an antiauthoritarian hero, newly relevant within social movements of the 1960s and 1970s—that far exceeds his influence within his own cultural moment. Intriguingly, ecocriticism has also yielded a partial recuperation of James Fenimore Cooper, whose representations of frontier settlement lend themselves to conversations about sustainability, waste, and the inevitable disruptions that human beings—and especially Anglo-Americans—bring to the landscapes they enter. In his rendering of settlers' heedless destruction of natural resources—the ill-fated fish and pigeons of *The Pioneers* come most immediately to mind—Cooper is newly available as an admirable, even prescient, figure, however much his depictions of women and native peoples may continue to disappoint.[10]

It is hardly shocking that moral economies shape ecocritical approaches, given the degree to which such inquires overlap with and draw energy from environmental activism and advocacy, investments whose moral bearings seem nearly axiomatic. And yet the field has begun to evince a distinct discomfort with its own moralism: Cristin Ellis, for example, drawing on theorists who advocate "a turn from ethical to systemic modes of conceiving nature," has used Frederick Douglass's macroeconomic argument against slavery in *My Bondage and My Freedom* as a way of thinking beyond ecocriticism's immersion in ethics-based appeals (what Douglass's contemporaries called *moral suasion*).[11] Taking up a more recent archive, Nicole Seymour's investigations of "bad environmentalism" seek alternatives to the "sanctimonious" tone of much ecocinema, films that routinely "solicit serious affective responses from viewers, such as reverence, guilt, dread, and conviction"; irony, she maintains, offers an alternative that need not be consigned to apolitical or ineffective realms.[12] David Ingram, meanwhile, asks if a film that treats environmental themes can "be moralist but not moralistic"—a question whose framing, I would argue, concedes what ought instead to be interrogated.[13] Even nature writers themselves are worried; Jenny Price laments in her essay "Thirteen Ways of Seeing Nature in L.A." that "the venerable American literature of nature writing has become distressingly marginal," owing to its "earnest, pious" reputation.[14] Insofar as nature writing reads like nineteenth-century didactic literature, she suggests, it's doomed to obscurity. And yet the anxieties erupting within ecocriticism seem more trained on tone than purpose; the problem is not that these texts have a moral agenda, but rather that they sound too much like they do.

I point to these ongoing investments in authorship's moral economies as evidence that the nineteenth century's preoccupations inform and adumbrate our own. My goal, though, is not to devise a means of arriving at a purer post-moralism. On the contrary, I rather like the idea that texts and their authors might improve us—though I admittedly have an unusually high tolerance for literary didacticism, relative to my peers—and I vehemently object to the notion that such aims inevitably forestall analytical complexity or aesthetic pleasure.[15] The claim that serious literary study requires a suspension of moral judgment is poorly premised and, in any case, unworkable, as my attention to the matter's various forms of reemergence demonstrates. I advocate instead that the field take these moral economies as objects of inquiry in their own right, so that we might arrive at more nuanced understandings of how reputation, markets, and literary value shape one another in the nineteenth century as well as in the current moment. As this book has suggested, the intersections between moral authority and aesthetic valuation have long been actively contested. To ignore them is to diminish our understanding not just of nineteenth-century literary culture, but of authorship more broadly conceived.

{ NOTES }

Introduction

1. "A Heroic Woman," *National Era*, Dec. 15, 1853, p. 197; "The Judgment Pronounced by Hon. Richard H. Baker upon Mrs. Douglass, for Learning Children to Read in Virginia—Her Fine and Final Imprisonment," *Frederick Douglass' Paper*, Feb. 24, 1854, p. 3.

2. "Selections. Reply to the Atrocious Decision of Judge Richard H. Baker," *Liberator*, Sept. 15, 1854, p. 145.

3. "Duties of Massachusetts. Speech of Hon. Charles Sumner, at the Republican Convention, at Worcester, September 7, 1854," *Liberator*, Sept. 15, 1854, p. 145. Curiously, the previous issue of the *Liberator* (Sept. 8, 1854) included a long excerpt from *Educational Laws*, in which Douglass specifically stated that she was not an abolitionist. The editorial headnote introduced this passage as a "frank declaration," but offered no further commentary on the matter ("Education a Criminal Offence," p. 142).

4. An important exception is a piece in the *Provincial Freeman*, which called Margaret Douglass "an active friend of, not the slave, but the slaveholder" ("Mrs. Douglass on Amalgamation," *Provincial Freeman* [Toronto, Canada West], Dec. 16, 1854, p. 2).

5. "The Case of Margaret Douglass," *National Anti-Slavery Standard*; rpt. in *Anti-Slavery Bugle* [New-Lisbon, OH], July 18, 1857, p. 1.

6. William Craft, *Running a Thousand Miles for Freedom; or, The Escape of William and Ellen Craft from Slavery*, ed. John Ernest (Acton, MA: Copley, 2000), p. 23. On Craft's appropriations, see Geoffrey Sanborn, "The Plagiarist's Craft: Fugitivity and Theatricality in *Running a Thousand Miles for Freedom*," *PMLA* 128.4 (2013): pp. 907–22.

7. Eliza Wigham, *The Antislavery Cause in America and Its Martyrs* (London: A. W. Bennett, 1863). Traces of Margaret Douglass's categorization as an antislavery author remain in the archiving of her narrative; a copy is included, for example, in the Samuel J. May Anti-Slavery Collection at Cornell University Library.

8. The excerpt reprinted in the *Liberator* hinted at this self-positioning, insofar as Douglass called herself "a Southern woman, in every sense of the word" ("Selections," p. 145).

9. Margaret Douglass, *Educational Laws of Virginia: The Personal Narrative of Mrs. Margaret Douglass, a Southern Woman, Who Was Imprisoned for One Month, in the Common Jail of Norfolk, under the Laws of Virginia, for the Crime of Teaching Free Colored Children to Read* (Boston: Jewett, 1854), p. 2, p. 33, p. 33.

10. Douglass, *Educational Laws*, p. 65.

11. *Frederick Douglass' Paper* also covered Margaret Douglass's case without reference to her proslavery politics (see "Decision of Judge Baker in the Case of Mrs. Douglass," *Frederick Douglass' Paper*, Feb. 24, 1854, p. 2). Apart from the *Provincial Freeman*'s critical coverage (see note 4), the only external reference I have found to Douglass's stated position on slavery appears in an article from the Dedham (MA) *Gazette*, which was reprinted in the November 9, 1855 issue of *Frederick Douglass' Paper*. Acknowledging that Mrs. Douglass was "brought up to

endure slavery," the article nevertheless praises her as "a kind and compassionate woman" who "felt a sympathy for the ignorance and suffering of its poor victims" ("Retribution," p. 3).

12. As Michael Everton has shown, publishers also cultivated, protected, and repaired their moral authority within the nineteenth century's expanding print marketplace. My emphasis on authors owes to an interest in the circulation of reputation in the broader culture, beyond "the trade" that Everton's book so effectively illuminates (*The Grand Chorus of Complaint: Authors and the Business Ethics of American Publishing* [New York: Oxford University Press, 2012]).

13. "To Mrs. Harriet Beecher Stowe," *Frederick Douglass' Paper*, Feb. 3, 1854, p. 3.

14. The reviewer writes that "Mrs. Stowe betrays a malignity so remarkable that the petticoat lifts of itself, and we see the hoof of the beast under the table" ("Art. VIII.—Stowe's Key to Uncle Tom's Cabin," *Southern Quarterly Review*, July 1853, p. 226).

15. Sean Latham, *The Art of Scandal: Modernism, Libel Law, and the Roman à Clef* (New York: Oxford University Press, 2009), p. 7; Nathaniel Hawthorne, *The Blithedale Romance and Fanshawe*, vol. 3 of *The Centenary Edition of the Works of Nathaniel Hawthorne*, ed. William Charvat, et al. (Columbus: Ohio State University Press, 1964), p. 2.

16. On the cultural resonances of character and its analogues in the nineteenth century, see Scott E. Casper, *Constructing American Lives: Biography and Culture in Nineteenth-Century America* (Chapel Hill: University of North Carolina Press, 1999); Karen Halttunen, *Confidence Men and Painted Women: A Study of Middle-Class Culture in America, 1830–1870* (New Haven, CT: Yale University Press, 1982); Judy Hilkey, *Character Is Capital: Success Manuals and Manhood in Gilded Age America* (Chapel Hill: University of North Carolina Press, 1997); Nancy Ruttenburg, *Democratic Personality: Popular Voice and the Trial of American Authorship* (Redwood City, CA: Stanford University Press, 1998); James Salazar, *Bodies of Reform: The Rhetoric of Character in Gilded Age America* (New York: New York University Press, 2010); and Warren I. Susman, "'Personality' and the Making of Twentieth-Century Culture," in *Culture As History: The Transformation of American Society in the Twentieth Century* (New York: Pantheon, 1984).

17. Thomas Augst, *The Clerk's Tale: Young Men and Moral Life in Nineteenth-Century America* (Chicago: University of Chicago Press, 2003), p. 4.

18. Augst, "Introduction: The Moral Economy of Literacy," *Clerk's Tale*, pp. 1–17; Hilkey, *Character Is Capital*, esp. pp. 126–41. Hilkey makes the apt point that a worker's good character often brought material gains to his or her employer rather than to the individual him/herself (p. 141).

19. Scott A. Sandage, *Born Losers: A History of Failure in America* (Cambridge, MA: Harvard University Press, 2005), p. 144.

20. Sandage, *Born Losers*, p. 100, 129.

21. E. P. Thompson, "The Moral Economy of the English Crowd in the Eighteenth Century," *Past and Present* no. 50 (1971): pp. 76–136; rpt. in *The Essential E. P. Thompson*, ed. Dorothy Thompson (New York: New Press, 2001), p. 318. The term *moral economy* has had a lively presence in the social sciences, especially among scholars interested in moral decision-making within industrialized and capitalist economies. See, for example, William J. Booth, *Households: On the Moral Architecture of the Economy* (Ithaca, NY: Cornell University Press, 1993) and "On the Idea of the Moral Economy," *American Political Science Review* 88.3 (1994): pp. 653–67; and Andrew Sayer, "Moral Economy and Political Economy," *Studies in Political Economy* 61 (Spring 2000): pp. 79–104.

22. What I am calling literary property accords with the increasing levels of abstraction that attended developing legal conceptions of property generally in the United States. As Chad Luck has written, "commercial nineteenth-century models...understood property more [compared with land-based understandings of a prior era] as an abstract set of intangible rights often associated with entirely nonphysical assets (for example, shares of a corporation)" (*The Body of Property: Antebellum American Fiction and the Phenomenology of Possession* [New York: Fordham University Press, 2014], p. 10). On American literature's preoccupation with property, see also Jeffory Clymer, *Family Money: Property, Race, and Literature in the Nineteenth Century* (New York: Oxford University Press, 2012) and Eric Wertheimer, *Underwriting: The Poetics of Insurance in America, 1722-1872* (Redwood City, CA: Stanford University Press, 2006). On the history of US property law, see Stuart Banner, *American Property: A History of How, Why, and What We Own* (Cambridge, MA: Harvard University Press, 2011).

23. Like many in the field, I reject the notion that religious faith lost influence or somehow "went private" in American culture across the nineteenth century. As Peter Coviello and Jared Hickman have declared, "the secularization thesis is dead" ("Introduction: After the Postsecular," special issue of *American Literature* 86.4 [2014]: p. 645). Scholars, meanwhile, have assigned to the term *secular* a range of alternative meanings that better align with post-Enlightenment American culture. Charles Taylor, for example, uses the term to describe a context in which religious faith becomes a choice rather than an imperative or axiom (*A Secular Age* [Cambridge, MA: Harvard University Press, 2007]), while John Lardas Modern writes that "secularism names a conceptual environment...that has made 'religion' a recognizable and vital thing in the world" (*Secularism in Antebellum America* [Chicago: University of Chicago Press, 2011], p. 7).

24. John Higham, "Hanging Together: Divergent Unities in American History," *Journal of American History* 61.1 (1974): p. 13; Catherine L. Albanese, *America: Religions and Religion*, 5th ed. (Boston: Wadsworth Cengage Learning, 2012), esp. pp. 278-81. Tracy Fessenden's analysis of Protestant-Catholic conflicts over the use of the King James Bible in public schools nicely complicates this rubric (*Culture and Redemption: Religion, the Secular, and American Literature* [Princeton, NJ: Princeton University Press, 2007], pp. 60-83).

25. In this respect, nineteenth-century literary markets mirrored organizations like the American Tract Society and the American Bible Society, which Modern calls "transdenominational media enterprises" (*Secularism in Antebellum America*, p. 29).

26. Gabriel Abend, *The Moral Background: An Inquiry into the History of Business Ethics* (Princeton, NJ: Princeton University Press, 2014), p. 31, 38.

27. Carretta's research suggests that Equiano may have been born in South Carolina rather than Africa. See *Equiano, the African: Biography of a Self-Made Man* (Athens: University of Georgia Press, 2005).

28. Augst, *Clerk's Tale*, p. 5.

29. On the reception of Melville's *Pierre*, see *Herman Melville: The Contemporary Reviews*, ed. Brian Higgins and Hershel Parker (New York: Cambridge University Press, 1995). Cooper's 1835 novel *The Monikins*, addressed briefly in chapter one, was widely ridiculed.

30. Michael Millner, *Fever Reading: Affect and Reading Badly in the Early American Public Sphere* (Durham: University of New Hampshire Press, 2012), p. 98.

31. These nonprint forms of social disapproval are often called *gossip*, though gossip has long had a printed presence as well, most obviously in the form of periodical offerings

termed *gossip pages* or *gossip columns*. (The *Oxford English Dictionary* lists 1859 as the first usage of "gossip column," though the phenomenon no doubt precedes this term.) On gossip's social roles and effects, see Karen V. Hansen, *A Very Social Time: Crafting Community in Antebellum New England* (Berkeley: University of California Press, 1994), pp. 114–36.

32. James Lull and Stephen Hinerman, "The Search for Scandal," in *Media Scandals: Morality and Desire in the Popular Culture Marketplace*, ed. Lull and Hinerman (New York: Columbia University Press, 1997), p. 17.

33. Laura Kipnis, *How to Become a Scandal: Adventures in Bad Behavior* (New York: Metropolitan, 2010), p. 14.

34. See, for example, *The Cyclopaedia of American Literature*, 2 vols., ed. Evert A. Duyckinck and George L. Duyckinck (New York: Scribner, 1855), which includes favorable accounts of Cooper and Child despite their reputational difficulties in the 1830s. (The *Cyclopaedia* discusses Stowe as well, though at this point the Byron scandal has not yet occurred.) Rufus Wilmot Griswold's *Prose Writers of America* also treats Child as an important, uncontroversial author; his account of Cooper attends to some of the author's disputes with critics, but is largely positive (Philadelphia: Carey and Hart, 1849). See also Henrietta Christian Wright, *American Men of Letters: 1660–1896*, vol. 1 (London: David Nutt, 1897); the lengthy entry on Stowe refers to her as "the first distinguished woman writer of America" and, crucially, does not mention the Byron scandal (p. 188).

35. See Susan M. Ryan, "Moral Authority As Literary Property in Mid-Nineteenth-Century Print Culture," in *The Cambridge History of American Women Writers*, ed. Dale Bauer (Cambridge: Cambridge University Press, 2012), pp. 333–72. Scholars who have emphasized Child's ostracism after 1833 include Carolyn Karcher (*The First Woman in the Republic: A Cultural Biography of Lydia Maria Child* [Durham, NC: Duke University Press, 1994], esp. pp. 152, 192); Heather Roberts ("'The Public Heart': Urban Life and the Politics of Sympathy in Lydia Maria Child's *Letters from New-York*," *American Literature* 76.4 [2004]: pp. 749–75); and Travis M. Foster ("Grotesque Sympathy: Lydia Maria Child, White Reform, and the Embodiment of Urban Space," *ESQ: A Journal of the American Renaissance* 56.1 [2010]: pp. 1–32).

36. "Critical Notices," *Southern Literary Messenger*, Sept. 1836, pp. 659–62.

37. Joan D. Hedrick, *Harriet Beecher Stowe: A Life* (New York: Oxford University Press, 1994), p. 370. It is also the case that the overwhelming success of *Uncle Tom's Cabin* was a cultural and marketplace outlier to a great extent; it's not surprising that it proved to be so within Stowe's career as well.

38. *The Slave*, though originally published anonymously, was widely acknowledged (at least by 1840) to be Hildreth's work; it is now better known by its 1852 title, *The White Slave: or, the Memoirs of Archy Moore*. The *Southern Quarterly Review*'s assessment of Hildreth's *History of the United States* (vol. 6), though mixed, makes no mention of his abolitionist authorship ("Art. XI.—Critical Notices," *Southern Quarterly Review*, Oct. 1852, p. 525). Stowe represents an exception to this trend. As I argue in chapter 5, her antislavery work very much informed how her writings on Byron were received.

39. Francis Amasa Walker, "The Planter's Northern Bride," *Liberator*, July 6, 1855, p. 108.

40. See Daniel Hack, "Close Reading at a Distance: The African Americanization of *Bleak House*," *Critical Inquiry* 34.4 (2008): pp. 729–53; on African American editors and literary offerings more generally, see Elizabeth McHenry, "Spreading the Word: The Cultural Work of the Black Press," *Forgotten Readers: Recovering the Lost History of African American Literary Societies* (Durham, NC: Duke University Press, 2002), pp. 84–140.

41. Elizabeth Renker, "Herman Melville, Wife Beating, and the Written Page," *American Literature* 66 (March 1994): pp. 123–50; *Strike through the Mask: Herman Melville and the Scene of Writing* (Baltimore: Johns Hopkins University Press, 1996), pp. 49–68.

42. Robert S. Levine, *Dislocating Race and Nation: Episodes in Nineteenth-Century American Literary Nationalism* (Chapel Hill: University of North Carolina Press, 2008), pp. 179–236.

43. Baym makes this assertion in the context of her claim that Hale should be understood as "a profoundly political writer" (*Feminism and American Literary History: Essays* [New Brunswick, NJ: Rutgers University Press, 1992], p. 168). Apart from Baym's study, the most substantive treatment of Hale is Patricia Okker's *Our Sister Editors: Sarah J. Hale and the Tradition of Nineteenth-Century American Women Editors* (Athens: University of Georgia Press, 1995).

44. I offer Hale as an example in part because I wrote one of the excoriating articles to which I have alluded—in other words, I am owning up to my participation in the nationalist project under discussion (Susan M. Ryan, "Errand into Africa: Colonization and Nation Building in Sarah J. Hale's *Liberia*," *New England Quarterly* 68.4 [1995]: pp. 558–83). See also Amy Kaplan, "Manifest Domesticity," *American Literature* 70.3 (1998): pp. 581–606; Beverly Peterson, "Mrs. Hale on Mrs. Stowe and Slavery," *American Periodicals* 8 (1998): pp. 30–44; and Etsuko Taketani, "Postcolonial Liberia: Sarah Josepha Hale's Africa," *American Literary History* 14.3 (2002): pp. 479–504.

45. June Howard, "What Is Sentimentality?" *American Literary History* 11.1 (1999): p. 65.

46. Meredith McGill, *American Literature and the Culture of Reprinting, 1834–1853* (Philadelphia: University of Pennsylvania Press, 2003), pp. 187–217.

47. "Art. IV.—Narrative of a Voyage to the Pacific and Behring's Strait....," *American Quarterly Review*, Sept. 1, 1832, p. 88.

48. Trish Loughran, *The Republic in Print: Print Culture in the Age of U.S. Nation Building, 1770–1870* (New York: Columbia University Press, 2007), esp. pp. xvii–xxv; pp. 1–15.

49. On US literary nationalism, see McGill, *American Literature and the Culture of Reprinting*; Loughran, *Republic in Print*; Edward L. Widmer, *Young America: The Flowering of Democracy in New York City* (New York: Oxford University Press, 1999); and especially Robert S. Levine, whose *Dislocating Race and Nation* emphasizes the riven, contingent nature of the period's literary nationalisms.

50. Cooper was preoccupied with a negative review of his novel *The Bravo*, which appeared in the *New York American* in June 1832. Convinced that the piece, signed "Cassio," was penned by a French antagonist, Cooper characterized its appearance in a US publication as proof of Americans' excessive deference to European critical judgment, an argument that figured prominently in his poorly received volume *A Letter to His Countrymen* (1834). Cassio was actually the pseudonym of the American writer Edward Sherman Gould, who had lived for a time in Paris. On Cooper's misidentification and its effects, see James Grossman, *James Fenimore Cooper* (n.p.: William Sloane, 1949), American Men of Letters Series, pp. 87–93 and Robert S. Levine, *Conspiracy and Romance: Studies in Brockden Brown, Cooper, Hawthorne, and Melville* (Cambridge: Cambridge University Press, 1989), pp. 99–100.

51. Aaron Jaffe, *Modernism and the Culture of Celebrity* (Cambridge: Cambridge University Press, 2005), p. 2. On nineteenth-century literary celebrity, see Thomas N. Baker, *Sentiment and Celebrity: Nathaniel Parker Willis and the Trials of Literary Fame* (New York: Oxford University Press, 1999); David Haven Blake, *Walt Whitman and the Culture of*

American Celebrity (New Haven, CT: Yale University Press, 2006); Ann R. Hawkins and Maura C. Ives, eds., *Women Writers and the Artifacts of Celebrity in the Long Nineteenth Century* (Burlington, VT: Ashgate, 2012); Leon Jackson, "'The Rage for Lions': Edgar Allan Poe and the Culture of Celebrity," in *Poe and the Remapping of Antebellum Print Culture*, ed. J. Gerald Kennedy and Jerome McGann (Baton Rouge: Louisiana State University Press, 2012), pp. 37–61; Bonnie Carr O'Neill, "'The Best of Me Is There': Emerson As Lecturer and Celebrity," *American Literature* 80.4 (2008): 739–67 and "The Personal Public Sphere of Whitman's 1840s Journalism," *PMLA* 126.4 (2011): pp. 983–98; Karah Rempe, "Intimacy in Print: Literary Celebrity and Public Interiority in Nineteenth-Century American Literature," PhD diss., University of North Carolina, 2009; and Brenda R. Weber, *Women and Literary Celebrity in the Nineteenth Century: The Transatlantic Production of Fame and Gender* (Surrey, UK: Ashgate, 2012). On literary tourism, see Alison Booth, "The Real Right Place of Henry James: Homes and Haunts," *Henry James Review* 25 (Fall 2004): pp. 216–27 and "Author Country: Longfellow, the Brontës, and Anglophone Homes and Haunts," *Romanticism and Victorianism on the Net* 48 (Nov. 2007): 29 paragraphs.

52. Herman Melville, *Pierre: or, The Ambiguities*, ed. Harrison Hayford, Hershel Parker, and G. Thomas Tanselle (Evanston and Chicago: Northwestern University Press and the Newberry Library, 1971), pp. 245, 246. Subsequent citations appear parenthetically in the text.

53. On the connection to Duyckinck, see the "Historical Note" in the Northwestern-Newberry edition of *Pierre* (p. 376). Marcy Dinius analyzes *Pierre*'s thematic treatment of daguerreotypy in depth (*The Camera and the Press: American Visual and Print Culture in the Age of the Daguerreotype* [Philadelphia: University of Pennsylvania Press, 2012], pp. 86–125). On Melville's relation to antebellum publishing and publicity more generally, see Everton, *Grand Chorus of Complaint*, pp. 115–39.

54. Gillian Silverman, *Bodies and Books: Reading and the Fantasy of Communion in Nineteenth-Century America* (Philadelphia: University of Pennsylvania Press, 2012), p. 85.

55. McGill, *American Literature and the Culture of Reprinting*, pp. 45–75. As McGill has shown, the mid-nineteenth century also saw the development of a decentralized system of reprinting, in which texts, often anonymous or misattributed, circulated broadly, unanchored by stable, known authorship (pp. 17–42). Melville comments on the coexistence of the system McGill treats and the emerging culture of authorial celebrity when he has Pierre express the wish that he had begun his writing career by publishing anonymously.

56. Caroline Kirkland's essay "Lion-Hunting" offers a tongue-in-cheek account of the culture's fascination with the personal qualities and habits of authors, a phenomenon she traces to eighteenth-century England: "May we not thank ferreting Boswell," she asks, "for putting the world upon the scent?" (*Sartain's Union Magazine of Literature and Art*, Feb. 1851, p. 111).

57. By *conventional* I mean a couple of things. First, Melville was one of many mid-nineteenth-century authors who registered a deep ambivalence about authorship's relationship to the market, though that expressed discomfort did not result in any wholesale isolation from market forces (see esp. Michael Gilmore, *American Romanticism and the Marketplace* [Chicago: University of Chicago Press, 1985]). Second, I'm using the term to suggest that authors since Melville and the fictional Pierre have continued to engage in this reflexive disavowal of and dependence on the market.

58. On developing conceptions of privacy and intimacy, see Katherine Adams, *Owning Up: Privacy, Property, and Belonging in U.S. Women's Life Writing* (New York: Oxford

University Press, 2009); Stacey Margolis, *The Public Life of Privacy in Nineteenth-Century American Literature* (Durham, NC: Duke University Press, 2005); Milette Shamir, *Inexpressible Privacy: The Interior Life of Antebellum American Literature* (Philadelphia: University of Pennsylvania Press, 2006); and Lisa Spiro, "Reading with a Tender Rapture: *Reveries of a Bachelor* and the Rhetoric of Detached Intimacy," *Book History* 6 (2003): pp. 57–93. On intimacy in relation to racial and national belonging, see Peter Coviello, *Intimacy in America: Dreams of Affiliation in Antebellum Literature* (Minneapolis: University of Minnesota Press, 2005).

59. Baker, *Sentiment and Celebrity*, p. 173.

60. Ralph Waldo Emerson, "Uses of Great Men," *Emerson: Essays and Lectures* (New York: Library of America, 1983), p. 628.

61. Caroline Kirkland noted this phenomenon in *A Book for the Home Circle*: as readers, "we love the intelligent and suggestive companion of our quiet hours. We rank [the author] among our benefactors, and we long for a nearer acquaintance. His person, his voice, his every-day habits and ordinaray [sic] sentiments, acquire a certain kind of importance; and for this reason, those biographies which let us most completely into these minutiae, have ever been esteemed the most precious." And yet, the beloved author, when actually encountered, "resembles anything rather than the graceful mental image; . . . considering his visitor as a mere stranger, and knowing nothing of the invisible chain so prized by the other, [the author] chills him with indifference" (New York: Scribner, 1853), pp. 48–49.

62. Leon Jackson, *The Business of Letters: Authorial Economies in Antebellum America* (Redwood City, CA: Stanford University Press, 2008). On American authorship's shifting economies, see also David Dowling, *Capital Letters: Authorship in the Antebellum Literary Market* (Iowa City: University of Iowa Press, 2009) and *The Business of Literary Circles in Nineteenth-Century America* (New York: Palgrave MacMillan, 2011).

63. The specific advertisement referenced here, featuring offerings from the firm of Ticknor, Reed, and Fields, appeared in the *Literary World*, Jan. 19, 1850, p. 69.

64. The term *didacticism* had some negative connotations even in the nineteenth century, when it was sometimes used to signify a heavy-handed or unaesthetic transmission of moral lessons. I depart from these sources—and from most of my contemporaries—in using *didacticism* more neutrally to signal only that a work has a teaching purpose or a "moral tendency," as antebellum commentators often termed it. Within midcentury regimes of literary valuation the presence of such a purpose was typically lauded, though critics sometimes commented on the quality of its expression, a matter that I explore in chapter 4.

65. Ralph Waldo Emerson, "The Poet," *The Collected Works of Ralph Waldo Emerson*, vol. 3, ed. Joseph Slater, et al. (Cambridge, MA: Belknap Press of Harvard University Press, 1983), pp. 7–8.

66. Hawthorne, *Blithedale*, p. 246.

67. In his essay "Character," Emerson describes this externalizing element as a figure's "power to make his talent trusted" ("Character," *Emerson: Essays and Lectures* [New York: Library of America, 1983], p. 496). Emerson here refers specifically to political candidates, but the phrase has wider applicability.

68. Bertram Wyatt-Brown, *Southern Honor: Ethics and Behavior in the Old South* (1982; New York: Oxford University Press, 2007), p. 14. On the confluence of honor, character, and reputation, see also Joanne B. Freeman, *Affairs of Honor: National Politics in the New Republic* (New Haven, CT: Yale University Press, 2001).

Chapter 1

1. The *North American Review*, for example, in evaluating Cooper's early career, praised his "power of description" but lamented his weakness in "the delineation of character"; "he seems to be afflicted," the review elaborated, "with a want of knowledge of human nature, which prevents him from giving a proper degree of distinctness and individuality, and above all, variety to the persons of the drama" ("Art. XI.—*The Water-Witch*," April 1831, pp. 515, 517). The *Ladies' Magazine and Literary Gazette* made the point in harsher terms: its review of *The Water Witch* averred that "we never knew the characters in a novel so uniformly dull and disagreeable" ("Literary Notices," Jan. 1831, p. 44). Cooper's "haste and carelessness…in composition" was often noted as well ("An Essay on Writings of the Author of The Spy," *Harvard Register*, July 1827, p. 146). A piece in the *New-York Mirror*, after mentioning that the author was at work on a new novel, urged "novel readers in general, to get up a petition to Mr. C., humbly praying him to take sufficient time for the completion of the forthcoming work, and to write it over a second time, making such alterations and improvements as his own taste and judgment may suggest" ("Cooper's Novels, No. 2," Aug. 11, 1827, p. 39). Whatever his shortcomings as a prose stylist, Cooper was remarkably prolific. According to Wayne Franklin, he wrote "fully 10 percent of all American novels in the 1820s" (*James Fenimore Cooper: The Early Years* [New Haven, CT: Yale University Press, 2007], p. xi).

2. See, for example, "The Pilot," *New-York Mirror*, Jan. 24, 1824, p. 207; "Literary Criticism. M'Henry and Cooper, the Novelists," *New-York Mirror*, July 19, 1834, p. 18; and "Article 1—No Title," *Saturday Evening Post*, March 8, 1828, p. 1. US periodicals reprinted English pieces that made the same claim: London's *New Monthly Magazine*, for example, called Cooper "the Sir Walter of the New World" (rpt. in "Selections," *Philadelphia Album and Ladies' Literary Portfolio*, June 4, 1831, p. 181, and elsewhere), while a review of *The Water Witch* that originally appeared in the *Athenaeum* [London] said that Cooper was the "yclept Sir Walter Scott of America," implying that the comparison was widely known. The same review asserts that Cooper and "Mr. Irving are the pillars that support the infant fabric of American Literature" (rpt. as "Review 2—No Title," *Museum of Foreign Literature, Science, and Art*, Jan. 1831, p. 79).

3. "Art. IX.," *North American Review*, July 1826, p. 150.

4. "Cooper," *Rural Repository Devoted to Polite Literature*, Nov. 23, 1833, p. 103; italics in original.

5. Originally published in London's *New Monthly Magazine*, the article was excerpted in the *Philadelphia Album and Ladies' Literary Portfolio* (June 4, 1831, p. 181) under the title "Selections."

6. One of Cooper's advocates, for example, lamented that "among so many men of genius that are now flourishing on the fertile soil of American literature, not one should have been found yet to stand up in defence of his distinguished contemporary" ("The History of the Navy of the United States of America" [review], *Expositor*, June 15, 1839, p. 304). Even Cooper's defenders were dismayed by some of his offerings, however. A commentator in the *Expositor* wrote that "we may condemn the paucity of thought exhibited in his late productions: we may lament the misapplication of splendid abilities: we may despise the egotism, which could betray him into such lamentable aberrations of conduct: but we cannot forget, that among the pioneers of American literature he has stood foremost" ("Our Library Table," Dec. 8, 1838, p. 11). Along similar lines, a generally positive career

review that appeared in the *Southern Literary Messenger* remarked that Cooper's "spirit seemed to languish beneath a foreign sky" ("Biographical Sketches of Living American Poets and Novelists. No. II. James Fenimore Cooper, Esq.," June 1838, p. 377).

7. "Critical Notices," *North American Magazine*, Nov. 1833, p. 70.

8. In a letter to his English publisher, Richard Bentley, Cooper wrote that while he "regret[ted] that Monikins has done no better" in terms of sales, it was nevertheless his "favorite book" (March 20, 1836, *The Letters and Journals of James Fenimore Cooper*, ed. James Franklin Beard, vol. 3 [Cambridge, MA: Belknap Press of Harvard University Press, 1964], p. 206).

9. "Literary Notices," *Knickerbocker*, Aug. 1835, p. 153.

10. "The Monikins," *American Monthly Magazine*, Aug. 1835, p. 487; "Biographical Sketches of Living American Poets and Novelists. No. II. James Fenimore Cooper, Esq." *Southern Literary Messenger*, June 1838, p. 378. For a thoughtful analysis of *The Monikins*, see Stephen Carl Arch, "Cooper's Turn: Satire and the Age of Jackson," *Literature in the Early American Republic: Annual Studies on Cooper and His Contemporaries* 2 (2010): pp. 173–201.

11. "Cooper's New Work," *American Monthly*, rpt in the *New-Yorker*, Oct. 7, 1837, p. 462.

12. "*Home as Found*," *New-Yorker*, Nov. 24, 1838, p. 158. Two of the editors whom Cooper would later sue for libel (Horace Greeley and Park Benjamin) were affiliated with this periodical, though this specific article appears not to have been at issue in the legal proceedings.

13. "Review of New Books," *Journal of Belles Lettres*, July 15, 1834, p. 1. For an early assertion of Cooper's declining "fame," see "Literature" [rev. of *Lionel Lincoln*], *Minerva*, May 7, 1825, p. 75.

14. "Review of New Books. The New American Novels," *Gentleman's Magazine*, Jan. 1839, p. 66.

15. "To the Famous Litigant" [open letter from William L. Stone, James Watson Webb, Thurlow Weed, and Park Benjamin, editors against whom Cooper had brought libel suits], *New World*, Oct. 3, 1840, p. 284.

16. "Literary Notices," *Knickerbocker*, Jan. 1841, p. 72.

17. "Art. II.—*England, with Sketches of Society in the Metropolis*," *Quarterly Review* [London], Oct. 1837, p. 328.

18. "Mr. Cooper's Last Novel," *New-Yorker*, Dec. 1, 1838, p. 173.

19. *Memorial of James Fenimore Cooper* (New York: Putnam, 1852). According to Letha Clair Robertson, the original painting was commissioned in 1857 and completed in 1860 ("The Art of Thomas Hicks and Celebrity Culture in Mid-Nineteenth-Century New York," PhD diss., University of Kansas, 2010, p. 74, 76). Its location is unknown. Alexander Hay Ritchie's 1866 engraving (see Figure 1), presumably made from the painting, has been widely disseminated.

20. "Art. I.—*Gleanings in Europe*," *North American Review*, Jan. 1838, p 6.

21. Meredith McGill, *American Literature and the Culture of Reprinting, 1834–1853* (Philadelphia: University of Pennsylvania Press, 2003), p. 39.

22. McGill, *American Literature and the Culture of Reprinting*, p. 1.

23. Alan Taylor, *William Cooper's Town: Power and Persuasion on the Frontier of the Early American Republic* (New York: Knopf, 1995), p. 416. Bryant's remarks appear in a letter to Richard H. Dana, dated Sept. 1, 1825 (*The Letters of William Cullen Bryant, vol. 1, 1809–1836*, ed. William Cullen Bryant II and Thomas G. Voss [New York: Fordham University Press, 1975], pp. 195–96).

24. The importance of Cooper's status as an early or foundational American novelist was remarked on during his lifetime. Edgar Allan Poe, for example, asked "is there any one so blind as not to see that Mr. Cooper...owes much...of his reputation as a novelist to his early occupation of the field?" ("The Literati of New York City.—No. III," *Godey's Lady's Book*, July 1846, p. 13).

25. Cooper's collected letters, though no doubt incomplete, suggest that he was an affectionate husband and father and that he enjoyed warm personal friendships.

26. Warren I. Susman, "'Personality' and the Making of Twentieth-Century Culture," in *Culture As History: The Transformation of American Society in the Twentieth Century* (New York: Pantheon, 1984), p. 273.

27. Reproduced in *Letters and Journals*, ed. Beard, vol. 3, p. 271.

28. Reproduced in *Letters and Journals*, ed. Beard, vol. 3, p. 272. A slightly different text is included in Ethel Outland, *The "Effingham" Libels on Cooper* (Madison: University of Wisconsin Studies in Language and Literature, No. 28, 1929), p. 33.

29. Outland, *"Effingham" Libels*, p. 201. On Cooper's libel suits, see also Charles Hansford Adams, *"The Guardian of the Law": Authority and Identity in James Fenimore Cooper* (University Park: Pennsylvania State University Press, 1990) and Stephen Railton, *Fenimore Cooper: A Study of His Life and Imagination* (Princeton, NJ: Princeton University Press, 1978), pp. 222–32.

30. Alan Taylor's *William Cooper's Town* recounts and analyzes the rise and fall of the Cooper fortune in exhaustive detail.

31. Franklin, *James Fenimore Cooper*, pp. xxxii–xxxiii.

32. Qtd. in Outland, *"Effingham" Libels*, p. 32.

33. Qtd. in Outland, *"Effingham" Libels*, pp. 42–43. The article appeared in the *Chenango Telegraph* [Norwich, NY], whose editor, E. P. Pellet, was sued by Cooper early in the controversy. The jury in this instance awarded the novelist $400 in damages.

34. According to Outland, Cooper filed at least two libel suits against editors who had, early on, published critical accounts of his behavior in the Three-Mile Point dispute. She argues, though, that "the flood of criticism" that emerged in response to *Home As Found* "constrained Cooper to undertake with zeal the prosecution of the cases filed in September, 1837" (*"Effingham" Libels*, p. 43). In other words, the novel's reception not only spurred new suits but also reenergized older filings that had languished.

35. *Home As Found* (1838; New York: Capricorn, 1961), p. 238; subsequent citations appear parenthetically in the text. Cooper rails against newspaper editors in both *Homeward Bound* and *Home As Found*. The most unsavory character in both books is an American editor named Steadfast Dodge, whose representation as a hypocritical, self-serving, and cowardly fool no doubt fueled journalistic ire toward Cooper.

36. "Review of New Books. The New American Novels," *Gentleman's Magazine*, Jan. 1839, p. 66; "Our Library Table," *Expositor*, Dec. 8, 1838, p. 11. The latter piece expressed regret that Cooper had been "so rudely handled" by another reviewer, who had mistaken "the gentle office of the critic for that of the butcher" (p. 11).

37. "Fenimore Cooper's Libels on America and Americans. (Concluded.)," *New World*, Sept. 5, 1840, p. 210.

38. "Art. VII.," *New York Review*, Jan. 1839, p. 214; "'Once More unto the Breach,'" *New World*, Aug. 29, 1840, p. 205.

39. "Art. VII.," *New York Review*, Jan. 1839, p. 215.

40. J. Fenimore Cooper, "The Effingham Controversy," *Brother Jonathan*, April 9, 1842, pp. 414–18. These disavowals eventually extended to *The Pioneers* as well. As Alan Taylor has noted, Cooper denied that there was any connection between that novel's characters and members of his own family (especially his father and sister) in a series of 1842 communications, though he had earlier played up the novel's fidelity to real life in early Cooperstown (*William Cooper's Town*, pp. 414–17).

41. "Literary Notices," *New-York Mirror*, Dec. 8, 1838, p. 192.

42. A number of sources refer mockingly to Cooper as "Mr. Effingham" or "handsome Mr. Effingham"; see Outland, *"Effingham" Libels*, pp 53–54; p. 65; p. 91; p. 143.

43. On US libel law prior to the twentieth century, see Norman Rosenberg, *Protecting the Best Men: An Interpretive History of the Law of Libel* (Chapel Hill: University of North Carolina Press, 1986) and Richard E. Labunski, *Libel and the First Amendment: Legal History and Practice in Print and Broadcasting* (New Brunswick, NJ: Transaction, 1987). Donna Dennis addresses nineteenth-century libel law as it pertains to matters of obscenity (*Licentious Gotham: Erotic Publishing and Its Prosecution in Nineteenth-Century New York* [Cambridge, MA: Harvard University Press, 2009]).

44. Qtd. in Outland, *"Effingham" Libels*, p. 186.

45. See Outland, *"Effingham" Libels*, p. 92.

46. Qtd. in Outland, *"Effingham" Libels*, p. 72.

47. "Mr. Cooper and His Libel Suits," *New World*, Nov. 27, 1841, p. 349.

48. Cooper's legal actions against William Stone relate to the latter's review of his *History of the Navy* and subsequent commentary rather than to the Three-Mile Point/Effingham controversy per se. Outland includes these proceedings in her study because they occurred within the same time frame as the Effingham sequence and because Stone allied himself with Cooper's Effingham antagonists.

49. Qtd. in Outland, *"Effingham" Libels*, p. 113; *Albany Evening Journal*, Nov. 22, 1841.

50. *New-York Tribune*, Nov. 30, 1841; qtd. in Outland, *"Effingham" Libels*, p. 136.

51. "Cooper's History of the Navy of the U.S.," *Army and Navy Chronicle*, July 18, 1839, p. 36.

52. Stephen Railton offers a similar assessment: "Beyond question the press slandered Cooper.... And no doubt their abuse eventually hurt the sale of Cooper's novels. Yet Cooper's compulsion to take the editors to court did just as much damage to his popularity, and his digressive rantings against the press in his later novels probably put off more readers than all the bad reviews" (*Fenimore Cooper*, p. 226).

53. William Cullen Bryant to Richard H. Dana, Sept. 1, 1825 (*Letters of William Cullen Bryant*, vol. 1, p. 196).

54. See, for example, "Cooperage of the Tribune," *New-York Daily Tribune*, Dec. 12, 1842; *Weekly Tribune*, Dec. 17, 1842.

55. "Mr. J. Fenimore Cooper," *New-York Tribune*, Nov. 30, 1841, p. 1.

56. "Monsieur Tonson Come Again!," *New-York Daily Tribune*, Jan. 24, 1843, p. 2.

57. [No title], *New York Tribune*, Feb. 15, 1843, p. 2.

58. [Thurlow Weed], "Mr Fennimore [sic] Cooper and His Libels," *Albany Evening Journal*, Nov. 22, 1841, qtd. in Outland, *"Effingham" Libels*, p. 113. Weed later referred to Cooper's lawsuits as his "libel career" ("The Law of Libel," *Albany Evening Journal*, May 20, 1845, qtd. in Outland, *"Effingham" Libels*, p. 128).

59. "Cooperage of the Tribune. Trial of the Publishers for Libel at the Suit of Mr. J. Fenimore Cooper," *New-York Daily Tribune*, Dec. 12, 1842, p. 3.

60. "To the Famous Litigant," *New World*, Oct. 3, 1840, p. 284.

61. Elisa Tamarkin, *Anglophilia: Deference, Devotion, and Antebellum America* (Chicago: University of Chicago Press, 2008). See also Christopher Hanlon, *America's England: Antebellum Literature and Atlantic Sectionalism* (New York: Oxford University Press, 2013).

62. "Cooper Coopered," *New World*, July 18, 1840, p. 108.

63. Qtd. in Outland, *"Effingham" Libels*, p. 112. The piece originally appeared in Weed's own paper, the *Albany Evening Journal*, Nov. 22, 1841; Cooper sued Horace Greeley for reprinting it in the *New York Tribune* a week later.

64. [No title], *New-Yorker*, May 16, 1840, p. 142.

65. The judge's remarks are printed in "Cooper Again," *New World*, Sept. 26, 1840, p. 269.

66. Cooper seems to have anticipated the novel's negative reception. He wrote in a letter to his wife that "Home As Found is published, and will not take, of course" (Nov. 15, 1838; *Letters and Journals*, vol. 3, p. 349.)

67. James Fenimore Cooper, *Homeward Bound: or, The Chase. A Tale of the Sea* (New York: Townsend, 1860), p. 13.

68. *Homeward Bound*, p. 12.

69. On the implications of the novel's marriage plot, see Eric J. Sundquist, "Incest and Imitation in Cooper's *Home As Found*," *Home As Found: Authority and Genealogy in Nineteenth-Century American Literature* (Baltimore: Johns Hopkins University Press, 1979), pp. 1–40. See also Stephen Carl Arch, "Fenimore Cooper's Literary Offense: The 'Homely' Truth of Cooper's Satire in *Home As Found*," in *Reading Cooper, Teaching Cooper*, ed. Jeffrey Walker (New York: AMS Press, 2007), pp. 375–91.

70. Taylor's chapter "Inheritance Lost" discusses these matters in detail (*William Cooper's Town*, pp. 372–405).

71. Leland Person situates Natty's appearances in *Home As Found* in the context of his development from a "historically active and vulnerable character" in the early Leatherstocking novels (those written in the 1820s, that is) to the "nearly mythic figure" he would become in *The Deerslayer* ("*Home As Found* and the Leatherstocking Series," *ESQ: A Journal of the American Renaissance* 27 [1981]: p. 170).

72. Frederick Jackson, *The Effinghams, or Home As I Found It* (New York: Colman, 1841), vol. 2, p. 198. See also W. B. Gates, "A Neglected Satire on James Fenimore Cooper's *Home As Found*," *American Literature* 35.1 (1963): pp. 13–21.

73. Jackson, *Effinghams*, vol. 2, pp. 235–36.

74. Jackson, *Effinghams*, vol. 2, p. 236.

75. "Living Literary Characters. James Fenimore Cooper," *London New Monthly Magazine*, rpt. in "Selections," *Philadelphia Album and Ladies' Literary Portfolio*, June 4, 1831, p. 181.

76. Cooper's contemporaries frequently noted this phenomenon. The *Southern Literary Messenger*, for example, remarked that "the British press…taught the Americans to appreciate [Cooper's] genius" ("Biographical Sketches of Living American poets and Novelists, No. II. James Fenimore Cooper, Esq.," June 1838, p. 375). An 1839 profile of Cooper made a more general point along these lines: "Although the case is less so now than formerly, it is still true, that no American has the meed of praise awarded to him by his own countrymen, until it is wrung from them by the popularity which he has obtained in England. His praise here is the mere echo of acclamation from the European shore" ("American Authors. No. II. James Fenimore Cooper," *American Museum of Literature and the Arts*, Jan. 1839, p. 2). Similarly, the *Christian Register* reprinted a piece from the London

Athenaeum that noted, with condescension, that "there are American books...which the Americans read—those which have been praised in England" ("Literature of the Nineteenth Century," *Christian Register*, March 7, 1835, p. 120). The article then lists Cooper, Irving, Catharine Sedgwick, and William Cullen Bryant as authors who have benefited from English esteem.

77. Scott was also famous for his poetry, but it was in his capacity as a novelist that he figured into critical discussions of Cooper.

78. "Literary Notices" [rev. of *Memoirs of the Life of Sir Walter Scott*, by J. G. Lockhart], *Knickerbocker*, Oct. 1838, p. 363.

79. "Reply to Cooper's Attack upon Sir Walter Scott," *New-Yorker*, Dec. 29, 1838, p. 228.

80. Wamba, "A Reply to the Attack on Sir Walter Scott, in the Knickerbocker for October," *Knickerbocker*, Dec. 1838, p. 520.

81. "Epaminondas Grubb, or, Fenimore Cooper, versus The Memory of Sir Walter Scott," rpt. in *Museum of Foreign Literature, Science, and Art*, April 1839, p. 529.

82. Jacopo, "Original Literary Criticism. J. Fenimore Cooper vs. Sir Walter Scott," *New-York Mirror*, Nov. 17, 1838, p. 165.

83. A search of the *American Periodicals* database (October 1838 through the end of 1840) does not yield a single article taking Cooper's side in the controversy.

84. Cooper attempted to forestall the former criticism, claiming that Scott had forfeited any right to posthumous privacy or protection when he "commanded that his personal history should be published" after his death ("Literary Notices," *Knickerbocker*, Oct. 1838, p. 350).

85. Jacopo, "Original Literary Criticism," *New-York Mirror*, Nov. 17, 1838, p. 164.

86. *Letters and Journals*, vol. 3, pp. 13–14.

87. It's worth noting that Cooper was an equal-opportunity irritant. The *Quarterly Review*'s assessment of his three-volume *England, with Sketches of Society in the Metropolis* (1837) offers an especially contentious example, calling the work "ill-written—ill-informed—ill-bred—ill-tempered, and ill-mannered" and ridiculing Cooper's "jealous, captious, and sour egotism"; the same piece accuses Cooper of an "avowed malignity against England" ("Cooper's England," *Quarterly Review*, Oct. 1837, pp. 327, 328, 329). Another English source took issue with Cooper's tone: "In what Mr. Cooper manufactures for the American market let him consult the taste of his customers, and be as fiercely national as he pleases; but it is a little too much to bring his prejudices and his caprices to the market of London" ("The Bravo.—Mr. Cooper," *Athenaeum*, rpt. in *Museum of Foreign Literature, Science, and Art*, Jan.–June 1832, p. 38).

88. *Letters and Journals*, vol. 3, p. 6.

89. James Fenimore Cooper, *A Letter to His Countrymen* (New York: Wiley, 1834), p. 59, p. 98.

90. "Art. VII.," *New York Review*, Jan. 1839, p. 209.

91. Reproduced in the *New-York Mirror*, Nov. 30, 1833, p. 175.

92. J. Fenimore Cooper to Gideon Lee, Jacob Morton, et al., Nov. 21, 1833 (*Letters and Journals*, vol. 3, pp. 13–14).

93. Qtd. in *Letters and Journals*, vol. 3, pp. 4–5.

94. "Public Dinners," *New-York Mirror*, Dec. 7, 1833, p. 183.

95. "Biographical Sketches of Living American Poets and Novelists, No. II, James Fenimore Cooper, Esq.," *Southern Literary Messenger*, June 1838, p. 378.

96. "James Fenimore Cooper. With a Portrait," *Hartford Pearl and Literary Gazette*, Aug. 20, 1834, p. 5.

97. "James Fenimore Cooper," *Hartford Pearl*, Aug. 20, 1834, p. 6.

98. "The Press and the Law of Libel," *New-York Tribune*, Jan. 14, 1843.

99. Dorothy Waples, *The Whig Myth of James Fenimore Cooper* (New Haven, CT: Yale University Press, 1938; rpt. Yale Studies in English, Vol. 88, [Archon, 1968]), p. 211.

100. Franklin, *James Fenimore Cooper*, p. xii.

101. *Letters and Journals*, ed. Beard, vol. 3, pp. 7, 273. For an intensive study of Cooper's political views, see John P. McWilliams, Jr., *Political Justice in a Republic: James Fenimore Cooper's America* (Berkeley: University of California Press, 1972).

102. *Graham's*, though generally supportive of Cooper (who was a frequent contributor to the magazine in the 1840s), noted in a review of *Ashore and Afloat* that "there is one grave fault running through this novel.... We refer to the guerilla war of sneers, sarcasms and inuendos [sic], which the author wages upon every thing in American manners and customs which he dislikes. The effect is not only to provoke prejudices against him, but it injures the novel artistically" (Oct. 1844, p. 192).

103. Outland corroborates my sense that publications affiliated with the Democratic Party did little to support Cooper in the Effingham controversy. "Only two prominent newspapers of the day," she notes, "the *Albany Argus* and the New York *Evening Post*, supported Cooper actively, although other journals occasionally protested against the treatment accorded the novelist by their brother editors" (*"Effingham" Libels*, p. 19). For a defense of Cooper along those lines, see "Crokerism," *Boston Weekly Magazine*, June 15, 1839, p. 327.

104. "Cooper's Last Novel," *United States Magazine, and Democratic Review*, Nov. 1847, p. 443. Even the *Democratic Review*'s brief assessment of *The Deerslayer*—for many readers, Cooper's "comeback novel"—was tepid at best ("Monthly Literary Record. Notices of New Books," Oct. 1841, pp. 404–05).

105. "Mr. Cooper's New Work," *New-Yorker*, March 21, 1840, p. 2.

106. "Review of New Books," *Casket*, April 1840, p. 192; "Literary Notices," *Knickerbocker*, Oct. 1841, p. 349.

107. "Literary Review," *Ladies' Companion*, Oct. 1841, p. 310. The *Ladies' Companion* published a negative review of Cooper's *Wyandotte*, however, remarking that it inspired "a smile of contempt" ("Literary Review," Oct. 1843, p. 308).

108. "The Two Admirals: A Tale" [review], *Southern Literary Messenger*, May 1842, p. 361.

109. "The Literary World," *New World*, April 30, 1842, p. 288.

110. "Review 3—No Title," *Graham's Lady's and Gentleman's Magazine*, June 1842, p. 356.

111. "Review of New Books," *Burton's Gentleman's Magazine and American Monthly Review*, July 1839, p. 56. Cooper's letters indicate that the *History of the Navy* sold well, but it did not mark an absolute departure from his controversial phase, as the book's reception prompted him to publish lengthy self-justifications and to pursue further legal action.

112. "Art. V.—*The Ways of the Hour*," *North American Review*, July 1850, p. 121. There was speculation as late as 1847 as to whether Cooper could get a fair review: "We regret that personal considerations should prevent any portion of the press from reviewing his works with candor and fairness" ("The Book Trade," *Merchants' Magazine and Commercial Review* [New York], Dec. 1, 1847, p. 644).

113. Prices derive from print advertisements published in 1850. Other US authors whose works were released in uniform editions at midcentury include Longfellow and Sedgwick.

Notes to Pages 50–56

114. "G. P. Putnam's Announcements," *Literary World*, Feb. 23, 1850, p. 190; "George P. Putnam's List of New Publications," *Literary World*, May 5, 1849, p. 401.

115. "G. P. Putnam's Announcements. Works in Press," *Literary World*, March 9, 1850, p. 240; "Advertisement 4—No Title," *Literary World*, April 20, 1850, p. 409.

116. "Notices of New Books," *United States Magazine, and Democratic Review*, Oct. 1850, p. 377.

117. Michael Anesko, "Collected Editions and the Consolidation of Cultural Authority: The Case of Henry James," *Book History* 12 (2009): p. 203.

118. *Memorial of James Fenimore Cooper* (New York: Putnam, 1852), p. 69.

119. *Memorial*, pp. 10, 71.

120. *Memorial*, p. 30.

121. *Memorial*, pp. 58, 59.

122. *Memorial*, p. 63.

123. *Memorial*, pp. 63, 64.

124. *Memorial*, pp. 69, 10, 10, 14, 31.

125. *Memorial*, p. 9. One of Cooper's obituaries remarked, similarly, that the author "rose with the dawn of our literature" ("Death of James Fenimore Cooper," *New York Evening Post*, rpt. in *Littell's Living Age*, Oct. 11, 1851, p. 87).

126. *Memorial*, p. 75.

127. *Memorial*, pp. 75–76. As early as 1841, the *Knickerbocker* cited scarcity as a factor in how critics ought to assess Cooper; referring to the harshness of recent commentary, the author asked, "is our literature so affluent in great names, that we can thus afford to impale the reputation of a writer whose genius has exalted the name and the fame of his country throughout the civilized world?" ("Literary Notices," *Knickerbocker*, Jan. 1841, pp. 72–73).

128. This search for literary progenitors was gendered male, not just in the mid-nineteenth century but in the twentieth as well. For a succinct account of this bias and an intriguing counternarrative, see Jane P. Tompkins, "Susanna Rowson, Father of the American Novel," in *Charlotte Temple*, ed. Marion L. Rust (New York: Norton, 2011), pp. 450–58.

129. *Memorial*, p. 70.

Chapter 2

1. Gérard Genette, *Paratexts: Thresholds of Interpretation* (1987), trans. Jane E. Lewin (Cambridge: Cambridge University Press, 1997), p. 2.

2. Genette, *Paratexts*, p. 408.

3. Beth A. McCoy, "Race and the (Para)Textual Condition," *PMLA* 121.1 (2006): p. 156. On paratexts, see also R.-L. Etienne Barnett, ed., *Poetics of the Paratext*, special issue of *Neohelicon* 37.1 (2010); Dorothee Birke and Birte Christ, "Paratext and Digitized Narrative: Mapping the Field," *Narrative* 21.1 (2013): pp. 65–87; Koenraad Claes, "Supplements and Paratext: The Rhetoric of Space," *Victorian Periodicals Review* 43.2 (2010): pp. 196–210; Craig Dworkin, "Textual Prostheses," *Comparative Literature* 57.1 (2005): pp. 1–24; Anthony Grafton, *The Footnote: A Curious History* (1997; Cambridge, MA: Harvard University Press, 1999); Christopher Looby, "Southworth and Seriality: *The Hidden Hand* in the *New York Ledger*," *Nineteenth-Century Literature* 59.2 (2004): pp. 179–211; and Lori Ween, "This Is Your Book: Marketing America to Itself," *PMLA* 118.1 (2003): pp. 90–102.

4. "From Lord Brougham," in Frank J. Webb, *The Garies and Their Friends*, ed. Robert Reid-Pharr (1857; Baltimore: Johns Hopkins University Press, 1997), p. xxi.

5. "From Lord Brougham," *The Garies and Their Friends*, p. xxi.
6. Preface to *The Garies and Their Friends*, p. xix.
7. Preface to *The Garies and Their Friends*, p. xx.
8. Scholarship on prefaces in American literature typically attends to individual authors (e.g., Hawthorne, Whitman, Henry James) who wrote especially influential or elaborate ones. On the preface as a literary form more generally, see, in addition to the work on paratexts cited in notes one and three, Eric Leuschner, "Prefacing Fictions: A History of Prefaces to British and American Novels," PhD diss, University of Missouri, 2004.
9. Catharine M. Sedgwick, *Married or Single?* (New York: Harper, 1857), pp. v–vi.
10. T. S. Arthur, *Sparing to Spend; or, The Loftons and Pinkertons* (New York: Scribner, 1853), n.p.
11. Mrs. Mary A. Denison, *Nobody's Child, and Other Stories* (Philadelphia: Lippincott, 1857), p. 3; F. Colburn Adams, *Justice in the By-Ways. A Tale of Life* (New York: Livermore and Rudd, 1856), p. iii.
12. Catharine M. Sedgwick, *A New England Tale, and Miscellanies* (New York: Putnam, 1852), p. 11. This edition's title page has "Catherine" rather than the generally accepted spelling.
13. "Publisher's Preface," in Emerson Bennett, *Intriguing for a Princess. An Adventure with Mexican Banditti* (Philadelphia: J. W. Bradley, 1859), p. 6.
14. Sarah J. Hale, *Northwood; or, Life North and South: Showing the True Character of Both* (New York: Long, 1852), p. iii.
15. Alice Granger, *A Tale of the West: By a Lady* (Cincinnati: Hart, 1852), n.p.
16. T. S. Arthur, *Leaves from the Book of Human Life* (Boston: L. P. Crown; Philadelphia: J. W. Bradley, 1855), p. iii.
17. Nathaniel Hawthorne, *Centenary Edition of the Works of Nathaniel Hawthorne*, vol. 1: *The Scarlet Letter*, ed. William Charvat, et al. (Columbus: Ohio State University Press, 1962), p. 44; p. 45. Many Salem residents took offense at Hawthorne's representations of his custom-house coworkers. As he wrote in the preface to the second edition of *The Scarlet Letter*, the "unprecedented excitement" that the sketch had caused "could hardly have been more violent, indeed, had he burned down the Custom-House, and quenched its last smoking ember with the blood of a certain venerable personage, against whom he is supposed to cherish a peculiar malevolence" (*The Scarlet Letter: A Romance* [New York: Penguin, 1983], p. 5). On the relationship between Hawthorne's dismissal and his authorship of "The Custom-House," see Gordon Hutner, *Secrets and Sympathy: Forms of Disclosure in Hawthorne's Novels* (Athens: University of Georgia Press, 1988), pp. 18–23; Stephen Nissenbaum, "The Firing of Nathaniel Hawthorne," *Essex Institute Historical Collections* 114 (April 1978): pp. 57–86; Donald Pease, "Hawthorne in the Custom-House: The Metapolitics, Postpolitics, and Politics of *The Scarlet Letter*," *Boundary 2* 32.1 (2005): pp. 53–70; and Bryce Traister, "The Bureaucratic Origins of *The Scarlet Letter*," *Studies in American Fiction* 29.1 (2001): pp. 77–92.
18. Nathaniel Hawthorne, *The House of the Seven Gables* (Boston: Ticknor, Reed, and Fields, 1851), pp. iv–v.
19. Herman Melville, *Typee: A Peep at Polynesian Life*, vol. 1 of *The Writings of Herman Melville*, ed. Harrison Hayford, et al. (Evanston and Chicago: Northwestern University Press and the Newberry Library, 1968), p. xiii.
20. Melville, *Typee*, p. xiv.
21. Herman Melville, *Omoo: A Narrative of Adventures in the South Seas*, vol. 2 of *The Writings of Herman Melville*, ed. Harrison Hayford, et al. (Evanston and Chicago: Northwestern University Press and the Newberry Library, 1968), p. xiv.

22. Melville, *Omoo*, p. xv.

23. Herman Melville, *Mardi: and a Voyage Thither*, vol. 3 of *The Writings of Herman Melville*, ed. Harrison Hayford, et al. (Evanston and Chicago: Northwestern University Press and the Newberry Library, 1970), p. xvii. Melville's next novel, *Redburn* (1849), includes a dedication to his brother Thomas Melville, but no preface; and *White-Jacket* (1850) begins with a straightforward "Note" identifying the author's experiences as an "'ordinary seaman' on board of a United States frigate" as the narrative's main source (*White-Jacket: or, the World in a Man-of-War*, vol. 5 of *The Writings of Herman Melville*, ed. Harrison Hayford, et al. [Evanston and Chicago: Northwestern University Press and the Newberry Library, 1970], p. ix).

24. Herman Melville, *Moby-Dick: or, The Whale*, vol. 6 of *The Writings of Herman Melville*, ed. Harrison Hayford, et al. (Evanston and Chicago: Northwestern University Press and the Newberry Library, 1988), pp. xv–xxviii.

25. Herman Melville, *Pierre: or, The Ambiguities*, vol. 7 of *The Writings of Herman Melville*, ed. Harrison Hayford, et al. (Evanston and Chicago: Northwestern University Press and the Newberry Library, 1971), n.p.

26. *Pierre* was scandalous on a number of registers—it was considered by many of its early readers to be morally corrupt, most notably in its "hint[ing] at" the "horrors of an incestuous relation," as Evert Duyckinck's review alleged (qtd. in Hershel Parker, *Herman Melville: A Biography*, vol. 2, 1851–1891 [Baltimore: Johns Hopkins University Press, 2002], p. 129). Moreover, the book's flirtation with autobiography (Pierre's genealogy mirrors Melville's own in many respects, as do his experiences of authorship, in terms of both celebrity and despair) exposed Melville and his family to scandalous comment. In particular, the narrative's treatment of Pierre's father drew on enough details of Melville's own father's life to inspire speculation with regard to the possibility of an illegitimate daughter. As Hershel Parker has written, "readers of *Pierre* who knew the Melville family would think the worst of Allan Melvill, regardless of what was true and what was fiction" (Parker, *Herman Melville*, vol. 2, p. 59).

27. Herman Melville, *Battle-Pieces*, in *Published Poems*, vol. 11 of *The Writings of Herman Melville*, ed. Harrison Hayford, et al. (Evanston and Chicago: Northwestern University Press and the Newberry Library, 2009), p. 3.

28. Herman Melville, *The Confidence-Man: His Masquerade*, vol. 10 of *The Writings of Herman Melville*, ed. Harrison Hayford, et al. (Evanston and Chicago: Northwestern University Press and the Newberry Library, 1984), p. 3.

29. The reviewer writes: "Perhaps the mild man in mourning [one of the Confidence-Man's avatars]...is an emblem of Mr. Melville himself, imploring toleration for three hundred and fifty-three pages of rambling, on the speculation of there being something to the purpose in the three hundred and fifty-fourth; which, by the way, there is not" (qtd. in "Historical Note," *Confidence-Man*, p. 325).

30. Melville, *Confidence-Man*, p. 226.

31. James Machor, *Reading Fiction in Antebellum America: Informed Response and Reception Histories, 1820–1865* (Baltimore: Johns Hopkins University Press, 2011), p. 139.

32. As Machor has noted, a few contemporary reviewers discerned in *The Confidence-Man* a conventional moral, but most did not (*Reading Fiction*, pp. 195–96).

33. See, for example, Robert Stepto, "Narration, Authentication, and Authorial Control in Frederick Douglass's *Narrative* of 1845" (1979), rpt. in *African American Autobiography: A Collection of Critical Essays*, ed. William L. Andrews (Englewood Cliffs, NJ: Prentice Hall, 1993), pp. 29–35.

34. William L. Andrews, *To Tell a Free Story: The First Century of Afro-American Autobiography, 1760–1865* (Champaign: University of Illinois Press, 1986), p. 2.

35. Ann Fabian situates slave narrators' bids for credibility within a broader context of experience-based narratives by variously marginalized figures (e.g., beggars, redeemed captives, criminals, disabled veterans), claiming that "these stories deal with questions of truth and authority in surprisingly similar ways" (*The Unvarnished Truth: Personal Narratives in Nineteenth-Century America* [Berkeley: University of California Press, 2000], p. 5). While I take her point that a common history of disadvantage contributed to these homologies, I wish to claim that such forms of authentication existed on a continuum with claims to moral authority that better-positioned and even elite authors were making as well in the antebellum period.

36. Nicole Aljoe, "'Going to Law': Legal Discourse and Testimony in Early West Indian Slave Narratives," *Early American Literature* 46.2 (2011): pp. 351–81; Sandra Pouchet Paquet, "The Heartbeat of a West Indian Slave: *The History of Mary Prince*," *African American Review* 26.1 (1992): pp. 131–46; Ifeoma Kiddoe Nwankwo, *Black Cosmopolitanism: Racial Consciousness and Transnational Identity in the Nineteenth-Century Americas* (Philadelphia: University of Pennsylvania Press, 2005); *African American Authors, 1745–1945: A Bio-Bibliographical Critical Sourcebook*, ed. Emmanuel S. Nelson (Westport, CT: Greenwood, 2000), pp. 357–65.

37. *Six Women's Slave Narratives*, ed. William L. Andrews (New York: Oxford University Press, 1988); the collection's other narratives treat US figures. *Three Narratives of Slavery* (Mineola, NY: Dover, 2008) groups Prince with Sojourner Truth and Harriet Jacobs. See also *The Classic Slave Narratives*, ed. Henry Louis Gates (New York: Mentor, 1987), which positions Prince's text alongside three of the most widely read slave narratives in Anglophone literature: Equiano's *Interesting Narrative*, Douglass's 1845 *Narrative*, and Harriet Jacobs's *Incidents in the Life of a Slave Girl*. Equiano's geographical origins have been debated, but his work is commonly taught in US literature classes; the other two are unequivocally American authors.

38. Strickland narrates her conversion to abolition in the preface to *Negro Slavery Described by a Negro: Being the Narrative of Ashton Warner, a Native of St. Vincent's* (London: Samuel Maunder, 1831), a text for which she also served as amanuensis. On Pringle's interventions, see Jessica L. Allen, "Pringle's Pruning of Prince: *The History of Mary Prince* and the Question of Repetition," *Callaloo* 35.2 (2012): pp. 509–19 and Rachel Banner, "Surface and Stasis: Re-reading Slave Narrative via *The History of Mary Prince*," *Callaloo* 36.2 (2013): pp. 298–311.

39. *The History of Mary Prince, A West Indian Slave. Related by Herself. With a Supplement by the Editor. To Which Is Added, the Narrative of Asa-Asa, a Captured African*, 3d ed. (London: F. Westley and A. H. Davis; Edinburgh: Waugh and Innes, 1831), p. 41. Subsequent references are to this edition and appear parenthetically in the text.

40. Pringle's introductory letter offers a different justification for this differential naming: "The names of all the persons mentioned by the narrator have been printed in full, except those of Capt. I—— and his wife, and that of Mr. D——, to whom conduct of peculiar atrocity is ascribed. These three individuals are now gone to answer at a far more awful tribunal than that of public opinion, for the deeds of which their former bondwoman accuses them; and to hold them up more openly to human reprobation could no longer affect themselves, while it might deeply lacerate the feelings of their surviving and perhaps innocent relatives, without any commensurate public advantage" (p. i).

41. Kathryn Temple analyzes the Prince scandal's implications for English national identity (*Scandal Nation: Law and Authorship in Britain, 1750–1832* [Ithaca, NY: Cornell University Press, 2003], pp. 172–206).

42. On the complex legal history relevant to Prince's status in England, see James Oldham, "New Light on Mansfield and Slavery," *Journal of British Studies* 27.1 (1988): pp. 45–68 and Temple, *Scandal Nation*, pp. 185–87.

43. Pringle's preface to the first edition is dated Jan. 25, 1831. He dated his postscript to the second edition almost two months later (March 22, 1831); this version of the text, according to Pringle, was a "Cheap Edition" designed "to facilitate the circulation of this Tract by Anti-slavery Societies" (p. ii).

44. On Macqueen's role in the controversy, see Sue Thomas, "Pringle v. Cadell and Wood v. Pringle: The Libel Cases over *The History of Mary Prince*," *Journal of Commonwealth Literature* 40.1 (2005): pp. 114–27.

45. James Macqueen, "The Colonial Empire of Great Britain. Letter to Earl Grey, First Lord of the Treasury, &c. &c. From James Macqueen, Esq.," *Blackwood's*, Nov. 1831, pp. 748–49; p. 750; p. 751.

46. Barbara Baumgartner, "The Body As Evidence: Resistance, Collaboration, and Appropriation in *The History of Mary Prince*," *Callaloo* 24.1 (2001): pp. 262–63.

47. On the *History*'s treatment (and elision) of sexuality, see Moira Ferguson, Introduction to the Revised Edition, *The History of Mary Prince, A West Indian Slave, Related by Herself* (Ann Arbor: University of Michigan Press, 1997), pp. 1–51; Ferguson, *Subject to Others: British Women Writers and Colonial Slavery, 1670–1834* (London: Routledge, 1992), pp. 281–98; and Jenny Sharpe, "Something Akin to Freedom: The Case of Mary Prince," *Differences* 8.1 (1996): pp. 42–53.

48. Baumgartner, "Body As Evidence," p. 262.

49. On abolition's strategic engagement with market forms, see Augusta Rohrbach, *Truth Stranger than Fiction: Race, Realism, and the U.S. Literary Marketplace* (New York: Palgrave, 2002), pp. 1–50 and Teresa Goddu, "The Antislavery Almanac and the Discourse of Numeracy," *Book History* 12 (2009): pp. 129–55. A bizarre manifestation of this commercial impulse appears in the preface to William J. Anderson's 1857 slave narrative, in which the author, having asserted that he has "been whipped about *three or four hundred times*," offers doubting readers the option of "see[ing] the receipts [i.e., his scars] by paying the stipulated sum of five dollars" (*Life and Narrative of William J. Anderson, Twenty-four Years a Slave; SOLD EIGHT TIMES! IN JAIL SIXTY TIMES!! WHIPPED THREE HUNDRED TIMES!!!; or the Dark Deeds of American Slavery Revealed* [Chicago: Daily Tribune Book and Job Printing Office, 1857], p. 3).

50. The preface to *Incidents Connected with the Life of Selim Aga, a Native of Central Africa* indicates, for example, that the author was "urged by several friends to write an account of his life" (Aberdeen, UK: W. Bennett, 1846), p. vii; James Roberts listed among his motivations a desire "to comply with the earnest request of many of my friends, both white and colored, who have strongly solicited me to publish a narrative of my long and eventful life" (*The Narrative of James Roberts, a Soldier under Gen. Washington in the Revolutionary War, and under Gen. Jackson at the Battle of New Orleans, in the War of 1812: "A Battle Which Cost Me a Limb, Some Blood, and Almost My Life"* [Chicago: Printed for the Author, 1858], p. iii); and Samuel Ringgold Ward noted in his preface that "the idea of writing some account of my travels was first suggested to me by a gentleman who has not a little to do

with the bringing out of this work. The Rev. Dr. Campbell also encouraged the suggestion" (*Autobiography of a Fugitive Negro: His Anti-Slavery Labours in the United States, Canada, and England* [London: John Snow, 1855], p. v). William Hayden stated twice in his preface that he was "induced" to write his life story (*Narrative of William Hayden, Containing a Faithful Account of His Travels for a Number of Years, Whilst a Slave, in the South. Written by Himself* [Cincinnati: Published for the Author, 1846], p. 4). By contrast, Thomas Pringle's preface to the *History of Mary Prince* begins with the claim that "the idea of writing Mary Prince's history was first suggested by herself" (p. i).

51. The apparently self-authored preface to J.W.C. Pennington's slave narrative notes that the author produced the volume because he "felt anxious to save professing Christians, and my brethren in the ministry, from falling into a great mistake"—that is, of considering slavery to be largely benign (*The Fugitive Blacksmith; or, Events in the History of James W. C. Pennington, Pastor of a Presbyterian Church, New York, Formerly a Slave in the State of Maryland, United States* [London: Charles Gilpin, 1849], p. iv); Henry Box Brown writes in his preface that he felt "impelled by the voice of my own conscience...to add yet one other testimony of, and protest against, the foul blot on the state of morals, of religion, and of cultivation in the American republic" (*Narrative of the Life of Henry Box Brown, Written by Himself* [Manchester: Lee and Glynn, 1851], p. i). (An earlier edition of Brown's narrative [Boston, 1849] had appeared under a more cumbersome title.) Daniel Peterson puts the matter more generally, remarking that his "sole aim" in writing a personal narrative is "to promote the happiness of the human family here and hereafter" (*The Looking-Glass: Being a True Report and Narrative of the Life, Travels, and Labors of the Rev. Daniel H. Peterson, a Colored Clergyman; Embracing a Period of Time from the Year 1812 to 1854, and Including His Visit to Western Africa* [New York: Wright, 1854], p. vi).

52. Henry David Thoreau, *Walden*, ed. Jeffrey S. Cramer (New Haven, CT: Yale University Press, 2004), p. 1.

53. Noah Davis, *A Narrative of the Life of Rev. Noah Davis, a Colored Man. Written by Himself, at the Age of Fifty-Four. Printed Solely for the Author's Benefit* (Baltimore: John F. Weishampel, Jr., 1859), p. 3.

54. *Memoirs of Elleanor Eldridge* (Providence: B. T. Albro, 1838), p. 3; *The Story of Mattie J. Jackson; Her Parentage—Experience of Eighteen Years in Slavery—Incidents during the War—Her Escape from Slavery. A True Story. Written and Arranged by Dr. L. S. Thompson (Formerly Mrs. Schuyler), As Given by Mattie* (Lawrence: Sentinel Office, 1866), p. 2.

55. Israel Campbell, *An Autobiography. Bond and Free: Or, Yearnings for Freedom from My Green Brier House. Being the Story of My Life in Bondage, and My Life in Freedom* (Philadelphia: Published by the Author, 1861), p. v. William Hayden wrote in his preface that the "Spirit," by which he appears to mean the Christian God, commanded him to write his narrative and "endowed [him] with an education suitable for the object allotted me" (*Narrative of William Hayden, Containing a Faithful Account of His Travels for a Number of Years, Whilst a Slave, in the South. Written by Himself* [Cincinnati: Published for the Author, 1846], p. 8).

56. Francis Fedric, *Slave Life in Virginia and Kentucky; or, Fifty Years of Slavery in the Southern States of America* (London: Wertheim, Macintosh, and Hunt, 1863), p. iii; *The Experience of Thomas H. Jones, Who Was a Slave for Forty-Three Years. Written by a Friend, As Related to Him by Brother Jones* (Boston: Bazin and Chandler, 1862), p. 80; *A Narrative of*

the Life and Labors of the Rev. G. W. Offley, a Colored Man, Local Preacher and Missionary; Who Lived Twenty-Seven Years at the South and Twenty-Three at the North (Hartford, CT: n.p., 1859), p. 2.

57. On marginalized white authors' uses of external authentication, see Fabian, *Unvarnished Truth*, pp. 9–48.

58. While these character references and appeals to moral authority typically pertained to individual narrators or authors, one editor's preface asserted that, collectively, "colored men are divine instrumentalities for Divine ends," a status that, the piece claimed, explained why "so many, of them have dodged their masters and their chains,—broken through the clouds, and become conspicuous in the intellectual and moral firmament" (J. W. Loguen, *The Rev. J. W. Loguen, As a Slave and As a Freeman. A Narrative of Real Life* [Syracuse, NY: J.G.K. Truair, 1859], p. viii).

59. On affiliation and moral legibility, see Karen Halttunen, *Confidence Men and Painted Women: A Study of Middle-Class Culture in America, 1830–1870* (New Haven, CT: Yale University Press, 1982), pp. 33–55.

60. Stepto, "Narration, Authentication, and Authorial Control in Frederick Douglass' Narrative of 1845," p. 27.

61. Lewis George Clarke, *Narrative of the Sufferings of Lewis Clarke, during a Captivity of More than Twenty-Five Years, among the Algerines of Kentucky, One of the So Called Christian States of North America* (Boston: David H. Ela, 1845; Seattle: University of Washington Press, 2012 [facsimile ed.]), p. vi.

62. Clarke, *Narrative of the Sufferings of Lewis Clarke*, p. viii.

63. *Chains and Freedom: or, The Life and Adventures of Peter Wheeler, a Colored Man Yet Living. A Slave in Chains, a Sailor on the Deep, and a Sinner at the Cross. Three Volumes in One. By the Author of the Mountain Wild Flower* (New York: E. S. Arnold, 1839), p. v; italics in original.

64. *Biography of a Slave: Being the Experiences of Rev. Charles Thompson, a Preacher of the United Brethren Church, While a Slave in the South* (Dayton, OH: United Brethren Publishing House, 1875), p. iii.

65. James Watkins, *Narrative of the Life of James Watkins, Formerly a "Chattel" in Maryland, U.S.; Containing an Account of His Escape from Slavery, Together with an Appeal on Behalf of Three Millions of Such "Pieces of Property," Still Held under the Standard of the Eagle* (Bolton, UK: Kenyon and Abbatt, 1852), p. iii.

66. Leonard Black, *The Life and Sufferings of Leonard Black, a Fugitive from Slavery. Written by Himself* (New Bedford, MA: Benjamin Lindsey, 1847), p. 2.

67. *Slavery in the United States: A Narrative of the Life and Adventures of Charles Ball* (New York: John S. Taylor, 1837), pp. i–ii, p. xi, pp. 13–16.

68. Philip Gould, "The Rise, Development, and Circulation of the Slave Narrative," in *The Cambridge Companion to the African American Slave Narrative*, ed. Audrey A. Fisch (Cambridge: Cambridge University Press, 2007), p. 19.

69. Robert Stepto, *From Behind the Veil: A Study of Afro-American Narrative* (Urbana: University of Illinois Press, 1979), p. 6.

70. Henry Bibb, *Narrative of the Life and Adventures of Henry Bibb, an American Slave, Written by Himself. With an Introduction by Lucius C. Matlack* (New York: Published by the Author, 1849), p. ii.

71. Bibb, *Narrative of the Life and Adventures*, p. ii, p. iii.

72. On Wheatley's spurious trial, see Joanna Brooks, "Our Phillis, Ourselves," *American Literature* 82.1 (2010): pp. 1–28.

73. *Narrative of the Life of J. D. Green, a Runaway Slave, from Kentucky, Containing an Account of His Three Escapes, in 1839, 1846, and 1848* (Huddersfield, UK: Henry Fielding, Pack Horse Yard, 1864), p. iii; *The Experience of Thomas H. Jones, Who Was a Slave for Forty-Three Years* (Boston: Bazin and Chandler, 1862), n.p.

74. Bibb, *Narrative of the Life and Adventures*, p. xi; Levin Tilmon, *A Brief Miscellaneous Narrative of the More Early Part of the Life of L. Tilmon, Pastor of a Colored Methodist Congregational Church in the City of New York* (Jersey City, NJ: W. W. & L. A. Pratt, 1853), p. 1; Charles Thompson, *Biography of a Slave*, p. iii; John Andrew Jackson, *The Experience of a Slave in South Carolina* (London: Passmore & Alabaster, 1862), p. iii.

75. Samuel Ringgold Ward, *Autobiography of a Fugitive Negro: His Anti-Slavery Labours in the United States, Canada, & England* (London: John Snow, 1855), p. vii, p. vi–vii.

76. See, for example, William Andrews's comparison of the 1845 and 1855 narratives (*To Tell a Free Story*, pp. 217–39).

77. "Textual Introduction," *The Frederick Douglass Papers. Series Two: Autobiographical Writings. Vol. 2: My Bondage and My Freedom*, ed. John W. Blassingame, et al. (New Haven, CT: Yale University Press, 2003), p. 288. Subsequent citations are to this edition.

78. Douglass, *My Bondage and My Freedom*, p. 5.

79. Douglass, *My Bondage and My Freedom*, p. 6.

80. Douglass, *My Bondage and My Freedom*, p. 5.

81. Douglass, *My Bondage and My Freedom*, p. 6; italics in original.

82. "A Self-Made Man," *Christian Advocate*, n.d.; rpt. in *Frederick Douglass Papers* (Ser. 2, Vol. 2), p. 411.

83. Frances Smith Foster, *Written by Herself: Literary Production by African American Women, 1746–1892* (Bloomington: Indiana University Press, 1993), p. 123–24.

84. A number of scholars have emphasized the ways in which Keckley's defiance complicates this apparent quiescence. See, for example, Katherine Adams, *Owning Up: Privacy, Property, and Belonging in U.S. Women's Life Writing* (New York: Oxford University Press, 2009), pp. 121–52 and Carme Manuel, "Elizabeth Keckley's *Behind the Scenes*; or, the 'Colored Historian's' Resistance to the Technologies of Power in Postwar America," *African American Review* 44 (Spring/Summer 2011): pp. 25–48.

85. Elizabeth Keckley, *Behind the Scenes; or, Thirty Years a Slave, and Four Years in the White House*, ed. William L. Andrews (1868; New York: Penguin, 2005), p. 3. Subsequent references appear parenthetically in the text.

86. Foster, *Written by Herself*, p. 128; Susan S. Williams, "Forwarding Literary Interests: James Redpath and the Authorial Careers of Marion Harland, Louisa May Alcott, and Sherwood Bonner," *Legacy* 25.2 (2008): p. 262; Barbara Ryan, "Behind the Scenes: A Case of Cross-Purpose Editing?" *American Studies in Scandinavia* 35.1 (2003): p. 38. Ryan overstates the degree to which the narrative's ghostwritten status is a consensus position. William Andrews's 2005 introduction to the Penguin edition, for example, represents Keckley unequivocally as the narrative's author, though he references Redpath (calling him Keckley's "white editor"). The only suggestion of editorial intervention is Andrews's assertion that it is "not known" whether the decision to publish Mary Todd Lincoln's letters was "the author's or her editor's" (p. xiv). Jennifer Fleischner, who has written extensively on Keckley, adopts a position closer to Susan Williams's, noting that Keckley wrote the narrative "evidently in

collaboration with James Redpath" ("When Bridget or Dinah Takes to Writing Books Instead: Reaction to Elizabeth Keckley's *Behind the Scenes*," in *Monuments of the Black Atlantic: Slavery and Memory*, ed. Joanne M. Braxton and Maria I. Diedrich [Münster: Lit-Verlag, 2004], p. 59).

87. In her rendering of life in Washington during the war, Keckley emphasizes her role in founding the "Contraband Relief Association" and engages in some energetic name-dropping (e.g., Wendell Phillips, Henry Highland Garnet, Frederick Douglass), thus aligning herself with an activist/abolitionist elite (pp. 51–52).

88. Mary Todd Lincoln to Rhoda White, May 2, 1868, in *Mary Todd Lincoln: Her Life and Letters*, ed. Justin G. Turner and Linda Levitt Turner (New York: Knopf, 1972), p. 476; italics in original.

89. See Foster, *Written by Herself*, p. 128–29; Ryan, "Behind the Scenes"; Susan S. Williams, *Reclaiming Authorship: Literary Women in America, 1850–1900* (Philadelphia: University of Pennsylvania Press, 2006), p. 135.

90. On the book's reception, see Jennifer Fleischner, "When Bridget or Dinah"; Frances Smith Foster, "Historical Introduction," in Elizabeth Keckley, *Behind the Scenes* (Urbana: University of Illinois Press, 2001), pp. lvii–lx; Foster, "Autobiography after Emancipation: The Example of Elizabeth Keckley," in *Multicultural Autobiography: American Lives*, ed. James Robert Payne (Knoxville: University of Tennessee Press, 1992), pp. 39–40; Xiomara Santamarina, *Belabored Professions: Narratives of African American Working Womanhood* (Chapel Hill: University of North Carolina Press, 2005), pp. 151–64; and Carolyn Sorisio, "Unmasking the Genteel Performer: Elizabeth Keckley's *Behind the Scenes* and the Politics of Public Wrath," *African American Review* 34.1 (2000): pp. 19–21.

91. "Indecent Publications," *New-York Citizen*, April 18, 1868, p. 4. On mid-nineteenth-century print pornography, especially the era's "sporting papers," see Michael Millner, *Fever Reading: Affect and Reading Badly in the Early American Public Sphere* (Durham: University of New Hampshire Press, 2012), pp. 73–83.

92. "Reviews and Literary Notices," *Atlantic Monthly*, July 1868, p. 128.

93. "Literary Notices," *Godey's*, July 1868, p. 86.

94. "Literature," *Putnam's*, July 1868, p. 119.

95. "An Indecent Book," *New-York Citizen*, April 25, 1868, p. 4.

96. I have found indirect evidence of other positive responses to *Behind the Scenes*: the *New-York Citizen's* outraged reviewer laments that Keckley's book "is compared by the *Evening Mail* to the journal of Queen Victoria, and is praised by a considerable portion of the press as a 'spicy and piquant volume of interesting gossip'" ("Reviews," *New-York Citizen*, April 25, 1868, p. 3). I have been unable to locate the primary sources alluded to here.

97. "Books of the Month," *Hours at Home: A Popular Monthly of Instruction and Recreation*, June 1868, p. 192.

Chapter 3

1. Some sources give 1848 as the year of Griffiths's arrival; see, for example, Waldo Martin, *The Mind of Frederick Douglass* (Chapel Hill: University of North Carolina Press, 1984), p. 40. Griffiths's own comments, however, suggest that it was 1849. She writes in the second of her "Letters from the Old World" that "the sun hid his face, the skies went into mourning, and the rain poured in torrents when I left Liverpool in March, 1849; and just

such a day greeted me, on my return, in the *summer* month of July [1855]," ("Our Correspondence," *Frederick Douglass' Paper*, Aug. 17, 1855, p. 3; italics in original).

2. William S. McFeely, *Frederick Douglass* (New York: Norton, 1991), p. 165.

3. "Frederick Douglass in Chicago," *Liberator*, Nov. 18, 1853, p. 182. Earlier in this paragraph, Garrison writes that Douglass, as a result of his criticism of the Garrisonians, has "lost much of his moral power." Janet Douglas has noted that "several Garrisonian newspapers began to refer to Griffiths as a 'Jezebel' who was exerting a poisonous influence on Douglass and destroying the domestic harmony of the Douglass family" ("A Cherished Friendship: Julia Griffiths Croft and Frederick Douglass," *Slavery and Abolition* 33.2 [2012]: p. 268). See, for example, "Frederick Douglass," *National Anti-Slavery Standard*, Sept. 24, 1853, p. 70, where Douglass is accused of enjoying "the aid of a *Jezebel*, whose capacity for making mischief between friends it would be difficult to match"; Griffiths is not directly named.

4. Frederick Douglass, "The Liberator, Anti-Slavery Standard, Pennsylvania Freeman, Anti-Slavery Bugle—William Lloyd Garrison and Frederick Douglass: or, A Review of Anti-Slavery Relations," *Frederick Douglass' Paper*, Dec. 9, 1853, pp. 2–3; rpt. in *Liberator*, Dec. 16, 1853, p. 195–96.

5. "The Mask Entirely Removed," *Liberator*, Dec. 16, 1853, p. 196.

6. The provenance of this note is unclear. Anna Murray Douglass remained unable to write throughout her life, according to McFeely (*Frederick Douglass*, p. 154). If in fact she authorized this note, someone probably wrote it on her behalf.

7. "Letter from Mrs. Douglass," *Liberator*, Dec. 2, 1853, p. 191; rpt. in *Liberator*, Dec. 16, 1853, p. 196.

8. Augusta Rohrbach reads Garrison's motives differently. "In this case," she writes, "the letter-to-the-editor is used to quell a rumor of domestic discord, and Garrison's publication of it indicates how closely knit he wanted the movement to appear despite various kinds of internal strife" (*Truth Stranger than Fiction: Race, Realism and the U.S. Literary Marketplace* [New York: Palgrave, 2002], p. 13). Given the apparent relish with which Garrison participated in the print war with Frederick Douglass, not to mention his overt dismissal of Anna Douglass's defense of her marriage, I am not persuaded that Garrison's goal was to create an illusion of unity within the movement.

9. See, for example, Benjamin Quarles, *Frederick Douglass* (1948; rpt. New York: Atheneum, 1976), pp. 103–07; Martin, *Mind of Frederick Douglass*, pp. 40–45; and McFeely, *Frederick Douglass*, pp. 161–78.

10. The first of Griffiths's "Letters from the Old World" gives the date of her departure as June 18, 1855 ("Our Correspondence," *Frederick Douglass' Paper*, Aug. 10, 1855, p. 3). Although Douglass's "Prospectus of the Ninth Volume" suggests that Griffiths planned to return to the United States and to the newspaper, her move to England proved permanent (*Frederick Douglass' Paper*, Dec. 7, 1855, p. 2).

11. Like many of his contemporaries, Douglass brought copies of his book to sell on his lecture tours ("Textual Introduction," *The Frederick Douglass Papers. Series Two: Autobiographical Writings, Vol. 2, My Bondage and My Freedom*, ed. John W. Blassingame, John R. McKivigan, and Peter P. Hinks [New Haven, CT: Yale University Press, 2003], p. 286). On the marketing of slave narratives generally, see Rohrbach, *Truth Stranger than Fiction*, pp. 29–50.

12. Saidiya Hartman, *Scenes of Subjection: Terror, Slavery, and Self-Making in Nineteenth-Century America* (New York: Oxford University Press, 1997), esp. pp. 6–7. On the former

slave's ongoing relationship to and figuration as property, see Stephen M. Best, *The Fugitive's Properties: Law and the Poetics of Possession* (Chicago: University of Chicago Press, 2004).

13. James McCune Smith's introduction frames Douglass's sometimes contentious print persona as an artifact of his personal strength: "The same strong self-hood, which led him to measure strength with Mr. Covey, and to wrench himself from the embrace of the Garrisonians, and which has borne him through many resistances to the personal indignities offered him as a colored man, sometimes becomes a hyper-sensitiveness to such assaults as men of his mark will meet with, on paper. Keen and unscrupulous opponents have sought and not unsuccessfully, to pierce him in this direction; for well they know, that if assailed, he will smite back" (*The Frederick Douglass Papers. Series Two: Autobiographical Writings, Vol. 2, My Bondage and My Freedom*, ed. John W. Blassingame, John R. McKivigan, and Peter P. Hinks [New Haven, CT: Yale University Press, 2003], p. 19).

14. Frederick Douglass, *My Bondage and My Freedom*, Frederick Douglass Papers (Ser. 2, Vol. 2), pp. 5, 6. Subsequent citations appear parenthetically in the text.

15. Robert S. Levine sees an analogous project in Douglass's 1845 narrative, in which the author "takes pains to establish his 'consecrated' status as a black Christ, black Jeremiah, and black Moses" (*Martin Delany, Frederick Douglass, and the Politics of Representative Identity* [Chapel Hill: University of North Carolina Press, 1997], p. 13).

16. "Literature," Edinburgh *Daily Scotsman*, Feb. 13, 1856, rpt. in *Frederick Douglass Papers* (Ser. 2, Vol. 2), pp. 422, 424.

17. "Editors' Book Table," *Independent*, Nov. 1, 1855, p. 352.

18. "American Literature and Reprints," *Putnam's*, Nov. 1855, p. 547.

19. "The Author Popular His Book in Demand," *Wesleyan*, n.d., rpt in *Frederick Douglass Papers* (Ser. 2, Vol. 2), p. 412.

20. "A Self-Made Man," *Christian Advocate*, n.d., rpt. in *Frederick Douglass Papers* (Ser. 2, Vol. 2), p. 411.

21. See esp. Martin, *Mind of Frederick Douglass*, pp. 42–43. Perhaps the portrait also served to remind Garrison that Douglass, unlike the biblical Samson, had kept his abundant hair intact.

22. Michael Newbury, *Figuring Authorship in Antebellum America* (Redwood City, CA: Stanford University Press, 1997), pp. 79–118.

23. Brook Thomas, *American Literary Realism and the Failed Promise of Contract* (Berkeley: University of California Press, 1997), pp. 56–63.

24. For an astute reading of Douglass's engagement with matters of faith in the mid-1850s, see Jared Hickman, "Douglass Unbound," *Nineteenth-Century Literature* 68.3 (2013): pp. 323–62.

25. As his newspaper's title suggests, Douglass was adamant in asserting his editorial control. Early in Douglass's conflict with Garrison, the latter published a "who's on first"-style critique of Douglass's choice of title: "Suppose an individual should ask his neighbor, 'What paper do you take?'—and the reply should be, 'Frederick Douglass's Paper'—would not the inquirer naturally ask, 'What is the name of his paper?' Still the reply would be, 'It is Frederick Douglass's Paper.' 'I know you said it is his paper, but what is the title of it?'" and so on ("Reply of Mr. Douglass," *Liberator*, Nov. 14, 1851, p. 187).

26. "Miller Orton & Mulligan's New Books," *Frederick Douglass' Paper*, July 27, 1855, p. 3.

27. "Advertisements," *Frederick Douglass' Paper*, Aug. 3, 1855, p. 3.

28. *Frederick Douglass' Paper*, Aug. 24, 1855, p. 3. In this issue, the advertisement for *My Bondage and My Freedom* appears immediately below an accounting of two weeks' worth of receipts for the newspaper, listing which subscribers had paid and in what amounts. This juxtaposition suggests that the autobiography's popularity, which the advertisement so energetically touts, and the paper's solvency and good bookkeeping practices were meant to be mutually reinforcing.

29. "Advertisements," *Frederick Douglass' Paper*, Aug. 31, 1855, p. 3.

30. "Other 6—No Title," *National Era*, Sept. 13, 1855, p. 148.

31. An advertisement that ran in the *American Publishers' Circular* placed Douglass's book at the top of a list of "Popular Anti-slavery Books" that included Richard Hildreth's *Archy Moore* and Solomon Northup's *Twelve Years a Slave* ("Miller, Orton & Mulligan," *American Publishers' Circular and Literary Gazette*, June 21, 1856, p. 369).

32. See, for example, the "Young America in Literature" chapter of Melville's *Pierre* (*Pierre: or, The Ambiguities*, vol. 7 of *The Writings of Herman Melville*, ed. Harrison Hayford, et al. [Evanston and Chicago: Northwestern University Press and the Newberry Library, 1971], pp. 244–56).

33. "New Publications," *Frederick Douglass' Paper*, Sept. 21, 1855, p. 4.

34. "Our Correspondence," *Frederick Douglass' Paper*, Nov. 9, 1855, p. 1.

35. "Southern Correspondence," *Frederick Douglass' Paper*, Oct. 26, 1855, p. 4.

36. *Frederick Douglass' Paper*, Sept. 14, 1855, p. 2.

37. *Frederick Douglass Papers* (Ser. 2, Vol. 2), p. 286. The Aug. 17, 1855 issue of *Frederick Douglass' Paper* includes the following notice: "'MY BONDAGE AND MY FREEDOM.'— We have just received a large supply of this new work fresh from the Publishers. Price $1.25. Copies can be sent to any part of the United States on receipt of price, postage *pre-paid*. Friends, send in your orders" (p. 2).

38. The interdependence of Douglass's roles as autobiographer and editor are evident in the Aug. 17, 1855 issue of *Frederick Douglass' Paper*. Here an advertisement for *My Bondage and My Freedom* appears where the newspaper's business notices and editorials usually run. A second mention of the book occurs on the far right side of the same page—a more typical placement.

39. McFeely, *Frederick Douglass*, p. 121.

40. "Prospectus for an Anti-Slavery Paper. North Star," *Anti-Slavery Bugle* [Ohio], Sept. 24, 1847, p. 3; "To Our Oppressed Countrymen," *North Star*, Dec. 3, 1847, p. 2.

41. "Our Paper and Its Prospects," *North Star*, Dec. 3, 1847, p. 2.

42. "The First Volume of the North Star Completed," *North Star*, Dec. 22, 1848, p. 2.

43. "Prospectus of the Eighth Volume of 'Frederick Douglass' Paper,' Published in Rochester, New York," *Frederick Douglass' Paper*, Dec. 8, 1854, p. 2.

44. All letters cited appear in "Correspondence," *North Star*, Jan. 7, 1848, p. 2.

45. [No title], *North Star*, Feb. 2, 1849, p. 2. The *Freeman*'s editor goes on to remark that Douglass ought to be "more rigid in regard to the literary merits of some other contributions to his paper." Douglass's response turns this alleged fault into a virtue: "We have not been insensible to the literary defects of many articles admitted into the columns of the North Star," he asserts, but claims to have "only admitted such when to do so served to encourage a class of persons whose literary advantages have been fewer than those of the editor of the Freeman" (p. 2).

46. "The Great Speech of Frederick Douglass, Delivered in Metropolitan Hall," *Frederick Douglass' Paper*, Nov. 10, 1854, p. 2.

47. "A Gratifying Testimonial," *Frederick Douglass' Paper*, Dec. 1, 1854, p. 2; [no title], *Frederick Douglass' Paper*, Feb. 16, 1855, p. 3; "Did You Hear Douglass?" [rpt. from the *Middlesex Journal*], *Frederick Douglass' Paper*, Feb. 23, 1855, p. 2. These commendations were in some sense a response to Douglass's many critics within the antislavery movement, who were especially active in 1854 and 1855. Douglass's note, appended to the Dec. 1, 1854 piece, indicates as much. After remarking that he is "profoundly grateful for such a distinguished mark of approbation," Douglass writes: "We have received more than we expected, or had ventured to hope for. Philadelphia has been especially the seat of the most insidious, mischievous, and lying attempts to destroy the confidence of the colored people in our integrity, as a man, and in our Paper, as a reliable advocate of their rights, and their elevation" (p. 2).

48. "Editorial Correspondence," *North Star*, May 26, 1848, p. 2.

49. "Letter from the Editor," *Frederick Douglass' Paper*, July 30, 1852, p. 2.

50. "In the Lecturing Field," *North Star*, Feb. 16, 1849 p. 2.

51. "Letter from the Editor" *North Star*, April 10, 1851, p. 2.

52. "The Great Speech of Frederick Douglass, Delivered in Metropolitan Hall. Fifteen Hundred People Present. Immense Enthusiasm. Full Report of the Speech" [rpt. from the *Chicago Daily Tribune*], *Frederick Douglass' Paper*, Nov. 10, 1854, p. 2. Julia Griffiths lamented in the paper's next issue that "the speech delivered by Frederick Douglass, at Chicago, was sadly marred, by several blunders, in reproducing it in our columns last week" ("Very Strange and Very Annoying," Nov. 17, 1854, p. 2). On the Western Reserve College speech, titled "The Claims of the Negro Ethnologically Considered," see Hickman, "Douglass Unbound."

53. Robert S. Levine, *Martin Delany, Frederick Douglass, and the Politics of Representative Identity* (Chapel Hill: University of North Carolina Press, 1997), p. 19. Garrison's comment appeared in a letter to Douglass, which the former published in the July 23, 1847 issue of the *Liberator*.

54. [No title], *North Star*, March 31, 1848, p. 2; "Home Again," *Frederick Douglass' Paper*, Feb. 17, 1854, p. 2; "The Campaign in Illinois," *Frederick Douglass' Paper*, Dec. 1, 1854, p. 2.

55. "Letter from the Editor," *North Star*, Nov. 23, 1849, p. 2.

56. "Letter from the Editor," *Frederick Douglass' Paper*, Oct. 29, 1852, p. 2.

57. [No title], *North Star*, Nov. 17, 1848 p. 2.

58. "Editorial Correspondence," *North Star*, Oct. 12, 1849, p. 2.

59. [No title], *North Star*, March 31, 1848, p. 2.

60. "Letter from the Editor," *North Star*, Nov. 30, 1849, p. 2.

61. "Editorial Correspondence," *North Star*, Oct. 12, 1849, p. 2.

62. Douglass occasionally shows a flash of humor in the face of these tensions. In a letter from the editor penned during one of his many absences from Rochester, he thanks readers for their patience with his diminished editorial output, but asks them to "observe... that I do not regard your singular forbearance as the result of any want of interest in my learned editorials! For to suppose that you do not *seriously* feel the loss of my valuable contributions would be wantonly to rob you of the high credit always due to generous self-sacrifice" (*Frederick Douglass' Paper*, Oct. 29, 1852, p. 2).

63. "About Ourselves," *North Star*, Dec. 7, 1849, p. 2.

64. Leon Jackson, *The Business of Letters: Authorial Economies in Antebellum America* (Redwood City, CA: Stanford University Press, 2008), pp. 164–65.

65. "The Cash System Adopted," *Frederick Douglass' Paper*, June 15, 1855, p. 2.

66. "Notice to Subscribers," *North Star*, Jan. 25, 1850, p. 2.

67. "To Our Subscribers—Bills! Bills! Bills!!" *Frederick Douglass' Paper*, Nov. 30, 1855, p. 2.

68. "To Our Friends and Subscribers," *Frederick Douglass' Paper*, June 16, 1854, p. 2.

69. *North Star*, Oct. 24, 1850, p. 2; see also "Pay Your Postage," *North Star*, April 17, 1851, p. 2.

70. Jackson, *Business of Letters*, p. 118.

71. According to David M. Henkin, the US Congress dramatically reduced the cost of sending a letter in 1845 (and further still in 1851) and introduced postage stamps in 1847 to facilitate prepayment; by 1855 prepayment was required. A year later the use of stamps (or prestamped envelopes) became mandatory (*The Postal Age: The Emergence of Modern Communications in Nineteenth-Century America* [Chicago: University of Chicago Press, 2006], pp. 18–22).

72. "To Our Friends and Subscribers," *Frederick Douglass' Paper*, June 16, 1854, p. 2.

73. "Our Paper and Its Prospects," *North Star*, Dec. 14, 1849, p. 2.

74. "The First Volume of the North Star Completed," *North Star*, Dec. 22, 1848, p. 2.

75. [No title], *Frederick Douglass' Paper*, Dec. 25, 1851, p. 2.

76. "Editorial Correspondence," *North Star*, April 27, 1849, p. 2.

77. "Perplexities of an Editor," *Frederick Douglass' Paper*, March 4, 1852, p. 2.

78. "To Our Readers and Patrons. Our Eighth Volume," *Frederick Douglass' Paper*, Dec. 15, 1854, p. 2.

79. Robert Fanuzzi has argued that the "bitter schism between Garrison and Douglass" is best understood "as a publicity war between two rivals in the newspaper trade in which libels and personal depredations were the accepted means of attack" (*Abolition's Public Sphere* [Minneapolis: University of Minnesota Press, 2003], p. 109). My claims in this chapter are largely congruent with Fanuzzi's characterization, though I suggest that, for Douglass, the risks of engaging those "libels" and "depredations" were especially keen.

80. Rev. of *Narrative of the Life of Henry Bibb*, *North Star*, Aug. 17, 1849, p. 2; "Slanderers," *North Star*, Oct. 26, 1849, p. 2.

81. Frederick Douglass, "The Liberator, Anti-Slavery Standard, Pennsylvania Freeman, Anti-Slavery Bugle," pp. 2–3.

82. "Rev. Henry H. Garnet," *North Star*, Aug. 17, 1849, p. 2. According to Douglass, the charge of instability was made in the course of Garnet's "speech at the Auburn celebration" (p. 2); contextual clues place the speech in late July or early August of 1849.

83. Douglass, "The Liberator, Anti-Slavery Standard, Pennsylvania Freeman, Anti-Slavery Bugle," p. 2.

84. Douglass, "The Liberator, Anti-Slavery Standard, Pennsylvania Freeman, Anti-Slavery Bugle," p. 2.

85. "To Our Readers and Patrons. Our Eighth Volume," *Frederick Douglass' Paper*, Dec. 15, 1854, p. 2.

86. Qtd. in Frederick Douglass, *Autobiographies* (New York: Library of America, 1994), p. 1079.

87. On the complexities of Douglass's representativeness, see Levine, *Martin Delany, Frederick Douglass, and the Politics of Representative Identity*.

88. As Douglass himself puts it, the failure of his newspaper would have "contribute[d] another proof of the mental and moral deficiencies of my race" (*My Bondage and My Freedom*, p. 226).

89. Of his daughter's segregation within and eventual expulsion from Seward Seminary, Douglass writes: "If this were a private affair, only affecting myself and family, I should possibly allow it to pass without attracting public attention to it; but such is not the case. It is a deliberate attempt to degrade and injure a large class of persons" ("H. G. Warner, Esq., [Editor of the Rochester Courier.]," *North Star*, Sept. 22, 1848, p. 2). For references to family illness, see [no title], *North Star*, March 30, 1849, p. 2 and [no title], *Frederick Douglass' Paper*, Oct. 27, 1854, p. 2. In the latter instance Julia Griffiths is reporting on Douglass's health.

90. Douglass writes that, while in hiding in New York, his "intended wife, Anna, came on from Baltimore... and, in the presence of... Mr. Ruggles, we were married" (p. 196). Douglass's rendering of David Ruggles, an African American active in New York City's Vigilance Committee, is far more detailed than his description of wife or wedding. A few pages later Douglass mentions his wife again, noting that she was "unable to work" during that first winter in New Bedford and that he had "supplied" her with "food and some necessary articles of furniture" (p. 201). Anna Douglass's circumstances may have been related to pregnancy; the couple's first child, Rosetta, was born the following June (of 1839) (see McFeely, *Frederick Douglass*, p. 81).

Chapter 4

1. For evidence of Arthur's status as a brand, see the following: "We have not been able to look over this work [the May 1845 issue of Arthur's *Lady's Magazine*], but can recommend it from the character of the editor" ("Books Received," *Littell's Living Age*, May 3, 1845, p. 201); "on the credit of Mr. Arthur's authorship we recommend [*The Wife: A Story for My Young Countrywomen*] to young ladies, although we have not yet read it" ("Books Received," *Littell's Living Age*, July 5, 1845, p. 10); and "Arthur's novels are always... morally instructive" ("Review of New Books," *Peterson's*, May 1852, p. 272).

2. "Literary Notices," *Godey's Lady's Book*, Jan. 1860, p. 83. The magazine's unstinting praise of Arthur had commercial entanglements: *Godey's* had a bundling agreement (sometimes called "clubbing") with *Arthur's Home Gazette* and later his *Home Magazine*, whereby a subscriber could order the two publications at a discounted price. *Godey's* advertised these options extensively in the 1850s and 1860s. *Godey's* bestowed a name-as-moral-guarantee status on less famous authors as well: a brief review of *Ida Norman; or, Trials and their Uses* (1848; 1854) by Mrs. Lincoln Phelps, for example, insisted that "it is unnecessary to say that the moral aim of the book is pure and high. The name of the authoress is a sufficient guarantee for that" ("Literary Notices," Feb. 1855, p. 178); referring to a volume of poems by William Tappan, the *Godey's* reviewer similarly noted that "it hardly need be said that this book is of excellent moral tendency—the name of the author is sufficient guaranty" ("Editors' Book Table," Jan. 1849, p. 66).

3. The longest magazine piece I have encountered about Arthur (published during his lifetime), apart from those that include extensive excerpts from works under review, runs to just five paragraphs ("A Baltimore Author—T. S. Arthur," *Littell's Living Age*, Dec. 29, 1855, p. 782); one- or two-paragraph notices were typical. Longer articles may have run in smaller-circulation papers, particularly those in the Baltimore and Philadelphia areas where Arthur lived, but I have not located any in the chief literary magazines of the day. A two-page retrospective piece on Arthur ran in *Arthur's Home Magazine* after his death (Ella Guernsey, "T. S. Arthur," *Arthur's Home Magazine*, Sept. 1888, pp. 277–78).

4. "Books Received," *Littell's Living Age*, June 7, 1845, p. 442.

5. "Review of New Books," *Peterson's*, April 1850, p. 196.

6. "Books of the Month," *Union Magazine*, March 1848, p. 144. *Insubordination*, which was issued with several different subtitles over time, was first published in 1841.

7. Nina Baym's study of antebellum novel reviewing affirms this observation. Many reviewers, Baym writes, "could not finally separate aesthetic from moral value" (*Novels, Readers, and Reviewers*, p. 56). When critics praised Arthur for other qualities, they often linked them to his moral vigor, as when *Peterson's* noted that his "merits" were "both intellectual and moral" ("Review of New Books," Sept. 1864, p. 217).

8. Barbara Hochman analyzes this investment in "reading for the author," with attention to its perceived risks (*Getting at the Author: Reimagining Books and Reading in the Age of American Realism* [Amherst: University of Massachusetts Press, 2001], pp. 11–28).

9. Caroline Kirkland, *Book for the Home Circle; or, Familiar Thoughts on Various Topics, Literary, Moral and Social* (New York: Scribner, 1853), p. 48.

10. E. D., "Modern Fiction," *Southern Literary Messenger*, May 1842, p. 345. The *North American Review* articulated a similar faith in novels as conveyers of an author's self: "The novel, indeed, is one of the most effective, if not most perfect forms of composition, through which a comprehensive mind can communicate itself to the world" ("Novels and Novelists: Charles Dickens," Oct. 1849, p. 384).

11. "The Literati of New York City.—No. IV," *Godey's*, Aug. 1846, p. 74.

12. "Editor's Table," *Harper's New Monthly Magazine*, July 1857, p. 270.

13. James L. Machor, *Reading Fiction in Antebellum America: Informed Response and Reception Histories, 1820–1865* (Baltimore: Johns Hopkins University Press, 2011), pp. 70–71.

14. "The Genius of Charles Dickens," *Putnam's*, March 1855, p. 272.

15. "Literary Notices," *Godey's*, March 1853, p. 279.

16. "Literary Notices," *Godey's*, June 1855, p. 565.

17. "Editors' Book Table," *Godey's*, Sept 1847, p. 155.

18. Baym, *Novels, Readers, and Reviewers*, p. 173; p. 21.

19. Machor, *Reading Fiction*, p. 40–41. A review that appeared in the December 1860 issue of *DeBow's* supports Machor's impression: "Didactic fiction," the author notes approvingly, "has become the chosen vehicle of information and instruction for the present generation of readers" ("Editorial Miscellany. Book Notices, Editorial, Etc.," p. 795).

20. This retrospective preoccupation with fiction seems to me largely an artifact of the genre's centrality to twentieth- and twenty-first-century literary studies, though some nineteenth-century commentators claimed that fiction had a special purchase on moral instruction. A contributor to the *American Whig Review*, for instance, remarked that "follies and vices exemplified in the progress of a well-written novel bear a better defined and a more repulsive aspect than when glossed over by the etiquette and disguised in the sophistries of life. Thus presented, they awaken a stronger disgust than the most forcible argument could produce, and point a moral which would be unread and unnoticed in the ever-open page of experience" ("Retribution," *American Review: A Whig Journal Devoted to Politics and Literature*, Oct. 1849, p. 376).

21. On the interpenetration of advertising and literature more generally, see Jennifer Wicke, *Advertising Fictions: Literature, Advertisement, and Social Reading* (New York: Columbia University Press, 1988). Wicke argues that advertising is "a language and a literature in its own right," though it "owes its momentum to its imitations of literary texts"

(p. 1; p. 55). On the emerging linkage of "moral and consumer choices" within the era's advertisements, see Augusta Rohrbach, "'Truth Stronger and Stranger Than Fiction': Reexamining William Lloyd Garrison's *Liberator*," *American Literature* 73 (Dec. 2001): pp. 727–55.

22. The best recent treatment of puffery is Lara Langer Cohen's chapter "'One Vast Perambulating Humbug': Literary Nationalism and the Rise of the Puffing System," *The Fabrication of American Literature: Fraudulence and Antebellum Print Culture* (Philadelphia: University of Pennsylvania Press, 2012), pp. 23–64. On the economic relations between publishers and reviewers that fueled the practice, see Ronald J. Zboray, *A Fictive People: Antebellum Economic Development and the American Reading Public* (New York: Oxford University Press, 1993), pp. 10, 17–18; on book marketing generally, see pp. 17–54. In one of his many attacks on puffery, Edgar Allan Poe asserted that print itself facilitated the dissemination of false praise: "We place on paper without hesitation a tissue of flatteries, to which in society we could not give utterance, for our lives, without either blushing or laughing outright" ("The Literati of New York City. Some Honest Opinions at Random," *Godey's*, May 1846, p. 194). On the complications of Poe's much-discussed critical independence, see Meredith McGill, *American Literature and the Culture of Reprinting*, pp. 187–97.

23. "Literary Notices," *Godey's*, Dec. 1852, p. 579.

24. A back-channel message could have been delivered easily enough—the publishing firm in question, T. B. Peterson, was located within a block or so of the *Godey's* editorial offices on Chestnut Street in Philadelphia.

25. Fletcher Harper conceded that the firm established *Harper's New Monthly Magazine* primarily "as a tender to our business" (qtd. in Frank Luther Mott, *A History of American Magazines*, vol. 2 [Cambridge, MA: Harvard University Press, 1938], p. 383).

26. See Leon Jackson, "Toward a History of Literary Debt," *The Business of Letters: Authorial Economies in Antebellum America* (Redwood City, CA: Stanford University Press, 2008), p. 142–85.

27. Zboray, *Fictive People*, p. 10.

28. *Frederick Douglass' Paper*, Aug. 31, 1855, p. 3. Although the advertisement lists Miller, Orton & Mulligan (at the bottom of the text) as the book's publisher, Douglass himself was intimately involved in its marketing. For a detailed analysis of his promotional strategies, see chapter 3.

29. "Literary Notices," *Godey's*, June 1855, p. 563.

30. A brief notice of *Ruth Hall* that appeared in *Godey's* referenced the novel's scandalous exposures while maintaining a decorous, albeit snide, distance: "As a writer, the author of this volume has been very successful and very popular. Her success and popularity may be increased by this 'domestic tale;' but, as we never interfere in family affairs, we must leave readers to judge for themselves" ("Literary Notices," Feb. 1855, p. 176).

31. "Book Notices," *Sartain's Union Magazine of Literature and Art*, March 1851, p. 221.

32. Charles Lanman, "Thoughts on Literature," *Southern Literary Messenger*, April 1840, p. 297.

33. "Mrs. Sigourney's New Book," *Harper's Weekly*, March 13, 1858, p. 176.

34. *Harper's Weekly*, Jan. 3, 1857, p. 16; italics in original.

35. *Harper's Weekly*, Jan. 10, 1857, p. 32.

36. "Miss Sedgwick's *Tales*," *North American Review*, Oct. 1837, p. 481.

37. "Novels and Novelists: Charles Dickens," *North American Review*, Oct. 1849, p. 391; "Review of New Books," *Peterson's*, Sept. 1862, p. 231.

38. Art. VIII.—Edgar Allan Poe," *North American Review*, Oct. 1856, pp. 430–31.

39. "Review of New Books," *Peterson's*, Nov. 1856, p. 342.

40. "Review of New Books," *Peterson's*, July 1850, p. 55; "Review of New Books," *Peterson's*, March 1856, p. 258.

41. "Editors' Book Table," *Godey's*, July 1847, p. 57; "Editors' Book Table," *Godey's*, Feb. 1842, p. 119.

42. "Literary Notices," *Godey's*, Feb. 1861, p. 179.

43. Professor J. Alden, "The Writings of Jane Taylor," *Lady's Book*, Jan. 1839, p. 47.

44. "Browne's Roman Literature," *Literary World*, Nov. 26, 1853, p. 276.

45. "Books of the Month," *Union Magazine*, March 1848, p. 144; "Review of New Books," *Peterson's*, May 1856, p. 400.

46. "Literary Notices," *Godey's*, March 1863, p. 308; "Literary Miscellanies," *Eclectic Magazine of Foreign Literature*, Oct. 1856, p. 283.

47. Among the few outright critiques of fictional moralism is the *Southern Quarterly Review*'s long condemnation of Stowe's *Key to Uncle Tom's Cabin* (and of the novel it referenced): "The attempt to establish a moral argument through the medium of fictitious narrative, is, *per se*, a vicious abuse of art and argument" ("Art. VIII.—Stowe's Key to Uncle Tom's Cabin," July 1853, pp. 216–17). Stowe's success as a didactic novelist no doubt contributed to this impulse to undermine the larger paradigm, though it's worth noting that this reviewer was preoccupied with Stowe's own moral status, despite his skepticism regarding didactic fiction.

48. "Review of New Books," *Peterson's*, July 1865, p. 75; "Editors' Book Table," *Godey's*, Jan. 1849, p. 67.

49. Art. X.—Miss Sedgwick's *Tales*," *North American Review*, Oct. 1837, p. 475.

50. "Literary Notices," *Godey's*, April 1865, p. 374; "Reviews and Literary Notices," *Atlantic Monthly*, Jan. 1859, p. 133.

51. *Ladies' Repository*, Feb. 1860, p. 125.

52. "Art. I.—*The False Heir*," *North American Review*, April 1844, p. 272.

53. Baym, *Novels, Readers, and Reviewers*, p. 125.

54. "Editorial," *Sartain's Union Magazine*, June 1852, p. 515.

55. "Review of New Books," *Peterson's*, Jan. 1849, p. 42.

56. "Editors' Book Table," *Godey's Lady's Book*, Dec. 1843, p. 287.

57. "Editors' Book Table," *Godey's Lady's Book*, Nov. 1845, p. 226.

58. "Review of New Books," *Peterson's*, Nov. 1856, p. 342.

59. "Influence of Morals," *Southern Literary Messenger*, July 1838, p. 420; p. 423.

60. "Notices of New Works," *Southern Literary Messenger*, Oct./Nov. 1851, p. 702. The reviewer could not resist the impulse to mix sectionalism with censure: "One little favor at least we must ask of Mr. Putnam. If he *will* put forth such volumes, let him keep them for his Northern friends. We want no such portraitures of Northern society on this side of the Potomac" (p. 702).

61. On the reception of *Uncle Tom's Cabin*, see Robin Bernstein, *Racial Innocence: Performing American Childhood from Slavery to Civil Rights* (New York: New York University Press, 2011), pp. 92–145; Barbara Hochman, *"Uncle Tom's Cabin" and the Reading Revolution* (Amherst: University of Massachusetts Press, 2011); Robert S. Levine, "A Nation within a Nation: Debating *Uncle Tom's Cabin* and Black Emigration," *Martin Delany, Frederick*

Douglass, and the Politics of Representative Identity (Chapel Hill: University of North Carolina Press, 1997), pp. 58–98; Sarah Meer, *Uncle Tom Mania: Slavery, Minstrelsy, and Transatlantic Culture in the 1850s* (Athens: University of Georgia Press, 2005); Beverly Peterson, "Mrs. Hale on Mrs. Stowe and Slavery," *American Periodicals* 8 (1998): pp. 30–44; David Reynolds, *Mightier than the Sword: Uncle Tom's Cabin and the Battle for America* (New York: Norton, 2011); Robert J. Scholnick, "'The Ultraism of the Day': Greene's *Boston Post*, Hawthorne, Fuller, Melville, Stowe, and Literary Journalism in Antebellum America," *American Periodicals* 18.2 (2008): pp. 163–91; and Cindy Weinstein, "*Uncle Tom's Cabin* and the South," in *The Cambridge Companion to Harriet Beecher Stowe*, ed. Weinstein (Cambridge: Cambridge University Press, 2004), pp. 39–57. On the novel's publication history, see Joan Hedrick, *Harriet Beecher Stowe: A Life* (New York: Oxford University Press, 1994), pp. 218–24; Claire Parfait, *The Publishing History of Uncle Tom's Cabin, 1852-2002* (Burlington: Ashgate, 2007); and Michael Winship, "'The Greatest Book of Its Kind': A Publishing History of *Uncle Tom's Cabin*," *Proceedings of the American Antiquarian Society* 109, pt. 2 (1999): pp. 309–32.

62. "Uncle Tomitudes," *Putnam's*, Jan. 1853, p. 98.

63. "Black Letters; or Uncle Tom-Foolery in Literature," *Graham's*, Feb. 1853, p. 209. A letter published a few years later in the *Provincial Freeman* suggested that the "bandwagon effect" was still active: "Since the great pecuniary profit to the authoress and publishers of *Uncle Tom's Cabin*, numerous aspirants for fame and 'tin' have been ... getting up, 'producing,' and multiplying works, in some way or other, relating to colored people; and so swelling the bulk of what is now known as 'Fugitive Literature.'" (*Provincial Freeman*, Feb. 16, 1856).

64. "Graham vs. Uncle Tom," *Frederick Douglass' Paper*, March 4, 1853, p. 1. George Graham's remarks, which Douglass reprints, had appeared in the March 1853 issue of his magazine ("Editor's Table," *Graham's*, March 1853, p. 365).

65. According to Sarah Meer, scholars have identified some thirty-four texts "that made some claim to be replies to *Uncle Tom's Cabin*," though not all were explicitly proslavery (*Uncle Tom Mania*, p. 75).

66. In order to reinforce those connections, a number of anti-Tom novels alluded to Stowe's book. See, for example, *Aunt Phillis's Cabin, The Cabin and the Parlor*, and the awkwardly titled *Uncle Robin, His Cabin in Virginia, and Tom without One in Boston*.

67. "Uncle Tomitudes," *Putnam's*, Jan. 1853, p. 100.

68. "Uncle Tomitudes," *Putnam's*, Jan. 1853, p. 98.

69. "Boston," *Round Table*, Feb. 27, 1864, p. 171.

70. "Literary Notices," *National Era*, April 22, 1852, p. 66; H. J. Seymour, "Letter 1—No Title," *Circular*, April 23, 1853, p. 184.

71. See "'Uncle Tom' in School," *Frederick Douglass' Paper*, March 31, 1854, p. 4.

72. Levine, *Martin Delany, Frederick Douglass, and the Politics of Representative Identity*, pp. 58–98.

73. "George Harris," *Provincial Freeman*, July 22, 1854, p. 2.

74. Rpt. in "From the New Orleans Picayune. UNCLE TOM'S CABIN," *Liberator*, March 4, 1853, p. 33.

75. "UNCLE TOM'S CABIN," *Southern Literary Messenger*, Dec. 1852, p. 722.

76. "Literature. 'Colored' Views," *Literary World*, April 24, 1852, p. 292.

77. "A Psalm of Life," *The Liberty Bell. By Friends of Freedom*, Jan. 1, 1856, p. 136. This parody of Longfellow's well-known poem excoriates the North for submitting to southern slave power.

78. Louisa McCord, "Art. III.—Uncle Tom's Cabin," *Southern Quarterly Review*, Jan. 1853, pp. 82, 81–82.

79. "From the New Orleans Picayune. UNCLE TOM'S CABIN," *Liberator*, March 4, 1853, p. 33.

80. "A Key To Uncle Tom's Cabin," *Southern Literary Messenger*, June 1853, p. 322.

81. "Mrs. Stowe and Dred," *Southern Literary Messenger*, Oct. 1858, p. 286.

82. "Article XII.—Critical Notices," *Southern Quarterly Review*, July 1854, p. 255.

83. "Notices of New Works," *Southern Literary Messenger*, Jan. 1859, p. 80.

84. "The True Story of Lady Byron's Life," *Haynesville Chronicle*, rpt. in *Moulton Advertiser* [AL], Sept. 10, 1869 (http://utc.iath.virginia.edu/proslav/prar181bt.html); "Mrs. Stowe and Lord Byron," *Moulton Advertiser* [AL], Oct. 15, 1869 (http://utc.iath.virginia.edu/proslav/prar181at.html). Both sources appear on the site "Uncle Tom's Cabin and American Culture: A Multi-Media Archive," directed by Stephen Railton.

85. On the complexities of southerners' responses to *Uncle Tom's Cabin*, see Thomas Chase Hagood, "'Oh, What a Slanderous Book': Reading *Uncle Tom's Cabin* in the Antebellum South," *Southern Quarterly* 49.1 (2012): pp. 71–93.

86. "Book Notices, Editorial, Etc.," *DeBow's*, Dec. 1860, p. 796.

87. The abolitionist press was not above taunting southern readers for their supposed inability to resist the attractions of Stowe's novel. The *National Era*'s notice of Caroline Lee Hentz's *The Planter's Northern Bride*, for instance, insisted that "Southern readers prefer Mrs. Stowe's work to any of the replies" ("Literary Notices," Aug. 3, 1854, p. 121).

88. "Boston," *Round Table*, Feb. 27, 1864, p. 171.

89. "English," *Putnam's*, Feb. 1853, p. 233.

90. "The Book of the Age" [advertisement], *Literary World*, April 30, 1853, p. 361.

91. "Announcement," *Independent*, Oct. 5, 1854, p. 320; "Notices of New Publications," *Gleason's Pictorial Drawing-Room Companion*, Dec. 9, 1854, p. 359. The *Liberator* groups *Ida May* with *Uncle Tom's Cabin* and Richard Hildreth's *White Slave* as "three novels…which have exerted, and undoubtedly will yet exert, a prodigious influence upon the solution of the great problem of slavery" ("The Anti-Slavery Novels," Jan. 5, 1855, p. 2).

92. Henry F. French, "Make Your Girls Independent," *New England Farmer*, Oct. 1854, p. 448.

93. Solomon Northup, *Twelve Years a Slave: Narrative of Solomon Northup, a Citizen of New-York, Kidnapped in Washington City in 1841, and Rescued in 1853* (Auburn, NY: Derby and Miller, 1853); Frank J. Webb, *The Garies and Their Friends* (London: Routledge, 1857).

94. "Mrs. Stowe," *Liberator*, June 10, 1853, p. 91. On Stowe's celebrity in England, see Sarah Ruffing Robbins, "Harriet Beecher Stowe, Starring As Benevolent Celebrity Traveler," in *Transatlantic Women: Nineteenth Century American Women Writers and Great Britain*, ed. Beth L. Lueck, Brigitte Bailey, and Lucinda L. Damon-Bach (Durham: University of New Hampshire Press, 2012), pp. 71–88.

95. Scholnick, "'Ultraism of the Day,'" p. 187. The review appeared in the May 3, 1852 issue of the *Boston Post* and was reprinted in *Littell's Living Age* just over two months later (July 10, 1852, pp. 61–62).

96. "Literary Celebrities," *Christian Parlor Magazine*, May 1, 1853, p. 305.

97. "Art. VI.—Literature of Slavery," *New Englander*, Nov. 1852, p. 588.

98. "Novels: Their Meaning and Mission," *Putnam's*, Oct. 1854, p. 395.

99. "Literariana," *Round Table: A Saturday Review of Politics, Finance, Literature, Society and Art*, May 7, 1864, p. 328. The article refers to a "collection of facsimiles" brought out by

the New York City-based publisher Appleton that included "choice selections from ninety distinguished American authors."

100. On Southworth's engagement with periodicals and publishing, see Nina Baym, introduction to *The Hidden Hand* (New York: Oxford University Press, 1997); Susan Coultrap-McQuinn, *Doing Literary Business: American Women Writers in the Nineteenth Century* (Chapel Hill: University of North Carolina Press, 1990), pp. 49–78; Sari Edelstein, "'Metamorphosis of the Newsboy': E.D.E.N. Southworth's *The Hidden Hand* and the Antebellum Story-Paper," *Studies in American Fiction* 37 (Spring 2010): pp. 29–53; Melissa Homestead, *American Women Authors and Literary Property, 1822–1869* (Cambridge: Cambridge University Press, 2005), pp. 44–49; Rachel Ihara, "'Like Beads Strung Together': E.D.E.N. Southworth and the Aesthetics of Popular Serial Fiction," in *Must Read: Rediscovering American Bestsellers: From Charlotte Temple to The Da Vinci Code*, ed. Sarah Churchwell and Thomas Ruys Smith (London: Continuum, 2012), pp. 79–99; and Christopher Looby, "Southworth and Seriality," *Nineteenth-Century Literature* 59 (Sept. 2004): pp. 179–211. On Southworth's reception, see Nina Baym, *Novels, Readers, and Reviewers* and Linda Naranjo-Huebl's "The Road to Perdition: E.D.E.N. Southworth and the Critics," *American Periodicals: A Journal of History, Criticism, and Bibliography* 16.2 (2006): pp. 123–50. My findings challenge Naranjo-Huebl's claim that Southworth's reviews were largely negative.

101. "Literary Notices," *Home Journal*, May 17, 1851, p. 3.; "Literary Notices," *Graham's*, April 1858, p. 374.

102. "Literary Notices," *Godey's Lady's Book*, Dec. 1854, p. 555; "New Publications," *Flag of Our Union*, July 7, 1855, p. 215; "Literary Notices," *Graham's*, April 1858, p. 374.

103. "*Retribution, or the Vale of the Shadows* [review]," *Holden's Dollar Magazine*, Oct. 1849, p. 636.

104. "Literary Notices," *Godey's Lady's Book*, April 1853, p. 371.

105. "Review of New Books," *Peterson's*, Dec. 1855, p. 412; "*The Deserted Wife*. A Novel," *Literary World*, Aug. 31, 1850, p. 171.

106. J.G.W., "Literary Notices," *National Era*, Sept. 20, 1849, p. 150; rpt. in *Littell's Living Age*, Nov. 10, 1849, p. 282.

107. "Literary Notices," *Home Journal*, Sept. 20, 1856, p. 3.

108. "New Publications," *Home Magazine*, July 1855, p. 56.

109. "Review 18—No Title," *International Monthly Magazine of Literature, Science and Art*, Jan. 1, 1851, p. 181.

110. "Literary Notices," *Frederick Douglass' Paper*, Oct. 19, 1855, p. 3. Of the six volumes noticed in this column, only Southworth's appears without a note indicating where it might be purchased.

111. "New Books," *Albion, A Journal of News, Politics and Literature*, Feb. 3, 1855, p. 57.

112. J.G.W., "Literary Notices," *National Era*, Sept. 20, 1849, p. 150.

113. "Retribution: A Tale of Passion," *National Era*, Sept. 18, 1856, p. 150. *Retribution* was originally published in 1849; this review addresses T. B. Peterson's 1856 edition.

114. "Review of New Books," *Graham's*, April 1853, p. 509.

115. "Art. IX.—Critical Notices," *Southern Quarterly Review*, July 1853, p. 266–67.

116. "Art. X.—Critical Notices," *Southern Quarterly Review*, April 1851, p. 566.

117. "Art. XI.—Critical Notices, *Southern Quarterly Review*, Oct. 1852, p. 532. A review of *The Mother-in-Law*, published just over a year earlier, offered a similar blend of advice ("[Southworth] must pause and go into solitude, and meditate") and excoriation ("Mrs.

Southworth does not improve") (Art. X.—Critical Notices," *Southern Quarterly Review*, July 1851, p. 268).

118. "New Publications, &c.," *Spirit of the Times*, Nov. 10, 1855, p. 457.
119. "Notices of New Works," *Southern Literary Messenger*, June 1851, p. 390.
120. "Advertisement 8—No Title," *Literary World*, Aug. 17, 1850, p. 137.
121. "Advertisement 1—No Title," *Saturday Evening Post*, Nov. 23, 1850, p. 2.
122. For details, including extracts from Peterson's correspondence with Southworth and an account of the collapse of their business relationship, see Coultrap-McQuin, *Doing Literary Business*, pp. 63–68.
123. "Advertisement," *Harper's Weekly*, Jan. 3, 1857, p. 16.
124. "The War Department," *The Huntress*, Nov. 30, 1850, p. 2. Some of Southworth's advocates took the more conventional route of emphasizing her own benevolence. A piece reprinted in the *National Era* remarked that the author "divide[d] her time, when not writing, between an invalid sister—her only own sister—who is fading away in consumption...and her only son, who is prostrate with the same incurable disease." Southworth's career, the author asserted, sprang from her desire to support her ailing dependents ([no title], *National Era*, May 13, 1858, p. 75).
125. "New Books, *Albion*, Feb. 3, 1855, p. 57.
126. "Criticism" *Saturday Evening Post*, Sept. 15, 1849, p. 2; "The Deserted Wife," p. 2.

Chapter 5

1. Harriet Beecher Stowe, "The True Story of Lady Byron's Life," *Atlantic Monthly*, Sept. 1869, p. 302. (The full text appears on pp. 295–313.) See also *Macmillan's Magazine*, Sept. 1869, pp. 377–96. I cite the *Atlantic* version throughout.
2. Teresa Guiccioli, *Lord Byron jugé par les témoins de sa vie* (Paris: Amyot, 1868). Harper and Brothers published an English translation in 1869, which was advertised in US periodicals prior to the appearance of Stowe's "True Story" (*My Recollections of Lord Byron; and Those of Eye-Witnesses of His Life* [New York: Harper and Brothers, 1869]). A British edition appeared the same year (London: R. Bentley, 1869).
3. "Wax Work," *Fun*, Oct. 2, 1869, p. 36.
4. One commentator remarked that the scandal "fascinated so many people, by the opportunities it gave to skilful [*sic*] talkers to beat about and about the confines of unmentionable crime, without quite becoming indecent or rude" (*Putnam's*, Feb. 1870, p. 244).
5. In keeping with nineteenth-century practice, periodicals often reprinted previously published articles addressing the scandal, while other pieces quoted or referred to prior interventions. Many of these exchanges and cross-references were transatlantic.
6. *Fun*, Oct. 16, 1869, p. 64; see also [H. Savile Clark], *Lord Byron's Defence* (London: The Strand, 1869); *The True Story of Mrs. Shakespeare's Life* (Boston: Loring, n.d.), pp. 22, 19.
7. On the Stowe/Byron scandal see especially Jennifer Cognard-Black, "The Wild and Distracted Call for Proof: Harriet Beecher Stowe's *Lady Byron Vindicated* and the Rise of Professional Realism," *American Literary Realism* 36.2 (2004): pp. 93–119; T. Austin Graham, "The Slaveries of Sex, Race, and Mind: Harriet Beecher Stowe's *Lady Byron Vindicated*," *New Literary History* 41.1 (2010): pp. 173–90; and Michelle Hawley, "Harriet Beecher Stowe and Lord Byron: A Case of Celebrity Justice in the Victorian Public Sphere," *Journal of Victorian Culture* 10.2 (2005): 229–56. Other treatments include Jean Willoughby Ashton, "Harriet

Stowe's Filthy Story: Lord Byron Set Afloat," *Prospects* 2 (1976): 372–84; Frank Lentricchia, "Harriet Beecher Stowe and the Byron Whirlwind," *Bulletin of the New York Public Library* 70.4 (1966): pp. 218–28; Susan McPherson, "Opening the Open Secret: The Stowe-Byron Controversy," *Victorian Review* 27.1 (2001): pp. 86–101; and Susan Wolstenholme, "Voice of the Voiceless: Harriet Beecher Stowe and the Byron Controversy," *American Literary Realism* 19.2 (1987): pp. 48–65. Joan Hedrick's biography of Stowe treats the scandal primarily in the context of Stowe's growing interest in woman's rights (*Harriet Beecher Stowe: A Life* [New York: Oxford University Press, 1994], pp. 354–70).

8. The quotation originally appeared in Quebec's *Weekly Chronicle* (Sept. 11, 1869) and was reprinted in *Public Opinion: A Weekly Review of Current Thought and Activity* (London), Sept. 25, 1869, p. 381. According to the *Saturday Evening Post*, the German press denounced Stowe in similar terms, accusing her of "'the greatest literary crime of the century'" ([no title], April 23, 1870, p. 6).

9. As Naomi Sofer points out, the *Atlantic Monthly* was an early proponent of literature's movement away from didacticism, as exemplified in its first issue, in which editor James Russell Lowell's poem "The Origin of Didactic Poetry" appeared. "By privileging 'beauty' over 'morals,'" Sofer writes, "Lowell announces the beginning of a new era in American literature, one that will exclude work produced under the premise that literary activity is an appropriate extension of women's role as guardians of their families', and the nation's, moral character" (*Making the "America of Art": Cultural Nationalism and Nineteenth-Century Women Writers* [Columbus: Ohio State University Press, 2005], p. 5). And yet, Stowe would publish the "True Story," that paradox of transgressive moralism, in the *Atlantic* some twelve years later. This contradiction reinforces my claim that American literature's drift away from an investment in moral character in the second half of the nineteenth century was an uneven and contradictory process.

10. See Dickinson's widely anthologized letter (April 25, 1862) to T. W. Higginson (*The Letters of Emily Dickinson*, ed. Thomas H. Johnson and Theodora Ward [Cambridge, MA: Belknap Press of Harvard University Press, 1986], p. 404).

11. David Haven Blake, *Walt Whitman and the Culture of American Celebrity* (New Haven, CT: Yale University Press, 2006); William Pannapacker, *Revised Lives: Walt Whitman and Nineteenth-Century Authorship* (New York: Routledge, 2004).

12. Blake, *Walt Whitman*, p. 185.

13. On the shifting definitions and perceptions of authorship in this period, see Nancy Glazener, *Reading for Realism: The History of a U.S. Literary Institution, 1850–1910* (Durham, NC: Duke University Press, 1997); Mary Poovey, "Forgotten Writers, Neglected Histories: Charles Reade and the Nineteenth-Century Transformation of the British Literary Field," *ELH* 71.2 (2004): pp. 433–53; Sofer, *Making the "America of Art"*; Claudia Stokes, "In Defense of Genius: Howells and the Limits of Literary History," *American Literary Realism* 40 (Spring 2008): pp. 189–203; Stokes, *Writers in Retrospect: The Rise of American Literary History, 1875–1910* (Chapel Hill: University of North Carolina Press, 2006); Sarah Wadsworth, *In the Company of Books: Literature and Its "Classes" in Nineteenth-Century America* (Amherst: University of Massachusetts Press, 2006); and Susan S. Williams, *Reclaiming Authorship: Literary Women in America, 1850–1900* (Philadelphia: University of Pennsylvania Press, 2006).

14. See William Dean Howells, *Criticism and Fiction* (New York: Harper and Brothers, 1891), esp. chapter 18 (pp. 92–104); while Howells tends to speak in terms of the novel's

(rather than the novelist's) obligations to truth and morality, he nevertheless retains here some allegiance to the notion of moral authorship. See also his remarks on Jane Austen, whose honesty he extols (pp. 73–77). The notion of the author's retreat, associated most strongly with what critics call high realism, takes a number of overlapping forms, including a movement toward less intrusive, less self-referential narrative personae; a growing suspicion of didacticism as a disruption of textual aesthetics; a disavowal of sentimental narrative strategies and assumptions; and a rejection of the notion that authorial character determined a text's legitimacy. For a range of meditations on these developments, see Daniel H. Borus, *Writing Realism: Howells, James, and Norris in the Mass Market* (Chapel Hill: University of North Carolina Press, 1989); Glazener, *Reading for Realism*, esp. pp. 111–46; Barbara Hochman, *Getting at the Author: Reimagining Books and Reading in the Age of American Realism* (Amherst: University of Massachusetts Press, 2001); and Melissa Homestead, "'Links of Similitude': The Narrator of *The Country of the Pointed Firs* and Author-Reader Relations at the End of the Nineteenth Century," in *Jewett and Her Contemporaries: Reshaping the Canon*, ed. Karen L. Kilcup and Thomas S. Edwards (Gainesville: University Press of Florida, 1999), pp. 76–98.

15. *Boston Times* article, qtd. in "The Right Nail," *Fun*, Feb. 26, 1870, p. 246; "The Byron Scandal," *Putnam's*, Feb. 1870, p. 244.

16. "Books Received," *Universalist Quarterly and General Review*, April 1870, p. 260.

17. For example, Ashton mentions the book just twice in "Harriet Stowe's Filthy Story," pp. 375, 382, while Hedrick's treatment (pp. 366–69) focuses primarily on Stowe's composing process. Cognard-Black, Graham, and Hawley treat the text itself more extensively.

18. I disagree with Cognard-Black's assertion that, in writing *Lady Byron Vindicated*, Stowe "reframed her rhetorical position from woman-Christian-citizen to that of professional realist writer" (p. 99). I am arguing instead that Stowe sought to reconcile and combine the two approaches, providing facts and evidence while simultaneously promoting herself as an authority in moral matters. Cognard-Black's later assertion that Stowe's book demonstrates "how necessary the sentimental was to realistic writing" (p. 105) is closer to my position.

19. Harriet Beecher Stowe, *Lady Byron Vindicated: A History of the Byron Controversy, From Its Beginning in 1816 to the Present Time* (Boston: Fields, Osgood, 1870), p. 160. Subsequent citations appear parenthetically in the text, with the abbreviation *LBV*.

20. In response to criticism heaped on the "True Story," Stowe reduced her reliance on literary exegesis in *Lady Byron Vindicated*, though she defended her reading of "Manfred," claiming that the poem's "allusion to the crime and consequences of incest is so plain...that it is astonishing that any one can pretend...that it had any other application" (*LBV*, p. 337).

21. Because *Blackwood's* was widely read and well regarded, Stowe saw its attack on Lady Byron as even more damaging than what had appeared in the Countess's book.

22. According to Lentricchia, Oliver Wendell Holmes first used the phrase "Byron whirlwind" to refer to the response to Stowe's article ("Harriet Beecher Stowe and the Byron Whirlwind," p. 221).

23. Philip Quilibet [George Edward Pond], "The Great Moral Drama," *Galaxy. A Magazine of Entertaining Reading*, Dec. 1869, p. 854.

24. Hedrick, *Harriet Beecher Stowe*, pp. 364–65.

25. Elizabeth Cady Stanton, "The Moral of the Byron Case," *Independent*, Sept. 9, 1869, p. 1.

26. Lydia Maria Child, "The Byron Controversy," *Independent*, Oct. 14, 1869, p. 1.

27. "Editor's Easy Chair," *Harper's New Monthly Magazine*, Oct. 1869, p. 767.

28. "The Byron Scandal," *Buffalo Express* [New York], Sept. 4, 1869; qtd. in Paul Baender, "Mark Twain and the Byron Scandal," *American Literature* 30.4 (1959): p. 470.

29. *The Stowe-Byron Controversy: A Complete Résumé of All That Has Been Written and Said upon the Subject, Re-printed from "The Times," "Saturday Review," "Daily News," "Pall Mall Gazette," "Daily Telegraph," etc. Together with an Impartial Review of the Merits of the Case. By the Editor of "Once a Week."* Ed. Eneas Sweetland Dallas (London: Thomas Cooper, 1869), p. 109.

30. *Stowe-Byron Controversy*, p. 21.

31. *Daily News*, Sept. 2, 1869, rpt. in *Stowe-Byron Controversy*, p. 29; Sampson Low, Jr., letter to the London *Times*, Sept. 7, 1869, rpt. in *Stowe-Byron Controversy*, pp. 91, 92. Low, Jr. was the son of Stowe's long-time British publisher (Sampson Low) and was himself active in the family business.

32. *Stowe-Byron Controversy*, p. 17.

33. *Echo* [London] article; rpt. in *Saturday Evening Post*, Oct. 16, 1869, p. 6; *Daily Telegraph*, Sept. 6, 1869, rpt in *Stowe-Byron Controversy*, p. 87. This attention to Stowe's financial arrangements was not new; in the 1850s the American press obsessed on Stowe's earnings from *Uncle Tom's Cabin*.

34. *Saturday Review*, Sept. 4, 1869; rpt in *Stowe-Byron Controversy*, p. 41.

35. James Russell Lowell expressed this view in a letter to Edmund Quincy, dated Sept. 15, 1869: "I am afraid that Madame was quite as eager to proclaim her intimacy with Lady B. as to defend her memory" (rpt. in *New Letters of James Russell Lowell*, ed. M. A. DeWolfe Howe [New York: Harper and Brothers, 1932], p. 147).

36. Letter to *Telegraph* [London]; noted in "Article 13—No Title," *Saturday Evening Post*, Sept. 25, 1869, p. 3. In Stowe's version of events, Byron asks Augusta and his wife when the three of them will meet again, to which Lady Byron responds, "'In Heaven, I trust'" ("True Story," p. 307).

37. See *Saturday Review*, Sept. 4, 1869, rpt. in *Stowe-Byron Controversy*, p. 41.

38. Qtd. in "The Byron Case," *Saturday Evening Post*, Oct. 23, 1869, p. 2.

39. See, for example, "The Byron Case," *Saturday Evening Post*, Nov. 13, 1869, p. 2 and "The Byron Scandal. The Unpublished Letters of Lady Byron," *New York Albion: A Weekly Journal of Literature, Art, Politics, Finance, Field Sports, and News*, Nov. 6, 1869, p. 668.

40. Qtd. in "The Byron Case," *Saturday Evening Post*, Nov. 13, 1869, p. 2.

41. "Was It a Mystification?" *Nation*, Sept. 2, 1869, p. 189.

42. "A Letter from George the Count Johannes to 'The New York Herald.'—September 4," rpt. in *Stowe-Byron Controversy*, appendix, p. 4.

43. Rpt. in *Stowe-Byron Controversy*, p. 36.

44. *Putnam's Magazine*, Dec. 1869, p. 752.

45. *Fun*, March 12, 1870, p. 6.

46. Theodore Tilton, "The Byron Revelations," *Independent*, Aug. 26, 1869, p. 4. Stowe was a frequent contributor to the *Independent* in the early 1860s and her brother, Henry Ward Beecher, the paper's former editor, was a friend and mentor of Tilton when the Byron scandal broke. Soon enough, Beecher and Tilton would become embroiled in a sex scandal of their own, in which Beecher was accused of a sexual liaison with Tilton's wife. See Richard Wrightman Fox, *Trials of Intimacy: Love and Loss in the Beecher-Tilton Scandal* (Chicago: University of Chicago Press, 1999) and Debby Applegate, *The Most Famous Man in America: The Biography of Henry Ward Beecher* (New York: Doubleday, 2006).

47. In a segment that serves as many contemporary readers' first exposure to the Stowe/Byron scandal, Ishmael Reed's *Flight to Canada* (1976) figures the 1869–1870 backlash against Stowe (here called "Naughty Harriet") as her punishment for having stolen the former slave Josiah Henson's story for use in *Uncle Tom's Cabin*. The arrogance that fueled her plagiarism, Reed suggests, also set her up for the Byron debacle.

48. *Spectator*, Sept. 4, 1869, rpt. in *Stowe-Byron Controversy*, p. 50.

49. *Fun*, Sept. 11, 1869, p. 6; Jan. 22, 1870, p. 196.

50. Rpt. in *Stowe-Byron Controversy*, p. 38.

51. *Saturday Review*, Sept. 4, 1869, rpt. in *Stowe-Byron Controversy*, p. 86; 86–87. On southern responses to the anti-Stowe backlash, see Lentricchia, "Harriet Beecher Stowe and the Byron Whirlwind," p. 224.

52. Rpt. in Cognard-Black, "Wild and Distracted Call," pp. 111–12; Cognard-Black, "Wild and Distracted Call," p. 110.

53. *Standard*, Sept. 4, 1869, rpt. in *Stowe-Byron Controversy*, p. 69.

54. "ETC.," *Overland Monthly and Out West Magazine*, Oct. 1869, p. 383.

55. According to a column in the *American Literary Gazette*, the Countess Guiccioli told "all her friends" that only an "'old American blue-stocking' could have been guilty" of such "an ignoble slander" as the incest charge against Byron ("Our Continental Correspondence," *American Literary Gazette and Publishers' Circular*, Nov. 15, 1869, p. 52).

56. See, for example, Cognard-Black, who describes Stowe's depiction in this cartoon as that of a "hag, scuttling up Byron's noble visage trailing muck from her hands and feet" ("Wild and Distracted Call," p. 112). She identifies this image as one of several that contributed to Stowe's "trivialization" as a literary figure (p. 112).

57. Eneas Sweetland Dallas, ed., *Stowe-Byron Controversy*, p. 3.

58. *Independent*, Aug. 26, 1869, p. 1; *Fun*, Sept. 25, 1869, p. 26; "Mrs. Stowe's Second Narrative," *New York Times*, Jan. 4, 1870, p. 4. James Russell Lowell expressed a similar sentiment in his letter to Edmund Quincy: "I have no doubt that Mrs. Stowe believes her own story, but she is essentially a romancer and has the inaccuracy of mind proper to the trade" (Sept. 15, 1869, rpt. in Howe, *New Letters*, p. 146).

59. "Review 1—No Title," *Overland Monthly and Out West Magazine*, April 1870, p. 385.

60. "Letter from George the Count Johannes to 'The New York Herald,'" p. 1.

61. On fiction's increasing prestige, see Lawrence Buell, "The Unkillable Dream of the Great American Novel: *Moby-Dick* As Test Case," *American Literary History* 20.1/2 (2008): p. 135; on poetry's decline, see Stokes, "In Defense of Genius," p. 192.

62. Rpt. in *Public Opinion*, Sept. 25, 1869, p. 381.

63. *Standard*, Sept. 4, 1869, rpt. in *Stowe-Byron Controversy*, p. 75.

64. *Fun*, Sept. 11, 1869, p. 6; *Standard*, Sept. 4, 1869, rpt. in *Stowe-Byron Controversy*, p. 87.

65. An exception is one author's assertion that a primary "fault" of Stowe's original *Atlantic* article "was its mixture of fact and feeling—the high-strung, sentimental, and, in some places, rhapsodical vein in which some of the most awful charges ever made against two human beings were brought before the public." Adopting the language of the legal system that so pervaded this controversy, the article added that "in charging a crime against a man, all displays of emotion on the part of the prosecutor are improper.... It is only to the defence that it is permitted to be pathetic." Stowe's book, according to this reviewer, exhibits the same inappropriateness of tone ("Mrs. Stowe's 'Vindication of Lady Byron,'" *Nation*, Jan. 13, 1870, p. 24).

66. See Baender, "Mark Twain and the Byron Scandal," pp. 469, 471. Baender makes a strong case for Twain's authorship of six editorials on the Stowe/Byron matter, which ran in the *Buffalo Express* in August and September of 1869. At least two of the editorials addressed the matter of sentimentalism in these terms.

67. "Books and Authors Abroad," *Hours at Home: A Popular Monthly of Instruction and Recreation*, Nov. 1869, p. 95.

68. Rpt. in *Stowe-Byron Controversy*, p. 20.

69. Rpt. in *Stowe-Byron Controversy*, p. 92; p. 55.

70. *Standard*, Sept. 4, 1869; rpt. in *Stowe-Byron Controversy*, p. 75.

71. "Notices of Books," *American Quarterly Church Review, and Ecclesiastical Register*, Oct. 1869, p. 471.

72. "Lord and Lady Byron," *Saturday Evening Post*, Aug. 28, 1869, p. 3; Francis Blandford, "Our English Correspondence," *American Literary Gazette and Publishers' Circular*, Oct. 15, 1869, p. 374.

73. Gustavus Stadler, *Troubling Minds: The Cultural Politics of Genius in the United States, 1840–1890* (Minneapolis: University of Minnesota Press, 2006), p. xiv. On American women and genius, see Victoria Olwell, "'It Spoke Itself': Women's Genius and Eccentric Politics," *American Literature* 77.1 (2005): pp. 33–63; Susan S. Williams, *Reclaiming Authorship*; and Williams, "Writing, Authorship, and Genius: Literary Women and Modes of Literary Production," *The Cambridge History of American Women's Literature*, ed. Dale M. Bauer (Cambridge: Cambridge University Press, 2012), pp. 204–31.

74. Stadler, *Troubling Minds*, p. xv.

75. *Daily News*, Sept. 2, 1869, rpt. in *Stowe-Byron Controversy*, p. 29.

76. *Times*, Sept. 3, 1869, rpt. in *Stowe-Byron Controversy*, p. 35.

77. M. H. Abrams, *The Mirror and the Lamp: Romantic Theory and the Critical Tradition* (Oxford University Press, 1953; New York: Norton, 1958), pp. 14, 21.

78. "The Byron Scandal," *Vanity Fair* [London], Sept. 11, 1869, p. 146.

79. John Morley, "Byron," *Critical Miscellanies* (London: Chapman and Hall, 1871), p. 255.

80. "Mrs. Stowe's Mistake," *Appletons' Journal of Literature, Science and Art*, Oct. 9, 1869, p. 247.

81. "Byron," *Saturday Evening Post*, Feb. 26, 1870, p. 2.

82. On William Dean Howells's disavowal of the relevance of genius to literary study, see Stokes, "In Defense of Genius."

83. See *LBV*, pp. 217–18. For scholarly analyses of Byron's influence on Stowe see Alice Crozier, "Harriet Beecher Stowe and Byron," in *Critical Essays on Harriet Beecher Stowe*, ed. Elizabeth Ammons (Boston: G. K. Hall, 1980), pp. 190–99 and Caroline Franklin, "Stowe and the Byronic Heroine," in *Transatlantic Stowe: Harriet Beecher Stowe and European Culture*, ed. Denise Kohn, Sarah Meer, and Emily B. Todd (Iowa City: University of Iowa Press, 2006), pp. 3–23.

84. Qtd. in *Lady Byron Vindicated*, p. 51.

85. On Byron's perceived seductiveness during his lifetime, see Ghislaine McDayter, *Byromania and the Birth of Celebrity Culture* (Albany: SUNY Press, 2009). On the homoerotics of Byron's literary friendships, see McPherson, "Opening the Open Secret."

86. Justin McCarthy, "Mrs. Stowe's Last Romance," (Letter to the Editor), *Independent*, Aug. 26, 1869, p. 1.

87. Citing M. A. De Wolfe Howe and Edwin H. Cady's vaguely sourced assertions, Lentricchia claims that the *Atlantic* lost some 15,000 subscribers as a result of the backlash against the "True Story" ("Harriet Beecher Stowe and the Byron Whirlwind," p. 228). Ellery Sedgwick offers a more cautious assessment. While he acknowledges that the magazine lost "at least 15,000" subscribers between 1865 and 1870, he suggests that "other factors, including a milder reaction against [Oliver Wendell] Holmes's serial 'The Guardian Angel' and particularly the increasing competition from other magazines, contributed to the decline" (*The Atlantic Monthly, 1857–1909: Yankee Humanism at High Tide and Ebb* [Amherst: University of Massachusetts Press, 1994], p. 110). This explanation seems more plausible than the notion that Stowe's article alone caused the decline.

88. "Mrs. Stowe's Mistake," p. 247.

89. *Newcastle Daily Chronicle*, Sept. 20, 1869, rpt. in *Public Opinion*, Sept. 25, 1869, p. 381.

90. "Article 4—No Title," *Saturday Evening Post*, Sept. 4, 1869, p. 3.

91. Both Hawley and Lentricchia (referring to English and American readers, respectively) claim that the scandal boosted Byron's literary reputation. Lentricchia's assertion that "Byron and Byronism in America were almost out of fashion" in the mid-nineteenth century bears rethinking, however. Byron's poems, offered in a number of formats by a range of publishers, were heavily advertised in US periodicals throughout the 1850s and 1860s, as was Moore's *Life of Byron*.

92. This figure compares advertisements that ran from Aug. 1, 1867 through July 31, 1869 to those running from Sept. 1, 1869 through Aug. 31, 1871. I excluded August 1869 from this count because it was the month in which Stowe's "True Story" began to circulate, both in England and the United States. By way of comparison, advertisements mentioning Stowe increased by approximately ten percent across the same period.

93. The *Gallery* was published in England as early as 1836 (other English editions are undated), with a US edition brought out by Appleton in 1860.

94. *Appletons'*, Nov. 27, 1869, p. 479.

95. "Byron and Byronana," *American Bibliopolist*, Dec. 1869, pp. 378–81.

96. *Saturday Evening Post*, Nov. 27, 1869, p. 3. The National Union Catalog lists only the Harper and Brothers edition, released earlier that year. One English edition (from R. Bentley) appeared as well.

97. *Nation*, Jan. 6, 1870, p. 11.

98. "The Byron Scandal," *Putnam's*, Feb. 1870, p. 244.

99. "Mrs Stowe's 'Vindication of Lady Byron,'" *Nation*, Jan. 13, 1870, p. 25

100. "Byron and the Controversy," *American Bibliopolist*, Feb. 1870, p. 69.

101. I have based this claim on searches of the following databases: *American Periodicals, Accessible Archives* (which includes *African American Newspapers*), *African American Newspapers, 1827–1998* (Readex), and the *Making of America* sites at Cornell and the University of Michigan. Fields, Osgood may have advertised the book in periodicals that do not appear in these databases or in the advertising pages of other books it published.

102. Some scholars have accepted this ruination thesis fairly uncritically. William Galperin, for example, writes that the Byron scandal "effectively marked the end of Stowe's remarkable run as a writer of consequence" ("Lord Byron, Lady Byron, and Mrs. Stowe," in Meredith L. McGill, ed., *The Traffic in Poems: Nineteenth-Century Poetry and Transatlantic Exchange* [New Brunswick, NJ: Rutgers University Press, 2008], p. 125).

103. Evert A. Duyckinck and George L. Duyckinck, *Cyclopaedia of American Literature* (2 vols), ed. M. Laird Simons (Philadelphia: William Rutter & Co., 1875; rpt. Detroit: Gale, 1965), vol. 2, p. 526.

104. Hedrick, *Harriet Beecher Stowe*, p. 370.

105. According to Joyce Warren's introduction to the Rutgers University Press edition of *Ruth Hall* (1986), the revelation of the author's true identity pushed the book's sales figures to 70,000 (p. xvii).

Epilogue

1. See, for example, Suzanna Andrews, "Arthur Miller's Missing Act," *Vanity Fair*, Sept. 2007; www.vanityfair.com/fame/features/2007/09/miller200709.

2. Thomas R. Mitchell, "Julian Hawthorne and the 'Scandal' of Margaret Fuller," *American Literary History* 7 (Summer 1995): p. 211.

3. William Goldhurst, "Edgar Allan Poe," *Heath Anthology of American Literature*, 3rd ed., vol. 1, ed. Paul Lauter, et al. (Boston: Houghton Mifflin, 1998), p. 1441. With the fourth edition (2002), Meredith McGill's biographical headnote on Poe replaced Goldhurst's.

4. Len Gougeon, *Virtue's Hero: Emerson, Antislavery, and Reform* (Athens: University of Georgia Press, 1990).

5. Carolyn Karcher, Introduction, *Hobomok and Other Writings on Indians* (New Brunswick, NJ: Rutgers University Press, 1986), p. ix, x, xi, xiii, xv.

6. Joyce W. Warren, Introduction, *Ruth Hall* (New Brunswick, NJ: Rutgers University Press, 1986), p. xxii; p. xxviii.

7. Elaine Showalter's introduction to *Little Women* departs from this strategy. Instead of demonstrating Alcott's congruence with late twentieth-century political and social attitudes, Showalter instead critiques her fellow feminist scholars who have excoriated the author for failing to live up to their standards. Negative assessments of the novel's resolution, she writes, "seem overstated and extreme, demanding from Alcott's nineteenth-century female Bildungsroman a twentieth-century feminist ending of separation and autonomy.... Jo's literary and emotional career is a happy one, even if it does not conform to our contemporary feminist model of a woman artist's needs" (Introduction, *Little Women* [New York: Penguin, 1989], pp. xxii–xxiii).

8. Rebecca Grant Sexton, ed., *The Correspondence of Augusta Jane Evans Wilson* (Columbia: University of South Carolina Press, 2002), p. xxiv, xxvi.

9. See, for example, Laurence Buell, *The Environmental Imagination: Thoreau, Nature Writing, and the Formation of American Culture* (Cambridge, MA: Harvard University Press, 1995); Greg Garrard, *Ecocriticism* (London: Routledge, 2004); *The ISLE Reader: Ecocriticism, 1993–2003*, ed. Michael P. Branch and Scott Slovic (Athens: University of Georgia Press, 2003); Daniel J. Philippon, "Is American Nature Writing Dead?" in *The Oxford Handbook of Ecocriticism*, ed. Greg Garrard (New York: Oxford University Press, 2014), pp. 391–407. On Thoreau and food, see Dana Phillips, "'Slimy Beastly Life': Thoreau on Food and Farming," *ISLE: Interdisciplinary Studies in Literature and Environment* 19.3 (2012): pp. 532–47 and Janet Fiskio, "Sauntering across the Border: Thoreau, Nabhan, and Food Politics," in *The Cambridge Companion to Literature and the Environment*, ed. Louise Westling (Cambridge: Cambridge University Press, 2014), pp. 136–51.

10. On Cooper and the environment, see David Mazel, "Performing 'Wilderness' in *The Last of the Mohicans*," in *Reading under the Sign of Nature: New Essays in Ecocriticism*, ed. John Tallmadge and Henry Harrington (Salt Lake City: University of Utah Press, 2000), pp. 101–14; Dana D. Nelson, "Cooper and the Tragedy of the Commons," in *What Democracy Looks Like: A New Critical Realism for a Post-Seattle World*, ed. Amy Schrager Lang and Cecilia Tichi (New Brunswick, NJ: Rutgers University Press, 2006), pp. 161–72; and Matthew Wynn Sivils, "'The Base, Cursed Thing': Panther Attacks and Ecotones in Antebellum American Fiction," *Journal of Ecocriticism* 2.1 (2010): pp. 19–32.

11. Cristin Ellis, "Amoral Abolitionism: Frederick Douglass and the Environmental Case against Slavery," *American Literature* 86.2 (2014): p. 277.

12. Nicole Seymour, "Irony and Contemporary Ecocinema: Theorizing a New Affective Paradigm," in *Moving Environments: Affect, Emotion, Ecology, and Film*, ed. Alexa Weik von Mossner (Waterloo, Can.: Wilfrid Laurier University Press, 2014): pp. 61–78.

13. David Ingram, "The Aesthetics and Ethics of Eco-Film Criticism," in *Ecocinema Theory and Practice*, ed. Stephen Rust, Salma Monani, and Sean Cubitt (New York: Routledge, 2013), p. 52.

14. Jenny Price, "Thirteen Ways of Seeing Nature in L.A.," *Believer Magazine*, April 2006, www.believermag.com/issues/200604/?read=article_price, p. 4/28.

15. A column in the *New York Times* book review (Sept. 7, 2014) exemplifies this reflexive fretting over reductiveness when considering the moral authority of authors and texts. In response to the query "Should literature be considered useful?" the poet and critic Adam Kirsch writes: "To reduce literature to its usefulness is to miss the sheer pleasure of word and sound that makes it literature in the first place," a statement that is highlighted as a pull-quote at the top of the column (p. 31). But why assume that talk of "usefulness" risks reduction any more than does talk of form or sound or narrative strategy? Why must it be figured as a mode of inquiry against which nuance and art require defense?

{ INDEX }

Abend, Gabriel, 8
abolition, 74, 77, 85, 96, 122, 191n87
   conflict within, 102–5, 195n47
   and England, 64–67, 69–70
   and Harriet Beecher Stowe, 122, 138–39, 147, 148–50
   and marketing, 1–3, 187n49
   and publishing, 1–5, 12–13, 95
   and Ralph Waldo Emerson, 165
Abrams, M. H., 156
Adams, F. Colburn, 58
advertising, 1–3, 12, 78, 112–15, 125, 160–61, 198n21, 210n101
   of collected editions, 50–51
   and literary status, 19
   and Lord Byron, 159–61, 210nn91–92
   of magazines, 131–33
   of *My Bondage and My Freedom* (Frederick Douglass), 94–95, 194n28, 194n31, 194n38
affect, 11, 42, 104–5, 141
Albanese, Catherine, 7
Albion, 129, 133
Alcott, Louisa May, 58, 211n7
Andrews, William, 63–64, 190n86
Anesko, Michael, 50
Anglophilia, 37, 44, 45
anonymity, 16, 28, 173n50, 174n55
Appletons' Journal of Literature, 156
Arthur, T. S., 58, 59, 109–10, 197n1, 197n3
Atlantic Monthly, 83, 118, 137, 140, 159, 161, 205n9, 210n87
Augst, Thomas, 5, 6, 9

Baker, Thomas N., 19
Ball, Charles, 74
Bancroft, George, 27, 47, 52
Baumgartner, Barbara, 68–69
Baym, Nina, 14, 111, 173n43, 198n7
Beard, James Franklin, 46, 48
Beecher, Henry Ward, 207n46
Benjamin, Park, 26, 35, 177n12
Bennett, Emerson, 58–59, 127
Bibb, Henry, 74–75, 80, 103
Blackwood's Magazine, 67, 142, 206n21
Blake, David Haven, 139

bluestocking, 3, 151, 208n55
book reviews, 109–35, 163, 198n7
   of *Behind the Scenes* (Elizabeth Keckley), 82–84, 191n96
   of Cooper's works, 26, 32–33, 35, 43, 48, 49–50, 176n1, 178n36, 182n102, 182n112
   of *Lady Byron Vindicated* (Harriet Beecher Stowe), 140–41
   of *My Bondage and My Freedom* (Frederick Douglass), 90
Brontë, Charlotte, 125
Brother Jonathan, 33–34
Brown, William Wells, 14, 65
Bryant, William Cullen, 27, 28, 36, 47, 51, 119, 181n76
Bulwer, Edward, 110, 119
Byron, Lady Anne Isabella (Milbanke) ["Lady Byron" or "Lady Noel Byron" in text], 8, 56, 57, 137–62

Campbell, Israel, 71
Carretta, Vincent, 8
celebrity, 16, 17–19, 28, 37–38, 56, 95, 121, 141, 163–64, 173n51, 202n94
Chapman, Maria Weston, 96
character, 4, 5–6, 18, 21, 23, 29, 38, 68, 72, 86, 92, 111, 140, 170n16, 170n18, 175nn67–68
Charvat, William, 52
Chesebro', Caroline, 118
Child, Lydia Maria, 11–12, 145, 166, 172nn34–35
Clarke, Lewis, 73
Cognard-Black, Jennifer, 141, 150, 206n18, 208n56
conduct manuals, 7
Cooper, James Fenimore, 10, 11, 12, 15, 20, 25–53, 105, 127, 172n34, 176n1, 178n25, 182n102
   Bravo, The, 173n50
   and Cooperstown 27, 29–31, 33–34, 179n40
   Deerslayer, The, 49, 182n104
   and the Democratic Party, 48, 182n103
   and ecocriticism, 167
   and *The Effinghams* (Frederick Jackson), 41–42
   and England, 42–45, 180n76, 181n87
   Headsman, The, 26

Cooper, James Fenimore (*continued*)
  History of the Navy of the United States of America, 49, 176n6, 179n48, 182n111
  Home As Found, 27, 32–35, 38–42, 45, 48, 50, 51, 178n35, 180n66
  Homeward Bound, 32, 33, 34, 39, 44–45, 51, 178n35
  Leatherstocking Tales, 49, 50, 51
  Letter to His Countrymen, A, 44, 45, 51, 173n50
  libel suits of, 16, 28, 29–38, 178n34
  as memorialized 27, 51–52, 183n125
  Monikins, The, 26, 50, 171n29, 177n8
  and Natty Bumppo, 40–42, 180n71
  Pathfinder, The, 49, 51
  Pioneers, The, 40, 41–42, 167, 179n40
  Spy, The, 25, 50
  and Three-Mile Point, 20, 30–32, 38, 178n34
  and the Whig Party, 47–48
  and William Cooper (father), 30, 31–32, 33
Coviello, Peter, 171n23
Craft, William, 3

Davis, Rev. Noah, 71
DeBow's Review, 122, 124
deference, 30–31, 37, 43–44
Delany, Martin, 103, 122
Democratic Review. See *United States Magazine and Democratic Review*
Denison, Mary, 58
Dickens, Charles, 111, 126–27
didacticism, 22, 156, 168, 175n64, 198n20, 200n47, 205n9
  and E.D.E.N. Southworth, 128, 129
  and Nathaniel Hawthorne, 59–60
  and nature writing, 167–68
  and nineteenth-century book reviewing, 111–12, 116–20, 185n32, 198n19
Douglas, Janet, 192n3
Douglass, Anna Murray, 86, 106, 192n6, 197n90
Douglass, Frederick, 14, 21, 85–107, 122, 191n87, 192n10, 193n13, 193n21
  as editor, 92, 96–107, 193n25, 194n38, 194n45, 195n62
  and family life, 13, 85–86, 106, 197nn89–90
  as lecturer, 87, 90–91, 92, 98–101
  My Bondage and My Freedom, 21, 76–78, 86–96, 103, 105, 106, 113–14, 167, 169n11, 194n28, 194n31, 194n37
  Narrative of the Life of Frederick Douglass, an American Slave (1845), 5, 60, 65–66, 85, 95–96, 186n37, 193n15
  See also *Frederick Douglass' Paper* and *North Star*
Douglass, Margaret, 1–4, 9, 16, 169nn3–4, 169n11
Duyckinck, Evert, 17, 160, 174n53

ecocriticism, 167–68
Eldridge, Elleanor, 71
Ellis, Cristin, 167
Emerson, Ralph Waldo, 13, 19, 89, 127, 165
  "Character," 175n67
  English Traits, 117
  "Poet, The," 22
Evans, Augusta Jane, 166
Everton, Michael, 170n12

Fabian, Ann, 186n35
Fanuzzi, Robert, 196n79
Fedric, Francis, 72
Fern, Fanny (Sara Willis Parton), 18–19, 95, 161, 166, 199n30
Fessenden, Tracy, 171n24
Fleischner, Jennifer, 82, 190n86
Forester, Fanny (Emily Chubbuck Judson), 19
Foster, Frances Smith, 78, 79
Franklin, Wayne, 29, 31, 48, 176n1
Frederick Douglass' Paper, 1, 5, 13, 76, 87, 95–105, 122, 128–29
Fulkerson, Gerald, 76
Fun, 147, 150, 152, 153

Galperin, William, 210n102
Garnet, Henry Highland, 103, 191n87, 196n82
Garrison, William Lloyd, 21, 72, 95
  as editor, 3, 4, 12–13
  and Frederick Douglass, 65–66, 72, 85–86, 96, 99, 103–5, 192n3, 192n8, 193n21, 196n79
  See also *Liberator*
Genette, Gérard, 55
genius, 21, 115, 119, 131, 147, 155–58
Godey's Lady's Book, 83, 109, 111, 113, 115, 116, 117, 118, 119, 127, 128, 197n2, 199n24
Goldhurst, William, 164–65
gossip, 85–86, 171n31
Gougeon, Len, 165
Gould, Philip, 74
Graham's Magazine, 48, 49, 120, 127, 128, 129, 182n102
Greeley, Horace, 35, 36–37, 38, 47, 177n12, 180n63
Green, J. D., 75
Greenwood, Grace (Sara Jane Lippincott), 19
Griffiths, Julia, 76–77, 85–86, 92–93, 191n1, 192n3, 192n10
Griswold, Rufus, 128, 172n34

Hale, Sarah Josepha, 14, 48, 59, 173nn43–44
Halttunen, Karen, 6
Harper, Frances E. W., 5
Harper's New Monthly Magazine, 110, 113, 145, 199n25
Harper's Weekly, 113, 116
Hart, Abraham, 12

Index

Hartman, Saidiya, 87
Hawthorne, Nathaniel, 32, 47, 127, 164, 184n8
  Blithedale Romance, The, 5, 22–23, 122
  "Custom-House, The," 59, 184n17
  House of the Seven Gables, The, 59–60
Hayden, William, 188n55
Hedrick, Joan, 12
Henkin, David, 196n71
Hentz, Caroline Lee, 12–13, 124, 202n87
Hickman, Jared, 171n23
Hicks, Thomas, 27, 177n19
Higham, John, 7
Hildreth, Richard, 12, 172n38, 202n91
Hilkey, Judy, 6, 170n18
Hinerman, Stephen, 10
Hochman, Barbara, 110, 198n8
honor, 23, 175n68
Howard, June, 14–15
Howells, William Dean, 140, 205n14

incest, 40, 130, 161, 164, 185n26
  and Lord Byron, 12, 21, 137, 139, 140–41, 147, 150–51
Independent, 90, 148, 153, 158–59, 207n46
Ingram, David, 167
intimacy, 16, 19, 29, 83, 144, 174n58
Irving, Washington, 25, 46, 181n76

Jackson, John Andrew, 75–76
Jackson, Leon, 19, 101
Jacobs, Harriet, 65, 78, 186n37
Jaffe, Aaron, 16
James, G.P.R., 118
Jewett, John P., 1, 4
Jones, Thomas H., 75

Karcher, Carolyn, 166
Keckley, Elizabeth, 20–21, 78–84, 190n84, 190n86, 191n96
Kipnis, Laura, 11
Kirkland, Caroline, 110, 174n56, 175n61
Kirsch, Adam, 212n15
Knickerbocker, 26, 27, 43, 48, 49, 183n127

Latham, Sean, 5
Leigh, Augusta, 137, 144, 146–47, 207n36
Lentricchia, Frank, 210n87, 210n91
Lever, Charles, 111
Levine, Robert S., 14, 99, 122, 193n15
Liberator, 1–3, 12–13, 16, 85, 94, 104, 125–26, 169n3, 202n91
Lincoln, Abraham, 82, 139
Lincoln, Mary Todd, 79, 80–84
Lippard, George, 118
literacy, 1–4, 64, 73–74, 89–90

literary nationalism, 13–14, 15, 146, 173n49
  and James Fenimore Cooper, 25, 27, 28, 37, 42, 46–47, 48, 50, 51–52, 183n127
literary value, 9, 19, 34, 57, 110, 139–40
  and didacticism, 116–19, 168
  and E.D.E.N. Southworth, 128–29, 131
  and Harriet Beecher Stowe, 125–27, 151–58
Literary World, 117, 123, 125, 128, 160
Lockhart, John G., 43, 44
Loguen, J. W., 95
Longfellow, Henry Wadsworth, 10, 19, 119, 127, 182n113, 201n77
Lowell, James Russell, 19, 205n9, 207n35
Luck, Chad, 171n22
Lull, James, 10

Machor, James L., 62, 110–111, 185n32
Macqueen, James, 67
marketing, 18, 109, 112–15, 158–61, 199n25
  and E.D.E.N. Southworth, 131, 133–34
  and Frederick Douglass, 86–87, 91, 93–96, 99, 192n11
  and Harriet Beecher Stowe, 121, 124–25
  and James Fenimore Cooper, 50–51
  misleading aspects of, 1–5
Matlack, Lucius, 74–75
McCoy, Beth A., 55
McFeely, William, 96
McGill, Meredith, 15, 16, 28, 174n55
Meer, Sarah, 201n65
Melville, Herman, 10, 13, 51, 93, 105–6, 174n55, 174n57, 185n23
  Battle-Pieces, 61–62
  Confidence-Man, The, 60, 61, 62–63
  Mardi, 61
  Moby-Dick, 61
  Omoo, 60–61
  and paratexts, 60–63
  Pierre, 17–18, 61, 93, 185n26
  Typee, 60
Miller, Arthur, 163
Millner, Michael, 10
Mitchell, Thomas, 164
Modern, John Lardas, 171n23, 171n25
moral authority, 8, 9, 18, 19, 22–23, 53, 127, 133, 135, 168, 189n58, 212n15
  and aesthetic value, 116
  and anger, 104–5
  and antislavery positions, 4–5, 121, 126
  and literary nationalism, 15
  and paratexts, 57, 65, 69, 70
  and popularity, 112
  and scandal, 4, 9–12, 86, 138, 141–42, 151–53, 161, 163
moral economies, 6–7, 9, 10, 13, 19, 138, 157, 165, 167–68, 170n21

National Era, 1, 95, 122, 128, 133, 202n87, 204n124
New Criticism, 13, 140
New Englander, 126
New World, 26, 33, 37, 49
New-York Citizen, 82, 83, 191n96
New-York Mirror, 34, 43, 44, 46, 48, 176n1
New-York Tribune, 36, 95
North, William, 111
North American Review, 19, 25, 27, 49, 109, 116, 118, 176n1, 198n10
North Star, 96–105
Northup, Solomon, 125

O'Brien, Fitz-James, 10
Outland, Ethel, 35, 178n34, 179n48, 182n103

Panic of 1837, 31
Pannapacker, William, 139
Paratexts, 20, 53, 55–84, 165–66, 185n23
Pennington, J.W.C., 98, 188n51
Pennsylvania Freeman, 98, 194n45
Person, Leland, 180n71
personality, 29, 48
Peterson, T. B., 204n122
Peterson's Magazine, 109, 116, 119, 128, 198n7
Poe, Edgar Allan, 15, 40, 110, 116, 164–65, 178n24, 199n22
popularity, 107, 112
postage, 102, 196n71
prefaces, 49, 55, 56, 57–63, 71–78, 79, 184n8, 188n51, 188n55
Price, Jenny, 167
Prince, Mary, 20, 64–70
Pringle, Thomas, 20, 65–70, 186n40
privacy, 9, 28, 29, 81, 83, 93, 105, 174n58
property, 5–6, 20, 30–32, 91, 97, 171n22, 192n12
 author as, 87, 93, 105–6, 164
 literary text as, 17–18
 reputation as, 28, 37–40
 secrets as, 81
proslavery ideology, 3–4, 5, 67, 121, 122–24
Provincial Freeman, 122, 169n4
public domain, 16–17, 38
puffery, 112, 199n22
Putnam, G. P., 50, 120, 200n60
Putnam's Magazine, 83, 109, 111, 121, 125, 127, 140, 147, 160

Railton, Stephen, 179n52
Randolph, J. Thornton, 113
Redpath, James, 79–80, 82, 190n86
Reed, Ishmael, 123, 208n47
Renker, Elizabeth, 13
reprinting, 16, 28, 35–36, 97, 173n55, 204n5

reputation, 5–6, 7 8, 9, 20–21, 92, 109–10, 112, 126, 144, 163–68
 damage to, 28, 48, 81
 differentiated from character, 23, 175n68
 and literary value, 19
 as property, 37–38
 recuperation of, 52, 138–40
Ritchie, Alexander Hay, 27, 177n19
Rohrbach, Augusta, 192n8, 199n21
roman à clef, 5, 19
Round Table, 127
Ryan, Barbara, 79, 190n86

Sandage, Scott, 6
Sartain's Union Magazine, 115, 109, 117
Saturday Evening Post, 131–32, 133, 134, 154, 157, 159, 161
scandal, 4, 9–11, 18, 20–22, 76–77, 85–86, 112, 137–62, 163, 185n26, 199n30, 204n4
 slavery debates and, 65, 67–70, 187n41
 unlikability as, 29, 30, 32
Scholnick, Robert, 126
Scott, Sir Walter, 25, 42–44, 176n1, 181n77, 181n84
secularism, 7, 171n23
Sedgwick, Catharine Maria, 14, 15, 58, 111, 116, 181n76, 182n113
Sedgwick, Ellery, 210n87
sensationalism, 1, 78, 109, 112, 118, 127, 133, 134, 139, 153, 154
sentimentalism, 12, 13, 14–15, 128, 142, 154, 157, 208n65
Sexton, Rebecca Grant, 166
Seymour, Nicole, 167
Showalter, Elaine, 211n7
Sigourney, Lydia, 116, 119
Silverman, Gillian, 17
Simms, William Gilmore, 14
slave narratives, 63–84, 86–96, 186n35, 187–88nn50–51, 188n55
slavery, 3–4, 13, 66–67, 88–90, 91, 97, 106, 120–21, 126, 138–39
Smith, Gerrit, 105
Sofer, Naomi, 205n9
Southern Literary Messenger, 11, 47, 48, 49, 109, 110, 115, 119, 123, 124, 130, 180n76
Southern Quarterly Review, 5, 123, 124, 129, 130, 172n38, 200n47
Southworth, E.D.E.N., 21, 107, 112, 127–35, 204n124, 209n66
 Curse of Clifton, The, 128, 129
 Deserted Wife, The, 128, 130, 131, 135
 Lost Heiress, The, 127–28
 Missing Bride, The, 128
 Mother-in-Law, The, 127, 130
 reception of, 127–35

Retribution, 128, 129, 135
  and the *Saturday Evening Post*, 131–33, 134–35
  Shannondale, 129
  Wife's Victory, The, 133–34
Stadler, Gustavus, 155
Stanton, Elizabeth Cady, 144–45
Stephens, Ann S., 133
Stepto, Robert, 73
Stoddard, Elizabeth, 116
Stowe, Harriet Beecher, 13, 21, 107, 112, 137–62, 172n34, 172n38, 210n102
  and the *Atlantic Monthly*, 137, 159, 205n9, 210n87
  Dred, 60, 124, 138
  and Frank J. Webb, 56–57
  Key to Uncle Tom's Cabin, A, 72, 141
  Lady Byron Vindicated, 138, 140–44, 147, 153, 158, 160, 161, 206n18, 210n101
  and Lord Byron 8–9, 12, 21, 137–62
  and prefaces, 60
  and sentimentalism, 154, 208n65
  "True Story of Lady Byron's Life, The," 11, 137, 145–47, 153–54
  Uncle Tom's Cabin, 4–5, 60, 95, 120–27, 138, 141, 148–50, 161, 172n37, 200n61, 207n33
Strickland, Susanna, 65, 66, 186n38
Sumner, Charles, 3
Susman, Warren, 29

Tamarkin, Elisa, 37
Taylor, Alan, 28, 31, 179n40
Taylor, Charles, 171n23

Thompson, Charles, 73, 75
Thompson, E. P., 6
Thoreau, Henry David, 5, 70–71, 167
Tilmon, Levin, 75
Tilton, Theodore, 148, 207n46
Tompkins, Jane, 166
transatlanticism, 8, 14, 20, 42–44, 64–65, 137–38, 147–48, 204n5
Twain, Mark (Samuel Clemens), 154, 209n66

Union Magazine. See *Sartain's Union Magazine*
United States Magazine and Democratic Review, 48, 50, 182n104

Waples, Dorothy, 47–48
Ward, Samuel Ringgold, 76, 103
Warner, Susan, 115
Warren, Joyce, 166
Watkins, Frances E. See Harper, Frances E. W.
Watkins, James, 73
Webb, Frank J., 56–57, 125
Webb, James Watson, 34–35
Weed, Thurlow, 35, 37, 38, 180n63
Wheatley, Phillis, 75
Wheeler, Peter, 73
Whitman, Walt, 13, 139–40, 163
Wicke, Jennifer, 198n21
Williams, Susan S., 79
Willis, N. P., 19, 115, 119
Wyatt-Brown, Bertram, 23

Zboray, Ronald J., 113

www.ingramcontent.com/pod-product-compliance
Ingram Content Group UK Ltd.
Pitfield, Milton Keynes, MK11 3LW, UK
UKHW042006230426
12048UKWH00009B/586